Sullivan County Tennessee

Death Records

1908-1918

Volume 1

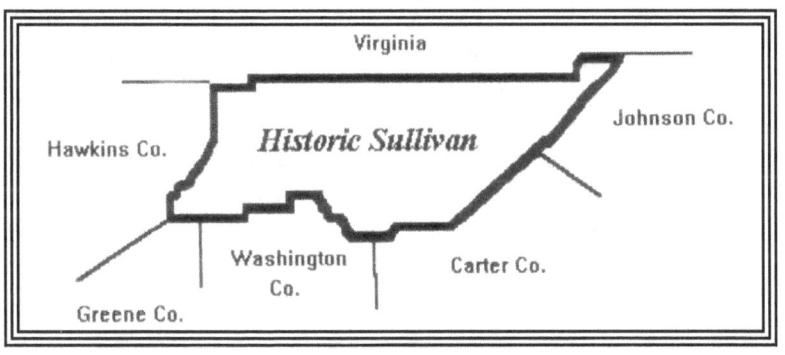

Eddie M. Nikazy

HERITAGE BOOKS
2007

HERITAGE BOOKS
AN IMPRINT OF HERITAGE BOOKS, INC.

Books, CDs, and more—Worldwide

For our listing of thousands of titles see our website
at
www.HeritageBooks.com

Published 2007 by
HERITAGE BOOKS, INC.
Publishing Division
65 East Main Street
Westminster, Maryland 21157-5026

Copyright © 1994 Eddie M. Nikazy

Other books by the author:

Abstracts of Death Records for Johnson County, Tennessee, 1908 to 1941

Carter County, Tennessee Deaths, 1926-1934

Carter County, Tennessee Record Abstracts, Death Records, 1908-1925

Carter County, Tennessee Record Abstracts, Marriages, 1871-1920

Forgotten Soldiers: History of the 2nd Tennessee Volunteer Infantry Regiment (USA), 1861-1865

Forgotten Soldiers: History of the 4th Tennessee Volunteer Infantry Regiment (USA), 1863-1865

Greene County, Tennessee Death Record Abstracts, Volume 1: 1908-1918

Sullivan County, Tennessee Death Records, 1919-1925, Volume 2

Unicoi County, Tennessee Death Record Abstracts, 1908-1936

Washington County, Tennessee Death Record Abstracts, 1908-1916

All rights reserved. No part of this book may be reproduced or transmitted in any form or by any means, electronic or mechanical, including photocopying, recording or by any information storage and retrieval system without written permission from the author, except for the inclusion of brief quotations in a review.

International Standard Book Number: 978-0-7884-0099-1

TABLE OF CONTENTS

Preface v
Abstracts of Death Records 1
Index 261

Foreword

This volume contains abstracts of death records for Sullivan County, Tennessee. Death records are available for rural Tennessee counties beginning in 1908. Currently, records of 1908 through 1941 are available for public access in the Tennessee State Library and Archives.

The area of Sullivan County was an early and important eastern Tennessee county which served as a major migration center.

In this compilation of Sullivan County death records:

1.) Where the reported place of birth is different from the local county, the place of birth is stated.

2.) Name spelling variations have been preserved. When looking for a particular surname, it is may be necessary to check other possible spelling variations.

3.) Where possible, the cause of death is quoted as it appears in the record.

4.) Parenthetical entries following parents names indicate the reported place of the parents birth.

5.) Parenthetical entries following the informants name indicate place of residence.

6.) Record numbers, except for 1914, correspond with the official death record numbers on file in the Tennessee State Archives. For the year 1914, record numbers are the record sequence number as it appeared in the micro-film.

Fannie CARTWRIGHT, female, age 68 years, married, death cause: "pneumonia", place of death: near Blountville, died: 22 Dec 1908, record (1908-12): 87120.

Hannah PANE, age 75 years, single, death cause: "pneumonia", place of death: near Blountville, died: 1 May 1909, record (1908-12): 87121.

Jennie CARTWRIGHT, age 27 years, married, death cause: "tuberculosis", place of death: near Blountville, died: 22 Feb 1909, record (1908-12): 87122.

Cora FICKLES, age 25 years, single, death cause: "tuberculosis", died: 18 Oct 1908.

Jerry WILLIAMS, age 68 years, married, born: near Newport, TN, death cause: "enlargement of liver", place of death: near Blountville, died: 22 May 1909, record (1908-12): 87123.

Buster ANDERSON, age: 3 weeks, 4 days, death cause: diphtheria, died: 16 Sep 1908, record (1908-12): 87125.

Ethel Cate CROSS, age 21 days, death cause: "dysentery", born/died: Buffalo, died: 19 Jun 1909, record (1908-12): 87126.

S.C. SMITH, female, age 8 years, death cause: "grippe", born/died: Buffalo, died: 25 Sep 1908, record (1908-12): 87127.

M.E. CROSS, female, age 47 years, born: Dunlap, death cause: "heart failure", died at Buffalo 23 Feb 1909, record (1908-12): 27128.

Cordelia SMITH, age 17 years, single, born/died: Sullivan Co., death cause: "typhoid fever", died: 30 May 1909, record (1908-12): 27129.

James MINGA, age 5 years, born/died: Sullivan Co., death cause: "diphtheria", died: 9 Sep 1908, record (1908-12): 27130.

David AKARD, age 80 years, married, death cause: "Brights disease", born/died: Sullivan Co., died: 18 May 1909, record (1908-12): 27131.

Annie MOODY, age 8 years, death cause:: "typhoid fever", born/died: Sullivan Co., died: 12 Aug 1908, record (1908-12): 27132.

Emeline SELLS, age 74 years, born in Washington Co., TN, death cause: "complication of disease", died: 6 Dec 1908, record (1908-12): 27133.

John S. GRAY, age 63 years, married, death cause: "organic kidney disease", born/died: Sullivan Co., died: 7 Jan 1909, record (1908-12): 87134.

Mary E. PEAKS, age 5 years, death cause: not stated, died: 12 Nov 1908, record (1908-12): 87135.

Ada Gertrude EDWARDS, age 7 months, death cause: not stated, died: 30 May 1908, record (1908-12): 87136.

Martha WARREN, age 54 years, marital status and death cause: not stated, died: 29 Jul 1908, record (1908-12): 87137.

W.B. HATCHER, age 65 years, married, death cause: not stated, died: 2 Feb 1908, record (1908-12): 87138.

Gray A. WAMPLER, age: 1 year, 11 days, death cause: not stated, died: 1 Jun 1909, record (1908-12): 87139.

Mary Ruth MOODY, age 7 days, death cause: "indigestion", died: 9 Feb 1909, record (1908-12): 37140.

Carl H. ARNOLD, age 3 years, death cause: "pneumonia fever", died: 31 Dec 1908.

Weeka MULLINS, age 2 months, death cause: "colic", died: 19 Jun 1909, record (1908-12): 87142.

Melvin C. BOWSER, age 2 weeks, death cause: "bowl hives", died: 2 Nov 1908, record (1908-12): 87143.

Frank MORRELL, age 13 years, death cause: "dropsy", born/died: Sullivan Co., died: 18 Aug 1908, record (1908-12): 87144.

Lida CONKIN, age 2 months, death cause: not stated, died: 25 Nov 1908, record (1908-12): 87144.

Rufus Logan WHITE, age 1 hour, death cause: "sick born", died: 27 Mar 1909, record (1908-12): 87145.

Unnamed Infant, female, death cause: "sick born", died: 29 Mar 1909, record (1908-12): 87147.

Sarah ENSLEY, age 70 years, married, death cause: "cancer", born/died: Sullivan Co., died: 2 May 1909, record (1908-12): 87148.

Sudie SIMPSON, age 18 years, single, death cause: "consumption", born/died: Sullivan Co., died: 22 Jan 1909, record (1908-12): 87149.

Lelona HILTON, age 33 years, married, death cause: not recorded, born/died: Sullivan Co., died: 9 May 1909, record (1908-12): 87150.

Infant HILTON, male, death cause: not stated, died: 23 May 1909, record (1908-12): 87151.

Nellie HOOD, age 11 months, death cause: "hooping cough", died: 13 Aug 1909, record (1908-12): 87152.

John FERGUSON, age 2 years, death cause: "hooping cough", died: 15 Jun 1909, record (1908-12): 87153.

William M. WOODS, age 61 years, married, death cause: not stated, born/died: Bluff City, died: 16 Dec 1908, record (1908-12): 87154.

Evaline NICHOLS, age 2 months, death cause: "mumps", born/died: Bluff City, died: 28 Jan 1909, record (1908-12): 87155.

Frank MILLARD, age 12 years, death cause: "tuberculosis", died at Bluff City, 22 Jun 1909, record (1908-12): 87156.
Thomas SMITH, age 13 years, death cause: "typhoid fever", born/died: Sullivan Co., died: 26 Sep 1908, record (1908-12): 87157.
Madeline KEESLING, age 5 years, born: Richmond, VA., death cause: "fever", died at Bristol 20 Aug 1910, record (1908-12): 87158.
Burnell ROLLER, age 2 years, death cause: "membranous croup", born/died: Bristol, died: 21 Oct 1910, record (1908-12): 87159.
Mandie BRIDGEMAN, age 4 years, born at Bristol, VA., died: 28 Mar 1911, record (1908-12): 87160.
Robert DICKERSON, age 39 years, married, born at Abingdon, died: Bristol on 26 Feb 1911, record (1908-12): 87161.
Mrs. Emma SHOEMAKER, age 29 years, married, born: Scott Co., VA., death cause: "consumption", died: Lugarsville on 29 Apr 1911, record (1908-12): 87162.
William SCHARF, age 21 years, single, death cause: "consumption", born/died: Bristol, died: (day not stated) Jan 1911, record (1908-12): 87163.
Mike, MURCERY, age 73 years, married, born: Greenville, TN., death cause: "heart dropsy", died at Bristol on 16 Jul 1910, record (1908-12): 87164.
Henry THOMPSON, colored, age 71 years, married, death cause: "unknown", died at Bristol on (day not stated) Mar 1911, record (1908-12): 87165.
Lizzie MURRY, colored, age 50 years, married, born: Carter Co., death cause: "dropsy", died at Bristol on 30 Jun 1910, record (1908-12): 87166.
Mary KINKEAD, age 15 years, death cause: "feaver", born/died: Bristol, died: 10 Nov 1910, record (1908-12): 87167.
Nora MILLER, age 7 months, death cause: "cholera infantum", died at Bristol on 9 Jun 1911, record (1908-12): 87168.
Henry WELCH, age 96 years, married, born: Carter Co., death cause: "age", died at Bristol on (day not stated) May 1911.
J.D. RICE, age 54 years, married, born at East, VA., death cause: "Brights disease", died at Bristol on 7 Nov 1910, record (1908-12): 87170.
George HOOVER, age 52 years, married, death cause: not stated, born/died: Bristol, died: (day not stated) Mar 1911, record (1908-12): 87171.

Mrs. Luther PIPPIN, age 30 years, married, death cause: "female trouble", born/died: Bristol, died: (day not stated) Apr 1911, record (1908-12): 87172.

Mr. LANE, age 22 years, born near Kingsport, death cause: "typhoid fever", died at Bristol (day not stated) Mar 1911, record (1908-12): 87173.

Ollie VANCE, age 32 years, married, death cause: "accident", died at "Withful" (Wytheville ?) on 1 Jun 1911, record (1908-12): 87174.

Elmer J. HAYNES, age 20 years, single, born at Washington Co., VA, death cause: "consumption", died at Bristol on 30 Jun 1910, record (1908-12): 87175.

Mary JONES, age 16 years, death cause: "dropsy", born/died: Bristol, died: 21 May 1911, record (1908-12): 87176.

Malindy GIBSON, colored, age 68 years, married, born at Russell Co., VA., death cause: "consumption", died at Bristol, 3 Jul 1910, record (1908-12): 87177.

Clem GIBSON, colored, age not stated, born at Shankles Mill, death cause: "heart trouble", died at Sugarsville on 30 Oct 1910, record (1908-12): 87178.

Susie HALE, age 32 years, married, born in "Missippi", death cause: "not known", died at Emmert on 20 Nov 1911, record (1908-12): 87179.

Mary LOYD, age 12 years, born in Virginia, death cause: "abscesses", died at Bristol on 12 May 1912, record (1908-12): 87180.

Infant BAKER, age 1 day, death cause: "unknown", born/died at Bluff City on 5 Jun 1912, record (1908-12): 87181.

Jackson BLEVINS, age 78 years, married, death cause: "organic heart disease", born/died: Emmert, died: 6 Apr 1912.

Estella I. HATCHER, age 42 years, single, death cause: "cancer", born/died: Emmert, died: 19 Jun 1912, record (1908-12): 87183.

Ernest J. ROYSTON, age 4 months, death cause: "stomacitis", born/died: Emmert, died: 31 Jul 1911, record (1908-12): 87184.

Elizabeth COWAN, age 86 years, married, death cause: "pneumonia", born: Sullivan Co., died: Holston Valley on 22 Oct 1911, record (1908-12): 87185.

Louisa MOORE, age 81 years, married, born at Carter Co., death cause: "old age", died at Holston Valley on 14 May 1912, record (1908-12): 87186.

Nathaniel GRUFF, age 18 months, death cause: "unknown", born/died: Holston Valley, died: 13 Dec 1911, record (1908-12): 87187.

Bettie D. KING, age 43 years, married, death cause: "consumption", born/died: Holston Valley, died: 27 Feb 1912, record (1908-12): 87188.

Infant Male, death cause: not stated, born/died: 20 Sep 1911, record (1908-12): 87189.

Addie L. MCKINZIE, age 15 years, death cause: "fever", born/died: Kingsport, died: 10 Jun 1910, record (1908-12): 87190.

Mrs. Nellie ROLLER, age 52 years, married, born in Greenville, TN, death cause: "consumption", died: 23 Feb 1910, record (1908-12): 87190.

P.G. HUMPHREYS, female, age 79 years, single, born at 7 Mile Ford, VA., death cause: "paralysis", died at Piney Flats on 18 Apr 1909, record (1908-12): 87192.

Toby PORTWOOD, female, age 21 years, married, death cause: "consumption", born/died: Piney Flats, died: 20 Mar 1909, record (1908-12): 87193.

Mrs. Jane MASSINGILL, age 84 years, married, death cause: "old age", born/died: Piney Flats, died: 27 Jun 1909, record (1908-12): 87194.

Ida COLE, age 34 years, married, born at Roanoke, VA., death cause: "consumption", died at Piney Flats on 6 Jun 1909, record (1908-12): 87195.

Nancy BRIGGS, age 82 years, single born in North Carolina, death cause: "dropsy", died in 9th District on 29 Mar 1909, record (1908-12): 87196.

Kniciley HATCHER, age 8 years, death cause: "diabetes", born/died: Piney Flats, died: 20 Dec 1909, record (1908-12): 87197.

Willey CROSS, age 4 years, death cause: "croup", born/died: 9th District, died: 17 Dec 1909, record (1908-12): 87198.

Ethel CRETSINGER, age 21 years, married, death cause: "consumption", born/died: Piney Flats, died: 9 Dec 1909, record (1908-12): 87199.

J.H.C. PIERCE, age 73 years, married, born at Wilkes Co., NC., death cause: "heart failure", died at Piney Flats on 1 Mar 1909, record (1908-12): 87200.

Infant WEBB, male, age 2 days, son of W.C. Webb, death cause: "hemorrge", died in 9th District on (day not stated) Jan 1909, record (1908-12): 87201.

John CANTER, Jr., age 1 day, death cause: "not known", born/died: Piney Flats, died: 4 Apr 1909, record (1908-12): 87202.

Annie PRICE, colored, age 25 years, married, death cause: "consumption", born/died: Bristol, died: 6 Jan 1911, record (1908-12): 87203.

Mary HAZZARD, colored, age 8 days, death cause: "jaundice", born/died: Bristol, died: 28 May 1911, record (1908-12): 87204.

Jennie SHELLY, age 54 years, married, born at Wytheville, VA., death cause: not recorded, died at Bristol on 30 Jan 1911.

Sallie MONTGOMERY, age 80 years, married, death cause: "general breakdown", born in Tennessee, died at Bristol on 25 Feb 1911, record (1908-12): 87206.

Unnamed Male, age 4 days, death cause: not stated, born/died: Bristol, died: 26 Jan 1911, record (1908-12): 87207.

Unnamed Male, age 4 hours, death cause: not stated, born/died: Bristol, died: (day not stated) Mar 1911, record (1908-12): 87208.

Rubie Lee WEAVER, age 2 months, death cause: "fever", born/died: Bristol, died: 15 Nov 1910, record (1908-12): 87209.

Maggie BLEVINS, age 63 years, death cause: "cancer", born/died: Big Creek, died: 13 Jan 1911, record (1908-12): 87210

King PETERS, age 14 years, death cause: "measles", died: 1st District on 27 Jul 1910, record (1908-12): 87211.

Celia SHIVER, age 31 years, married, death cause: "cancer", died: 16 Nov 1910, record (1908-12): 87212.

Unnamed Male, age 1 day, death cause: not stated, died at Big Creek on 23 Jun 1911, record (1908-12): 87213.

John PHIPPS, age 72 years, married, death cause: "pneumonia", born in Sullivan Co., died at Emmert on 20 Jan 1911, record (1908-12): 87214.

Unnamed Male, age 24 hours, death cause: not stated, born/died: Emmert, died: 6 Sep 1910. record (1908-12): 87215.

Mart STONE, male, age 71 years, born in Virginia, married, death cause: "pneumonia", died at Emmert on 19 Jan 1911, record (1908-12): 87216.

Hugh J. PIPPIN, age 84 years, born in Washington Co., VA., married, death cause: "pneumonia", died at Emmert on 11 Mar 1911, record (1908-12): 87217.

S   CROSS, male, age 1 month, death cause: "spinal meningitis", died at Emmert on 18 Jan 1911, record (1908-12): 87218.

Sary Akers BURNETT, age 66 years, married, death cause: "stomach trouble", died in 1st District on 11 Dec 1911, record (1908-12): 87219.

Jasper NEWMANS, age 28 years, married, death cause: "typhoid fever", born/died: 1st District, died: 12 Oct 1910, record (1908-12): 87220.

Marry MORRELL, age 66 years, born in Virginia, married, death cause: "dropsy", died in 1st District on 1 Sep 1910, record (1908-12): 87221.

Laura SHIPLEY, age 19 years, single, death cause: "appendicitis", died in 1st District on 12 Nov 1910, record (1908-12): 87222.

Adie SMITHTON, age 11 months, death cause: not stated, died in 1st District on 20 Aug 1910, record (1908-12): 87223.

Alice Catherine MORTON, age 63 years, married, death cause: "cancer", died in 1st District on 18 Jun 1911, record (1908-12): 87224.

Sallie SEMKIN, age 76 years, married, death cause: "consumption of bowels", died in 1st District on 8 Aug 1910, record (1908-12): 87225.

Mr. J.W. PAINTER, age 74 years, born in "With" Co., VA., married, death cause: "parylized", died at Bristol on 18 Nov 1910, record (1908-12): 87226.

Dr. J.T. WILLIAMS, age 59 years, born in Floyd Co., VA., married, death cause: "asthma", died at Bristol on 24 Apr 1911, record (1908-12): 87227.

Myrtle CANTER, age 18 years, married, death cause: "fever", born/died: Horse Creek, died: 28 Nov 1908, record (1908-12): 87228.

Eddie PINN, colored, age 30 years, born at Gate City, VA., married, death cause: "consumption", died at Bristol on (day not stated) Jan 1911, record (1908-12): 87229.

Hallie V. THOMAS, age 1 week, death cause: "spasmc", died at Bristol on 4 Aug 1910, record (1908-12): 87230.

Janie May RIGGS, age 6 years, death cause: "dyptheria", died at Bristol on 30 Sep 1910, record (1908-12): 87231.

Joseph WHITE, age 16 months, death cause: "cholera", died at Bristol on 3 Jul 1911, record (1908-12): 87232.

George KING, colored, age 65 years, born in Georgia, married, death cause: "consumption", died at Bristol on 1 Mar 1911, record (1908-12): 87233.

Albert BRAUDAUS, colored, age 1 year, death cause: "spasms", died at Bristol on 7 Apr 1911, record (1908-12): 87234.

Bessie Lee QUARLS, age 17 months, death cause: "indigestion", died at Bristol on 1 Aug 1910, record (1908-12): 87235.

Noah COX, age not stated, married, death cause: "heart failure", born/died: Fordtown, died: 24 Jan 1910, record (1908-12): 87236.

L.H. WHALEY, age 41 years, 6 months, married, death cause: "paralysis", born/died: Gotts Cross Roads, died: 6 Dec 1909, record (1908-12): 87237.

Infant HITE, male, age 1 day, death cause: not stated, died at Gotts Cross Roads on 9 Jan 1910, record (1908-12): 87238.

Infant HITE, male, age 4 days, death cause: not stated, died at Gotts Cross Roads on 13 Jan 1910, record (1908-12): 87239.

Rufus CLEEK, age 3 years, death cause: not stated, died in 14th District on 20 Oct 1910, record (1908-12): 87240.

W.H. KIDWELL, age 52 years, born in Virginia, married, death cause: "cancer of stomach", died in 21st District on 12 Dec 1909, record (1908-12): 87241.

Gertie EDWARDS, age 4 months, death cause: "cholera", died in 21st District on 1 Jun 1910, record (1908-12): 87242.

Louvena HOLT, age 50 years, married, death cause: "epathelic fits", died at Indian Springs on 25 Oct 1909, record (1908-12): 87243.

Joe LYNN, age 13 years, born at Arcadia, TN., death cause: "spinal mental jedus", died at Indian Springs on 9 Feb 1910, record (1908-12): 87244.

Katie RUTLIDGE, age 3 years, death cause: "croup", died at Indian Springs on 26 Sep 1909, record (1908-12): 87245.

Mary E. LADY, age 52 years, married, death cause: "pneumonia", born/died: Indian Springs, died: 28 Aug 1909, record (1908-12): 87246.

W.M. BOWERY, age 62 years, married, death cause: "tuberculosis", born/died: Indian Springs, died: 27 Mar 1910, record (1908-12): 87247.

C.D. COLE, age 37 years, married, death cause: "tuberculosis", born/died: Indian Springs, died: 12 Dec 1910, record (1908-12): 87248.

Mary R. ISLEY, age 8 years, death cause: "pneumonia", born/died: Indian Springs, died: 1 Nov 1909, record (1908-12): 87249.

W.A. HOLT, age 61 years, married, death cause: "pneumonia", born/died: Indian Springs, died: 6 Mar 1910, record (1908-12): 87250.

Mrs. L.E. HOLT, age 55 years, married, death cause: "pneumonia", born/died: Indian Springs, died: 2 Mar 1910, record (1908-12): 87251.

Fannie Kate CROSS, age 8 years, death cause: "she fell", died in 8th District on 18 Sep 1909, record (1908-12): 87252.

Matilda HICKS, age 47 years, married, death cause: "flux", died in the 8th District on 2 Jul 1909.

Susan MILLER, age 63 years, married, death cause: "stomach trouble", died in the 8th District on 31 Oct 1909, record (1908-12): 87254.

Mary Catherine MORRELL, age 38 years, death cause: "rhumatism", died in the 1st District on 20 Dec 1910, record (1908-12): 87255.

Roda E. BLEVINS, age 80 years, born in Carter Co., TN., married, death cause: "pneumonia", died at Emmert on 15 Aug 1910, record (1908-12): 87256.

Nathan BRACH, age 31 years, married, death cause: "pneumonia", died in the 1st District on 13 Jul 1910, record (1908-12): 87257.

Elvina ROGGERS, age 92 years, born in Virginia, married, death cause: not recorded, died in 1st District on 9 Mar 1911, record (1908-12): 87258.

Nannie MATTOX, age 75 years, born in Virginia, married, death cause: "rhumatism", died at Paperville on 12 Dec 1910, record (1908-12): 87259.

Unnamed Male, age 6 hours, death cause: not stated, died in the 8th District on 6 Jul 1910.

French DEAKIN, age 7 years, death cause: "membranous croup", died in the 8th District on 4 Nov 1909, record (1908-12): 87261.

Unnamed Male, age 6 hours, death cause: not stated, died in the 8th District on 5 Jul 1910, record (1908-12): 87262.

Susan WINE, (rest of record illegible), died: 16 Jul 1910, record (1908-12): 87264.

Annie TRICKLE, age 16 years, death cause: "tuberculosis", died in 8th District on 21 Apr 1910, record (1908-12): 87264.

John TRICKLE, age 20 years, death cause: "tuberculosis", died in Bakersfield, CA., on 2 Jan 1910, record (1908-12): 87265.

Sallie MILARD, age 78 years, single, death cause: "old age", died in the 8th District on 20 Mar 1910, record (1908-12): 87266.

Thomas CARROLL, age 85 years, born in Tennessee, married, death cause: "dropsy", died in 8th District on 15 Mar 1910, record (1908-12): 87267.

C.M. HODGE, age 65 years, married, death cause: "consumption", died in the 18th District on 18 Nov 1910, record (1908-12): 87268.

Myrtle PITS, age 13 years, death cause: "dropsy", born/died: Holston, died: 15 Jan 1911, record (1908-12): 87269.

Mabel NEWLAND, age 3 months, death cause: "unknown", born/died: Newland Store, died: 17 Jun 1911, record (1908-12): 87270.

Paskel MORSE, age 1 year, death cause: "membranous croup", died at the 18th District on 6 Nov 1911, record (1908-12): 78271.

Guy BARND, age 21 years, single, death cause: "heart failure", died in the 18th District on 13 Apr 1911, record (1908-12): 87272.

A.A. HAMILTON, age 57 years, single, death cause: "tuberculosis", died in the 18th District on 13 May 1911, record (1908-12): 87273.

Samuel CRAWFORD, age 69 years, married, death cause: "pneumonia", born/died: Holston, died: 18 Mar 1911, record (1908-12): 87274.

Georgie LITE, age 6 years, death cause: "diphtheria", died at Holston on 20 Oct 1911, record (1908-12): 87275.

John Ernist SMITH, age 2 months, death cause: "skinolmongetis", died in the 18th District on 27 Jul 1910, record (1908-12): 87276.

Emma MONK, age 54 years, married, death cause: "rhumatism", died in the 18th District on 5 Jul 1910, record (1908-12): 87277.

Henry Etta FRAZIER, age 34 years, death cause: "childbirth", died in the 18th District on 13 Aug 1910, record (1908-12): 87278.

Nannie WHITAKER, age not stated, death cause: "unknown", died in the 18th District on 6 Jan 1911, record (1908-12): 87279.

Viv LAVISON, female, age 34 years, married, death cause: "consumption", died in the 18th District on 9 Jun 1911, record (1908-12): 87280.

Ralph Gentry HARMON, age 1 month and 28 days, death cause: "neumone fever", born/died in the 3rd District, died: 18 Mar 1911, record (1908-12): 87281.

M Elizabeth HANSOM, female, age 26 years, married, death cause: "consumption", born/died in the 3rd District, died: 25 Dec 1908, record (1908-12): 87282.

Charlotte GUIN, age 3 months, death cause: "hives", born/died in the 3rd District, died: 15 Jun 1908, record (1908-12): 87283.

Hila Catham MILLARD, age 55 years, married, death cause: "cancer of stomach", born/died in the 3rd District, died: 1 Apr 1909, record (1908-12): 87284.
William COMBS, age about 78 years, married, death cause: "new mona fever", born/died in the 3rd District, died: 11 Apr 1909, record (1908-12): 87285.
John GUIN, female, age 57 years, born in North Carolina, married, death cause: "cancer of stomach", died in the 3rd District on 11 Jun 1909, record (1908-12): 87286.
Anna Jeeter MILLER, age 5 years, death cause: "croup", born/died: Bristol, died: 18 Dec 1908, record (1908-12): 87287.
William S. ANDERSON, age 61 years, married, death cause: "rhumatism and kidney trouble", died at Blountville on 31 Jan 1909, record (1908-12): 87288.
William G. MORSE (or Moore ?), age 66 years, single, death cause: "paralysis", died: 4 Sep 1908, record (1908-12): 87288.
Beky MOORE, age 80 years, death cause: "heart failure", died in the 5th District on 12 Mar 1908, record (1908-12): 87290.
Lola HARR, age 17 years, single, death cause: "typhoid fever', died at Blountville on 3 Sep 1908, record (1908-12): 87291.
James CARDEN, age 27 years, married, death cause: "shot by Frank Leonard", died at Blountville on 8 Aug 1908, record (1908-12): 87292.
Mrs. Louisa SMITH, age 83 years, death cause: "old age", died at Blountville on 12 May 1909, record (1908-12): 87293.
James K.P. MINNICK, age 64 years, death cause: "kidney trouble", born/died in the 5th District, died: 24 Oct 1908, record (1908-12): 87294.
Laura Gerturde FAIR, age 36 years, married, born at Bluff City, death cause: "tuberculosis", died at Blountville on 20 Jan 1909, record (1908-12): 87295.
Lily CASTEEL, age 6 months, death cause: "indigestion", died: 30 Jun 1909, record (1908-12): 87296.
Sarah CASTEEL, age 23 years, born at Blountville, married, death cause: "childbirth", died: 13 Dec 1909, record (1908-12): 87297.
Dr. A.J. HAIDLY, age 69 years, married, died in the 5th District on 10 Jan 1909, record (1908-12): 87298.
Mattie CROSS, age 30 years, single, death cause: "tuberculosis", died in the 5th District on 19 Apr 1909.

Infant ADAMS, male, death cause: "stillborn", died in the 5th District on 6 Jan 1909, record (1908-12): 87300.

Emma CARTER, age 3 weeks, death cause: "hives", died at Indian Springs on 1 Apr 1909, record (1908-12): 87301.

Sana BURGESS, age 5 years, born in North Carolina, death cause: "croup", died at Emmett on 9 Dec 1910, record (1908-12): 87302.

Infant MALONE, female, age 6 days, death cause: "heart trouble", died in the 5th District on 1 Jun 1911, record (1908-12): 87303.

William DISHNER, age 77 years, married, death cause: "Brights disease", died in the 5th District on 14 Feb 1911, record (1908-12): 87304.

Willie CRUSSELL, male, age 52 years, married, death cause: "consumption", died in the 5th District on 2 May 1911, record (1908-12): 87305.

Elbert CRUSSELL, age 55 years, married, death cause: "pneumonia", died in the 5th District on 2 Feb 1911, record (1908-12): 87306.

Abe LEONARD, age 55 years, married, death cause: "rheumatism", died in the 5th District on 29 Mar 1911, record (1908-12): 87307.

Hanna JOHNSON, age 34 years, married, death cause: "consumption", born/died: 5th District, died: 15 Apr 1911, record (1908-12): 87308.

George HARR, age 40 years, married, death cause: "typhoid", died in the 5th District on 1 Aug 1910, record (1908-12): 87309.

Mrs. Martha CAMPBELL, age 40 years, married, death cause: "consumption", born/died: 5th District, died: 1 Jun 1911, record (1908-12): 87310.

Mrs. Adaline HOLLY, age 60 years, married, death cause: "consumption", died in the 5th District on 6 Nov 1910, record (1908-12): 87311.

John C. HULL, age 70 years, married, death cause: "paralysis", died in the 5th District on 20 Sep 1910, record (1908-12): 87312.

Johnnie BOOKER, age 94 years, married, death cause: "old age", died in the 5th District on 1 Nov 1910, record (1908-12): 87313.

Dr. N.J. DELANEY, age 77 years, born: Tennessee, married, death cause: "dysentery", died in the 5th District on 3 Oct 1910, record (1908-12): 87314.

Elizabeth RUSSELL, age 63 years, married, death cause: "consumption", died in Poor House, 5th District on 12 Jul 1910, record (1908-12): 87315.

John TOLLMAN, age 66 years, born in Virginia, married, death cause: "rhumatism", died in the 5th District on 25 Sep 1910, record (1908-12): 87316.
Corthena CAMPBELL, age 40 years, single, death cause: "fits", died in the Poor House, 5th District, on 15 JUn 1911, record (1908-12): 87317.
Mrs. Lorena E. HENDRICKSON, age 76 years, married, death cause: "paralysis", died in the 5th District on 5 Dec 1910, record (1908-12): 87318.
Mrs. Amanda PIERSON, age 62 years, married, death cause: "heart trouble:, died in the 5th District on 11 Apr 1911, record (1908-12): 87319.
Mrs. Emma POWELL, age 80 years, born: Tennessee, married, death cause: "asthma", died in the 5th District on 15 Mar 1911, record (1908-12): 87320.
Mrs. Martha DOOLEY, age 74 years, born: Tennessee, married, death cause: "penumonia", died in the 5th District on 3 Mar 1911, record (1908-12): 87321.
Hubert Hawk BLACKMAN, age 6 weeks, death cause: "spinal menengitis", died in the 5th District on 1 Nov 1910, record (1908-12): 87322.
Mrs. Lucy MASSEY, age 52 years, married, death cause: "rheumatism", died in the 5th District on 3 May 1911, record (1908-12): 87323.
Homer H. SMITH, Jr., age 2 years, 1 month and 1 day, death cause: "croup", died in the 5th District on 28 Dec 1910, record (1908-12): 87324.
Mrs. Susan ROGERS, age 78 years, married, death cause: "old age", born/died: 5th District, died: 3 Jan 1911, record (1908-12): 87325.
Urias RIDDLE, male, age 90 years, married, death cause: "old age", died in the Poor House, 5th District, on 6 Jan 1911, record (1908-12): 87326.
Emiline FLYNN, age 80 years, married, death cause: "dropsy", born/died: Rock Springs, died: 17 May 1911, record (1908-12): 87327.
G.W. BOYD, age 73 years, born at Depews Chapel, married, death cause: "paralysis", died at Rock Springs on 26 Mar 1911, record (1908-12): 87328.
Alfred L. CAMPBELL, age 59 years, born at Rock Springs, married, death cause: "dropsy", died at Pactalus on 9 Mar 1911, record (1908-12): 87329.
Charlotte OWENS, age 2 years, death cause: "pneumonia fever", died at Pactalus on 3 Jan 1911, record (1908-12): 87330.
Roxy COX, age 3 years, death cause: "croup", died at Rock Springs on 13 Dec 1910, record (1908-12): 87331.

Thomas HUNT, age 52 years, married, death cause: "pneumonia", born/died: Pactalus, died: 4 Jan 1911, record (1908-12): 87332.
George HUNT, age 77 years, married, death cause: "paralysis", born/died: Pactalus, died: 18 Feb 1911, record (1908-12): 87333.
Alfred K. LISEMAY, age 62 years, married, death cause: "pneumonia", born/died; Pactalus, died: 13 Apr 1911, record (1908-12): 87334.
Infant DIXON, age 5 months, death cause: "measles", died at Pactalus, (day not stated) Jun 1911, record (1908-12): 87335.
John FORD, age 40 years, born at Rock Springs, married, death cause: "tuberculosis", died at Pactalus on 25 Mar 1911, record (1908-12): 87336.
Infant FORD, male, age 1 day, death cause: "not known", died at Pactalus on (day not stated) Dec 1910, record (1908-12): 87337.
William FLEENOR, age 19 years, single, death cause: "typhoid fever", born/died: Horse Creek, died: 14 Sep 1910, record (1908-12): 87538.
Anne COX, age 47 years, born at Depew Chapel, married, death cause: "heart dropsy", died at Horse Creek on 29 Jun 1911, record (1908-12): 87339.
Retta BLAKELY, age 30 years, married, death cause: "tuberculosis", born/died: Rock Springs, died: 26 Apr 1911, record (1908-12): 87340.
Rufus BROWN, age 1 year, death cause: "spinal mengitis", born/died: Depew Chapel, died: 15 Jul 1910, record (1908-12): 87341.
George HICKMAN, age 75 years, married, death cause: "not known", born/died: Depew Capel, died: 22 Dec 1910, record (1908-12): 87342.
Bersheba HICKMAN, age 74 years, married, death cause: "not known", born/died: Depew Chapel, died: 25 Jul 1910, record (1908-12): 87343.
John BARRS, age 52 years, born in Virginia, married, death cause: "cancer", died at Rock Springs on 30 Sep 1910, record (1908-12): 87344.
Mrs. Henry LIGHT, age 23 years, born: Depew Chapel, married, death cause: "tuberculosis", died at Horse Creek on 23 Mar 1911, record (1908-12): 87345.
July Mandy NETHERLAND, black, age 12 days, death cause: "unknown", died at Kingsport on 27 Nov 1910, record (1908-12): 87346.
Cathleen Robinson CLOUD, age 5 years, death cause: "fever and measles", born/died: Kingsport, died: 10 May 1911, record (1908-12): 87347.

Thomas LIGHT, age 84 years, born at Horse Creek, married, death cause: "old chronic troubles", died at Kingsport on 14 Jan 1911, record (1908-12): 87348.

W.M. DIXON, age 68 years, born in Scott Co., VA., married, death cause: "rhumatism", died at Bloomingdale on 17 Mar 1911, record (1908-12): 87349.

Annie Loura HICKS, age 10 months and 2 days, death cause: "congested lungs", born/died: Bloomingdale, died: 5 Aug 1910, record (1908-12): 87350.

Elizabeth KETRON, age 65 years, born: Kingsport, married, death cause: "cattarah of stomach", died at Bloomingdale on 8 Oct 1910, record (1908-12): 87351.

Maud E. KETRON, age 26 years, born at Jonesville, Lee Co., VA., married, death cause: "child birth", died at Bloomingdale on 14 Jul 1910, record (1908-12): 87352.

Mary C. HUFFMAN, age 26 days, death cause: "bold hives", born/died: Arcadia, died: 13 Aug 1910, record (1908-12): 87353.

Suella KETRON, age 7 years, death cause: "tuberculose meningitis", born/died: Bloomingdale, died: 18 Mar 1911, record (1908-12): 87354.

Gerturde HOBBS, age 27 years, married, death cause: "tuberculosis", born/died: Bloomingdale, died: 17 Mar 1911, record (1908-12): 87355.

James H. HUMPHREYS, age 10 days, death cause: "unknown", died: 9 Aug 1909, record (1908-12): 87365.

Theopholis GREENWAY, age 18 months, death cause: "whooping cough", died in the 4th District on 19 May 1910, record (1908-12): 87357.

Sidney EARHART, age 3 years, death cause: "locked bowels", died in the 4th District on 8 Aug 1909, record (1908-12): 87358.

S.F. HUGHES, age 61 years, single, death cause: "consumption", died in the 4th District on 19 Oct 1909, record (1908-12): 87359.

Joseph RHEA, age 79 years, born in Tennessee, married, death cause: "senility", died in the 4th District on 13 Aug 1909, record (1908-12): 87360.

William CROSS, age 75 years, born in Tennessee, married, death cause: "old age",, died in the 4th District on (day not stated) Jan 1910, record (1908-12): 87361.

Infant MAHAFFEY, male, death cause: "stillborn", died in the 4th District on 2 Apr 1910, record (1908-12): 87362.

Infant TAYLOR, female, age 3 days, death cause: "unknown", died in the 4th District on 20 Mar 1910, record (1908-12): 87363.

May TAYLOR, age 26 years, married, death cause: "childbirth", died in the 4th District on 27 Jul 1909, record (1908-12): 87364.
W.O. GOTT, age 59 years, born at Gott Cross Road, married, death cause: "tuberculosis", died int eh 18th District on 15 Apr 1912, record (1908-12): 87365.
Dalis ROLLER, age 1 month, death cause: "hives", died in the 18th District on (day not stated) May 1912, record (1908-12): 87366.
Joseph GOFORTH, age 9 days, death cause: "yellow jaundice", died in the 18th District on (day illegible) May 1912, record (1908-12): 87367.
Daniel T. HILTON, age 4 months, death cause: "bealed head", died in the 18th District on 18 Mar 1912, record (1908-12): 87368.
Elalina G..(Illegible), age 87 years, married, death cause: "old age", died in the 18th District on 19 Jun 1912, record (1908-12): 87369.
Bascom BIBBER, age 1 year, death cause: "membranous croup", born/died: Washington Co., VA., died: 26 Jan 1912, record (1908-12): 87370.
Vada WATSON, age 8 years, born in North Carolina, death cause: "birnt", died in Abingdon, VA. on 29 Mar 1912, record (1908-12): 87371.
M.B. SMITH, age 62 years, born in Washington Co., VA., married, death cause: "piles and stomach trouble", died in the 19th District on 25 Dec 1911, record (1908-12): 87372.
Nelley E. RUSH, age 2 years, born in Virginia, death cause: "hooping cough", died in the 19th District on 27 Mar 1912, record (1908-12): 87373.
Gordin RUSH, age 1 year, death cause: "hooping cough", born/died in Washington Co., VA., died; 17 Mar 1912, record (1908-12): 87374.
Thomas CALAHAND, age 3 montsh, death cause: "bold hives", died in the 19th District on 15 Dec 1911, record (1908-12): 87375.
Lillie CALIHAN, age 1 year, death cause: "bold hives", died in the 19th District on 1 May 1912, record (1908-12): 87376.
L.B. HARR, female, age 18 years, single, death cause: "water and cancer", died in Chicago, Illinois on 12 Jan 1912, record (1908-12): 87377.
William WRIGHT, age 3 years and 6 months, death cause: "dyptheria", died in the 19th District on 20 Nov 1911, record (1908-12): 87378.

Infant CALLAND, age 6 days, death cause: "not known", died in the 19th District on 22 Jun 1912, record (1908-12): 87379.

William GROSS, age 10 years, death cause: "hook worm", died in the 19th District on 27 Mar 1912, record (1908-12): 87380.

Infant JOHNSON, male, age 1 day, death cause: not stated, died in the 19th District on 14 Apr 1912, record (1908-12): 87381.

Infant OFFIELD, male, death cause: not stated, died in the 19th District on 25 Dec 1911, record (1908-12): 87382.

John DICKSON, age 87 years, married, death cause: "Brights disease", born/died: Kingsport, died: 1 Apr 1910, record (1908-12): 87383.

James William SHARP, age 1 year, 26 days, death cause: "whooping cough", died in the 3rd District on 10 Oct 1910, record (1908-12): 87384.

Orvill CARRIER, age 9 months, death cause: "spinal affection", died in the 3rd District on 17 Dec 1910, record (1908-12): 87385.

Susan JONES, age about 51 years, married, death cause: "abscess of stomach", died in the 3rd District on 2 Mar 1911, record (1908-12): 87386.

Unnamed Infant, male, death cause: "born dead", died 3rd District on 21 Apr 1911, record (1908-12): 87387.

Sarah MICKLAS, age 66 years and 11 months, single, death cause: "cancer of breast", died in the 3rd District on 7 Apr 1911, record (1908-12): 87388.

Elbert STEVENS, age 1 year and 10 months, born in Carter County, death cause: "collery", died in Carter County on 8 Jun 1911, record (1908-12): 87398.

Jessie CHISADYS, age 17 years and 2 months, born in North Carolina, death cause: "consumption", died in the 3rd District on 9 Apr 1911, record (1908-12): 87390.

Catherine ELSWICK, age 58 years, married, death cause: "lung trouble", born/died: 3rd District, died: 10 Feb 1911, record (1908-12): 87391.

Edna PATRICK, age 1 year, 6 months and 6 days, death cause: "spinal affection", died in the 3rd District on 10 May 1911, record (1908-12): 87392.

Flancey ALFORD, age 7 months, death cause: "spinal minagets", died in the 3rd District on 30 Nov 1910, record (1908-12): 87393.

Cinthy An CURSIEA, age 67 years, married, death cause: "heart failure", born/died in 3rd District, died: 5 Apr 1911, record (1908-12): 87394.

Robbie HILLIARD, female, age 1 year, 9 months and 1 day, death cause: "flux", died in the 3rd District on 25 Jun 1911, record (1908-12): 87395.

Robart William BOYD, age about 15 years, death cause: not stated, born/died: 3rd District, died: 16 Aug 1913, record (1908-12): 87396.

Sidney HATCHER, age 10 days, death cause: "bold hives, died in the 3rd District on 22 Dec 1910, record (1908-12): 87397.

Virginia NAVE, age 1 year and 11 months, death cause: "consumption", born/died: Emmitt, died: 13 Apr 1910, record (1908-12): 87398.

Lafayette MORRELL, age 13 years, death cause: "Brights disease", born/died: Bluff City, died: 31 May 1910, record (1908-12): 87399.

Paul MORRELL, age 4 years, born at Hemlock, death cause: "scarlet fever", died at Bluff City on (day not stated) Nov 1909, record (1908-12): 87400.

J.A. CURRIER, age 65 years, married, death cause: "heart failure", died at Bluff City on 12 Feb 1910, record (1908-12): 87401.

J.E.C. HALE, age 52 years, born in Washington Co., married, death cause: illegible, died in the 1st District on 21 Jun 1910, record (1908-12): 87402.

Georgie BLEVINS, age 13 months, death cause: "pneumonia", born/died: Emmett, died: 13 May 1910, record (1908-12): 87403.

William (Illegible), age 1 month, 15 days, death cause: illegible, died at Emmett on 9 Apr 1910, record (1908-12): 87404.

J.A. BEIDLEMAN, age 82 years, born in Sullivan Co., married, death cause: "pneumonia", died at Emmett on 14 May 1910, record (1908-12): 87405.

Susan RODGERS, age 60 years, married, death cause: "consumption", died at Emmett on 4 May 1910, record (1908-12): 87406.

Mary TRIVET, age 19 years, married, death cause: "pneumonia", died in the 1st District on 28 Mar 1910, record (1908-12): 87407.

Hampton SHOUN, age 28 years, born in Carter Co., married, death cause: "mashed by log, blood poison", died at Bristol on (day not stated) Mar 1910, record (1908-12): 87408.

James CHAPPEL, age 18 years, single, death cause: "accidental suicide, pistol", died at Emmett on 24 May 1910, record (1908-12): 87409.

Tommy HICKS, age 6 years, born at Arcadia, death cause: "brain fever", died at Bloomingdale on 18 Oct 1910, record (1908-12): 87410.
Elizabeth M. KING, age 85 years, 7 months and 5 days, born in Washington Co., TN., married, death cause: "old age", died at Kingsport on 22 Jun 1911, record (1908-12): 87411.
Unnamed Infant, female, death cause: "born dead", died at Kingsport on 11 Nov 1910, record (1908-12): 87412.
James STEADMAN, death cause: "silent birth", died at Kingsport on 22 Sep 1910, record (1908-12): 87413.
Unnamed Infant, male, age 55 days, death cause: "weakness", died at Kingsport on 2 May 1911, record (1908-12): 87414.
Unnamed Infant, male, death cause: "silent birth", died at Bloomingdale on 27 Jan 1911, record (1908-12): 87415.
Daniel ELLIS, age 68 years, born in North Carolina, married, minister, death cause: "cancer", died at Big Creek on 15 Dec 1909, record (1908-12): 87416.
Francis BALL, age 65 years, born in Jefferson Co., married, death cause: illegible, died in the 1st District on 15 Mar 1910, record (1908-12): 87417.
George BALL, age 72 years, born in Jefferson Co., married, death cause: "pneumonia", died in the 1st District on 17 Dec 1909, record (1908-12): 87418.
Unnamed Infant, male, age 1 day, death cause: not stated, died in the 1st District on 10 May 1910, record (1908-12): 87419.
Ellen HICKS, age 49 years, born in Johnson Co., married, death cause: "paralysis", died in Washington Co., TN. on 2 Mar 1910, record (1908-12): 87420.
J. DAVIDSON, age 69 years, married, death cause: "pneumonia", died in the 20th District on 8 Jul 1909, record (1908-12): 98421.
Elizabeth ALISON, age 73 years, born in Carter Co., married, death cause: "pneumonia", died in the 20th District on 16 Feb 1910, record (1908-12): 87422.
R.F. KING, age 61 years, married, minister, death cause: "consumption", died in the 20th District on 10 May 1910, record (1908-12): 87423.
Victoria MASTER, age 40 years, married, death cause: "abcess on brain", died in the 20th District on 6 Jul 1909, record (1908-12): 87424.
John ALLISON, age 61 years, married, death cause: "broken blood vessel", died in the 20th District on 7 Feb 1910, record (1908-12): 87425.

Winfred WOLFE, age 76 years, born in Indiana, married, death cause: "heart trouble", died in the 20th District, 9 Oct 1909, record (1908-12): 87426.

Infant GEISLER, male, age not stated, death cause: "unknown", died in the 20th District on 1 Apr 1910, record (1908-12): 87427.

Lula SHIPLEY, age 4 years, death cause: "burned", died in the 20th District on 26 Oct 1909, record (1908-12): 87428.

Joel A.G. COLE, age 74 years, 6 days, born near Abingdon, married, death cause: "heart failure", died at Arcadia on 15 Aug 1909, record (1908-12): 87429.

Fannie Catherine BOOHER, age 1 month and 21 days, death cause: "hives", died at Mill Point on 26 Apr 1910, record (1908-12): 87430.

Job H. CLARK, age 72 years, born at Abingdon, VA., married, death cause: "complication of disease", died at Mill Point on 5 Jul 1909, record (1908-12): 87431.

Belle HOLT, age 18 years, single, death cause: "complication of disease", died at Mill Point on 1 Jun 1910, record (1908-12): 87432.

Mamie Eliza SENIKER, age 19 years, 1 month, 3 days, married, death cause: "tuberculosis", died at McMinnville, TN., died: 18 Apr 1910, record (1908-12): 87433.

Bessie May SHEFFEY, age 15 years, 1 day, death cause: "heart failure", born/died: Mill Point, died: 20 Jan 1910, record (1908-12): 87434.

Infant BARR, male, age 1 day, child of Henry Barr, death cause: "not known", died at Blountville on 8 Feb 1910, record (1908-12): 87435.

Infant GARRETT, female, child of George Garrett, born/died: Holston Valley on 24 Mar 1911, record (1908-12): 87436.

Mary Elzora STONE, age 18 months, death cause: "cholera", died at Holston Valley on 6 Aug 1910, record (1908-12): 87437.

Nancy FRITZ, age 60 years, born in Johnson Co., married, death cause: "gripp", died at Holston Valley on 5 Feb 1911, record (1908-12): 87438.

Infant LONET, male, child of E.D. Lonet, death cause: "not known", died at Sinking Creek on 5 Jun 1911, record (1908-12): 87439.

Infant JONES, male, child of Floyd Jones, death cause: "not known", died at Holston Valley on 25 Oct 1910, record (1908-12): 87440.

Charley CATE, age 21 years, born in Sevier Co., single, death cause: "consumption", died at Holston Valley on 3 Feb 1911, record (1909-12): 87441.
Zilpha GARRETT, age 42 years, married, died at Holston Valley on 24 Mar 1911, record (1909-12): 87442.
Sam THOMAS, age 72 years, married, death cause: "heart disease", died at Holston Valley on 16 Apr 1911, record (1909-12): 87443.
Infant PINDERGRASS, male, child of John Pindergrass, death cause: "unknown", died at Holston Valley on 31 Mar 1911, record (1909-12): 87444.
Lonie L. BARNES, age 7 years, death cause: "pneumonia fever", died in the 18th District on 22 Jan 1910, record (1909-12): 87445.
Infant HICKS, female, age 2 days, death cause: "unknown", died in Holston Valley on 29 Apr 1910, record (1909-12): 87446.
Jack GRUBB, age 18 years, single, death cause: "typhoid fever", born/died: Holston Valley, died: 19 Nov 1909, record (1909-12): 87447.
Claten LOUDY, age 15 months, death cause: "scarlet fever", died at Holston Valley on 11 Mar 1910, record (1909-12): 87448.
John SHUFFLESTREET, age 73 years, born in Johnson Co., married, death cause: "heart failure", died in Holston Valley on 14 May 1910, record (1909-12): 87449.
Sue E. PYLE, age 24 years, single, school teacher, death cause: "appendicitis", born/died: Holston Valley, died: 26 Dec 1909, record (1909-12): 87450.
Cathern PETERS, age 21 years, single, death cause: "consumption", died at Holston Valley on 26 Nov 1909, record (1909-12): 87451.
S.P. SHIPLEY, age 60 years, born at Shipley's Ferry, married, death cause: "unknown", died at Kendrick Creek on 12 Mar 1909, record (1909-12): 87452.
Nanie STRICKLER, age 3 months, death cause: "thrash", born and died: Fordtown, died: 25 Aug 1908, record (1909-12): 87453.
Charley JONES, age 82 years, married, death cause: "sudon death", born and died: 14th District, died: 12 May 1909, record (1909-12): 87454.
A.H. HALL, male, age 72 years, married, death cause: "heakups", died at Fordtown on 25 Oct 1908, record (1909-12): 87455.
Wilson HAMILTON, age 3 weeks, death cause: "bold hives", born and died: near Fordtown, died: 7 Jan 1909, record (1909-12): 87456.

Benjamin SMITH, age 54 years, born at Vance, TN., married, death cause: "tuberculosis", died at Bristol on 4 Oct 1908, record (1908-12): 87457.

Callie CAMPBELL, age 6 years, death cause: "tuberculosis", died at Bristol on 24 May 1909, record (1908-12): 87458.

T.E. CARRIER, male, age not recorded, married, born at Bluff City, death cause: "tuberculosis", died at Bristol on 2 Aug 1908, record (1908-12): 87459.

Sarah SWINEY, age 64 years, born at Vance, TN., married, death cause: "pneumonia fever", died near Bristol on 3 Mar 1909, record (1908-12): 87460.

D.L. COMBS, age 51 years, born at Bluff City, married, death cause: "pneumonia", died near Bristol on 17 Jul 1908, record (1908-12): 87461.

William H. STONE, age 59 years, married, death cause: "pneumonia fever", died at Holston Valley on 28 May 1909, record (1908-12): 87462.

John FEATHERS, age 17 years, born: Kings Mill, VA., single, death cause: "diabetes", died at Holston Valley on 28 May 1909, record (1908-12): 87463.

Louise HODGE, age 48 years, born at Carter Co., married, death cause: "cancer", died at Holston Valley on 31 Jan 1909, record (1908-12): 87464.

James C. GRUBB, age 1 day, death cause: "not known", died at Holston Valley on 8 May 1909, record (1908-12): 87465.

Ann PARE, age 49 years, single, death cause: "cancer" born and died at Edens Ridge, died: 15 May 1909, record (1908-12): 87466.

Elizabeth MOODY, age 78 years, single, death cause: "cancer", born and died at Indian Springs, died: 20 Jan 1909, record (1908-12): 87467.

T.A. COX, male, age 28 years, born at Blountville, married, death cause: "consumption", died at Indian Springs on 12 Jun 1909, record (1908-12): 87468.

Vine RETHFORD, age 50 years, single, death cause: "typhoid fever", born and died at Indian Springs, died: 8 Jul 1908, record (1908-12): 87469.

Medie HARR, female, age 29 years, married, death cause: "typhoid fever", born and died at Indian Springs, died: 30 Oct 1908, record (1908-12): 87470.

Sallie E. LYNN, age 45 years, born at Bidleman, TN., married, death cause: "cancer", died at Indian Springs on 31 May 1909, record (1908-12): 87471.

Lafayette CLARK, age 28 days, death cause: "brain trouble", died at Indian Springs on 3 Jun 1909, record (1908-12): 87472.

Dave RUTLEDGE, age 52 years, born in Hawkins Co., married, death cause: "abscess in head", died at Fall Branch on 25 Jan 1909, record (1908-12): 87473.

Lizzie Naoma FORD, age 8 years, death cause: "burned", died at Fall Branch on 10 Dec 1908, record (1908-12): 87474.

Elizabeth MCCULLY, age 85 years, born at Rock Springs, married, death cause: "dropsy", died at Pactalus on 24 Jan 1909, record (1908-12): 87475.

Jane EASLEY, age 76 years, born in Wythe Co., VA., married, death cause: "kidney trouble", died at Rock Springs on 22 Nov 1908, record (1908-12): 87476.

Eliza RATCLIFFE, age 65 years, married, death cause: "dropsy", died at Pactalus on (day not stated) May 1909, record (1908-12): 87477.

Mrs. C.R. BELL, age 70 years, born at Kendrick Creek, married, death cause: "ulcer of stomach", died near Rock Springs on 20 Jan 1909, record (1908-12): 87478.

Fannie BOND, age 43 years, married, death cause: "typhoid fever", died at Horse Creek on 7 Aug 1908, record (1908-12): 87479.

Verlan CRAWFORD, age 2 years, death cause: "unknown", died at Horse Creek on (day not stated) Jan 1909, record (1908-12): 87480.

Dan SHORT, age 15 months, death cause: "whooping cough", died at Depew Chapel on 12 Jun 1909, record (1908-12): 87481.

Rev. William DEPEW, age 82 years, born at Rock Springs, married, death cause: "heart failure", died at Depew Chapel on 10 Apr 1909, record (1908-12): 87482.

Tenny HITE, age 18 years, born in Hawkins Co., married, death cause: "abortion", died at Pactalus on 14 Feb 1909, record (1908-12): 87483.

Nancy HICKMAN, age 57 years, single, death cause: "consumption", died at Horse Creek on 6 Dec 1909, record (1908-12): 87484.

W.C.C. CHURCHWELL, age 73 years, married, death cause: "ulcerous sores", born and died at Kingsport, died: 3 Mar 1909, record (1908-12): 87485.

Jess BARE, age 75 years, single, death cause: "chronic complications", born and died at Kingsport, died: 11 Aug 1908, record (1908-12): 87486.

Lessie HOLT, age 4 months, death cause: "hives", died at Kingsport on 22 May 1908, record (1908-12): 87487.

Bettie ROSE, age 35 years, born in Scott Co., VA., married, death cause: "tuberculosis", died at Indian Springs on 20 Feb 1910, record (1908-12): 87488.

Unnamed Infant, female, death cause: "hurt and strangulation", born and died at Kingsport on 11 Feb 1909, record (1908-12): 87489.

Robert MCINTOSH, age 2 years, death cause: "bowel troubles", died at Kingsport on 11 May 1909, record (1908-12): 87490.

James D. COX, age 18 years, single, death cause: "epileptic fits", died at Kingsport on 23 Jun 1909, record (1908-12): 87491.

Eva DICKERSON, black, age 43 years, born at Chattanooga, married, death cause: "consumption", died at Kingsport on 20 Dec 1908, record (1908-12): 87492.

Nathan HAMMONS, age 16 years, born in Scott Co., VA., death cause: "blood poison", died at Kingsport on 2 Aug 1908, record (1908-12): 87493.

William CHRISTIAN, age 17 years, born in Hawkins Co., death cause: "consumption", died at Kingsport on 23 May 1908, record (1908-12): 87494.

Mrs. Emma SMITH, age 35 years, born "in the West", death cause: "cancer of the womb", died at Bristol on 16 Dec 1910, record (1908-12): 87495.

Sallie MCCRARY, age 3 years, born at Pulaski, death cause: "pneumonia", died at Bristol on 25 Dec 1910, record (1908-12): 87496.

Ward VERNON, age 1 year, born in Virginia, death cause: "flux", died at Bristol on 8 Feb 1911, record (1908-12): 87497.

Harry LOWE, age 7 years, death cause: "hooping cough", died at Bristol on 30 Jul 1910, record (1908-12): 87498.

Ollie BURNETT, female, age 32 years, married, death cause: "consumption", died at Bristol on 27 Apr 1911, record (1908-12): 87499.

(Illegible) G. BUCKLES, female, age 20 years, single, teacher, death cause: "appendicitis", died at 11 Mile Ford 29 Jan 1911, record (1908-12): 87500.

Fred CARTWRIGHT, age 9 days, death cause: "paralitis", died at Bristol on 30 Oct 1910, record (1908-12): 87501.

Henry SEXTON, age 1 day, death cause: "not known", died at Bristol on 14 Nov 1910, record (1908-12): 87502.

Lucy DAVIS, age 22 years, born at Tazwell, VA., married, death cause: "consumption", died at Bristol on 22 Feb 1911, record (1908-12): 87503.

Mr. J.P. WHITE, age 55 years, born in Virginia, married, death cause: "dropsy" died at Bristol on (day not stated) Oct 1910, record (1908-12): 87504.

Elizabeth BROWN, age 62 years, born at Bluff City, married, death cause: "(illegible) of brain", died at Bristol on 21 May 1911, record (1908-12): 87505.

Maggie ARWOOD, age 27 years, married, death cause: "consumption", born and died at Bristol, died: 25 Jul 1910, record (1908-12): 87506.

Loucile WHITTEN, colored, age 20 years, single, death cause: "feaver", born and died at Bristol, died: 30 Dec 1910, record (1908-12): 87507.

Harvey LAUGHTUS, age 3 years, death cause: "fever", died at Bristol on 2 Feb 1911, record (1908-12): 87508.

Georgie LOVE, age 3 years, death cause: "indigestion", died at Bristol on 1 Oct 1910, record (1908-12): 87509.

Henry THOMAS, age 76 years, born in North Carolina, married, death cause: "consumption", died at Bristol on 13 Mar 1911, record (1908-12): 87510.

Absolom BURN (?), age 78 years, born in North Carolina, married, minister, death cause: "unknown, sudden death", died at Bristol on 15 Dec 1910, record (1908-12): 87511.

Ike SIMMONS, colored, age 50 years, born at Saltville, VA., widower, death cause: "dropsy", died at Bristol on 29 Jun 1911, record (1908-12): 87512.

Docia COMBS, age 17 years, single, death cause: "typhoid fever", died in the 16th District on 4 Sep 1908, record (1908-12): 87513.

Anner WATSON, female, age 14 years, death cause: "appendicitis", died in the 16th District on 22 Jun 1909, record (1908-12): 87514.

J. Parks MILLER, age 2 months, death cause: "pneumonia" born and died at Bluff City, died: 4 Jun 1909, record (1908-12): 87515.

Gernia ADAMS, male, age 1 day, death cause: not stated, died at Bluff City on 15 May 1909, record (1908-12): 87516.

Jacob N. HICKS, age 75 years, married, death cause: "Brights disease", died in the 16th District on 13 May 1909, record (1908-12): 87517.

James JENKINS, age 11 months, death cause: "pneumonia", died in the 16th District on 3 Mar 1909, record (1908-12): 87518.

Harsie JENKINS, male, death cause: "pneumonia", died in the 16th District on 18 Mar 1909, record (1908-12): 87519.

Belle BOUTIN, age 18 years, single, death cause: "typhoid fever", died in the 16th District on 14 Nov 1908, record (1908-12): 87520.

Buford LOVE, age 8 months, death cause: "flux", died at Bluff City on 13 Sep 1908, record (1908-12): 87521.

James CARDEN, age 31 years, married, death cause: "accidental gun shot wound", died in the 4th District on 1 Aug 1908, record (1908-12): 87522.

Gladys GALLOWAY, age 7 years, death cause: "diphtheria", died in the 4th District on (day not stated) Dec 1908, record (1908-12): 87523.

George MURRAY, age 24 years, born in Virginia, married, death cause: "typhoid fever", died in the 4th District on 24 Aug 1908, record (1908-12): 87524.

Sarahphenia BURNETT, age 35 years, death cause: "catarrh of throat", died in the 4th District on 15 Dec 1908, record (1908-12): 87525.

Eliza BURNETT, age 63 years, married, death cause: "consumption of bowels", died in the 4th District on 28 Apr 1909, record (1908-12): 87526.

Virginia May BISHOP, age 15 months, death cause: "stomach trouble", died in the 4th District on 21 Oct 1908, record (1908-12): 87527.

W.J. GODSEY, age 4 years, born in Virginia, death cause: "accidental gun shot", died in the 4th District on 31 Dec 1908, record (1908-12): 87528.

Eliza A. SMITH, age 69 years, born in Virginia, married, death cause: "paralysis", died in the 4th District on 18 May 1909, record (1908-12): 87529.

Barbara MILLER, age 58 years, married, death cause: "cancer", died in the 4th District on (day not stated) Sep 1908, record (1908-12): 87530.

Samuel THOMAS, age 74 years, married, death cause: "thrown from a horse", died in the 4th District on 29 Sep 1908, record (1908-12): 87531.

James LEONARD, age 2 years, death cause: "pneumonia", died in the 4th District on 26 Dec 1908, record (1908-12): 87532.

Mary Jane HITE, age 54 years, born at Fordtown, married, death cause: "catarrh of stomach", died at Rock Springs on 14 Sep 1908, record (1908-12): 87533.

Annie BAILEY, age 20 years, born in North Carolina, married, death cause: "shot", died at Pactalus on (day not stated) Sep 1908, record (1908-12): 87534.

James H. HUNT, age 3 years, death cause: "bowel trouble", died in the 13th District on 14 May 1909, record (1908-12): 87535.

Perry BAILEY, age 2 years, death cause: "bowel trouble", died in the 13th District on 11 May 1909, record (1908-12): 87536.

Mary MYERS, age 79 years, born in Washington Co., TN., married, death cause: "old age", died in Bloomingdale on 16 Aug 1910, record (1908-12): 87537.

Henry Stewart RAY, age 5 months, born in Scott Co., VA., death cause: "pneumonia", died in Kingsport on 3 Mar 1911, record (1908-12): 87538.

Hattie J. JAYNE, age 50 years, born in Scott Co., VA., married, death cause: "cancer", died in Kingsport on 18 Jun 1911, record (1908-12): 87539.

Frank HARR, age 20 years, single, death cause: "rheumatism", died in the 19th District on 4 Feb 1909, record (1908-12): 87540.

Infant RUTHERFORD, female, age 1 day, death cause: "not known", died in the 19th District on 12 Jun 1909, record (1908-12): 87541.

Dora RUTHERFORD, age 28 years, married, death cause: "lock bowels", died in the 19th District on 7 Dec 1908, record (1908-12): 87542.

Mack BUTEN, age 48 years, born: Watauga Co., NC., married, death cause: "pneumonia fever", died in the 19th District on 12 Mar 1909, record (1908-12): 87543.

Infant Male, name illegible, age 2 days, death cause: "not known", died in the 19th District on 3 Feb 1909, record (1908-12): 87544.

Gladdis ROUSE, age 11 months, death cause: "spinal trouble", died in the 19th District on 19 May 1909, record (1908-12): 87545.

Lillie Bell ROUSE, age 1 day, death cause: "not known", died in the 19th District on 16 May 1909, record (1908-12): 87546.

W.M. FINK, female, age 71 years, death cause: "consumption", born and died in the 2nd District, died: 21 Oct 1909, record (1908-12): 87547.

Sarah, DILLOW, age 36 years, married, death cause: "paralyzed", died in the 2nd District on 2 Aug 1909, record (1908-12): 87548.

W.D. KETRON, age 46 years, 9 months, married, death cause: "ruptured blood vessel", born/died Bloomingdale, died: 26 Mar 1909, record (1908-12): 87549.

Margaret LEONARD, age 6 days, death cause: "not known", died at Bloomingdale on 14 Dec 1909, record (1908-12): 87550.

Katherine Elizabeth MYERS, age 27 years, married, death cause: "cancer", born and died at Arcadia, died: 11 Dec 1908, record (1908-12): 87551.

David CARRIER, age 10 years, death cause: "killed by a log falling on him", born and died at Bluff City, died: 16 Dec 1911, record (1908-12): 87552.

Lauretia ODELL, age 29 years, death cause: "consumption", married, died at 3rd District on 16 May 1912, record (1908-12): 87553.

Thomas CARRIER, age 14 days, death cause: "bold hives", died at 3rd District on 17 Dec 1911, record (1908-12): 87554.

George CRUMLEY, age 67 years, single, death cause: "Brights disease", died at 3rd District on 28 Dec 1911, record (1908-12): 87555.

Owen SAMS, age 18 years, single, death cause: "consumption", died at 3rd District on 15 Apr 1912, record (1908-12): 87556.

William O. CRUMLEY, age 48 years, married, death cause: "organic heart trouble", died at 3rd District on 30 Apr 1912, record (1908-12): 87557.

Martha BAUTAN, age 78 years, widow, death cause: "general break down", died at the 3rd District on 10 Feb 1912, record (1908-12): 87558.

Laura JANES, age 29 years, single, death cause: "consumption", died at the 3rd District on 18 Mar 1912, record (1908-12): 87559.

Martha E. JANES, age 59 years, married, death cause: "Brights disease", died in the 3rd District on 2 Apr 1912, record (1908-12): 87560.

Ollie PERRY, female, age 1 year, death cause: "pneumonia", died in the 3rd District on 17 Dec 1911, record (1908-12): 87561.

John CARTER, age 50 years, married, death cause: "rheumatism", died near Bristol on 21 Aug 1911, record (1908-12): 87562.

Blanch GOLIE, age 15 years, death cause: "fever", died at Bristol on 26 May 1912, record (1908-12): 87563.

Mrs. Sarah HAWK, age 50 years, born at Bluff City, married, death cause: "dropsy", died at Bristol on 24 May 1912, record (1908-12): 87564.

Nannie SHROLEY, age 32 years, born in Virginia, married, death cause: "cancer", died in the 4th District on 2 Apr 1912, record (1908-12): 87565.

Margaret MCCRARY, age 64 years, married, death cause: "old age and blind", died in the 4th District on 19 Mar 1912, record (1908-12): 87566.

Chassie B. GREENWAY, age 5 months, death cause: "bold hives", died in the 4th District on 16 Dec 1911, record (1908-12): 87567.
George E. HEADEN, age 52 years, married, death cause: "tuberculosis", died near Blountville on 18 Feb 1912, record (1908-12): 87568.
Infant Male, death cause: "born dead", died at Bloomingdale on 18 May 1909, record (1908-12): 87569.
Mattie S. HOBBS, age 48 years, 1 month and 20 days, born at Scott Co., VA., married, death cause: "blood poison", died at Bloomingdale on 9 Dec 1908, record (1908-12): 87570.
Eleanor CARR, age 5 years, 2 months and 4 days, death cause: "typhoid fever", died at Bloomingdale on 24 Jun 1909, record (1908-12): 87571.
William OFFIELD, age 28 years, 3 months and 24 days, single, death cause: "appendicitis", died at Atlanta, GA., on 7 Sep 1908, record (1908-12): 87572.
Charlie LOYD, age 3 months and 25 days, death cause: "pneumonia", died near Bloomingdale on 25 Jan 1908, record (1908-12): 87573.
Pank N. POORE, age 49 years, widow, death cause: "cancer", died in the 10th District on 17 May 1908, record (1908-12): 87574.
Laura E. POORE, age 32 years, married, death cause: "bone scroffula", died in the 10th District on 23 Jan 1908, record (1908-12): 87575.
R. Wiley BARE, age 30 years, married, death cause: "typhoid fever", died 14 Jul 1908, record (1908-12): 87576.
Robert Franklin CARROLL, age 10 months and 19 days, born in Scott Co., VA., death cause: "spinal meningitis", died at Arcadia on 26 Mar 1909, record (1908-12): 87577.
John G. LYNN, age 70 years, married, death cause: "brights disease", died near Bloomingdale on 12 Jul 1909, record (1908-12): 87578.
Infant MALONE, female, age 1 day, death cause: not stated, died in the 5th District on 1 Aug 1911, record (1908-12): 87579.
Fannie ALMAROAD, age 3 months, death cause: not stated, died in the 5th District on 20 Jun 1912, record (1908-12): 87580.
Infant EATON, male, death cause: not stated, died in the 5th District on 14 Feb 1912, record (1908-12): 87581.

Charlie DAVIS, age 24 years, single, born in North Carolina, death cause: "unknown", died in the 5th District on 20 Jul 1911, record (1908-12): 87582.

Mrs. Nannie SHRIVELY, age 29 years, married, death cause: "cancer", died in the 5th District on 2 Mar 1912, record (1908-12): 87583.

Mrs. Mary SHORT, age 64 years, married, death cause: "paralysis", born and died in the 5th District, died: 28 Apr 1912, record (1908-12): 87584.

Infant REED, female, death cause: not stated, died in the 5th District on 23 Sep 1911, record (1908-12): 87585.

Dewey HAGY, age 12 years, death cause: "measles", died in the 5th District 26 Apr 1912, record (1908-12): 87586.

Infant BARNES, death cause: not stated, died in the 5th District on 10 Jul 1911, record (1908-12): 87587.

Thomas J. CATES, age 63 years, married, death cause: "heart failure", died in the 5th District on 27 Dec 1911, record (1908-12): 87588.

Mrs. Bonie SPANGLER, age 82 years, married, death cause: "old age", died at the poor house, 5th District on 2 Jun 1912, record (1908-12): 87489.

Reba SMITH, age 9 years, death cause: "pneumonia", died in the 5th District on 28 Mar 1912, record (1908-12): 87590.

William CARMACK, age 77 years, married, death cause: "consumption", died in the 5th District on 27 Jul 1911, record (1908-12): 87591.

Mrs. James PIERCE, age 63 years, married, death cause: "dropsy", died in the 5th District on 8 Feb 1912, record (1908-12): 87592.

Lulu May HOUTZ, age 41 years, married, death cause: "consumption", died in the 5th District on 12 Aug 1911, record (1908-12): 87593.

Mrs. Addie COWAN, age 67 years, born at Holston Valley, married, death cause: "apoplexy", died in the 5th District on 17 Feb 1912, record (1908-12): 87594.

Hollie DUNN, age 44 years, married, death cause: "pneumonia", died at Kingsport on 14 Mar 1911, record (1908-12): 87595.

Unnamed Infant, male, colored, born at Rome, GA., death cause: "hives", died at Rome, GA., on 12 Jan 1911, record (1908-12): 87596.

Walice F. DALTON, age 4 months, death cause: "heart failure", died at Kingsport on 3 Feb 1911, record (1908-12): 87597.

Walker Tipton THOMPKINS, age 11 months and 18 days, death cause: "measles", died at Kingsport on 12 Jun 1911, record (1908-12): 87598.
Arthur Virgil DOTSON, age 10 months and 9 days, born at Johnson City, death cause: "bronchial pneumonia", died at Kingsport on 1 Jun 1911, record (1908-12): 87599.
Minnie Pearl MCCLAIN, age 3 years, death cause: "sucture of bowels", died at Bloomingdale on 4 Jan 1911, record (1908-12): 87600.
Rufus WADKINS, age 66 years, married, death cause: "organic heart trouble', died at Bloomingdale on 6 Mar 1911, record (1908-12): 87601.
George Thomas PILE, age 50 years, married, death cause: "spinal trouble", died at Bloomingdale on 27 Mar 1911, record (1908-12): 87602.
Martha Jane MCFAW, age 4 years, born at Lee Co., VA., death cause: "heart trouble", died at Lee Co., VA., on 20 Aug 1910, record (1908-12): 87603.
Thurston JENKINS, age 29 years, born in Virginia, married, death cause: "pneumonia", died in the 6th District on 27 Mar 1911, record (1908-12): 87604.
A.J. DROKE, age 71 years, married, death cause: "consumption", died in the 6th District on 30 Dec 1910, record (1908-12): 87605.
John J. LESLIE, age 58 years, married, death cause: "typhoid fever", died in the 6th District on 28 Jan 1911, record (1908-12): 87606.
Mrs. Harriett SNAPP, age 64 years, married, death cause: "fever", died in the 6th District on 1 Apr 1911, record (1908-12): 87607.
E.D. WOLFORD, age 78 years, married, death cause: "pneumonia fever", died in the 6th District on 1 Mar 1911, record (1908-12): 87608.
A.W. DROKE, age 70 years, married, death cause: "complication of disease", died in the 6th District on 15 Mar 1911, record (1908-12): 87609.
Mrs. Ellen HARR, age 65, married, death cause: "pneumonia", died in the 6th District on 2 Apr 1911, record (1908-12): 87610.
Mrs. Lydia HARR, age 68 years, married, death cause: "pneumonia", died in the 6th District on 27 Apr 1911, record (1908-12): 87611.
Priscilla JACKSON, age 75 years, widow, death cause: "old age", died in the 6th District on 21 Aug 1910, record (1908-12): 87612.

Will Rhea BARGER, age 3 months, death cause: "brain fever", died in the 6th District on 27 Jan 1911, record (1908-12): 87613.

Infant LANE, age 2 months and 5 days, death cause: not stated, died in the 6th District on 9 Aug 1910, record (1908-12): 87614.

Abe CAIN, age 83 years, born in Tennessee, death cause: "old age", died in the 6th District on 1 Sep 1910, record (1908-12): 87615.

Melvin ELSEA, age 22 years, born: 6th District, death cause: "killed by engine", died in Ohio on 20 Dec 1910, record (1908-12): 87616.

Joe CURRIC, age about 45 years, married, death cause: "spinal cone affected", died in the 1st District on 22 Jun 1909, record (1908-12): 87617.

Unnamed Infant, female, age not stated, death cause: not stated, died in the 3rd District on 2 Mar 1909, record (1908-12): 87618.

James ROSS, age 38 years, born in Mississippi, married, death cause: "tree fell upon him", died at Bristol on 27 Apr 1909, record (1908-12): 87619.

John Sanford BLEVINS, death cause: "stillborn", born/died at Blountville on 30 Jan 1909, record (1908-12): 87620.

Rebecca BOLING, age 66 years, married, death cause: "cancer", died near Bristol on 19 Apr 1911, record (1908-12): 87621.

Luther BOLING, age 39 years, single, death cause: "paralysis of brain", died near Bristol on 24 Sep 1911, record (1908-12): 87622.

John GRIMES, age 56 years, married, death cause: "consumption", died at Bristol on 11 Mar 1911, record (1908-12): 87623.

Catherine FORD, age 78 years, born in Sullivan Co., widow, death cause: "pneumonia", died at Blountville on 29 Jan 1911, record (1908-12): 87624.

Mary HENDRICKSON, age 55 years, married, death cause: "spinal nervousness", died at Blountville on 7 Sep 1910, record (1908-12): 87625.

Mary FRAZIER, age 44 years, married, death cause: "pneumonia", died at Blountville on 6 Dec 1910, record (1908-12): 87626.

William BEARD, age 70 years, born in Sullivan Co., married, death cause: "pneumonia", died at Blountville on 8 Feb 1911, record (1908-12): 87627.

John CRESS, age 78 years, married, death cause: "heart trouble", died at Piney Flats on 22 Aug 1910, record (1908-12): 87628.

Adelia TOMLINSON, age 79 years, born at Richmond, VA., single, death cause: "rheumatism", died at Indian Springs on 18 Nov 1910, record (1908-12): 87629.

Dr. D.M. MILLER, age 71 years, born in Washington Co., TN., married, death cause: "paralysis", died at Indian Springs on 8 Jan 1911, record (1908-12): 87630.

Susan ROLLER, age 26 years, single, death cause: "tuberculosis", born/died at Indian Springs, died: 9 May 1911, record (1908-12): 87631.

Alice Marie ISLEY, age 3 years, born at Kingsport, death cause: "stomach trouble", died at Indian Springs on 14 Apr 1911, record (1908-12): 87632.

David HORN, age 60, married, death cause: "typhoid fever", born/died at Indian Springs, died: 10 Feb 1911, record (1908-12): 87633.

Isac ROBERSON, age 5 years, born in Scott Co., VA., death cause: "croup", died at Indian Springs on 7 May 1911, record (1908-12): 87634.

Edith CRAWFORD, age not stated, death cause: not stated, died in 15th District on 14 Jun 1911, record (1908-12): 87635.

Coy C. CRAWFORD, age 5 months, death cause: "flux", died in the 15th District on 1 Jul 1911, record (1908-12): 87636.

Roosevelt CONKINS, age 14 months, death cause: "croup", died in 15th District on 19 Oct 1910, record (1908-12): 87637.

Bonnie M. WHESEL, age 18 months, death cause: "croup", died in the 15th District on 16 Sep 1910, record (1908-12): 87638.

Infant MELEAR, male, age not stated, death cause: not stated, died in the 15th District on 17 Mar 1911, record (1908-12): 87639.

John W. HARTESS, age 2 years, death cause: "flux", died in 15th District on 4 Jun 1911, record (1908-12): 87640.

Thomas W. FINCHER, age 3 years, death cause: "spinal", died in 15th District on 25 Mar 1911, record (1908-12): 87641.

Guy GREGG, age 2 months, death cause: "hives", died in 15th District on 7 Feb 1911, record (1908-12): 87642.

Infant LESTER, age not stated, death cause: not stated, died in 15th District on 15 Jan 1911, record (1908-12): 87643.

Willie COX, age not stated, death cause: not stated, died in 15th District on 6 Feb 1911, record (1908-12): 87644.

Josie D. COX, age 6 years, death cause: "croup", died at Fordtown on 3 Nov 1911, record (1908-12): 87645.

John JONES, age 54 years, married, death cause: "fever", born/died at Fordtown, died: 26 Nov 1911, record (1908-12): 87646.

Elbert DILLOW, age 2 months and 12 days, death cause: "bold hives", died at Fordtown on 30 Aug 1910, record (1908-12): 87647.

Unnamed Infant, female, death cause: "born dead", died at Fordtown on 8 Jan 1911, record (1908-12): 87648.

Mrs. Sallie RITCHARDSON, age 82 years, married, born/died: Kendrick Creek, died: 13 May 1911, record (1908-12): 87649.

Perry MILLER, age 6 years, death cause: "croup", died at Gotts Cross Roads on 1 Jan 1911, record (1908-12): 87650.

Mrs. Ben OVERBY, age 35 years, married, death cause: "tuberculosis", born/died: Kendrick Creek, died 11 Jul 1911, record (1908-12): 87651.

John M. DEMCY, age 76 years, born in South Carolina, death cause: "complication of disease", died at Bluff City on 7 May 1911, record (1908-12): 87652.

Hyder SIMS, age 14 years, death cause: "drowned in Holston River", died at Bluff City on 5 May 1911, record (1908-12): 87653.

Sarah E. DEMCY, age 35 years, married, death cause: "pneumonia", died at Bluff City on 8 Mar 1911, record (1908-12): 87654.

Stella ODELL, age 1 years, death cause: "tuberculosis", died at Bluff City on 24 Aug 1910, record (1908-12): 87655.

Robert NICKELS, age 1 year, death cause: "complication of measles", died at Bluff City on 3 Jun 1911, record (1908-12): 87656.

N. Darhula HICKS, female, age about 68 years, widow, death cause: "cancer", died at Bluff City on 9 Apr 1911, record (1908-12): 87657.

Sarah GLOVER, age 68 years, widow, death cause: "consumption", died at Bluff City on 12 Jul 1910, record (1908-12): 87658.

Francis J. COX, age 33 years, born at Mitchell Co., NC., single, death cause: "cancer", died at Bluff City on 11 Jul 1910, record (1908-12): 87659.

Infant RICHARDS, female, age 3 hours, death cause: not stated, died in the 16th District on 3 Aug 1910, record (1908-12): 87660.

Hayns Ernest GEISLER, age 15 years, death cause: "neuritis", died in the 16th District on 8 Jan 1911, record (1908-12): 87661.

Aris TESTER, age 6 years, born in North Carolina, death cause: "caught in sawmill belt", died at Southerlan on 25 Oct 1911, record (1908-12): 87662.

Carrie S. HARMON, age 6 months and 22 days, death cause: "brain fever", died in the 16th District on 4 Nov 1910, record (1908-12): 87663.

Ira SPARRY, age 1 year and 7 months, born in North Carolina, death cause: "darhea", died in the 16th District on (day not stated) Jun 1911, record (1908-12): 87664.

Charles F. JONES, age 17 years, 9 months and 21 Days, death cause: "pneumonia", died in the 16th District on 27 Dec 1910, record (1908-12): 87665.

Daniel Milton SIGMAN, age 30 years, born in 3rd District, single, death cause: "typhoid fever", died at Harlan, KY., on 11 Sep 1910, record (1908-12): 87666.

Francis M. BOY, male, age 85 years, widower, death cause: "old age", born/died: 16th District, died: 4 Jan 1911, record (1908-12): 87667.

James N. GUIN, age 79 years, born in Scott Co., VA., married, death cause: "chronic complications", died at Kingsport on 3 Mar 1910, record (1908-12): 87668.

Tack HAWK, age 45 years, married, death cause: "tuberculosis", died in 18th District on 31 Dec 1910, record (1908-12): 87669.

Emaline MONK, age 58 years, married, death cause: "rheumatism", died in 18th District on 5 Jul 1910, record (1908-12): 87670.

Harret SHARP, age 66 years, 9 months and 29 days, married, death cause: "heart trouble", died in 3rd District on 26 Jun 1910, record (1908-12): 87671.

Infant NEWLAND, sex and age not stated, death cause: not stated, died in the 18th District on 30 May 1910, record (1908-12): 87672.

D.J. CRUMLEY, age 89 years, 4 months and 7 days, born in Sullivan Co., married, death cause: "old age", died in the 3rd District on 1 Jun 1910, record (1908-12): 87673.

Infant GALLOWAY, male, death cause: "deformity", died in the 3rd District on 24 Apr 1910 (?), record (1908-12): 87674.

L.W. JONES (? or Janes), age 88 years, born in Sullivan Co., married, death cause: "heart (illegible)", died in the 3rd District on 14 Feb 1910, record (1908-12): 87675.

Infant HARMON, male, death cause: "born dead", 3rd District on 29 May 1910, record (1908-12): 87676.

Rosana MORRELL, age 79 years, 3 months and 16 days, married, death cause: "paralysis", born/died in 3rd District, died: 8 Nov 1909, record (1908-12): 87677.

Mollie MCKINNEY, age about 25 years, born in North Carolina, married, death cause: "pneumonia", died 18 Oct 1910, record (1908-12): 87679.

Oliver BARNES, age 1 year, death cause: "pneumonia", died in the 18th District on 6 Feb 1910, record (1908-12): 87680.

J.R. BARNES, age 56 years, married, death cause: "pneumonia", died in 18th District on 25 Jan 1910, record (1908-12): 87681.

L.R. BARNES, age 29 years, single, death cause: "pneumonia", died in the 18th District on 5 Feb 1910, record (1908-12): 87682.

J.N. SMITH, age 40 years, married, death cause: "pneumonia", died in 18th District on 6 Apr 1910, record (1908-12): 87683.

John Ernest SMITH, age 1 year, death cause: "cholera", died in the 18th District on 22 Jul 1910, record (1908-12): 87684.

Judson KITZMILLER, age 36 years, married, death cause: "consumption", died in 18th District on 22 Jun 1910, record (1908-12): 87685.

Lester KING, age 18 years, single, death cause: "pneumonia", died in 18th District on 5 Mar 1910, record (1908-12): 87686.

Mary KING, age 1 year, death cause: "pneumonia", died in 18th District on 5 Mar 1910, record (1908-12): 87687.

Lula SELLS, age 0, death cause: not stated, died in 18th District on 28 Feb 1910, record (1908-12): 87688.

John KITZMILLER, age 0, death cause: not stated, died in 18th District on 4 Mar 1910, record (1908-12): 87689.

Judson KITZMILLER, age 2 months, death cause: not stated, died in 18th District on 18 Apr 1910, record (1908-12): 87690.

Kiltie FORD, age 72 years, death cause: "old age and grippe", died in 18th District on 9 Mar 1910, record (1908-12): 87691.

Barbara SELLS, age 69 years, married, death cause: "lagrippe", died in the 18th District on 8 Dec 1909, record (1908-12): 87692.
Bessie BULLIS, age 7 years, death cause: "curved spin", died in the 18th District on 30 Oct 1909.
Ida BULLIS, age 35 years, married, death cause: "pneumonia", died in 18th District on 27 Feb 1910, record (1908-12): 87694.
Daniel HILTON, age 59 years, married, death cause: "pneumonia", died in 18th District on 12 Feb 1910, record (1908-12): 87695.
John COFFEE, age: 0, death cause: not stated, died in 18th District on 30 Nov 1909, record (1908-12): 87696.
Sallie R. HONSER, age 65 years, married, death cause: "dropsy", died in the 1st District on 3 Dec 1911, record (1908-12): 87697.
Golda A. BOOHER, age 10 years, married, (note: either age or marital status is in error), death cause: "heart trouble", died in 1st District on 23 May 1912, record (1908-12): 87698.
Rothern PLESS, female, age 82 years, born in Indiana, single, death cause: "paralysis", died in 1st District on 2 Jan 1912, record (1908-12): 87699.
Fannie J. SMITH, age 72 years, born in Virginia, married, death cause: "consumption", died in 1st District on 18 Mar 1912, record (1908-12): 87700.
William J. SMITH, age 66 years, married, death cause: "kidney trouble", died in the 1st District on 2 Apr 1912, record (1908-12): 87701.
John M. BOOHER, age 40 years, married, death cause: "measles", died in 1st District on 9 Mar 1912, record (1908-12): 87702.
Isaac OSBORN, age 55 years, born in Johnson Co., married, death cause: not stated, died in the 1st District on 16 May 1912, record (1908-12): 87703.
Brookie CARRIER, female, age 25 years, born in Carter Co., married, death cause: "epelitic fits", died in 1st District on 18 Mar 1912, record (1908-12): 87704.
Floyd PETERS, age 18 years, single, death cause: "measles", died in 1st District on 15 Feb 1912, record (1908-12): 87705.
Charles SIMMONS, age 28 years, born in Johnson Co., married, death cause: "Brights disease", died in 1st District on 28 Oct 1911, record (1908-12): 87706.
Kate TAYLOR, age 62 years, married, death cause: "dropsy", died in 1st District on 25 Aug 1911, record (1908-12): 87707.

Ellen MORRELL, age 27 years, single, death cause: "consumption", died in 1st District on 9 Apr 1912, record (1908-12): 87708.

Jud E. MCGARRY, age 56 years, single, death cause: "consumption", died in 1st District on 19 Jul 1911, record (1908-12): 87709.

David CARRIER, age 11 years, death cause: "killed by a tree", died in 1st District on 16 Dec 1911, record (1908-12): 87710.

Sallie MORRELL, age 29 years, married, death cause: "consumption", died in 1st District on 18 Jul 1912, record (1908-12): 87711.

Infant ROSENBALM, age 5 days, death cause: "pneumonia", died in 1st District on 3 Mar 1912, record (1908-12): 87712.

Mary VAUGHT, age 48 years, born in Wythe Co., VA., married, death cause: "heart trouble", died near Bristol on 4 May 1910, record (1908-12): 87713.

Emmert ARNOLD, age 42 years, married, death cause: "heart trouble", died near Bristol on 8 Mar 1910.

Ferby ROBERTS, female, age 68 years, born in Johnson Co., married, death cause: "general break down", died near Bristol on 3 Jun 1910, record (1908-12): 87715.

John MCDANIEL, age 45 years, married, death cause: "heart failure", died at Bristol on 10 Mar 1910, record (1908-12): 87716.

Grace CLOYD, age 6 months, death cause: not stated, died at Bristol (month and day not stated) 1909, record (1908-12): 87717.

Neal NEVISTON, colored, age 26 years, born at Gate City, VA., married, death cause: "neuralgia of bowels", died at Bristol on 10 Mar 1909, record (1908-12): 87718.

Martin DELANEY, colored, age 73 years, born at Blountville, death cause: "pneumonia", died at Bristol on 25 Feb 1909, record (1908-12): 87719.

Luther HINDERSON, age 22 years, single, bridge builder, death cause: "accident on railroad bridge", born/died at Kingsport, died: 15 Apr 1909, record (1908-12): 87720.

Mr. I.B. LEONARD, age 42 years, married, death cause: "tiford fever", died at Bristol on 3 Jun 1909, record (1908-12): 87721.

Joseph WHEATLY, age 4 months, death cause: "indigestion", died at Bristol on 20 May 1909, record (1908-12): 87722.

Walter BLANKENSHIP, age 36 years, born at Statesvlle, NC., married, death cause: not recorded, died at Bristol on 26 Dec 1908, record (1908-12): 87723.

Norman BARR, age 6 months and 3 days, death cause: not stated, died at Mill Point, 6th District on 14 Nov 1908, record (1908-12): 87724.

Bessie SMALLWOOD, age 28 years, born in Virginia, single, death cause: "invalid from birth", died at Bristol on 1 May 1909, record (1908-12): 87725.

Mrs. Frank SEARCH, age 30 years, born at Wytheville, VA., married, death cause: "consumption", died at Bristol on 11 Jul 1909, record (1908-12): 87726.

J. Benjamine DROKE, age 27 years, single, death cause: "tuberculosis", born/died at Mill Point, died: 15 Feb 1909, record (1908-12): 87727.

Frank Alexander MORRELL, age 2 months and 15 days, death cause: "indigestion", died at Arcadia on 22 May 1909, record (1908-12): 87728.

Fred Walker MORRELL, age 3 months and 5 days, death cause: "indigestion", died at Arcadia on 12 Jun 1909, record (1908-12): 87729.

Daniel BOOHER, age 70 years, 1 month and 3 days, born at Three Springs, VA., married, death cause: "cancer of stomach", died at Blountville on 26 May 1909, record (1908-12): 87730.

Seebert Thomas PHIPPS, age 4 years, born at Ruthton, death cause: "ditheria", died at Bristol on 19 Nov 1911, record (1908-12): 87731.

Hal EMMERT, age 6 years and 6 months, death cause: "measles and pneumonia", died at Bristol on 28 Feb 1912, record (1908-12): 87732.

Infant PHELPS, sex not stated, death cause: "born dead", died at Bristol, 17th District, on 15 Mar 1912, record (1908-12): 87733.

Georgie DOVE, age 11 months and 16 days, death cause: "indigestion", died in East Bristol on 22 Sep 1911, record (1908-12): 87734.

Burnie LOVEGROVE, age 11 years, born at Jonesborough, TN., death cause: "measles", died at Bristol on 25 Feb 1912, record (1908-12): 87735.

James Clive HINES, age 28 years, single, death cause: "cancer of stomach", died at Bristol on 14 Dec 1911, record (1908-12): 87736.

Virgie Lee TILLISON, female, age 3 years, death cause: "measles and pneumonia", died at Bristol on 3 Mar 1912, record (1908-12): 87737.

Mrs. Bettie Elizabeth BLEVINS, age 50 years, married, death cause: "tuberculosis of the lungs", died at Bristol on 26 Nov 1911, record (1908-12): 87738.

Margarette FELTY, age 10 months, death cause: "brain fever and spinal meningitis", died at Bristol on 4 Apr 1911, record (1908-12): 87739.

Adam HUNT, age 72 years, 7 Months and 15 Days, born in Carter Co., married, death cause: "paralysis", died at Bristol on 29 Sep 1910, record (1908-12): 87740.

Jennings CARRIER, age 4 months, death cause: "fever", died at South Bristol on 13 Feb 1911, record (1908-12): 87741.

Elic JOHNSON, age 23 days, death cause: "brain fever", died: Bristol on 20 Aug 1910, record (1908-12): 87742.

Lula ARNOLD, age 27 years, born in Warrington, VA., married, death cause: "tuberculosis", died at East Bristol on 8 Jun 1911, record (1908-12): 87743.

Harvey Payne BROCE, age 4 days, death cause: "stomach trouble", died at South Bristol on 11 Apr 1911, record (1908-12): 87744.

Charlie WISDOM, black, age 50 years, death cause: "heart disease", born at Bristol on (day not stated) Sep 1910, record (1908-12): 87745.

Sarah C. SMALLING, age 70 years, born at Piney Flats, single, death cause: "cancer", died at Bristol on 30 Apr 1911, record (1908-12): 87746.

Franklin C. SMITH, age 24 years, born at Blountville, single, death cause: "tuberculosis", died at Bristol on 18 Jun 1911, record (1908-12): 87747.

Clarence H. BAYS, age 2 years and 7 months, death cause: "whooping cough", died at Bristol on 24 Aug 1910, record (1908-12): 87748.

Mary MCCLAY, born: 4 Apr 1910, death cause: illegible, died in the 4th District on 12 Aug 1910, record (1908-12): 87749.

Carrie Ruth HENLEY, age 10 months, death cause: "bronchitis and whooping cough", died at South Bristol on 26 Aug 1910, record (1908-12): 87750.

John H. LITTLEFORD, age 71 years, born at Albermarle Co., VA., widower, death cause: "cancer of bowels", died in the 16th District on 30 Oct 1910, record (1908-12): 87751.

Winnie Clinton PETERS, age 2 years, and 8 months, death cause: "pneumonia", died at Bluff City on 3 Dec 1910, record (1908-12): 87752.

Charles Lee WASHINGTON, black, age 20 years, single, death cause: "tuberculosis", died at Bluff City on 26 Mar 1911, record (1908-12): 87753.

Maude WASHINGTON, black, age 18 years, single, death cause: "tuberculosis", died at Bluff City on 13 Jun 1911, record (1908-12): 87754.

Marie V. RUTLEDGE, age 58 years, born in Jefferson Co., married, death cause: "consumption", died in the 4th District on 28 Apr 1911, record (1908-12): 87755.

George D. RUTLEDGE, age 23, single, death cause: "pneumonia", died in the 4th District on 4 Feb 1911, record (1908-12): 87756.

Samuel HUGHES, age 62 years, married, death cause: "consumption", died in 4th District on 19 Oct 1910, record (1908-12): 87757.

Rober Rhea TAYLOR, age 66 years, married, death cause: "consumption", died in the 4th District on 21 Mar 1911, record (1908-12): 87758.

Mary Elizabeth CROOSENBERRY, age 1 year, death cause: "whooping cough", died in 4th District on 27 Oct 1910, record (1908-12): 87759.

Ollie STEWART (?), age 32 years, married, death cause: "not known", died in 4th District on 27 Apr 1911, record (1908-12): 87760.

Emma Line CARDEN, age 66 years, married, death cause: "dropsy", died in 4th District on 9 Mar 1911, record (1908-12): 87761.

Stella Gale GUESS, age 1 year and 7 months, born in Washington Co., TN., death cause: "fever", died in 4th District on 5 Jun 1911, record (1908-12): 87762.

Maggie MOORE, age 22 years, married, death cause: "pneumonia", died at 1234 W. State St., Bristol on 2 Jun 1910, record (1908-12): 87763.

Unnamed Infant, male, death cause: "not known", died at 1234 W. State St., Bristol on 2 Jun 1910, record (1908-12): 87764.

George MYATT, age 1 day, death cause: "don't know", died at 12, 13th St., Bristol, died: 12 Jun 1910, record (1908-12): 87765.

LaFayette TOMLINSON, age: not stated, married, death cause: "pneumonia", died at 1229 Broad St., Bristol on 23 Dec 1909, record (1908-12): 87766.

Addie YOUNCE, age not stated, married, death cause: "heart trouble", died at 1219 Winsor Ave, Bristol, died: day and month not stated, recorded: 1 Jul 1910, record (1908-12): 87767.

O.F. HUGHES, age 69 years, born at Holston, VA., married, death cause: "grip", died at 695 Winsor Ave., Bristol on 12 Jan 1910, record (1908-12): 87768.

Lucie DOBYNS, age 5 months, death cause: "pneumonia", died at 851 Winsor Ave., Bristol on 29 Oct 1909, record (1908-12): 87769.
W.Y. POINTER, age 85 years, born in New Jersey, married, death cause: "old age", died at 1019 Shelby St., Bristol on 9 Aug 1909, record (1908-12): 87770.
William MITCHELL, age 75 years, born in Eastern VA., death cause: "indigestion", died at 918 Broad St., Bristol on 2 Sep 1909, record (1908-12): 87771.
Mary Elizabeth HOLMES, age 2 years, born in Abingdon., death cause: "pneumonia", died in Abingdon on 16 Apr 1910, record (1908-12): 87772.
Elizabeth MERRY (or Murry ?), age 50 years, born in Carter Co., married, death cause: "dropsy", died at 108, 10th St., Bristol on 21 Jun 1910, record (1908-12): 87773.
Paul ARCUT, age 20 months, death cause: "pneumonia", died at 1116 Shelby St., Bristol on 23 Feb 1910, record (1908-12): 87774.
Lillie CALLAHAND, age 6 months, death cause: "bold hives", died in 19th District on 1 May 1911, record (1908-12): 87775.
Lizzie HILTON, age 59 years, born in Greenville, married, death cause: "pneumonia fever", died at Woodlawn Ave., Bristol on 17 Mar 1910, record (1908-12): 87776.
J.H. EVERETT, age 78 years, born in North Carolina, married, death cause: "old age", died at 223 3rd St., Bristol on 22 Feb 1910, record (1908-12): 87777.
Mrs. Elizabeth SMITH, age 39 years, born at Greenville, married, death cause: "consumption", died at 105 Second High St., Bristol on 1 Dec 1909, record (1908-12): 87778.
Mrs. Annie THOMAS, age 65 years, born in Smyth Co., VA., married, death cause: "consumption", died at 17 Linwood Ave., Bristol on 31 Mar 1910, record (1908-12): 87779.
Frank GREEN, age 7 months, death cause: "don't know", died at Piney Flats on 23 Jan 1911, record (1908-12): 87780.
Newton RHEA, age 59 years, born in Jefferson Co., married, death cause: "stomach trouble", died at Piney Flats on 23 May 1911, record (1908-12): 87781.
Eli ANDERSON, age 82 years, born: Sullivan Co., married, death cause: "old age", died at Piney Flats on 25 May 1911, record (1908-12): 87782.

Miles PENIX, age 72 years, married, death cause: "Brights disease", died at Piney Flats on 23 Jun 1911, record (1908-12): 87783.

B.L. FORD, age 41 years, married, death cause: "typhoid fever", died at Piney Flats on 30 Jul 1911, record (1908-12): 87784.

Lee BARNES, age 30 years, born in Washington Co., married, death cause: "injured at furniture factory", died at Piney Flats on 31 Jul 1911, record (1908-12): 87785.

T.J. FAGAN, age 74 years, married, death cause: "lagrippe", died at Piney Flats on 18 Sep 1910, record (1908-12): 87786.

Earl SMITH, age 18 years, single, death cause: "drowned", born/died at Piney Flats, died: 24 Jul 1911, record (1908-12): 87787.

Rosana WHITE, age 74 years, married, death cause: "pneumonia fever", died at Piney Flats on (date not stated), recorded 3 Jul 1911, record (1908-12): 87788.

(Name not given) WHITAKER, female, age 13 years, death cause: "lagrippe", died at Piney Flats on 18 Mar 1911, record (1908-12): 87789.

Amanda PIERCE, age 74 years, married, death cause: not stated, died at Piney Flats on 10 Mar 1911, record (1908-12): 87790.

Willie HATCHER, age 33 years, single, death cause: not stated, died at Piney Flats on 20 Oct 1910, record (1908-12): 87791.

Mildred Lee BARNES, age 8 months, death cause: "don't know", died at Piney Flats on 14 Sep 1910, record (1908-12): 87792.

James Gilbert COX, age 35 years, single, death cause: "consumption", died at Washington Co., VA. on 22 Sep 1910, record (1908-12): 87793.

Gladus WIDNER, age 8 weeks, death cause: "indigestion", died in 19th District on 17 Jul 1910, record (1908-12): 87794.

Unnamed Infant, female, age not stated, death cause: "not known", died in 19th District on 3 Feb 1911, record (1908-12): 87795.

Maud SWEET, age 4 years, death cause: "diphtheria", died in 19th District on 12 Oct 1910, record (1908-12): 87796.

Julia V. ROGERS, age 33 years, born in Carter Co., married, death cause: "typhoid fever", died in 19th District on 17 Feb 1911, record (1908-12): 87797.

Orbin F. SHIPLEY, age 1 year and 2 months, death cause: "pneumonia fever", died in 11th District on 15 Nov 1909, record (1908-12): 87798.
Mollie DUNN, age 45 years, born in Bloomingdale, married, death cause: "pneumonia fever", died at Kingsport on 14 Mar 1910, record (1908-12): 87799.
Perry BAILEY, age 2 years, death cause: "not known", died at Pactalus on (day not stated) May 1910, record (1908-12): 87800.
William YOUNG, black, age 45 years, born in North Carolina, married, death cause: illegible, died in the 13th District on (day not stated) Jan 1910, record (1908-12): 87801
Charles BOYD, age 45 years, born at Horse Creek, married, death cause: "typhoid fever", died at Rock Springs on 15 Oct 1909, record (1908-12): 87802.
Cora EADES, age 15 years, death cause: "typhoid fever", died at Horse Creek on 18 Oct 1909, record (1908-12): 87803.
Mary STADMAN, age 42 years, married, death cause: "consumption", born/died: Depew Chapel, died: 2 Nov 1909, record (1908-12): 87804.
Infant BOYD, age/sex not stated, death cause: "born dead", died at Rock Springs on (day not stated) Mar 1910, record (1908-12): 87805.
Georgie R. CRAWFORD, age 3 months, death cause: "croup", died at Depew Chapel on (day not stated) Jan 1910, record (1908-12): 87806.
Bob SMILEY, age 35 years, married, death cause: "hemorage", born/died: Horse Creek, died: 24 Mar 1910, record (1908-12): 87807.
Anna BACHMAN, age 57 years, single, death cause: "pneumonia", born/died: Horse Creek, died: 24 Mar 1910, record (1908-12): 87808.
Infant RUTLEDGE, female, age 4 days, death cause: "don't know", died at Horse Creek on (day not stated) Jul 1909, record (1908-12): 87809.
Mary E. DEVAULT, age 58 years, married, death cause: "heart failure", born/died: Horse Creek, died: 7 Apr 1910, record (1908-12): 87810.
Eliza OWENS, age not known, single, death cause: "heart disease", died at Pactalus on (day not stated) Mar 1910, record (1908-12): 87811.
Maggie HITE, age 18 years, single, death cause: "typhoid fever", born/died: Rock Springs, died: (day not stated) Jan 1910, record (1908-12): 87712.

Mary MODY, age 61 years, single, death cause: "consumption", born/died: Rock Springs, died: (day not stated) Sep 1909, record (1908-12): 87813.

John M. NOE, age 78 years, married, death cause: "consumption", born/died: Kingsport, died: 28 May 1910, record (1908-12): 87814.

Malissa HARMAN, age 93 years, born at Watauga Co., NC., death cause: "old age", died at Bluff City on 5 May 1910, record (1908-12): 87815.

Henry Walter HARMON, age 24 years, born at Watauga Co., NC., single, death cause: "typhoid fever", died 9 Nov 1909, record (1908-12): 87816.

Mattie E. JESSIE, age 30 years, born at Bluff City, married, death cause: "consumption", died at Bristol on 29 Jun 1910, record (1908-12): 87817.

Thurman THURSTON, age 3 years, death cause: "indigestion", died at Bristol on 8 Apr 1910, record (1908-12): 87818.

Millhom WILLIAMS, age 59 years, married, married, death cause: not recorded, died in 20th District on 29 Jan 1909, record (1908-12): 87819.

Miles MILLER, age 3 years and 11 months, death cause: "spinal affection", died in 20th District on 8 Apr 1909, record (1908-12): 87820.

John SANDERS, age 60 years, 2 months and 7 days, married, death cause: "consumption", died in 20th District on 17 Mar 1909, record (1908-12): 87821.

R.C. MCQUEEN, age 25 years, 4 months and 9 days, born in Washington Co., TN., single, death cause: "consumption", died in 20th District on 24 Mar 1909, record (1908-12): 87822.

Jacob GROSS, age 72 years, born in Sullivan Co., married, death cause: "consumption", died in 20th District on 22 Oct 1908, record (1908-12): 87823.

Alla CLAY, age 41 years and 1 months, single, death cause: "consumption", died in 20th District on 29 Mar 1909, record (1908-12): 87824.

Susan HICKS, age 4 years, death cause: "diphtheria", died in 20th District on 14 Nov 1908, record (1908-12): 87825.

Samuel OWENS, age not known, married, death cause: "heart disease", died at Pactalus, 13th District on (day not stated) Mar 1910, record (1908-12): 87826.

C.P. JANES, age 52 years, married, death cause: "typhoid fever", born/died: Kendrick Creek, died: 22 Sep 1909, record (1908-12): 87827.

Tommy BIRDWELL, age 33 years, born at Telford, TN., married, death cause: "consumption", died at Pactalus on 23 Nov 1909, record (1908-12): 87828.
Dora E. BIRDWELL, age 4 years, death cause: not known, died at Pactalus on 8 May 1910, record (1908-12): 87829.
Mr. Ham SHOUN, age not stated, married, lumberman, death cause: "log", died at Bristol, date not stated, death registered: 21 May 1910, record (1908-12): 87830.
Unknown female, age 100 years, married, death cause: not stated, died at Bristol, date not stated, death recorded on 19 Jul 1910, record (1908-12): 87831.
Clifford DEMCY, born: 1909, death cause: "tuberculosis of bowels", died at Bluff City on 10 Sep 1909, record (1908-12): 87832.
Dora Bessie EADS, age 2 years and 8 months, death cause: "diphtheria", died at Bluff City on 17 Dec 1909, record (1908-12): 87833.
Rebecca Ann GLOVER, age 62 years, single, death cause: "nervous prostration", died in 16th District on 4 Jul 1909, record (1908-12): 87834.
Jerry CARR, age 36 years, married, death cause: "tonging logs", died at Taylor's Valley on 27 Aug 1909, record (1908-12): 87835.
Nola CARR, age 2 months, death cause: "croup", died at Bluff City on 1 Dec 1909, record (1908-12): 87837.
Garfield H. PRESNELL, age 30 years, born in Carter Co., married, death cause: "tuberculosis", died at Bluff City on 24 May 1910, record (1908-12): 87838.
Charles Howard SCALF, age 5 hours, died at Bluff City on 30 Mar 1910, record (1908-12): 87839.
Wade DETHRAGE, age 27 years, born in Lee Co., VA., death cause: "pholegra", died in Bristol on 13 Jun 1910, record (1908-12): 87840.
Elizabeth (illegible), age 3 months and 2 days, death cause: "cholera", died at Bristol on 21 Jul 1910, record (1908-12): 87840.
Margaret CLARK, age 11 years and 8 months, born in Knoxville, death cause: "heart failure", died at Bristol on 30 May 1910, record (1908-12): 87841.
Mrs. M.J. HENDERSON, age 77 years, born at Halafax Co., VA., widow, death cause: "stomach trouble", died at Bristol on 14 May 1910, record (1908-12): 87842.
Mrs. Robert KING, age 30 years, married, death cause: "pneumonia", died at Bristol on 16 Feb 1910, record (1908-12): 87843.

John MCGOLDRIC, age not stated, born at Abingdon, married, death cause: "fractured skull", died at Bristol on 1 Jan 1910, record (1908-12): 87844.
Fred HALE, age not stated, single, death cause: "fever", died at Bristol, date not stated, death registered on 10 Jul 1910, record (1908-12): 87845.
Kathleen MINNIC, age 6 weeks, death cause: "pneumonia", died at Bristol on 4 Jan 1910, record (1908-12): 87846.
Edgar HAYNES, age 21 years, born in Virginia, single, death cause: "consumption", died at Bristol on 13 Oct 1909, record (1908-12): 87847.
Mrs. DAVIS, age 47 years, married, death cause: "consumption", died at Bristol on 24 Dec 1909, record (1908-12): 87848.
Elmer HAYNES, age 19 years, single, death cause: "consumption", died at Bristol on 18 Jun 1910, record (1908-12): 87849.
Mrs. Harriett J. MOORMAN, age 57 years, born at Culpepper, VA., married, death cause: "tuberculosis", died at Bristol on 2 Mar 1910, record (1908-12): 87850.
Maj. H.C. WOOD, age 71 years, born in Scott Co., VA., single, death cause: "paralysis", died 8 Dec 1909, record (1908-12): 87851.
Bettie BROWN, age 63 years, born in Lynchburg, single, death cause: "dropsy", died at Bristol on 23 Nov 1909, record (1908-12): 87852.
Lacy E. RODGERS, age 1 year, death cause: "pneumonia fever", died in 19th District on 29 Jan 1911, record (1908-12): 87858.
John M. RODGERS, age 34 years, married, death cause: "pneumonia fever", died in 19th District on 1 Dec 1910.
Luisy RODGERS, age 65 years, born in Johnson Co., married, death cause: "pneumonia fever", died in 19th District on 2 Dec 1910, record (1908-12): 87860.
Margt RODGERS, age 40 years, born in Johnson Co., death cause: "pneumonia fever", died in 19th District on 3 Dec 1910, record (1908-12): 87861.
William P. SOUTH, age 42 years, married, death cause: "killed by shooting him", died in 19th District on 2 Jul 1910, record (1908-12): 87862.
Hywathis BULLIAN, male, lived 1 hour, death cause: not known, died in 19th District on 12 Feb 1911, record (1908-12): 87863.

William O'NEAL, age 89 years, born in Wilkes Co., NC., married, death cause: "cold and old age", died in 19th District on 22 Mar 1911, record (1908-12): 87864.
Lelas FORD, female, lived one-half hour, death cause: "not known", died in 19th District on 13 Nov 1910, record (1908-12): 87865.
Oliva MINTON, age 1 year, born in Johnson County, death cause: "hooping cough", died in 19th District on 13 Nov 1910, record (1908-12): 87866.
Hessie POE, age 21 years, 7 months and 27 days, single, death cause: "heart failure", died in 20th District on 4 Jan 1911, record (1908-12): 87867.
Diadema CLAY, age 78 years, born in Floyd Co., VA., married, death cause: "spinal trouble", died in 20th District on 4 Aug 1910, record (1908-12): 87868.
George P. COX, age 4 months, death cause: not stated, died in 19th District on 2 Aug 1910, record (1908-12): 87869.
Joe M. ALLISON, age 52 years, married, death cause: "festulous opening", died in 20th District on 5 Oct 1910, record (1908-12): 87870.
Sarah Jane GROSS, age 45 years, 7 months and 25 days, married, death cause: "pneumonia", died in 20th District on 1 Apr 1911, record (1908-12): 87871.
Pearl HODGES, age 24 years, born in Washington Co., TN., married, death cause: "pneumonia", died in 20th District on 17 Oct 1910, record (1908-12): 87867.
Infant SELLS, female, age 2 months, death cause: "unknown", died in 20th District on 29 Nov 1910, record (1908-12): 87868.
Lucy GEISLER, age 41 years, single, death cause: "dropsy", died in 20th District on 1 Nov 1910, record (1908-12): 87869.
Benjamin L. SELLS, age 70 years and 11 months, born: Sullivan Co., married, death cause: "heart and liver trouble", died in 20th District on 22 Dec 1910, record (1908-12): 87870.
Lucy HODGES, age 34 years, 4 months and 19 days, single, death cause: "epilepsy", died in 20th District on 3 Jun 1911, record (1908-12): 87871.
Stacy HATCHER, female, age 5 years, death cause: not stated, died in 21st District on 20 Oct 1910, record (1908-12): 87872.
David CROSS, age 60 years, married, death cause: "old age", died in 21st District on 1 Nov 1910, record (1908-12): 87873.

J. Kass ENSOR, age 76 years, born in Washington Co., TN., married, death cause: "consumption", died in 20th District on 21 Aug 1910, record (1908-12): 87874.

J.L. VANCE, age 55 years, married, death cause: "consumption", died in 21st District on 11 Jun 1911, record (1908-12): 87875.

Andrew GOODMAN, age 47 years, 5 months and 8 days, married, death cause: "tuberculosis", died in 20th District on 22 Aug 1910, record (1908-12): 87876.

Mary E. HARKLEROAD, age 68 years, married, death cause: "consumption", born/died: Kingsport, died: 18 May 1910, record (1908-12): 87877.

M.M. CHILDRESS, age 78 years, born: Sullivan Co., married, death cause: "paralysis and rheumatism", died at Bloomingdale on 29 Apr 1910, record (1908-12): 87878.

Samuel LIGHT, age 56 years, married, death cause: "consumption", died at Bloomingdale on 8 Aug 1909, record (1908-12): 87879.

Infant TAYLOR, female, death cause: "still birth", child of John TAYLOR, died at Kingsport on 1 Aug 1909, record (1908-12): 87880.

L.D. WATERMAN, age 75 years, born in Sullivan Co., married, death cause: "consumption", died at Bloomingdale on 10 Jun 1910, record (1908-12): 87881.

Matilda BIRDWELL, age 42 years, widow, death cause: "rheumatism", born/died: Bloomingdale, died: 25 Oct 1909, record (1908-12): 87882.

Walker D. KETRON, age 1 year, 4 months and 2 days, death cause: "pneumonia", died at Bloomingdale on 8 Feb 1910, record (1908-12): 87883.

Infant HUFFMAN, male, death cause: "stillborn", died at Arcadia on 24 Jun 1910, record (1908-12): 87884.

William H.H. GAINES, age 73 years, 9 months and 28 days, born at Arcadia, married, death cause: "gastritis", died at Bloomingdale on 14 May 1910, record (1908-12): 87885.

Clarence E. HUDSON, age 1 year, 4 months and 22 days, death cause: "stomach trouble", died at Bloomingdale on 9 Dec 1908, record (1908-12): 87886.

Melvin A. KETRON, age 55 years, 9 months and 15 days, married, death cause: "spinal trouble", born/died: Bloomingdale, died: 28 Jun 1910, record (1908-12): 87887.

George Clifton MCCRARY, age 5 months, death cause: "unknown", died at Bloomingdale on 21 Feb 1910, record (1908-12): 87888.

Johnathan GARLAND, age 73 years, born in Carter Co., married, death cause: not recorded, died at Blountville on 18 Feb 1910, record (1908-12): 87889.

Unnamed Infant, female, age 21 days, death cause: "croup", died at Blountville on 20 Nov 1909, record (1908-12): 87890.

Mollie SLAUGHTER, age 47 years, married, death cause: "complication of disease", died at Blountville on 25 Aug 1909, record (1908-12): 87891.

Fannie Jane SPANGLER, age 5 years, death cause: "pneumonia", died at Blountville on 29 Mar 1910, record (1908-12): 87892.

Eva V. RADER, age 54 years, single, death cause: "paralysis", born/died: Blountville, died 2 Apr 1910, record (1908-12): 87893.

Doc CHAPMAN, age 40 years, married, death cause: "typhoid fever", died in 5th District on 30 Nov 1909, record (1908-12): 87894.

Letcher MCNUTT, lived 1 hour, born at Gate City, VA., death cause: not stated, died at Gate City, Scott Co., VA., on 28 Feb 1909, record (1908-12): 87895.

B.A. COX, age 51 years, single, death cause: "pneumonia", born/died: 5th District, died 7 Mar 1910, record (1908-12): 87896.

Unnamed Infant, female, death cause: "stillborn", died at Blountville on 9 Aug 1909, record (1908-12): 87897.

Bruce Adam GRUFF, age 17 years and 5 months, single, death cause: "pneumonia", died in 5th District on 14 Feb 1910, record (1908-12): 87898.

Lizzie RUSSELL, age 54 years, widow, death cause: "consumption", died at poor house, 5th District on 12 Jul 1909, record (1908-12): 87899.

Daniel GREEN, age 100 years, single, death cause: "old age", died at poor house, 5th District on 30 Dec 1909, record (1908-12): 87900.

Kenney SOUTH, age 20 years, single, death cause: "fits", died at poor house, 5th District on 18 Apr 1910, record (1908-12): 87901.

Mrs. Francis BALL, age 50 years, married, death cause: "insanity", died at poor house, 5th District on 17 Aug 1909, record (1908-12): 87902.

Infant DUFREECE, male, death cause: "born dead", born/died: 5th District, 1 Sep 1909, record (1908-12): 87903.

Nannie JOHNSON, age 26 years, single, death cause: "consumption", died in 5th District on 14 Jul 1909, record (1908-12): 87904

Mrs. Hannah JOHNSON, age 84 years, born in Washington Co., widow, death cause: "old age", died in 5th District on 24 Sep 1909, record (1908-12): 87905.
Infant DAVIS, female, lived one-half hour, death cause: not stated, died in 5th District on 1 Apr 1910, record (1908-12): 87906.
Infant HICKMAN, female, death cause: "born dead", died in 5th District on 14 Apr 1910, record (1908-12): 87907.
Mrs. Polly LARGE, age 45 years, married, death cause: "not known", died in 5th District on 27 Jul 1909, record (1908-12): 87908.
Mrs. Margaret LEONARD, age 71 years, born in Virginia, married, death cause: "heart failure", died in 5th District on 12 Apr 1910, record (1908-12): 87909.
Infant MOORE, female, death cause: "born dead", child of James MOORE, died in 5th District on 17 Feb 1910, record (1908-12): 87910.
C.O. KENNEDY, age 41 years, born in Virginia, married, death cause: "run over by wagon", died in 5th District on 1 Oct 1909, record (1908-12): 87911.
James TAYLOR, age 86 years, married, death cause: "paralysis", died in 5th District on 6 Mar 1910, record (1908-12): 87912.
G.A. WILLIAMS, age 72 years, born in Virginia, married, death cause: "pneumonia", died in Blountville, 5th District on 25 Apr 1910, record (1908-12): 87913.
J.J. SMITH, age 78 years, born in Sullivan Co., married, death cause: "old age", died in 5th District on 20 May 1910, record (1908-12): 87914.
Virginia A. WOLFE, age 78 years, born in Virginia, married, death cause: "dropsy", died in 5th District on 10 May 1910, record (1908-12): 87915.
Anderson JOHNSON, age 50 years and 10 days, born in Grayson Co., VA., married, death cause: "unknown", died in 20th District on 13 Aug 1911, record (1908-12): 87916.
Carrie BARKEN, age 27 years and 6 months, born in Washington Co., TN., single, death cause: "burned", died in 20th District on 28 Jan 1912, record (1908-12): 87917.
Lula BARGUS, age 21 years and 11 months, married, death cause: "birth of child", died in 20th District on 10 Dec 1911, record (1908-12): 87918.

Cash VANBUREN, age 74 years and 11 months, born in Washington Co., TN., married, death cause: "consumption", died in 20th District on 17 Jul 1911, record (1908-12): 87919.

Unnamed Infant, male, lived 4 hours, death cause: "unknown", died in 20th District on 30 Oct 1911, record (1908-12): 87920.

Robert VESTER, colored, age 23 years, born in Santa Fe, TN., married, death cause: "tuberculosis", died at Mount Pleasant on 1 Mar 1912, record (1908-12): 87921.

Cleo WEBB, age 15 years, born at Henderson, KY., death cause: "tuberculosis", died at Mount Pleasant on 22 Jun 1912, record (1908-12): 87922.

Ida MARSH, age 24 years, born at Columbia, TN., married, death cause: "tuberculosis", died at Mount Pleasant on 7 Oct 1911, record (1908-12): 87923.

Alberta GARDNER, age 13 years, death cause: "tuberculosis", born/died: Mount Pleasant, died: 23 Nov 1911, record (1908-12): 87924.

Morrel JONES, age 16 years, death cause: "sirofula", died at Mount Pleasant on 7 May 1912, record (1908-12): 87925.

Percy BECKETT (?), colored, age 9 years, death cause: "tuberculosis", born/died: Mount Pleasant, died: 6 May 1912, record (1908-12): 87926.

J.L. ALEXANDER, age 64 years, born at Maury Co., TN., married, death cause: "paralysis", died at Mount Pleasant on 28 Jul 1911, record (1908-12): 87927.

Unnamed Infant, male, lived 1 day, death cause: "unknown", died at Mount Pleasant on 17 Nov 1912, record (1908-12): 87928.

Mrs. Charles CHAFIN, age 30 years, born at Columbia, TN., married, death cause: "child birth", died at Mount Pleasant on 17 Nov 1911, record (1908-12): 87929.

Unnamed Infant, female, death cause: "born dead", died at Mount Pleasant on 22 Nov 1911, record (1908-12): 87930.

Lena Cook DORRIS (?), age 33 years, born at Maury Co., TN., married, death cause: "cancer liver", died at Columbia, TN. on 19 Nov 1911, record (1908-12): 87931.

Margaret Louise JONES, age 9 months, death cause: "pneumonia fever", died at Mount Pleasant on 10 May 1912, record (1908-12): 87932.

Sammie SIMPKINS, age 11 years, born at Columbia, TN., death cause: "scarlet fever", died at Mount Pleasant on 12 Nov 1911, record (1908-12): 87933.

Unnamed Infant, male, death cause: "born dead", died at Mount Pleasant on 10 Feb 1912, record (1908-12): 87934.

Moses REYNOLDS, black, age 74 years, born at Giles Co., TN., married, death cause: "paralysis", died at Mount Pleasant on 30 Sep 1911, record (1908-12): 87935.

Carolina Elizabeth GRAY, age 37 years, born at Nashville, death cause: "tuberculosis of lungs", died at Emmett, 21st District on 11 Jun 1912, record (1908-12): 87936.

Mary E. DURHAM, age 65 years, married, death cause: "lumbago", born/died: Indian Springs, died on 23 Mar 1912, record (1908-12): 87937.

Warda GOODMAN, age 4 years and 11 months, death cause: "diphtheria", died in 20th District on 30 Nov 1910, record (1908-12): 87938.

J.M. MORTON, age 73 years, married, death cause: "cancer", died in 21st District on 13 Dec 1910, record (1908-12): 87939.

VIRGIE, male, age 4 years, death cause: "croup", died in 21st District on 9 Dec 1910, record (1908-12): 87940.

Beulah Edith LYONS, age 9 years, born at Bluff City, death cause: "tuberculosis of brain", died in 21st District on 23 Oct 1910, record (1908-12): 87941.

BAKER, age not stated, death cause: not stated, died in 21st District on 25 May 1911, record (1908-12): 87942.

C.B. MILLARD, age 49 years, married, death cause: "cancer of mouth", died in 21st District on 1 Sep 1910, record (1908-12): 87947.

Ruth FARRIS, age 5 months, death cause: "indigestion", died in Bristol on 30 Oct 1908, record (1908-12): 87948.

Rosa GODSEY, colored, age 28 years, born in Virginia, married, death cause: "typhoid fever", died at Bristol on 5 Jun 1909, record (1908-12): 87949.

John ROGERS, age 35 years, married, death cause: "pneumonia", died at Bristol on 6 Mar 1909, record (1908-12): 87950.

John DAGGS, colored, age 68 years, born in Virginia, married, death cause: "don't know", died at Bristol on (day not stated) May 1909, record (1908-12): 87951.

Unnamed Infant, male, lived 3 days, death cause: not stated, died at Bristol on 15 Jun 1909, record (1908-12): 87952.

Mattie SHERMAN, age 11 months and 12 days, death cause: "stomach trouble", died at Bristol on 21 Sep 1908, record (1908-12): 87953.
Samuel Carl COX, age 2 years and 6 months, born at Morristown, death cause: "pneumonia", died at Indian Springs on 31 Jan 1912, record (1908-12): 87954.
J.N. COX, age 31 years, married, death cause: "kidney trouble", born/died: Indian Springs, died 11 Apr 1912, record (1908-12): 87955.
Julia Ann SMITH, age 62 years, married, death cause: "pneumonia", born/died: Indian Springs, died: 5 Jan 1912, record (1908-12): 87956.
S.E. COX, age 77 years, born at Blountville, single, death cause: "eurine poisoning", died at Indian Springs on 15 Jul 1911, record (1908-12): 87953.
J.D. LADY, age 53 years, married, death cause: "paralysis", born/died: Indian Springs, died: 8 Aug 1911, record (1908-12): 87954.
Rae DICKSON, female, age 44 years, married, death cause: "typhoid fever", born/died: Indian Springs, died: 10 Dec 1911, record (1908-12): 87955.
John BOWEARY, age 68 years, married, death cause: "rheumatism", born/died: Indian Springs, died: 11 Apr 1912, record (1908-12): 87956.
Willie BARGES, age 25 years, born at Kingsport, single, death cause: "rheumatism", died at Indian Springs on 6 Aug 1911, record (1908-12): 87957.
Jacob JONES, age 84 years, born: Sullivan Co., single, death cause: "old age and kidney trouble", died at Blountivlle on 25 Mar 1912, record (1908-12): 87958.
Mrs. Julia CROSS, age 77 years, born: Sullivan Co., widow, death cause: "pneumonia", died at Blountville on 25 Feb 1912, record (1908-12): 87959.
Jacob SMITH, age 53 years, married, death cause: "rheumatism", died at Blountville on 27 Nov 1911, record (1908-12): 87960.
Michael DAVENPORT, age 80 years, born in Indiana, married, death cause: "Brights disease", died at Piney Flats on 12 Mar 1912, record (1908-12): 87961.
James WATKINS, age 86 years, born in Sullivan Co., widower, death cause: "old age", died at Blountville on 5 Feb 1912, record (1908-12): 87962.
Reece CROSS, age 47 years, married, death cause: "pneumonia", died in the 8th District on 23 May 1912, record (1908-12): 87963.
John CLIFFORD (?), age 1 year, death cause: illegible, died at 8th District on 1 Feb 1912, record (1908-12): 87964.

William HUDSON, age 59 years, married, death cause: "cattarr of stomach and bowels", born/died: Piney Flats, died: 5 Jun 1912, record (1908-12): 87965.
Abner PARMILEE, age 84 years, born at Silver Creek, NY., married, death cause: "paralysis", died at Piney Flats on 26 May 1912, record (1908-12): 87966.
James JETER, age 63 years, married, death cause: "cancer of bowels", died at Piney Flats on 22 May 1912, record (1908-12): 87967.
Hiram LIPPS, age 72 years, born in Carter Co., married, death cause: "softening of brain", died at Piney Flats on 11 Dec 1911, record (1908-12): 87968.
W.G. WHITAKER, age 2 months, death cause: "fever", died at Piney Flats on 18 Mar 1912, record (1908-12): 87969.
John W. HICKS, age 10 months and 7 days, death cause: "indigestion", died at Bloomingdale on 31 Jul 1911, record (1908-12): 87970.
Mary E. MYERS, age 66 years, 7 months and 23 days, born at Indian Springs, married, death cause: "nervous dyspepsy indigestion", died at Arcadia on 30 May 1912, record (1908-12): 87971.
Sallie H. FULK, age 43 years, married, born/died: Arcadia, died on 16 Aug 1911, record (1908-12): 87972.
Alice Agatha KETRON, age 1 year, 2 months and 23 days, death cause: not stated, died at Bloomingdale on 27 Dec 1911, record (1908-12): 87973.
Samuel DUNN, age 72 years, born in Wythe Co., VA., married, death cause: "paralysis", died at Bloomingdale, 10th District on 20 Jan 1912, record (1908-12): 87974.
Rena DAVIS, age 29 years, born in Burke Co., VA., married, death cause: "cancer of liver", died at Bristol on 4 Mar 1909. record (1908-12): 87975.
Fannie DOWLER, age 73 years, born in Snowville, TN., married, death cause: "dropsy", died at Bristol on 6 Apr 1909, record (1908-12): 87976.
Maxia B. CATRON, age 3 years and 3 months, death cause: "whooping cough", died in 4th District on 9 Jul 1910, record (1908-12): 87977.
Sallie E. MILLERD, age 58 years and 4 days, born in Carter Co., married, death cause: "enlargement of liver", died in 4th District on 25 Nov 1910, record (1908-12): 87978.
Elizabeth CRANE, age 75 years, married, born: Sullivan Co., death cause: "old age", died in 4th District on 18 Dec 1910, record (1908-12): 87979.

Jake B. HOBSON, age 58 years, single, death cause: "catarr of stomach", died in 4th District on 25 Jun 1911, record (1908-12): 87980.

Samuel B. MILLER, age 77 years, married, death cause: "pneumonia", died in 4th District on 15 Mar 1911, record (1908-12): 87981.

Johnnie EATON, age 1 year and 10 months, death cause: "brain trouble", died in 4th District on 5 Oct 1910, record (1908-12): 87982.

Lura Lee LEONARD, age not stated, single, death cause: "bold hives", died in 4th District on 2 Dec 1910, record (1908-12): 87983.

Ike LEONARD, age 50 years, married, death cause: "tumor of stomach", died in 4th District on 27 Feb 1911, record (1908-12): 87984.

James LOVE, age 45 years, married, death cause: "fever", born/died: Bristol, died on 24 Nov 1910, record (1908-12): 87985.

Mary E. GOODMAN, age 2 years, death cause: "fever", died at Bristol on 29 Aug 1910, record (1908-12): 87986.

Charles SCORAFT, age 54 years, born in Carter Co., married, death cause: "appendicitis", died at Bristol on 1 Oct 1910, record (1908-12): 87987.

Martha and Mary BROWN, age 21 days, death cause: "fever", died at South Bristol on 16 Jan 1911, record (1908-12): 87988.

Peter Mimish KESERY, age 79 years, born in Washington Co., VA., married, death cause: "fever", died near Bristol on 27 Mar 1910, record (1908-12): 87989.

Jacob WEAVER, age 39 years, born at Weaver, TN., death cause: "fever", died at South Bristol on 24 Dec 1910, record (1908-12): 87990.

E.M. BLEVINS, age 58 years, married, death cause: "heart failure", died at Emmett, 1st District on 28 Aug 1909, record (1908-12): 87991.

Mrs. S.C. JONES, age 79 years, born at Hall Co., GA., widow, death cause: "fever", died at Kingsport on 23 Feb 1910, record (1908-12): 87992.

James B. CRUM, age 63 years, born in Green Co., married, died at Kinssport on 2 Feb 1911, record (1908-12): 87993.

Jake ADAMS, age 45 years, born at Wythe Co., VA., married, death cause: "fever", died at Kingsport on 27 Feb 1910, record (1908-12): 87994.

J.H. COX, age 66 years, born in Sullivan Co., married, death cause: "heart failure", died in 19th District on 7 Apr 1910, record (1908-12): 87995.

Steven WYATT, age 72 years, born in Grayson Co., VA., married, death cause: "gravel", died in 19th District on 16 Apr 1910, record (1908-12): 87996.

Kate DENTON, age 3 months, death cause: "consumption", died in 19th District on 3 Oct 1910, record (1908-12): 87997.

N.D. PARKS, age 2 years, death cause: "fever", died in 19th District on 3 May 1910, record (1908-12): 87998.

David C. SWIFT, age 4 weeks, death cause: not stated, died in 19th District on 6 Sep 1909, record (1908-12): 87999.

Infant SAUL, male, lived one-half hour, death cause: not stated, died in 19th District on 5 Mar 1910, record (1908-12): 88000.

Lehoy CASH, male, age 2 years, born in Washington Co., VA., death cause: "consumption", died at Washington Co., VA., on 29 Aug 1909, record (1908-12): 88001.

Lee GENTRY, age 1 year, death cause: "hooping cough", died in 19th District on 28 Jun 1910, record (1908-12): 88002.

Helen HARKLEROAD, age 7 months, death cause: "unknown", died age 808 Ga. Ave., Bristol on 10 Mar 1912, record (1908-12): 88003.

Vollie MOORE, male, age 18 years, death cause: "spinal tuberculosis", died age 622 Florida Ave., Bristol on 21 Feb 1912, record (1908-12): 88004.

Andrew GLOVER, age 18 months, death cause: "measles", died at Bristol on 3 Mar 1912, record (1908-12): 88005.

Infant DALTON, age 4 months, death cause: "morphane form mother's milk", died at 846 Shelby St., Bristol on 3 Jun 1912, record (1908-12): 88006.

Loucinda LITZ, age 78 years, born in Sullivan Co., married, death cause: "heart failure", died at Kingsport on 10 Feb 1912, record (1908-12): 88007.

Annie Elizabeth KETRON, age 7 weeks, death cause: "unnown", died at Kingsport on 16 Oct 1911, record (1908-12): 88008.

David E. QUARLES, age 83 years, 5 months and 7 days, born at Scott Co., VA., married, death cause: "not known", died at Kingsport on 4 Jan 1912, record (1908-12): 88009.

Lyda Kate DAVIS, age 20 years, born at Bloomingdale, single, death cause: "pneumonia fever", died at Kingsport on 26 Feb 1912, record (1908-12): 88010.

Edward S. JOHNSON, age 30 years, married, death cause: "rheumatism", died at Kingsport on 8 Aug 1911, record (1908-12): 88011.

Unnamed Infant, female, lived 12 hours, death cause: "not known", died at Kingsport on 20 Aug 1911, record (1908-12): 88012.

Unnamed Infant, female, lived 10 days, death cause: "not known", died at Kingsport on 1 Sep 1911, record (1908-12): 88013.

Unnamed Infant, male, lived 5 days, death cause: "weakness", died at Kingsport on 29 Jun 1912, record (1908-12): 88014.

Aura D. THOMPSON, male, age 18 months, death cause: "pneumonia", died at Kingsport on 12 may 1912, record (1908-12): 88015.

Nellie V. BENNETT, age 4 months and 11 days, born in Johnson City, death cause: "colera", died in Johnson City on 11 Jul 1911, record (1908-12): 88016.

Andy T. BYERS, age 7 years and 5 months, death cause: "consumption of bowels, died at Kingsport on 1 Nov 1911, record (1908-12): 88017.

John W. FELTY, age 8 months and 23 days, death cause: "bronchial pneumonia", died at Kingsport on 8 Apr 1912, record (1908-12): 88018.

Minnie May PERKINS, age 2 years, death cause: "spinal trouble", died at Kingsport on 14 Aug 1911, record (1908-12): 88019.

Charles S. ADAMS, age 20 years, born in Wythe Co., VA., single, death cause: "typhoid fever", died at Kingsport on 11 Jan 1912, record (1908-12): 88020.

William SCALF, age 53 years, married, death cause: "heart failure", died at Kingsport on 1 May 1912, record (1908-12): 88021.

Sallie Ann VAUGHN, age 55 years, single, death cause: "cancer", died at Kingsport on 15 Feb 1912, record (1908-12): 88022.

Thomas PARKER, age 83 years, born in Virginia, married, death cause: "chronic", died at Kingsport on 7 Mar 1912, record (1908-12): 88023.

Sallie BLAKELY, age 64 years, married, death cause: "chronic trouble", died at Kingsport on 6 Mar 1912, record (1908-12): 88024.

Maud MCKINZIE, age 26 years, married, death cause: "consumption", died at Kingsport on 28 Sep 1212, record (1908-12): 88025.

Mrs. G.G. KEENER, age 28 years, married, death cause: "appendicitis", died at Knoxville on 1 Jul 1912, record (1908-12): 88026.

John L. PILE, age 75 years, single, death cause: "pneumonia fever", born/died: Kingsport, died: 20 Feb 1912, record (1908-12): 88027.

Emalin CLOUD, age 81 years, born in Wytheville, VA., single, death cause: "pneumonia fever", died at Kingsport on 15 Apr 1912, record (1908-12): 88028.
J.W.T. PELTIER, age 61 years, born: Kingsport, single, death cause: "railroad accident", died in Scott Co., VA. on 19 Feb 1912, record (1908-12): 88029.
Mrs. Annie ARMSTRONG, age not stated, widow, death cause: "dropsy", died at Kingsport on 20 Feb 1912, record (1908-12): 88030.
Minnie Mable PARKER, age 10 days, death cause: "scarlet fever", died at Kingsport on 30 Jun 1912, record (1908-12): 88031.
John Henry JONES, age 17 months, death cause: "pneumonia fever", died at Kingsport on 17 Jun 1912, record (1908-12): 88032.
Unnamed Infant, male, age 7 weeks, death cause: "hives", died at Indian Springs, 13th District on 15 Sep 1911, record (1908-12): 88033.
Lizzie FOX, age 23 years, married, death cause: "consumption", born/died: Pactalus, died: 10 Mar 1912, record (1908-12): 88034.
Ellen SHORT, age 40 yearws, married, death cause: not recorded, born/died: Depew's Chapel, died: 20 Dec 1911, record (1908-12): 88035.
Talmage SHORT, age 16 years, death cause: "typhoid fever", born/died: Depew's Chapel, died: 20 Mar 1912, record (1908-12): 88036.
Mirinda SMILY, age 71 years, married, death cause: "stomach trouble", born/died: Horse Creek, died: 10 Aug 1911, record (1908-12): 88037.
Isaac MODY, age 36 years, married, death cause: "consumption", born/died: Pactalus, died: (day not stated) Sep 1911, record (1908-12): 88038.
Cecil HORN, age 10 days, death cause: "hives", died at Pactalus on 9 Aug 1911, record (1908-12): 88039.
Jerry MCCULLEY, age 62 years, married, death cause: "pneumonia", born/died: Pactalus, died: 31 Mar 1912, record (1908-12): 88040.
Sarah FLEENOR, age 70 years, born in Virginia, married, death cause: "heart failure", died at Rock Springs on 10 Mar 1912, record (1908-12): 88041.
Unnamed Infant, male, age 6 weeks, death cause: "hives", died at Indian Springs on 10 Sep 1911, record (1908-12): 88042.
Margaret A. GEISLER, age 54 years, married, death cause: "dropsy", born/died: 16th District, died: (day not stated) Mar 1912, record (1908-12): 88043.

Steven Lee ELLER, age 4 months, death cause: "measles", died at E. Mary St., Bristol on 22 Feb 1912, record (1908-12): 88044.
Robert REYNOLDS, age 44 years, born in Henry Co., VA., married, death cause: "dropsy", died E. State St., Bristol, (day not stated) Oct 1911, record (1908-12): 88045.
Wiley JONES, age 4 years and 6 months, death cause: "measles", died at E. State St., Bristol on 1 Mar 1912, record (1908-12): 88046.
Lola Birdwell LANE, age 22 years, married, death cause: "dropsy", died at 340 Woodlawn Ave., Bristol on 6 Jul 1911, record (1908-12): 88047.
Rody POWELL, age 3 weeks and 2 days, death cause: "unknown, died suddenly", died at 505 Woodlawn Ave., Bristol on 30 Jun 1912, record (1908-12): 88048.
Isom PRITCHARD, age 75 years, born in Russell Co., VA., married, death cause: "paralysis", died at 609 Woodlawn Ave., Bristol on 26 Jan 1912, record (1908-12): 88049.
George Montgomery WILLETT, age 5 years, death cause: "measles", died at 603 Woodlawn Ave., Bristol on 14 Feb 1912, record (1908-12): 88050.
Jennie WIDENER, age 38 years, born in Virginia, single, death cause: "tuberculosis", died at 112, 6th St., Bristol on 17 Jun 1912, record (1908-12): 88051.
Infant BOWERY, male, lived 1 day, child of Thomas BOWERY, death cause: "inanition", died at 104, 16th St., Bristol on 19 Apr 1912, record (1908-12): 88052.
A.J. BRIDGEMAN, age 48 years, born in Smith Co., VA., married, death cause: "dropsy", died at 1425, 14th St., Bristol on 22 Jun 1912, record (1908-12): 88053.
Andrew C. HARKLEROAD, age 53 years, married, death cause: "ulcer of brain", died at Bristol on 9 Apr 1912, record (1908-12): 88054.
Levi GROSECLOSE, age 67 years, born in Wythe Co., VA., married, death cause: "dropsy", died at 1317 Broad St., Bristol on 20 Dec 1911, record (1908-12): 88055.
Mrs. W.D. KINKEAD, age 39 years, born at Gate City, married, death cause: "cancer", died at 1301 Broad St., Bristol on 20 Sep 1911, record (1908-12): 88056.
Charles Nelson SMITH, age 1 years, death cause: "measles and pneumonia", died at 1237 Broad St., Bristol on 9 Mar 1912, record (1908-12): 88057.
Mrs. E.B. WEXLER, age 48 years, born in Smith Co., VA., married, death cause: "overturning of buggy", died in Bristol on 7 Jul 1912, record (1908-12): 88058.

Mrs. A.B. WHITAKER, age 50 years, born in Giles Co., VA., married, death cause: "cancer", died at 1004 Anderson St., Bristol on 22 May 1912, record (1908-12): 88059.

Beatrice BOWERS, age 13 months, death cause: "measles", died at 308, 8th St., Bristol on 31 Jan 1912, record (1908-12): 88060.

Patton, POSTON, age 65 years, born at Horse Creek, married, death cause: "not known", died at Depew's Chapel on (day not stated) Mar 1912, record (1908-12): 88061.

Infant CRAWFORD, female, age not stated, death cause: not stated, died at Depew's Chapel on 16 Dec 1911, record (1908-12): 88062.

Isaac D. MOUDY, age 41 years, married, death cause: "tuberculosis", died in 14th District on 7 Sep 1911, record (1908-12): 88063.

William MILLER, age 72 years, born near Jonesboro, married, death cause: "old age and complication of disease", died at Fordtown on 11 Oct 1911, record (1908-12): 88064.

Infant LARKINS, male, lived 3 months, death cause: "heart trouble", died in 15th District on 27 Dec 1911, record (1908-12): 88065.

Ellen MORRISON, lived 2 months, death cause: "found dead in bed", died in 15th District on 28 Nov 1911, record (1908-12): 88066.

Hellen MORRISON, lived 2 months, death cause: "found dead in bed", died in 15th District on 28 Nov 1911, record (1908-12): 88067.

Lucil FERGUSON, lived 3 days, death cause: not stated, died in 15th District on 6 Feb 1912, record (1908-12): 88068.

Connie COPASS, age 6 months, death cause: not stated, died in 15th District on 10 Apr 1912, record (1908-12): 88069.

Andrew J. BURNETT, age 62 years, born in Overton Co., TN., single, death cause: "cancer", died in 16th District on 10 Nov 1911, record (1908-12): 88070.

Andrew BOOHER, age 6 years, born at Big Creek, TN., death cause: "tuberculosis of brain", died at Bristol on 20 Apr 1912, record (1908-12): 88071.

Georgie STONE, age 3 years, death cause: "measles", died at 1204, Ga., Ave., Bristol on (day not stated) Feb 1912, record (1908-12): 88072.

Earl ODELL, black, age 8 months, death cause: "fever", died in 16th District on 23 Apr 1912, record (1908-12): 88073.

Texie COWEN, age 11 years, born in Johnson Co., death cause: "fever", died in 16th District on 5 Jul 1911, record (1908-12): 88074.
Gracie COWEN, age 20 years, born in Johnson Co., single, death cause: "fever", died in 16th District on 19 Jul 1911, record (1908-12): 88075.
Rebecca COWEN, age 18 years, born in Johnson Co., single, death cause: "fever", died in 16th District on 16 Aug 1911, record (1908-12): 88076.
James WILLIAMS, age 65 years, born in Charleston, SC., married, death cause: "dropsy", died at 408 Waterloo St., Bristol on 7 Dec 1911, record (1908-12): 88077.
Jessie James LUTTRELL, age 4 years, born at Pulaski, VA., death cause: "pneumonia", died in Bristol, VA., on 1 Mar 1912, record (1908-12): 88078.
Walter FERGUSON, black, age 22 years, born at Athens, TN., single, death cause: "tuberculosis", died at 508 College Ave., Bristol on 5 Mar 1912, record (1908-12): 88079.
Mattie Victoria WORSHAM, age 1 year and 6 months, born in Erwin, TN., death cause: "measles", died at 619, 5th St., Bristol on (day not stated) Feb 1912, record (1908-12): 88080.
Burt R. SMITH, age 50 years, born in Kentucky, married, president of King College, death cause: "Brights disease", died (day not stated) Jan 1912, record (1908-12): 88081.
Belle MCCLELLAN, age 65 years, born in Blountville, single, death cause: "paralysis", died at 320, 5th St., Bristol on 11 Jun 1912, record (1908-12): 88082.
Infant INGLE, male, child of L.D. INGLE, death cause: "born dead", born/died: 212, 6th St., Bristol on 29 Mar 1912, record (1908-12): 88083.
James GREEN, black, age 35 years, born in Blountville, divorced, death cause: "shot", died at 1020 Broad St., Bristol on 31 Aug 1911, record (1908-12): 88084.
Annie May ENGLISH, age 2 years, death cause: "measles", died at 1021 Broad St., Bristol on 21 Feb 1912, record (1908-12): 88085.
Erschel HARDY, black, age 3 weeks, death cause: "hemorrhage", died at 1011 Broad St., Bristol on 25 Apr 1912, record (1908-12): 88086.
Columbus DOW, black, death cause: "born dead", died at 946 Broad St., Bristol on 3 Jun 1912, record (1908-12): 88087.
Infant PAYNE, male, lived 11 hours, death cause: "paralysis", died at 944 State St., Bristol on 27 May 1912, record (1908-12): 88088.

Clara Lee MORSE, age 20 months, born in Wytheville, death cause: "measles", died at 802 State St., Bristol on 24 Jan 1912, record (1908-12): 87089.

Infant NEAL, female, lived 3 weeks, child of W.H. NEAL, death cause: "inanition", died at 511 Holston Ave., Bristol on 26 Jun 1912, record (1908-12): 88090.

Charles Bradford CABLE, age 74 years, born near Louisville, KY., married, death cause: "hardening of arteries", died at 319, 7th St., Bristol on 3 Apr 1912, record (1908-12): 88091.

Charles R. VANCE, age 76 years, born near Jonesboro, married, death cause: "hardening of arteries", died at 412, 6th St., Bristol on 18 Nov 1911, record (1908-12): 88092.

Julia CARLTON, age 65 years, married, death cause: "hemorrhage of lungs", died at 54, 4th St., Bristol on (day not stated) Dec 1911, record (1908-12): 88093.

Infant SMITH, female, child of J.W. SMITH, death cause: "born dead", died at 360, 4th St., Bristol on 26 May 1912, record (1908-12): 88094.

Infant CURTIS, male, lived 1 hour, child of Ed. CURTIS, death cause: "infanition", died at 406 English St., Bristol on * Nov 1911, record (1908-12): 88095.

Infant PAINTER, male, lived 5 months, child of E.S. PAINTER, death cause: "spinal tuberculosis", died at 716, 4th St., Bristol on 29 Jun 1912, record (1908-12): 88096.

Zilphia WATERS, age 42 years, born in North Carolina, married, death cause: "tuberculosis", died at 730, 4th St., Bristol on 15 Jun 1912, record (1908-12): 88097.

Daniel SHEETS, age 14 years, born in Carter Co., death cause: "fever", died in 16th District on * Mar 1912, record (1908-12): 88098.

Robert SHEETS, age not stated, death cause: "fever", born/died in 16th District, died: 17 Mar 1912, record (1908-12): 88099.

Elbert Hartsel, HEABERLIN, age 20 years, single, death cause: "measles", died at 730 Ky., Ave., Bristol on 15 Mar 1912, record (1908-12): 88100.

Matilda PENN, age 55 years, born in Tampa, FL., married, death cause: "female trouble", died at 929 E. State St., Bristol on 27 Dec 1911, record (1908-12): 88101.

John J. COPESS, age 61 years, widower, death cause: "by accident", born/died: near Fordtown, died: 14 Sep 1911, record (1908-12): 88102.

Unnamed Infant, male, death cause: "born dead", died near Fordtown on 25 Dec 1911, record (1908-12): 88103.

Gary SPICER, age 2 years, death cause: "tomaine poisoning", died at 212, 6th St., Bristol on 2 Jan 1912, record (1908-12): 88104.

Infant COLLINS, male, child of Burly COLLINS, death cause: "born dead", died at 328 Woodlawn Ave., Bristol on 17 May 1912, record (1908-12): 88105.

George W. MORRELL, age 88 years, born in Sullivan Co., married, death cause: "old age", died at Emmett on 10 Mar 1919, record (1908-12): 88106.

Jeasie MILLER, age 85 years, born in North Carolina, married, death cause: "kidney trouble", died at Big Creek, 1st District on 7 Jun 1908, record (1908-12): 88108.

William SIMERLY, age 6 years, death cause: "pneumonia fever", died in 1st District on 28 Sep 1908, record (1908-12): 88109.

Jane S. O'DELL, age 86 years, born in Jefferson City, TN., married, death cause: not stated, died at Emmett on 29 Jun 1908, record (1908-12): 88110.

Nathan M. BOYD, age 55 years, married, death cause: "apoplexy", died 27 Mar 1908, record (1908-12): 88111.

Susan JOHNSON, age 56 years, married, death cause: "cancer", died at Bloomingdale, 11th District on 5 Mar 1909, record (1908-12): 88112.

Doc ROGERS, age 60 years, born in Sullivan Co., married, death cause: "heart trouble", died at Bloomingdale, date of death not stated (probably 1909), record (1908-12): 88113.

Birty Ann PRICE, lived 3 days, death cause: not known, died at Kingsport on 19 Jun 1909, record (1908-12): 88114.

Unnamed Infant, female, death cause: "born dead", died at Kingsport on 20 Oct 1908, record (1908-12): 88115.

Unnamed Infant, male, death cause: "still born", died at Kingsport on 13 Nov 1908, record (1908-12): 88116.

Unnamed Infant, male, death cause: "born dead", died near Fordtown on 7 Dec 1911, record (1908-12): 88117.

Mrs. Jane COX, age 49 years, born at Sulphur Springs, married, death cause: "brain lesion", died at Hemlock on 27 Jun 1911, record (1908-12): 88118.

Isac P. CHASE, age 72 years, married, death cause: "senile pneumonia", died at Hemlock on date not stated, death registered on 20 Jul 1912, record (1908-12): 88119.

Mattie DEAKIN, age 21 years, single, death cause: "asthma", died in 8th District on (day illegible) Feb 1912, record (1908-12): 88120.

Wiley B. POORE, age 33 years, born at Childress, TN., married, death cause: "typhoid fever", died at Kingsport on 13 Jul 1908, record (1908-12): 88121.
D.R. DEVAULT, age 58 years, married, death cause: "pneumonia fever", born/died: Kingsport, died: 24 Jan 1909, record (1908-12): 88122.
Infant PRICE, male, child of Joe PRICE, death cause: "stillborn", died at Kingsport on 3 Dec 1908, record (1908-12): 88123.
Annise JOHNSON, female, age 43 years, married, death cause: "consumption", died at Kingsport on 6 Jun 1909, record (1908-12): 88124.
John M. HOMEL, age 77 years, married, death cause: "catarr of stomach", died at Kingsport on 14 Jun 1909, record (1908-12): 88125.
Jesse Albert WALLACE, age 66 years, born at Soddy, TN., married, death cause: "weakness of heart", died at 535 Alabama St., Bristol, on 23 Jun 1912, record (1908-12): 88126.
J.H.C. PIERCE, age 62 years, born in North Carolina, married, death cause: "kidney and heart", died at Piney Flats on 18 Nov 1910, record (1908-12): 88127.
Clyde CURTIS, lived 7 days, death cause: "croup", died at Piney Flats on 15 Apr 1910, record (1908-12): 88128.
Rachel SMITH, age 64 years, single, death cause: "general break down", died in 9th District on 9 Jun 1910, record (1908-12): 88129.
Granville PROFFITT, age 1 years, death cause: "croup", died at Piney Flats on 25 Aug 1909, record (1908-12): 88130.
Garfield PRESNELL, age 30 years, born at Butler, TN., married, death cause: "consumption", died at Piney Flats on 24 May 1910, record (1908-12): 88131.
George A. BLEVINS, age 6 months, death cause: "stomach disease", died at Piney Flats on 14 Mar 1910, record (1908-12): 88132.
Adam L. WEBB, age 3 months, death cause: "fever", died at Piney Flats on 17 Jan 1910, record (1908-12): 88133.
Infant CAUTERN, female, death cause: "born dead", died at Piney Flats on 4 Mar 1910, record (1908-12): 88134.
Mary OLIVER, age 74 years, married, death cause: "dropsy", born/died: Tennessee, died: 17 Dec 1909, record (1908-12): 88135.
Infant HEYETT, female, lived 6 days, death cause: "not known", died at Piney Flats on 8 May 1910, record (1908-12): 88136.

Infant HEYETT, male, lived 10 days, death cause: "not known", died at Piney Flats on 10 May 1910, record (1908-12): 88137.

George HUDSON, age 74 years, single, death cause: "heart trouble", died at Piney Flats on 2 Jan 1910, record (1908-12): 88137.

Marry J. NAVE, age 35 years, married, death cause: "consumption", died 8 Apr 1909, record (1908-12): 88138.

Daniel O. SHIPLEY, age 50 years, married, death cause: "heart trouble", died 23 Jun 1908, record (1908-12): 88139.

Maggie NAVE, age 4 years, death cause: "consumption", died: 29 May 1908, record (1908-12): 88140.

Albert MORRELL, age 8 years, death cause: "hooping cough", died: 19 Oct 1908, record (1908-12): 88141.

Lizzie GRUB, age 19 years, married, death cause: "dropsy", died: 5 May 1908, record (1908-12): 88142.

John H. SENIKER, age 80 years, married, death cause: "heart failure", born/died: Sullivan Co., died: 26 Aug 1908, record (1908-12): 88143.

Sarah E. MCGARRY, age 78 years, married, death cause: "apoplexy", born/died: Sullivan Co., died: 4 Jun 1909, record (1908-12): 88144.

Carson BOOHER, age 63 years, married, death cause: "pneumonia fever", died in 1st District on 5 Dec 1908, record (1908-12): 88145.

Unnamed Infant, female, lived 5 days, death cause: "unknown", died at Emmett on 2 Oct 1908, record (1908-12): 88146.

Smith CAMPBELL, age 17 years, single, death cause: not stated, died at Emmett on 25 Sep 1908, record (1908-12): 88147.

George MORRELL, age 5 years, death cause: "hooping cough", died in 1st District on 15 Nov 1908, record (1908-12): 88148.

William HORTON, age 75 years, born in North Carolina, married, death cause: "tuberculosis", died at Paperville on 11 Jul 1909, record (1908-12): 88149.

Margaret AKERS, age 79 years, born in Virginia, married, death cause: "heart failure", died at Bristol on 25 May 1909, record (1908-12): 88150.

Newton ARNOLD, age 30 years, born in Virginia, married, death cause: "tuberculosis", died at Bristol on 18 Jun 1909, record (1908-12): 88151.

James RUTHERFORD, age 72 years, born near Bristol, married, death cause: "brights disease", died at Paperville on 13 Oct 1908, record (1908-12): 88152.

Nannie BURTON, age 69 years, born in Virginia, single, death cause: "heart disease", died at Paperville on 31 Mar 1909, record (1908-12): 88153.
Fannie BOUTON, lived 1 day, death cause: "unknown", died at Bulors on 20 Jan 1909, record (1908-12): 88154.
Clyde PRIVETT, age 2 years and 6 months, death cause: "measles and pneumonia", died at 817 Alabama St., Bristol, on 21 Feb 1912, record (1908-12): 88155.
Fannie Carrier CROSS, age 23 years, married, death cause: "tuberculosis", died at So., 6th St, Bristol on 25 Apr 1912, record (1908-12): 88155A.
Harvey William CROSS, age 10 months, death cause: "tuberculosis", died at So., 6th St., Bristol on 29 Apr 1912, record (1908-12): 88156.
Nannie Ellane LAMBERT, age 44 years, born in Smith Co., VA., married, death cause: "tuberculosis", died at 408 Garland Ave, Bristol, on 6 Mar 1912, record (1908-12): 88157.
Alfred Walters BLEVINS, age 58 years, born in Carter Co., married, death cause: "weakness of heart", died at 608 E. State St., Bristol on 5 Jun 1912, record (1908-12): 88158.
Mrs. J.A. QUARLES, age 66 years, born in North Carolina, married, death cause: "gall stones", died at 601 E. State St., Bristol, on 13 Apr 1912, record (1908-12): 88159.
Cecilia GRIER, black, age 44 years, born in Christianburg, VA., married, death cause: "convulsions", died at 405 McDowell ST., Bristol, on 28 Jun 1912, record (1908-12): 88160.
Bertie RHEA, black, age 16 years, born in Big Stone Gap, VA., death cause: "bronchitis", died at 412 E. State St., Bristol, on 12 May 1912, record (1908-12): 88161.
Thomas SMITH, black, age 50 years, born in Virginia, single, death cause: "paralysis", died at Blackleg's Alley on* Apr 1912, record (1908-12): 88162.
Josiah BOOHER, age 62 years, married, death cause: "weakness of heart", died at Taylor St., Bristol on 4 May 1912, record (1908-12): 88163.
Emma RICHARDS, age 21 years, married, death cause: "fever", died in 16th District on 30 Dec 1911, record (1908-12): 88164.
Mollie MAZE, age 17 years, single, death cause: "fever", died in 16th District on 31 Oct 1911, record (1908-12): 88165.

Martha CARRIER, age 77 years, born in 3rd District, single, death cause: "dropsy", died in 16th District on 30 Oct 1911, record (1908-12): 88166.

Nancy CARRIER, age 79 years, born in 3rd District, single, death cause: "dropsy", died in 16th District on * Oct 1911, record (1908-12): 88167.

William B. ROYSTON, age 19 years, born in 16th District death cause: "hurt by machinery", died in Lenore City, TN., died: 26 Feb 1912, record (1908-12): 88168.

Elizabeth CARLTON, age 61 years, married, death cause: "cancer", died in 18th District on 16 May 1912, record (1908-12): 88169.

Ralph S. DROKE, age 3 years and 9 months, death cause: "croup", died in 6th District on 4 Dec 1911, record (1908-12): 88170.

Rebecca HARR, age 69 years, married, death cause: "dropsy", died in 6th District on 15 Jun 1912, record (1908-12): 88171.

Hester HODGES, age 31 years, married, death cause: "paralysis", died in 20th District on 10 Aug 1908, record (1908-12): 88172.

Allie DICKSON, age 72 years, married, born: Sullivan Co., death cause: "heart trouble", died at Indian Springs on 22 Mar 1912, record (1908-12): 88173.

Infant EDWARDS, female, parents: David C. EDWARDS (VA) and Nancy N. BISHOP (VA), death cause: "stillborn", died at Kingsport on 2 Jan 1914, record (1914): 1.

Dalton Delaney MOODY, born: 19 Apr 1881, single, parents: William L. MOODY and Sarah J. ROLLER, death cause: "chronic Brights disease", died at Indian Springs on 3 Jan 1914, record (1914): 2.

Virginia Emaline COLLINS, born: 5 Mar 1870, single, parents: William D. COLLINS (VA) and Rebecca M. HULL, death cause: "pneumonia fever", died at Kingsport on 9 Jan 1914, record (1914): 3.

Mary Ann HARKLEROAD, born: 23 Jan 1830 in Tennessee, widow, parents: (illegible) VAUGHN (Washington) and Nancy LANE, death cause: "catarrhal dysentery", informant: William L. HARKLEROAD, buried: Reedy Creek Cemetery, died: 9 Jan 1911, record (1914): 4.

Rebecca M. COLLINS, born: 5 Oct 1846, married, parents: David HULL and Isabella BARNES (NC), death cause: "bronchial pneumonia", informant: W.D. COLLINS, buried: Piles Cemetery, died: 14 Jan 1914, record (1914): 5.

Infant PIERCE, female, parents: William PIERCE (Carter Co.) and Ida May PARLIER, death cause: "stillborn", buried: Preston Cemetery, died: 20 Jan 1914, record (1914): 6.

Margie JONES, born: 11 Jan 1831 in Mitchell Co., NC., widow, parents: John THOMAS (NC) and Sinda WILSON (NC), death cause: "acute nephritis", informant: D.B. JONES (Kingsport), buried: Depew Chapel, died: 26 Jan 1914, record (1914): 7.

George DILLARD, born: 8 Mar 1913, parents: Wesley DILLARD and Lillian DEPEW, death cause: "broncho pneumonia", informant: Elijah DEPEW (Kingsport), buried: Depew Chapel, died: 26 Jan 1914, record (1914): 8.

Infant GRINER, male, lived 1 day, parents: J.W. GRINER and Ada BOUTIN, death cause: not stated, informant: J.M. BOUTIN (Bristol), buried: Crumley Cemetery, died: 3 Jan 1914, record (1914): 9.

Charlie CASTER, Negro, born: 22 Apr 1875, married, parents: H.W. CARTER and Mary M. RAY, death cause: "tuberculosis and mitral insufficiency", informant Mary M. CARTER (Bristol), buried: Tennessee Cemetery, died: 12 Jan 1914, record (1914): 10.

Lillie PACE, Negro, born: 15 Feb 1878, single, parents: Binks PACE (VA) and Eliza KEEN (VA), death cause: "tuberculosis", informant: J.J. PACE (Bristol), died: 3 Jan 1914, record (1914): 11.

Hana GODSEY, Negro, born: 1862 in Virginia, married, parents: Fin TURNER (VA) AND mother's name unknown, death cause: "acute nephritis", informant: Andrew Godsey (Bristol), buried in Virginia, died: 30 Jan 1914, record (1914): 12.

Infant WHITLOCK, parents: Clarence WHITLOCK (Fall Branch) and Mary L. HIX (Blountville), death cause: "stillborn", informant: Mary L. HIX (Blountville), born/died: 11 Jan 1914, record (1914): 13.

Name Illegible, female, born: 12 Feb 1836, parents: Walter JOHNSON and Mary BARBE, death cause: "chronic nephritis", informant: Mrs. S.S. BAILEY (Blountville), died: 8 Jan 1914, record (1914): 14.

George DOANE, born: 27 Dec 1838, single, parents: William DOANE and Emeline LADY, death cause: illegible, died 4 Jan 1914, record (1914): 15.

Elacnah DOANE, born: 12 Apr 1853, married, parents: William DOANE and Emeline LADY, death cause: illegible, died: 1 Jan 1914, record (1914): 16.

Jesie B. SAUNDERS, born: 4 Jul 1859, married, parents: J.B. SAUNDERS and (first name illegible) YOAKLEY, death cause: "acute nephritis", informant: John BARNES (Blountville), died: 11 Jan 1914, record (1914): 17.
Mrs. Eliza HATCHER, born in 1856, married, parents: Henry Clay MILLHORN and Nancy A. (surname illegible), death cause: "spinal apoplexy", died in 21st District on 7 Jan 1914, record (1914): 18.
William CLIFFORD, born: 16 Nov 1831 in Tennessee, widower, parents: Joseph CLIFFORD and Betsy BOLING, death cause: "general senility", informant: William M. CLIFFORD (Big Creek), buried: Grants, TN., died: 16 Jan 1914, record (1914): 19.
Georgie TURNER, age 23 years, parents: George TURNER and Jane GLOVER, death cause: "brights disease", informant: G.P. BOLING (Emmett), died: 18 Dec 1913, record (1914): 20.
Mrs. Letta Sproles BULLOCK, age about 64 years, married, parents: Samuel SPROLES (VA) and Nancy F. (illegible), death cause: "pneumonia", informant: J.A. BULLOCK (Bristol), died: 14 Jan 1914, record: 21.
John KING, record illegible, record (1914): 22.
Infant EATON, age 11 days, parents: George EATON and Lucy GRAY, death cause: "pneumonia", informant: W.S. SPROLES (Bluff City), died: 15 Jan 1914, record (1914): 23.
Joseph KUHN, born: 10 Dec 1833 in North Carolina, married, parents: not stated, death cause: "Brights disease", informant: Malinda KUHN (Bluff City), died: 14 Jan 1914, record (1914): 24.
Billie BLALOCK, born: 10 Jan 1849, married, parents: not stated, death cause: "tuberculosis", died in 20th District on 20 Jan 1914, record (1914): 25.
Jeanette Gilmor FAIR, born: 23 Jun 1913 in Virginia, parents: James FAIR and Gastona HITE, death cause: "bronchial pneumonia", informant: James FAIR (Jonesboro), died: 4 Jan 1914, record (1914): 26.
Mary Ann SHIPLEY, born: 14 Aug 1852, single, parents: Frederick SHIPLEY and Louise ELSEA, death cause: "influenza", informant: G.A. SLAUGHTER (Fordtown), buried: Lebanon Cemetery, died: 11 Jan 1914, record (1914): 27.
Mary Mosie BOWERY, born: 18 Sep 1889, married, parents: James HALL and Mary Ellen BARNES, death cause: "pulmonary tuberculosis", informant: J.R. BOWERY (Jonesboro), buried: 14th District, died: 23 Jan 1914, record (1914): 28.

Infant GALLOWAY, male, parents: Noah GALLOWAY and Annie Eldon HOOD, death cause: "premature, stillbirth", informant: S.P. GALLOWAY (Fordtown), died: 24 Jan 1914, record (1914): 29.

Georgie Etta GRIMSLEY, born: 20 Jul 1896, single, parents: Sam Houston GRIMSLEY and Laura Etta GRIMSLEY, death cause: "pulmonary tuberculosis", informant: S.H. GRIMSLEY (Fall Branch), died: 28 Jan 1914, record (1914): 30.

Warneda NORDIKE, black, age 14 years, parents: James NORDIKE (VA) and Ann GODSEY (Russell Co., VA), death cause: "tuberculosis of kidney", informant: James NORDIKE (Bristol), died: 20 Feb 1914, record (1914): 31.

John M. MCCUE, born: 4 Jul 1876 in Nelson Co., VA., single, parents: Charles W. MCCUE (VA) and Virginia PULLIAM (VA), death cause: "paralysis", informant: J.H. MCCUE (Bristol), buried: E. Hill Cemetery, Bristol, VA., died: 26 Feb 1914, record (1914): 32.

Mary Catherine BINHANG, born: 3 Dec 1846, widow, parents: William O'DELL and Mary CRUMLEY, death cause: "tuberculosis", informant: Mrs. Belle SCOTT (Bristol), died: 24 Feb 1914, record (1914): 33.

Conrod BOWERY, born: 13 Feb 1841, widower, Confederate pensioner, parents: Conrad BOWERY and Sarah SHIPLEY, death cause: "abscess of liver", buried: Lebanon Cemetery, 14th District, died: 9 Feb 1914, record (1914): 34.

Darthula Marshall FORD, born: 9 Jun 1850 in Kentucky, widow, parents: "unknown", death cause: "pneumonia", informant: P.F. MCCLURE (Jonesboro), buried: Lebanon Cemetery, 14th District, died: 14 Feb 1914, record (1914): 35.

Robert S. SPROLES, born: 15 Aug 1848 in Virginia, married, parents: John SPROLES (VA) and Elizabeth SPARKS (VA), death cause: "cystitis", informant: E.M. HALL (Fordtown), buried: Mount Lebanon, died: 17 Feb 1914, record (1914): 36.

Mary E. BRADLEY, born about 1849 in Washington Co., TN., married, parents: Isaac MUSSLEMAN (Philadelphia, PA) and Mary MUSSLEMAN (PA), death cause: "intestinal tuberculosis", informant: Olive M. STEWART (Fall Branch), buried: Depews Chapel, died: 20 Feb 1914, record (1914): 37.

Elizabeth MINNICK, age 11 months, parents: Jim MINNICK and Emma MINNICK, death cause: "pneumonia", died: 9 Mar 1914, record (1914): 38.

Robert ALLISON, born: 24 Feb 1836, married, parents: Joseph ALLISON and (illegible) HALL, death cause: "mitral regurgitation heart", informant: Rob ALLISON, Jr. (Piney Flats), buried: New Bethel Cemetery, died: 24 Feb 1914, record (1914): 37.

Mollie C. JONES, born: 19 Jan 1868, married, parents: Darbey WEBB, and mother's name not stated, death cause: "carcinoma of arterus", informant: G.W. JONES (Piney Flats), buried: Poplar Ridge Cemetery, died: 9 Feb 1914, record (1914): 40.

Rhal A. WOODS, age 78 years, widow, parents: David FRAZIER (NC) and Rachel A. FRAZIER (NC), death cause: "tuberculosis", informant: W.W. WOODS (Bluff City), buried: Webb Cemetery, died: 14 Feb 1914.

Ellen Parlee WRIGHT, born: 29 Jun 1863, married, parents: Joel C. GILLENWATER and Mary Ann BROOKS, death cause: "chronic nephritis", informant: C.L. WRIGHT (Bristol), buried: Rogersville, died: 4 Feb 1914, record (1914): 42.

Raymond Franklin FOGARTY, born: 4 Oct 1894 in Washington Co., VA., parents: John FOGARTY and Lettie MUMPOWER (VA), death cause: "typhoid fever", informant; E.A. COMBS (Bristol), died: 1 Feb 1914, record (1914): 43.

Sallie Kate WHITE, born: 30 Nov 1913, parents: Mack WHITE (VA) and Lillie HUTSON, death cause: "lobar pneumonia", informant: Steve FIELDS (Kingsport), buried: Liberty, TN., Died: 5 Feb 1914, record (1914): 44.

Bessie DIXON, black, born: 9 Mar 1901, parents: Hugh DIXON and Mary GOINS, death cause: "pulmonary tuberculosis", informant: John DULANEY (Kingsport), buried: Kingsport Cemetery, died: 9 Feb 1914, record (1914): 45.

James Miller DEVALUT, born: 27 Jun 1828 in Kingsport, parents: Daniel DEVALUT (PA), and Mary ROLLER, death cause: "valvular heart disease", buried: Kingsport Cemetery, died: 11 Feb 1914, record (1914): 46.

Amanda Ethel MOODY, born: 25 Apr 1898, parents: G.W. MOODY and Martha E. ARNOLD, death cause: "tuberculosis", buried: Emory Cemetery, died: 1 Mar 1914, record (1914): 47.

Infant DOWELL, colored, parents: James DOWELL (NC) and Ella MITCHELL (VA), death cause: "stillborn", buried: Colored Cemetery, Bristol, died: 6 Jan 1914, record (1914): 48. (twin below)

Infant DOWELL, colored, parents: James DOWELL (NC) and Ella MITCHELL (VA), death cause: "stillborn", buried: Bristol, died: 6 Jan 1914, record (1914): 49.
Ancil GEORGE, male, born: 13 Sep 1833 in Kentucky, widower, parents: James GEORGE (VA) and Mary RUTHERFORD (VA), death cause: "old age", informant: Mrs. Eliza GEORGE (Bristol), buried: Lancaster, KY., died: 20 Feb 1914, record (1914): 50.
John R. GILLESPIE, born: 17 Jun 1867 in Virginia, married, parents: P.F. GILLESPIE (VA) and Malinda HENEGER (VA), death cause: "Brights disease", informant: J.S. GILLESPIE (Johnson City), buried: Abingdon, VA., died: 26 Feb 1914, record (1914): 51.
Moses BROOKS, colored, age about 60 years, born in Virginia, parents: "unknown", death cause: "chronic intestinal nephritis", informant: M.J. WATSON (Bristol), died: 26 Feb 1914, record (1914): 52.
Thomas W. MAURY, born: 10 May 1877, single, parents: C.E. MAURY and Katherine A. (illegible), death cause: "cerebral hemorrhage", buried: Marion, VA., died: 13 Feb 1914, record (1914): 53.
Alex CORNICE, born: 25 Aug 1847 in Wytheville, VA., married, parents: Isaac CORNICE (VA) and Bettie HOOVER (VA), death cause: "paralysis", informant: Bessie CORNICE (Bristol), died: 18 Feb 1914, record: 54.
Rachel BOYD, colored, age about 90 years, born in Virginia, parents: not stated, death cause: "carcinoma", informant: A.P. WASHINGTON (Bristol), died: 22 Mar 1914, record (1914): 55.
Infant HAMMETT, female, parents: G.W. HAMMETT (Washington Co., TN) and Mary TROBAUGH, death cause: "no physician", buried: E. Hill Cemetery, Bristol, born/died: 24 Mar 1914, record (1914): 56.
Cecil COOPER, born: 10 Oct 1912, parents: father not stated and Charmis COOPER, death cause: "pneumonia", informant: L.A. COOPER (Bristol), buried: East Hill Cemetery, died: 25 Mar 1914, record (1914): 57.
Lillian B. DYER, born: 22 Mar 1914, parents: W.P. DYER and Bessie POORE, death cause: "premature", informant: Will POORE (Bristol), buried: East Hill Cemetery, died: 29 Mar 1914, record (1914): 58.
Mary Elizabeth SMITH, born: 28 Dec 1865 in Glasgow, KY., widow, parents: B.F. DICKEY (Boonesboro, KY) and Mary A. DICKEY (Barren Co., KY), death cause: "cancer", informant: Miss S.J. DICKEY (Bristol), buried: Glasgow, KY, died: 26 Mar 1914, record: 59.

Infant ROYSTON, age: 8 days, parents: Frank ROYSTON and Belle (illegible), death cause: "unknown, found dead in bed", died: 2 Mar 1914, record (1914): 60.
Thomas BOWMAN, age 82 years, born in Tennessee, married, parents: not stated, death cause: "Brights Disease", informant: J.L. CAMPBELL (Bluff City), buried: Crumley Cemetery, died: 2 Feb 1914, record (1914): 61.
Louis S. BROYLES, born: 11 Jun, in Monroe Co., VA., age: 75 years, 9 months and 13 days, married, parents: Allen BROYLES and Bettie WILLIAMS, death cause: "lobar pneumonia", informant: H.L. BROYLES (Bluff City), buried: Weaver, TN., died: 24 Mar 1914, record (1914): 62.
Pearl Beard LEWIS, colored, age: about 24 years, born in Hawkins Co., married, parents: George BEARD (NC) and Cawzadia MANUEL (Hawkins Co.), death cause: "perperal pertonitis", informant: James LONG, died: 20 Mar 1914, record (1914): 63.
Matilda Adelade DOLEN, born: 22 Feb 1847, married, parents: Benjamin BIRDWELL and Lydia DUNCAN, death cause: "angina pectoris", informant: Lydia BACON (Fordtown), buried: Dolen Cemetery, 13th Dist., died: 25 Mar 1914, record (1914): 64.
Amanda Ethel MOODY, born: 25 Apr 1898, parents: G.W. MOODY and Martha E. ARNOLD, death cause: "tuberculosis of lungs", informant: A.L. ISELEY (Indian Springs), buried: Emory, TN., died: 27 Feb 1914, record (1914): 65.
Infant HICKMAN, female, parents: Sam E. HICKMAN and Susie DYKES, death cause: "stillborn", informant: C.W. AGEE (Kingsport), buried: Depew Chapel, died: 8 Mar 1914, record (1914): 66.
George D. HAWK, born: 3 Aug 1857, married, parents: Martin R. HAWK and Sarah HORNE, death cause: "epileptic, fell in fire, died from burns", informant: A.S. JACKSON (Indian Springs), buried: Pleasant Hill, died: 21 Mar 1914, record (1914): 67.
James A. ARNOLD, born: 15 Jul 1872 in Hawkins Co., married, parents: A.J. ARNOLD (Hawkins Co.) and Martha E. MOODY, death cause: "tuberculosis of lungs", informant: J. William DICKSON (Indian Springs), buried: Galloway Cemetery, died: 27 Mar 1914, record (1914): 68.
Joshua COX, born: Aug 1845, married, parents: John J. COX and Rachel SHIPLEY, death cause: "chronic intestinal nephritis", informant: Dr. F. Childress

(Indian Springs), buried: Emory Cemetery, died: 28 Mar 1914, record (1914): 69.
Nelson Woodrow MCMURRAY, born: 23 Dec 1913, parents; E.L. MCMURRAY (Scott Co., VA) and Bertie SHAFFER (Scott Co., VA), death cause: "whooping cough, meningitis", buried: Booher Cemetery, 7th District, died: 29 Mar 1914, record (1914): 70.
Mrs. J.G. KUHNART, born: 4 Apr 1888 in Middle Tennessee, married, parents: A.H. YOUNG (Glascow, KY) and Alice BRYAN (Middle TN), death cause: "appendectomy", informant: J.P. YOUNG (Bristol), buried: East Hill Cemetery, died: 4 Mar 1914, record (1914): 71.
Robert H. MILLER, born: 4 Dec 1884, married, parents: James MILLER and Deliah WHITE (VA), death cause: "pulmonary tuberculosis", informant: A. HOOVER (Bristol), buried: East Hill, died: 5 Mar 1914, record (1914): 72.
Eva EVANS, Negro, age 57 years, married, parents: Roderick ROYSTON and Agnes HUNTER, death cause: "chronic intestinal nephritis", informant: Rev. N.H. EVANS (Bristol), died: 10 Mar 1914, record (1914): 73.
William RAMSEY, age 33 years, born in Virginia, married, parents: not stated, death cause: "dropsy", informant: C. MONTGOMERY (Bristol), buried: Weaver Cemetery, died: 13 Mar 1914, record (1914): 74.
Mamie VAULT, born: 13 Nov 1875 in Smith Co., VA., married, parents: Philip (illegible) and Becky WEST (Smith Co.), death cause: "malignant disease of foot", died in 17th District on 18 Mar 1914, record (1914): 75.
Mrs. Jane JONES, age 80 years, born in Tennessee, widow, parents: Joseph JONES and Milly BIRCH (VA), death cause: "stomach trouble", informant: R.J. POORE (Emmett), buried: Brown Cemetery, died: 18 Feb 1914, record (1914): 76.
W.J. DYER, Jr., parents: W.J. DYER and Bessie POORE, death cause: not stated, born/died: 22 Mar 1914, buried: East Hill, record (1914): 77.
Zora OFFIELD, born: 23 Apr 1892, married, parents: Alfred BLEVINS and Josephine BROWN, death cause: "pneumonia", informant: George OFFIELD (Big Creek), died: 14 Apr 1914, record (1914): 78.
Ellen CROSS, age 34 years, born in Russell Co., VA., married, parents: Wash MASSEY (VA) and Catherine (illegible) (VA), death cause: "lobar pneumonia", died in the 5th District on 27 Mar 1914, record (1914): 79.

Alfred MOORE, born: 7 Apr 1837, married, parents: Nathan MOORE (Claiborne Co., TN.) and Martha MOORE, death cause: not stated, informant: J.A. MOORE (Blountville), buried: Johnson Cemetery, died: 29 Mar 1914, record (1914): 80.

Eliza A. HODGES, born: 10 Oct 1837, widow, parents: John LOUDEWILL and _____ BEARD, death cause: "carcinoma", informant: W.J. KIDD (Blountville), died: 21 Mar 1914, record (1914): 81.

Melvenia FRAZIER, born: 17 May 1867, widow, parents: not stated, death cause: not stated, died in the 5th District on 23 Mar 1914, record (1914): 82.

George W. LADY, born: 18 Aug 1830, widower, parents: William LADY (PA) and Jennie TREADWAY (Carter Co.), death cause: "bronchial pneumonia", informant: S.N. MCCULLY (Fordtown), buried: Lady Cemetery, died: 14 Mar 1914, record (1914): 83.

Harriet BAKER, born: 22 Sep 1863 in Washington Co., TN., married, parents: William GIBSON (Wash Co) and Hannah CURTIS (Carter Co.), death cause: "lobar pneumonia", died at Piney Flats on 8 Mar 1914, record (1914): 84.

Minnie MILLHORN, born: 5 Mar 1896, single, parents: Ray MILLHORN and Jennie JONES, death cause: "appendicitis", buried: New Bethel Cemetery, 5th Dist., died: 5 Mar 1914, record (1914): 85.

William Calvin GREENWAY, born: 1 Jan 1837 at Craig Co., VA., married, parents: Nathan GREENWAY (VA) and Margaret BOLTON, death cause: "meningitis", died in the 16th District on 3 Mar 1914, record (1914): 86.

Infant CARRIER, born: 23 Feb 1914, female, parents: William C. CARRIER and Myrtle E. RIDER (Anderson Co., TN), death cause: "premature birth", died at Bluff City on 24 Feb 1914, record (1914): 87.

Claudie Hubert CRAWFORD, born: 24 Jun 1912, parents: Lawrence CRAWFORD and Cordia CONKIN (Washington Co., TN), death cause: "lobar pneumonia", died in the 15th District, buried: Dykes Cemetery, Hawkins Co., died: 1 Mar 1914, record (1914): 88.

Albert L. OVERBY, born: 30 Nov 1859, married, parents: Jacob OVERBY (NC) and Sarah K. DUNN (Albermarle Co., VA), death cause: "peritoneal abscess, thrown from a horse", informant: John OVERBY (Church Hill, TN), buried: Fall Branch, died: 5 Apr 1914, record (1914): 89.

Infant COX, female, parents: John Emory COX and Mary JOBE, death cause: "stillborn", informant: John Cox

(Fall Branch), buried: Lone Star Cemetery, born/died: 20 Apr 1914, record (1914): 90.
Thomas CRAWFORD, born: 15 Mar 1874, married, parents: Shadrack CRAWFORD and Catherine MORRELL, death cause: "pulmonary tuberculosis", informant: S.H. CONKIN (Fall Branch), buried: Will Murray Cemetery, died: 22 Apr 1914, record (1914): 91.
Margaret Jane WHITSEL, born: 12 Dec 1835 in Greene Co., TN., widow, parents: Joshua GREEN and Amelia FELLERS (Green Co.), death cause: "paralysis", buried: Solomans Temple Cemetery, died: 26 Apr 1914, record (1914): 92.
William BOWLON, age 54 years, married, parents: James BOWON and ____ CARRIER, death cause: "uremic poison", died in the 1st District on 5 May 1914, record (1914): 93.
Christena Morton DROKE, born: 30 Apr 1844, widow, parents: James MORTON and ____ HARR, death cause: "pneumonia", informant: J.B. DROKE (Blountville), buried: Mill Point Cemetery, died: 28 Apr 1914, record (1914): 94.
Mrs. L. Beulah HARRELL, born: 21 May 1871 at Church Hill, TN., parents: William Lewis CLICK and Elizabeth (illegible), death cause: "hemorrhage", died in the 17th District on 18 Apr 1914, record (1914): 95.
Infant WOOD, sex: not stated, parents: R.D. WOOD (VA) and M.G. TYRE, death cause: "premature", died in the 17th District on 24 Apr 1914, record (1914): 96.
J.W. BOWLING, age 52 years, widower, parents: Larkin BOWLING and Jennie STEWARD (VA), death cause: "blood poison", informant: Alf BOWLING (Big Creek), buried: Brown Cemetery, died: 27 Apr 1914, record (1914): 97.
Mrs. Myrtle BOOHER, age 26 years, married, parents: Samuel MORRELL and Florence BOOHER, death cause: "tuberculosis", informant: S.W. MORRELL (Big Creek), buried: Shipley Cemetery, died: 27 Apr 1914, record (1914): 98.
Laura G. HODGES, born: 23 Jun 1910, parents: John HODGES (Mt. Airy, NC.) and Maggie CORVIN, death cause: "meningitis", informant: John HODGES (Bristol), buried: Bluff City, died: 27 Apr 1914, record (1914): 99.
Mrs. Bessie Pooer DYER, born: 2 Dec 1897, married, parents: Will C. POORE and Sallie E. HARTSOCK (VA), death cause: "pneumonia", informant: Will C. POORE (Bristol), buried: East Hill Cemetery, died: 1 Apr 1914, record (1914): 100.

William H. SHERFEY, born in 1870, married, parents: Isaac SHERFEY (VA) and Elizabeth CAMPBELL (VA), death cause: "uremic poisoning", informant: J.S. SHERFEY (Bristol), buried: East Hill, died: 5 Apr 1914, record (1914): 101.

Margaret Jane VANCE, born: 28 Mar 1838 in Scott Co., VA., widow, parents: Joseph NEWLAND (Arcadia) and Rebecca ANDERSON (Scott Co., VA), death cause: "pneumonia", informant: Miss Margaret VANCE (Bristol), buried: East Hill, died: 8 Apr 1914, record (1914): 102.

Nelson GORNES, Negro, age about 60 years, married, death cause: "aortic insufficiency", informant: Josie GORNES (Bristol), buried: E. Radford, VA., died: 9 Apr 1914, record (1914): 103.

Mary Jane BUCKLES, born: Jan 1872, married, parents: James SAMS and Elsira WEAVER, death cause: "pregnancy, vomiting", informant: J.R. GALLOWAY (Bluff City), buried: Weaver Cemetery, died: 9 Apr 1914, record (1914): 104.

Mrs. Louisa H. DEZEIERN (?), born: 20 Mar 1866 at Speers Ferry, VA., married, parents: Hezakiah FALIN (VA) and Polly SLOAN (Scott Co., VA.), death cause: "general perit..(illegible), informant: John DIZECRN (Speers Ferry, VA), buried in Virginia, died: 21 Apr 1914, record (1914): 105.

Walter M. DETHERAGE, born: 19 Aug 1837 in Virginia, widower, parents: John T. DETHERAGE (VA) and mother not stated, death cause: "nephritis, cardiac (illegible), informant: C.C. DETERAGE (Bristol), buried: Steels Cemetery, died: 24 Apr 1914, record (1914): 106.

Samuel Bernard BUCHANAN, born: 13 May 1884 in Carter Co., single, parents: W.B. BUCHANAN (Kingsport) and Sarah D. STOVER, death cause: "pulmonary tuberculosis", informant: A.J. BUCHANAN (Bluff City), died: 3 Apr 1914, record (1914): 107.

Mary Jane BUCKLES, age 38 years, married, parents: George SAMS and Eliza WEAVER, death cause: "pregnancy, vomiting", informant: Frank J. BUCKLES (Bluff City), buried: Weaver Church, died: 9 Apr 1914, record (1914): 108.

Edna LEE, born: 8 Jul 1904, parents: Edward Lee and Nannie BRUSHAN, death cause: "diabetes and pneumonia", died at Bluff City on 23 Apr 1914, record (1914): 109.

Infant WATSON, female, parents: Wiley WATSON and Jennie MOSER, death cause: "premature", died at Bluff City on 7 Apr 1914, record (1914): 110.

Maggie KETRON, born: 16 Dec 1851 in Virginia, widow, parents: Nathan GREEN (NC) and Maggie C. GREEN (VA), death cause: "acute gastritis", informant: T.M. KETRON (Bloomingdale), buried: Reedy Creek, died: 6 Apr 1914, record (1914): 111.

Samuel A. CLYCE, born: 11 May 1887, married, parents: William CLYCE and Elizabeth KENEDY, death cause: "typhoid fever", died at Kingsport on 8 Apr 1914, record (1914): 112.

Mary Annie CHILDRESS, born: 1 May 1878, married, parents: William SHIPLEY and Mary MOODY, death cause: "tuberculosis of lungs", informant; I.T. CHILDRESS (Indian Springs), buried: Emory, died: 29 Apr 1914, record (1914): 113.

Thomas HALE, black, age estimated to be 77 years, widower, parents: not stated, death cause: "acute indigestion", informant: J.S. VANCE (Kingsport), died: 30 Apr 1914, record (1914): 114.

William Ambros COLLINS, age 52 years, widower, parents: not stated, death cause: "Brights disease", buried: New Bristol Cemetery, died: 19 May 1914, record (1914): 115.

Laura Christina PENIX, born: 16 Oct 1913, parents: Preston PENIX and Ethel FRYE, death cause: "acute dysentery", died at Piney Flats on 28 May 1914, record (1914): 116.

Mary Jane RUTHERFORD, born: 23 Jun 1877 in Watauga Co., NC., married, parents: John MORETZ (Yancey Co., NC) and Jane MILLER (Watauga Co., NC), death cause: "tuberculosis of lungs", informant: John P. RUTHERFORD (Emmett), died: 7 May 1914, record (1914): 117.

Nany WHEELER, colored age about 74 years, born in Johnson Co., parents; ____ LUNCEFORD and Syndy LUNCEFORD, death cause: "pneumonia", informant: James WHEELER (Emmett), died: 20 Apr 1914, record: 118.

Harry Spurgeon BURGER, born: 1 Jun 1914, parents: G.S. BARGER and Bettie FARR, death cause: "acute indigestion", informant: Mary MOBLEY (Blountville), died: 1 Jun 1914, record (1914): 119.

Sarah HANDCOCK, born: 5 May 1852, widow, parents: Sam VILES and mother unknown, death cause: "acute heart dilatation", informant: Berry HANDCOCK (Kingsport), died: 13 May 1914.

Margaret ADAMS, born: 15 May 1865 in Wythe Co., VA., widow, parents: Madison DEEN (Wythe Co.) and Susan AKERS (VA), death cause: "nail punctured foot", informant: Mrs. Mamie SMALLWOOD (Kingsport), died: 22 May 1914, record (1914): 121.

Isaac Enoch SMITH, born: 12 Jan 1914, parents: Isaac SMITH and Kate HANPT (?) (Scott Co.), death cause: "gastritis", informant: D.R. SEVIER (Kingsport), buried: Pile Cemetery, died: 24 May 1914, record (1914): 122.

John Columbus MOREFIELD, age 29 years, born in Tazewell Co., VA., married, parents: Joseph MOREFIELD (NC) and Mary STRATTON (VA), death cause: "caught in a belt at work, crushed to death", informant: J.A. COLLINS (Kingsport), buried: Pile Cemetery, died: 25 May 1914, record (1914): 123.

Clyde Paul MARTIN, born: 19 Aug 1912, parents: Ed. MARTIN and Mattie BUISON (VA), death cause: "measles", informant: Will DOTSON (Kingsport), buried: Reedy Creek, died: 28 May 1914, record (1914): 124.

Mattie O'DELL, colored, age 42 years, married, parents: Jessie ROBINSON and mother not stated, death cause: "tuberculosis of bowels", informant: Will O'DELL (Bluff City), died: 29 May 1914, record: 125.

Paul Henry O'DELL, colored, age 7 months, parents: Will O'DELL and Mattie O'DELL, death cause: "pneumonia fever", informant: Will O'DELL (Bluff City), died: 24 May 1914, record (1914): 126.

Victoria G. EWING, born: 25 Sep 1851 in Scott Co., VA., single, parents: Henry Wood EWING (Scott Co.) and Emaline P. BOSTIC, death cause: "carcinoma of stomach", informant: L.M. EWING (Knoxville), died at Bluff City on 2 May 1914, record (1914): 127.

William B. RILEY, born: 2 Aug 1885, single, parents: William RILEY and Rebecca Elizabeth AKARD, death cause: "suicide, shot himself in abdomen", informant: William RILEY (Bluff City), buried: Bays Cemetery, died: 23 May 1914, record (1914): 128.

John Elbert HICKS, born: 22 Sep 1848, married, parents: Ruben HICKS and Mary MOTTERN (Carter Co.), death cause: "cerebral apoplexy", informant: Miss Alice HICKS (Bluff City), died: 5 May 1914, record (1914): 129.

Infant REED, male, parents: Hardy REED (NC) and M.E. ADAMS (Watauga, Co., NC), death cause: "not known", informant: Mary ADAMS (Bluff City), born/died: 13 May 1914, record (1914): 130.

Laura LITTLE, born: 21 Feb 1892, single, parents: Henry LITTLE and Martha HOUCHIN, death cause: "suicide, cut throat with a razor", informant: George LITTLE (Bluff City), died: 24 May 1914, record (1914): 131.

Mrs. Rhoda BROWN, age about 67 years, married, parents: Jesse HUGHES and Rena BLEVINS, death cause: "intestinal obstruction", informant: J.R. BROWN (Bluff City), buried: Weaver Cemetery, died: 20 May 1914, record (1914): 132.

Wilbur Henly SHEPARD, born: 28 Jun 1912, parents: S.H. SHEPARD and Hettie HENLEY (VA), death cause: "dysentery", informant: S.H. SHEPARD (Bristol), died: 28 May 1914, record: 133.

Evaline MONROE, Negro, age 34 years and 2 months, single, parents: Robert MONROE (VA) and Mary ASHLY (VA), death cause: "pulmonary hemorrhage", informant: Nannie HUDSON (Bristol), buried: Citizens Cemetery, died: 27 May 1914, record (1914): 134.

Infant COOPER, female, born: 23 May 1914, parents: father not stated and Maggie COOPER, death cause: "malnutrition", informant: Gay JONES (Bristol), buried: East Hill, died: 26 May 1914, record: 135.

Lillian Francis May DAVIS, born: 17 Oct 1911, parents: Nick L. DAVIS and Mignon MUMPOWER (VA), death cause: "meningitis", informant: Mrs. Mignon MUMPOWER (Bristol), buried: East Hill, died: 25 May 1914, record (1914): 136.

Miss May GRAY, age illegible, parents: James GRAY and Eliza FULK, death cause: "pulmonary tuberculosis", informant: Miss Ada J. PAYNE (Bristol), died: 22 May 1914, record (1914): 137.

James M. BROWN, age 10 years, born in Pennignton Gap, VA., parents: Roy BROWN (Mighigan) and Marie RASINE (VA), death cause: "accidental gun shot wound", informant: Roy BROWN (Dryden, VA), buried: Pennington Gap, died: 21 May 1914, record (1914): 138

John Henry OWEN, born: 10 May 1862, married, parents: John Henry OWEN and mother not stated, death cause: illegible, informant: Andrew OWEN (Bristol), died: 20 May 1914, record (1914): 139.

William PERRY, Negro, age about 40 years, married, parents: William WILSON and Sallie RANGE, death cause: "heart leison", informant: Charles PERRY (Bristol), died: 20 May 1914.

Mrs. Bettie M. MAXWELL, born: 1866, married, parents: J.C. MATHIS and Elizabeth HOOVER, death cause: "indocarditis", informant: W.H. COLE (Bristol), buried: East Hill, died: 15 May 1914, record: 141.

Richard CALLOWAY, Negro, born: 1849 in Virginia, single, parents: "don't know", death cause: "chronic intestinal nephritis", died: 14 Mar 1914, record (1914): 142.

John Wesley BURNS, born: 1 Jul 1910 at Knoxville, parents: J.B. BURNS (Bryson City, NC.) and Zettie WARWICK (Luttrell), death cause: "diptheria", informant: J.B. BURNS (Bristol), record (1914): 143.

Rhoda Hughes BROWN, age 38 years, 8 months and 16 days, married, parents: Jese HUGHES and Rena BLEVINS, death cause: "paralysis", died at Bluff City on 23 May 1914, record (1914): 144.

Susan VANCE, age 63 years, widow, parents: Billie MORRELL and mother not stated, death cause: "tuberculosis", died in the 5th District on 15 May 1914, record (1914): 145.

Mildred E. CLOUD, born: 15 Apr 1914, parents: F.S. CLOUD and Paisey Lee HULLETT (Ashville, NC), death cause: "stomatitis", informant: F.S. CLOUD (Fordtown), buried: Cloud Cemetery, 12th District, died: 21 May 1914, record (1914): 146.

Theodore JENKINS, born: 16 May 1914, parents: Benjamin JENKINS (Washington Co., TN) and Norma COX (Washington Co., TN), death cause: "premature birth", informant: Ben H. Jenkins (Fordtown), buried: Pactalus Cemetery, died: 17 May 1914, record (1914): 147.

John CRAWFORD, born: 5 Mar 1842, widower, parents: Thomas CRAWFORD and Bettie BARNETT (Hawkins co), death cause: "chronic gastritis", informant: G.H. CRAWFORD (Fall Branch), buried: Depew Capel, died: 22 May 1914, record (1914): 148.

Lillie Adelade MCCULLEY, born: 2 May 1914, parents: William Franklin MCCULLEY and Lucy A. EASLEY, death cause: "premature birth", informant: W.W. EASLEY (Fall Branch), died: 27 May 1914, record (1914): 149.

Elbert Gibson BOND, born: 28 Dec 1845, married, parents: James BOND and Elizabeth STOKES (Hawkins Co), death cause: "Brights disease and paralysis", buried: Lebanon Church, died: 28 May 1914, record (1914): 150.

John W. RAGAN, born: 4 Aug 1837, widower, parents: Daniel RAGAN and Isabell SMITH, death cause: "chronic nephritis", informant: Earnest RAGAN (Bristol), buried: East Hill, died: 30 May 1914, record: 151.

Aaron J. FOUCH, age 56 years, married, parents: James FOUCH and Petey BASS, death cause: "pulmonary tuberculosis", informant: W.J. LITTLE (Bristol), buried: Avoca Cem, died: 29 May 1914, record: 152.

Annie Jane LOWE, born: 11 Aug 1854 in Yancey Co., NC., married, parents: Thomas ARWOOD (NC) and Charisey PRESLEY (NC), death cause: "apoplexy", informant: A.J. LOWE (Bristol), buried: E. Hill Cemetery, died: 18 Jun 1914, record (1914): 153.

Mary A. SPRINKLE, born: 28 Nov 1871 in Virginia, married, parents: John B. SIEFORS (Watauga, VA) and Sarah MITCHELL (VA), death cause: "tuberculosis", informant: G.W. SPRINKLE (Watauga, VA), buried: Mt. View Cemetery, died: 20 Jun 1914, record (1914): 154.
Edith Evelyn GRAY, born: 24 Oct 1913, parents: William GRAY (Richmond) and Mary E. BELL (Bristol, VA), death cause: "broncho pneumonia", informant: Mrs. Willie GRAY (Bristol), buried: E. Hill Cemetery, died: 20 Jun 1914, record (1914): 155.
John Robert CHAMBERS, born: 28 Feb 1914, parents: J.B. CHAMBERS (VA) and Huelah HENNING (KY), death cause: "acute colitis", informant: J.B. Chambers (Bristol), buried: Pleasant Grove, died: 28 Jun 1914, record (1914): 156.
Henry PEOPLES, age 27 years, 6 months and 10 years, single, parents: illegible, death cause: "tuberculosis", buried: Weaver Cemetery, died: 4 Jul 1914, record (1914): 157.
Celia PAYNE, date of birth illegible, married, parents: illegible, death cause: illegible, died: 28 Jun 1914, record (1914): 158.
William SHEPHARD, born: 3 Feb 1869 in Washington Co., VA, married, parents: Henry SHEPHARD (Washington Co., VA) and ___ HUMPHREY (Washington Co., VA), death cause: "tuberculosis of throat, stomach and bowels", informant: G.W. JONES (Piney Flats), buried: Poplar Ridge, died: 18 Jun 1914, record (1914): 159.
Infant GEISLER, female, born: 4 Jun 1914, parents: Ernest James GEISLER and Etta Vestie HALL (Washington Co.), date illegible, record (1914): 160.
Infant ARCHER, born: 11 Jun 1914, parents: G.M. ARCHER and Fanny HICKMAN, death cause: "premature birth", informant: G.M. ARCHER (Fall Branch), buried: Lone Star Cemetery, died: 12 Jun 1914, record (1914): 161.
L. LONG, male, born: 14 Apr 1914, parents: Joseph LONG (Cocke Co.) and May SEAVERS (Hawkins Co.), death cause: "cholera infantum", informant: S.J. WILLIAMS (Kingsport), died: 19 Jun 1914, record (1914): 162.
Thomas J. COX, born: 15 May 1837 in Sullivan Co., married, parents: Thomas COX (VA) and Sallie BAKER (VA), death cause: "lagrippe and Brights disease", buried: Emory Cemetery, 7th District, died: 9 Jun 1914, record (1914): 163.
Infant FOALDEN, born: 20 May 1914, parents: A.J. FOALDEN (Pulaski Co., VA) and Dora Edna DICKINSON (Floyd Co., VA), death cause: "don't know", informant:

father (Bristol), buried: Paperville, died: 2 Jun 1914, record (1914): 164.

Albert RUSSELL, born: 30 May 1914, parents: A.R. RUSSELL and Annie May HORNER, death cause: "purpura", informant: father (Bristol), buried: East Hill, died: 8 Jun 1914, record (1914): 165.

Infant HUNT, male, born: 11 Jun 1914, parents: Ernest V. HUNT and Nettie PRICE, death cause: "stillborn", informant: father (Bristol), record (1914): 166.

Charles E. BRYAN, age 65 years, born in Virginia, married, parents: Henry W. BRYAN (Culpepper, VA) and Rebecca SWITZER (Bedford Co., VA), death cause: "disease of heart", informant: W.H. BRYAN (Myers, TN), buried: Weaver Cemetery, died: 12 Jun 1914, record (1914): 167.

Jessie BRYANT, age 2 months, parents: father not stated and Bessy BRYANT (NC), death cause: "marasmus", informant: Frank KEENER (Bristol), died: 14 Jun 1914, record (1914): 168.

Lelia Belle ROE, born: 30 Aug 1894, single, parents: H.C. ROE and Larilu BLEVINS, death cause: "palegra", buried: Bluff City, died: 16 Jun 1914, record: 169.

Marshal COLE, age 58 years, parents: Jack COLE and mother not stated, death cause: "Brights disease", buried: Bluff City, died: 19 Jul 1914, record: 170.

Noah HARDEN, age 63 years, 4 months and 21 days, born in Virginia, parents: John HARDEN (VA) and mother not stated, death cause: "gangrene", buried: Bluff City, died: 3 Jul 1914, record (1914): 171.

Rachel Buckles (illegible), age 72 years, widow, parents: _____ BUCKLES and mother's name illegible, death cause: "cerebral apoplexy", informant: Mrs. Flora SIMERLY (Emmett), buried: Weaver Cemetery, died: 4 Aug 1914, record (1914): 172.

Mrs. Nannie PYLE, born: 1 Sep 1868 in Virginia, widow, parents: Sparriel RESGUE (VA) and Sallie JONES, death cause: "pulmonary tuberculosis", informant: Mrs. Mattie PYLE (Kingsport), buried: Morrison Chapel, died: 1 Jul 1914, record (1914): 173.

Robert Earl RUPE, born: 1 Oct 1912, parents: Dennis C. RUPE and Lura E. ROLLER, death cause: "cerebro spinal meningitis", informant: L.B. LEEDY (Indian Springs), died: 9 Jul 1914, record (1914): 174.

Maxie LITE, born: 22 Apr 1914, parents: Clarence LITE and Eppie DIXON, death cause: "cholera infantum", informant: Frank DIXON (Kingsport), buried: Lites Cemetery, died: 20 Jul 1914, record (1914): 175.

Infant STEADMAN, female, parents: C.W. STEADMAN and Lillie RUTLEDGE (Hawkins Co.) death cause: "stillborn", informant: father (Blountville), buried: Rock Springs, died: 25 Jul 1914, record (1914): 176.
Mrs. Lovie M. SMITH, age not stated, married, parents: Dr. W.E. JONES and mother's name not stated, death cause: "tuberculosis", informant: R.M. JOHNSON, (Bristol), buried: Kingsport, died: 1 Jul 1914, record (1914): 177.
William PARKER, age not stated, single, born in Washington Co., VA., parents: Wyatt PARKER and Elizabeth KUYLE, death cause: "acute brights", informant: Mrs. Alice LOVE (Bristol), buried: Booher Cemetery, died: 2 Jul 1914, record (1914): 178.
Mrs. Alice DYER, born: 10 Oct 1853, married, parents: Robert N. HENRY (VA) and Malinda KETRON, death cause: "phthisis pulnonalis", informant: J.R. DYER (Bristol), died: 22 Jul 1914, record (1914): 179.
Jackson GODSEY, age 82 years, married, parents: Henry P. GODSEY and mother not stated, death cause: "paralysis", informant: Cain GODSEY (Bristol), died: 26 Jul 1914, record (1914): 180.
Lela Kate BALL, born: 9 Jul 1904, parents: George BALL (Washington Co., VA) and Pearl MILLS, death cause: "flux", informant: father (Bristol), buried: Ordway Cemetery, died: 27 Jul 1914, record (1914): 181.
Freddie BLAKE, Negro, born: 24 Jun 1914, parents: George BLAKE (VA) and Annie AUSTIN, death cause: "lobar pneumonia", informant: father (9th Street, Bristol), buried: Citizen Cemetery, died: 28 Jul 1914, record (1914): 182.
Thomas Jackson BURROW, born: 3 Nov 1903, parents: Robert BURROW (Elizabethton) and Belle LYLE (Kingsport), death cause: illegible, informant: father (Bristol), buried: E. Hill Cemetery, died: 31 Jul 1914, record (1914): 183.
John TOLBERT, age about 42 years, married, parents: Charles TOLBERT (VA) and Jane FERGUSON (VA), death cause: "crushed ..illegible", informant: N.T. TOLBERT (Bristol), buried: Oak Grove, VA., died: 31 Jul 1914, record (1914): 184.
Illegible EADS, male, born: 24 Sep 1909, parents: Charlie EADS and Maggie MORRELL, death cause: "rupture liver and bowels from falling against wagon tongue", buried: Bluff City, died: 12 Jul 1914, record (1914): 185.

Infant PATTON, male, parents: W.S. PATTON and Lena PATTON, death cause: "stillborn", buried: Bluff City, died: 17 Jul 1914, record (1914): 186.

Rev. R.A. SWAN, Negro, born: 6 Jun 1852 in Virginia, married, parents: Alexander SWAN (VA) and Patti FALINES (VA), death cause: "chronic intestinal nephritis", informant: Susie C. SWAN (Bristol), buried: Wytheville, VA., died: 18 Aug 1914, record (1914): 187.

Alvin H. BRAY, born: 2 Nov 1883 in Hawkins Co., married, parents: Thomas BRAY and Mahaley HENRY, death cause: "consumption", informant: F.G. WOODS (Bristol), buried: Ordway Cemetery, died: 18 Aug 1914, record (1914): 188.

William Henry CROWELL, born: 18 Oct 1858 in Virginia, married, parents: John W. CROWELL (VA) and Mary H. .. illegible, death cause: "diabetes", informant: W.M. CROWELL, (Rome, GA), buried: East Hill, died: 19 Aug 1914, record (1914): 189.

Mamie F. GAINS, colored, born: 23 Feb 1891 in Ringold, VA., married, parents: Elder C.L. RAGLAND (Halafax, VA) and Mary F. DAVIS (Ringold, VA), death cause: "pulmonary tuberculosis", buried: Danville, VA., died: 22 Aug 1914, record (1914): 190.

Margaret Wood GIBSON, born: 6 Aug 1875 in Virginia, single, parents: T.M. GIBSON (VA) and Ester FUGATE (VA), death cause: illegible, informant: Neil GIBSON (Bristol), buried: East Hill, died: 22 Aug 1914, record (1914): 191.

O. SITGNAVES (?), born: 15 Jan 1837 in South Carolina, married, parents: John SITHNAVES (NC) and Anna LOVE (GA), death cause: "pulmonary tuberculosis", buried: East Hill Cemetery, died: 22 Aug 1914, record (1914): 192.

Ivan L. HAWK, born: 3 May 1913, parents: J.A. HAWK and Effie B. HAYES, death cause: "gastro ..(illegible) infection", informant: father (Bristol), buried: Weaver Cemetery, died: 25 Aug 1914, record (1914): 193.

Jacob Edward WEAVER, born: 25 Apr 1913, parents: James Edward WEAVER and Minnie RADER (Green Co.), death cause: "ileo colitis", buried: Weaver Cemetery, died: 28 Aug 1914, record (1914): 194.

Vadella CAMPBELL, born: 14 Aug 1914, parents: Trigg CAMPBELL (Abingdon) and Martha WITT (VA), death cause: "penumonia", buried: East Hill Cemetery, died: 31 Aug 1914, record (1914): 195.

Grac May BALL, age 2 years, 6 months and 14 days, parents: George BALL (Washington Co., VA) and Pearl MILLS, death cause: "meningitis", buried: Ordway Cemetery, died: 1 Aug 1914, record (1914): 196.

Eliza Alice HATCHER, born: 30 Jan 1896, single, parents: R.L. HATCHER and Leona RICHARDSON, death cause: "typhoid fever", informant: father (Bristol), buried: Weaver Cemetery, died: 4 Aug 1914, record (1914): 197.

Infant WASHINGTON, colored, lived 11 days, parents: Lornes WASHINGTON (Washington Co., VA) and Nelly WASHINGTON (Albermaryle Co., VA), death cause: "convulsions", died in 17th District on 8 Aug 1914, record (1914): 198.

Infant STONE, female, parents: F.M. STONE (VA) and Sallie G..(illegible), death cause: "still born", informant: father (Bristol), buried: East Hill Cemetery, died: 7 Aug 1914, record (1914): 199.

Magnolia ROBERTS, Negro, age 26 years, married, parents: LaSalle SHEPHARD and Leachie CALLOWAY, death cause: "malignat jaundice", informant: Ethel JOHNSON (Bristol), buried: Jefferson Wall Cemetery, died: 8 Aug 1914, record (1914): 200.

Coleman HARRISON, Negro, age 62 years, married, parents: Matt HARRISON (VA) and mother unknown, death cause: "senile dementia", informant: Mearia HARRISON (Bristol), buried: Citizen Cemetery, died: 9 Aug 1914, record (1914): 201.

Sam CRAWFORD, age 40 years, born in Virginia, married, parents: John CRAWFORD (VA) and Polly LENARD (VA), death cause: "typhoid fever", died in 17th District on 12 Aug 1914, record (1914): 201.

Vance CARR, born: 4 Oct 1913, parents: Charles CARR and mother not stated, death cause: "meningitis", informant: W.P. BLEVINS (Bristol), buried: Arcadia, died: 13 Aug 1914, record (1914): 203.

Infant PATTERSON, male, born: 15 Aug 1914, parents: D.A. PATTERSON and Lillian MCNEIL (VA), death cause: "birth injury", infomant: E.S. MCNEIL (Bristol), died: 16 Aug 1914, record (1914): 204.

Mrs. E.J. WILSON, born: 16 Feb 1835 in Virginia, widow, parents: David KESHIER and Kate MINNICK, death cause: "diarrhea", informant: Mrs. Joe WORLEY (Bristol), buried: Maple Grove, VA, died: 16 Aug 1914, record (1914): 205.

John Andrew KEESLING, born: 10 Feb 1914, parents: John A. KEESLING (Wytheville) and Bessie Virginia DETHRIDGE, death cause: "tubercular meningitis",

informant: father (Bristol), buried: E. Hill Cemetery, died: 16 Aug 1914, record (1914): 206.
Henry MITCHELL, Negro, age 58 years, born in Pennsylvania, married, parents: Ed MITCHELL (PA) and mother unknown, death cause: "mitral insufficiency", informant: Millie MITCHELL (Locust), buried: Citizen Cemetery, died: 17 Aug 1914, record (1914): 207.
Maria BROYLES, black, age 75 to 80 years, widow, parents: "unknown", death cause: "uremia", informant: Dennis SMITH (Kingsport), died: 6 Aug 1914, record (1914): 208.
Cordie Ray HURST, born: 22 Sep 1892, single, parents: George T. HURST and Cynthia HARKLEROAD, death cause: "pellagra", died ath Indian Springs, buried: Pile Cemetery, died: 8 Aug 1914, record (1914): 209.
Harry DICKENS, born: 13 Mar 1913, parents: Arthur J. DICKENS and Addie AGEE (Hawkins Co.), death cause: "pneumonia", informant: C.W. AGEE (Kingsport), buried: Mt. Carmel Cemetery, died: 13 Aug 1914, record (1914): 210.
Carrie Elizabeth ROBERTS, born: 5 Oct 1912, parents: Ruben ROBERTS and Dorrie HUTSON, death cause: "whooping cough", informant: father (Kingsport), buried: Mt. Carmel Cemetery, died: 13 Aug 1914, record (1914): 211.
Elizabeth WHITE, age 78 years, born in North Carolina, widow, parents: Odom C. DUNN and mother's name unknown, death cause: "heart disease", informant: Frank DUNN (Bristol), buried: Pile Cemetery, died: 13 Aug 1914, record (1914): 212.
William Lester MCKINZIE, born: 17 Aug 1914, parents: Frank MCKINZIE and Annie LARKINS, death cause: "unknown", died at Kingsport on 19 Aug 1914, buried: Morrison Cemetery, record (1914): 213.
Sarah ALSGUE, born: 8 Jan 1837, widow, parents: Peter JONES and Mary TURNER, death cause: "aortic regrugitation", informant: Robert KYLE (Kingsport), buried: Morrison Chapel, died: 26 Aug 1914, record (1914): 214.
Mrs. Martha L. COX, age 83 years, 6 months and 6 days, widow, parents: John J. SMITH and Mary HICKS, death cause: "mitral regurgitation, nephritis", informant: J.T. COX (Bristol), buried at Blountville, died: 14 Aug 1914, record (1914): 215.
John MILLER, born: Jan 1831, widower, parents: not stated, death cause: "tuberculosis and paralysis", died in the 8th District on 1 Aug 1914, record (1914): 216.

Annie HOOD, parents: Lafayette HOOD and Hattie May MOORE (Green Co.), death cause: "asphysia neonaterum", buried: Depew Chapel, born/died: 13th District on 8 Jul 1914, record (1914): 217.

Jane Parker CONKIN, born: 18 Jul 1839 in Sullivan Co., widow, parents: "unknown", death cause: "dropsy", informant: C.M. HICKS (Fordtown), buried: Pactalus Church, died: 20 Jul 1914, record (1914): 281.

Infant HAMILTON, female, born: 29 Jul 1914, parents: William P. HAMILTON and Soloma HALL, death cause: "premature birth", informant: J.B. HAMILTON (Fordtown), died: 30 Jul 1914, record (1914): 219. (twin below)

Infant HAMILTON, female, born: 29 Jul 1914, parents: William P. HAMILTON and Soloma HALL, death cause: "premature birth", informant: J.B. HAMILTON (Fordtown), buried: Fordtown Church Cemetery, died: 31 Jul 1914, record (1914): 220. (twin above)

John William STUART, Jr., born: 4 Jun 1914, parents: J.W. STUART (Murphey, NC) and O.M. EASLEY, death cause: "cholera", informant: father (Fall Branch), buried: Depew Chapel, died: 30 Jul 1914, record (1914): 221.

Samuel M. RIGGS, born: 9 JUl 1855, married, parents: William B. RIGGS and Lueretia PEOPLES, death cause: "apoplexy", informant: Alfred A. RIGGS (Fall Branch), buried: Baptist Cemetery, 7th District, died: 11 Aug 1914, record (1914): 222.

Jacob C. ZIMMERMAN, born: 6 Mar 1847, married, parents: Samuel ZIMMERMAN and Sarah HAMILTON, death cause: "ulcer of stomach, probably malignant", informant: Mrs. Sarah ZIMMERMAN (Jonesboro), died: 22 Aug 1914, record (1914): 223.

John JOYCE, age about 68 years, born in Ireland, parents: "not known", death cause: "indigestion following a hearty meal", informant; Harry COLPERS (Fordtown), died: 23 Aug 1914, record (1914): 224.

Infant ROSE, male, born: 15 Aug 1914, parents: Oscar ROSE and Ella KING, death cause: "not known", buried: Poplar Ridge, Piney Flats, died: 16 Aug 1914, record (1914): 225.

Jessie D. PERRY, born: 30 May 1914, parents: Preston PERRY and Ethel FRY, death cause: "whooping cough", buried: Piney Flats Cemetery, died: 30 Aug 1914, record (1914): 226.

Infant GENTRY, female, born: 12 Aug 1914, parents: E. Roy GENTRY (NC) and mother's name illegible, death cause: not stated, informant: father (Bluff City), died; 14 Aug 1914, record (1914): 227.

Nellie NEWTON, born: 20 Apr 1899, parents: John NEWTON and Julia JONES, death cause: illegible, buried: Weaver Cemetery, died: 19 Aug 1914, record (1914): 228.

Rachel FEATHERS, age illegible, widow, parents: illegible BUCKLES and mother's name illegible, death cause: "apoplexy", died at Emmett, date illegible, record (1914): 229.

R.F. MALONEE, born: 7 May 1914, female, parents: Alfred M. MALONEE and Theodocia HUGHES, death cause: "diarrhoea", informant: father (Kingsport), buried: Johnson City, died: 3 Aug 1914, record (1914): 230.

Infant DEPEW, female, parents: Oscar DEPEW and Rose PRAYTER, death cause: "still birth", informant: Ernest DEPEW (Kingsport), buried: Morrison Chapel, died: 3 Aug 1914, record (1914): 231.

Lucy BARE, born: 8 Mar 1845, single, parents: William BARE and Susan BARE, death cause: "cirrhosis liver", informant: Tom DIXON (Kingsport), buried: Easley Cemetery, died: 5 Aug 1914, record (1914): 232.

Noah BRABSON, Negro, age about 70 years, widower, parents: father's name unknown and Patsy BRABSON, death cause: "pellagra", informant: Kittie BRABSON (Bristol), buried: Chuckey, TN., died: 13 Sep 1914, record (1914): 233.

Infant ROBINSON, male, colored, lived 6 days, parents: Pat ROBINSON (Abingdon) and Ida WHITE (Abingdon), death cause: "strangulaton", died: 14 Sep 1914, record (1914): 234.

J. HAUN, age about 46 years, married, parents: Pleas A. HAUN and Nancy FARRIS, death cause: "fall from trussle", informant: R.N. HAUN (Bristol), died: 15 Sep 1914, record (1914): 235.

William WALKER, age 42 years, single, parents: Cyrus WALKER (Vermont) and ____ DAVIS, death cause: "fell from trussle", informant: R.N. HAUN (Bristol), buried: Bluff City, died: 15 Sep 1914, record (1914): 236.

Mrs. Mary SHERFEY, born: 7 Aug 1871 in Green Co., widow, parents: Turk MITCHELL (Green Co.) and Martha MORELOCK (Green Co.), death cause: "pellagra", informant: J.S. SHERFEY (Bristol), buried: E. Hill Cemetery, died: 20 Sep 1914, record (1914): 237.

Leon HAYES, colored, born: 24 Jul 1892, parents: Henry HAYES (VA) and mother not stated, death cause: "pulmonary tuberculosis", informant: Alex HAYES

(Bristol, VA), buried: New Cemetery, Bristol, died: 27 Sep 1914, record (1914): 238.
Infant ANDERSON, male, parents: C. ANDERSON and (illegible) JOHNSON, death cause: "still birth", buried: East Hill Cemetery, died: 28 Sep 1914, record (1914): 239.
William White WATSON, born: 20 Apr 1857 in Washington Co., VA., married, parents: Robert WATSON (Scotland) and Jane WHITE (Washington Co., VA), death cause: "lock bowels", informant: Miss Nannie WATSON (Bristol), buried in Virginia, died: 29 Sep 1914, record (1914): 240.
George TRINKLE, born: 18 Oct 1887, married, parents: Joseph TRINKLE (Pulaski, VA) and Mattie HOOVER (VA), death cause: "pellagra", informant: Joseph TRINKLE (Bristol), buried: Ordway Cemetery, died: 30 Sep 1914, record (1914): 241.
Lucinda KING, age about 58 years, born in Smith Co., VA., married, parents: Woodson LLOYD (VA) and Sallie SAUNDERS (VA), death cause: illegible, informant: T.C. KING (Bristol), died: 22 Sep 1914, record (1914): 242.
Mary Elizabeth GALLOWAY, born: 1 Aug 1913, parents: Thomas M. GALLOWAY and Annie M. MCKINZIE, death cause: "meningitis", informant: father (Kingsport), buried: Morrison Chapel, died: 14 Sep 1914, record (1914): 243.
Andrew Jackson BREEDING, born: 1 Dec 1825 in Pulaski, Co., VA., widower, parents: William BREEDING (VA) and FUGATE (VA), death cause: "catarrhal dysentery", informant: J.K. BREEDING (Kingsport), buried: Breeding Cemetery, died: 17 Sep 1914, record (1914): 244.
Kate Eugene BOLTON, born: 21 Aug 1914, parents: George BOLTON and Nellie BARE, death cause: "whooping cough", informant: Robert BOLTON (Kingsport), buried: Backman Cemetery, died: 21 Sep 1914, record (1914): 245.
Infant CRUM, female, parents: J.R. CRUM and Nora ADAMS (VA), death cause: "still birth", informant: C.W. CRUM (Kingsport), buried: Groseclose Cemetery, died: 29 Sep 1914, record (1914): 246.
John FORD, age 66 years, widower, parents: "unknown", death cause: "pellagra", informant: Richard FORD (Kingsport), died: 30 Sep 1914, record (1914): 247.
Celia PAYNE, born: 26 Oct 1842 in Virginia, parents: Joseph FELTS (VA) and Polly KESTER (VA), death cause: "heart complications", informant: N.V. PAYNE (Big Creek), died: 28 Jun 1914, record (1914): 248.
Eula Fay OSBORN, age 5 months and 7 days, parents: Charles OSBORN and Lillian HICKS, death cause:

"dysentery", informant: father (Big Creek), died: 22 Aug 1914, record (1914): 249.

James CARR, age about 68 years, married, parents: not stated, death cause: "carcinoma of face", died in the 9th District on 30 Sep 1914, record (1914): 250.

Sally PEREGAY, age illegible, widow, death cause: "apoplexy", buried: Peregoy Cemetery, died in the 9th District on 30 Sep 1914, record (1914): 251.

Watson ANDERSON, born: 17 Jun 1844 in Grayson Co., VA., married, parents: not stated, death cause: "Brights disease", buried: Sanders Cemetery, Piney Flats, died: 16 Sep 1914, record (1914): 252.

Jennie FEATHERS, born: 21 Sep 1882, married, parents: George WATSON and Nancy WATKINS, death cause: "tuberculosis of lungs", buried: Morrell Cemetery, died: 21 Sep 1914, record (1914): 253.

Pauline HARKLEROAD, born: 30 Dec 1910, parents: J.T. HARKLEROAD and mother's name illegible (Erwin), death cause: "acute meningitis", died at Bluff City on 21 Sep 1914, record (1914): 254.

Rhena MILLER, born: 4 Mar 1858, widow, parents: James MORRELL and mother not stated, death cause: "tuberculosis of bowels", died at Bluff City on 4 Sep 1914, record (1914): 255.

Mrs. R.R. ANDERSON, born: 14 Sep 1834, widow, parents: Andrew BOY and Mary A. HOBAUGH, death cause: illegible, informant: Phil J. BOY, died at Bristol on 29 Aug 1914, record (1914): 256.

Thomas HARRIGAN, age about 93 years, born in Ireland, parents: Thomas Harrigan (Ireland) and Mary CARROLL (Ireland), death cause: illegible, informant: Mrs. E. LERUE (Bristol), died: 1 Sep 1914, record (1914): 257.

Mrs. Jane BLEVINS, born: 16 Apr 1840, widow, parents: William DYER and Savery PETERS (VA), death cause: "heart failure", informant: Mrs. Dave MONTGOMERY (Knoxville), buried: Knoxville, died: 1 Sep 1914, record (1914): 258.

W.N. TAYLOR, age about 25 years, born in Scott Co., VA., married, parents: Abram TAYLOR (VA) and Bettie STARNES (Scott Co.), death cause: "general perelonis", informant: E.M. STARENS (Gate City), buried: Gate City, died: 9 Sep 1914, record (1914): 259.

Mrs. Elizabeth MOORE, born: 20 Mar 1874 in North Carolina, married, parents: John UTSMAN (NC), and Nancy SHOEMAKER (NC), death cause: "typhoid fever" informant: Mart MOORE (Kingsport), died: 2 Oct 1914, record (1914): 260.

Nettie Francis BARNES, born: 9 Sep 1914, parents; Robert Wesley BARNES (Scott Co.) and Elsie Mae BELLER (Dickson Co., Nebr.), death cause: "infection through meningocete", informant: W.D. BARNES (Indian Springs), buried: Thomas Cemetery, died: 4 Oct 1914, record (1914): 261.
Henry Clay PYLE, born: 3 Nov 1908, parents: Samuel P. PYLE and Amanda DAVIS, death cause: "tumor of base of brain", informant: D.A. PYLE (Kingsport), buried: Pyle Cemetery, died: 24 Oct 1914, record (1914): 262.
Fred Keever DAY, born: 13 Oct 1911, parents: James DAY (NC) and Mary WATSON (NC), death cause: "diphtheria", informant: Pearl PYLE (Kingsport), buried: Morrison Chapel, died: 24 Oct 1914, record (1914): 263.
Verden Rasp MARTIN, born: 13 Jun 1914, parents; Charles P. MARTIN and Bell MARTIN, death cause: "acute gastritis", informant: Joe PHILLIPS (Kingsport), buried: Liberty, died: 27 Oct 1914, record (1914): 264.
E. HATCHER, female, age 67 years, widow, parents: Abe SAMS and mother not stated, death cause: "valvular cardiac lesion", buried: Weaver Cemetery, Bluff City, died: 15 Oct 1914, record (1914): 265.
Henry HAYETT, born: 10 Aug 1898, parents: James HAYETT and Nannie HAYETT, death cause: "typhoid", died at Piney Flats on 9 Oct 1914, record (1914): 266.
Rev. John W. WATSON, born: 8 Aug 1847, married, parents: Johnathon WATSON and Susan FEATHERS, death cause: "gall stones", informant: Sam WATSON (Bluff City), buried: Chinquapin Cemetery, died: 24 Oct 1914, record (1914): 267.
Lizzie HUNT, born: 24 Apr 1869, widow, parents: Thomas Jefferson DILLONS and Nancy CHASE, death cause: "cancer right breast", informant: C.R. BELL (Fordtown), buried: Pactolus, died: 5 Aug 1914, record (1914): 268.
Robert L. HOOD, born: 14 Mar 1874, married, parents: Henry H. HOOD (Hawkins Co.) and Sinora F. COLEY, death cause: "accident by team running away, brain injury", informant: T.O. HOOD (Fall Branch), buried: 7 Dist, Washington Co., died: 6 Sep 1914, record (1914): 269.
Usely CONKIN, born: 2 Jun 1884, single, parents: Thomas J. CONKIN and Sallie MULLENNIX (VA), death cause: "pulmonary tuberculosis", informant: J.J. WHITE (Fall Branch), buried: Fairview Church, 15 District, died: 15 Sep 1914, record (1914): 270.
Mary Ann BAXTER, born: 24 Jun 1849, widow, parents: J. Henderson DEVAULT and Mary Ann SMITH (VA), death

cause: "intestinal tuberculosis", informant; Jennie E. HENDMAN (Fairfax, MO.) buried: Baxter Cemetery, 15th District, died: 30 Sep 1914, record (1914): 271.

Infant LIGHT, male, parents: George Washington LIGHT and Mary Bessie MOWDY, death cause: "still born", informant: A.G. LIGHT (Fordtown), died: 20 Oct 1914, record (1914): 272.

Beatrice MCCULLEY, born: 13 Oct 1914, parents: Jeremiah Proffitt MCCULLEY and Daisy ISENBERG, death cause: "premature birth", buried: Pactolus Church, died: 28 Oct 1914, record (1914): 277.

Alfred TAYLOR born: 18 Jul 1840, married, parents: Nick CARTER and Polly TAYLOR, death cause: "pellagra", informant: Mrs. Alfred TAYLOR (Bristol), buried: Shipley Cemetery, died: 6 Oct 1914, record (1914): 274.

Mrs. Hassie J. SAMPSON, born: 28 Sep 1869 in Unicoi, Co., widow, parents: Isaac NELSON (Unicoi) and Rebecca PHILLIPS (Unicoi), death cause: illegible, informant: Mrs Lizzie HOLTON (Bristol), buried: East Hill Cemetery, died: 7 Oct 1914, record (1914): 275.

Cleo Crystal TOLBERT, born: 12 Aug 1914, parents: Charles TOLBERT and Clara MCKAY (VA), death cause: illegible, informant: father (Bristol), buried: Paperville, died: 8 Oct 1914, record (1914): 276.

Rachel Iscue HICKS, born: 2 Sep 1914, parents: Frank HICKS and Sinthy POOLE, death cause: "indigestion", informant: A.M. HICKS (Bristol), buried: Webb Cemetery, died: 19 Oct 1914, record (1914): 277.

Mattie ELLER, born: 15 Jan 1913, parents: John ELLER (NC) and Rosie THOMAS (VA), death cause: "marasmus", informant: father (Bristol), buried: East Hill, died: 22 Oct 1914, record (1914): 278.

F.T. ELLIOTT, age about 35 years, born in Ashe Co., NC., married, parents: J.C. ELLIOTT (Ashe Co.) and Rousie OSBORNE (Alleghany Co., NC), death cause: "appendicitis", informant: Andrew ELLIOTT (Clifton, NC), buried: Ashe Co., died: 22 Oct 1914, record (1914): 279.

Mrs. Isaac DOYLE, born: 23 Feb 1873, married, parents: R.M. KEESEE (VA) and Mattie KEESEE, death cause: "pellagra", informant: W.B. KEESEE (Bristol), buried: Walnut Grove, VA., died: 25 Oct 1914, record (1914): 280.

Earl BARR, born: 28 Jun 1913 at Jacksboro, TN., parents: J.S. BARR (Rushton, TN) and Mary Luther STONE (Carroll Co., VA), death cause: "infection due to circumcision, blood poison", informant: J.S. BARR

(Bristol), buried: Rushton, TN., died: 29 Oct 1914, record (1914): 281.

Virgil BOWERS, age 32 years, born in Virginia, single, parents: D.C. BOWERS (VA) and Emma MARDEN (VA), death cause: "typhoid", informant: father (Bristol), buried: Abingdon, VA., died: 30 Oct 1914, record (1914): 282.

Cora CARRIER, age 38 years, married, parents: David SMITH and mother not stated, death cause: not stated, informant: Henry CARRIER (Bristol), buried: Smith Cemetery, died: 5 Oct 1914, record (1914): 283.

Howard HARMON, born: 7 Apr 1912, parents: John HARMON (NC) and Clair EGGERS (NC), death cause: "croup", informant: Clair HARMON (Bluff City), buried: Crumley Cemetery, died: 7 Dec 1914, record (1914): 284.

Barbara Ann WHITLOCK, born: 9 Nov 1839 in Roanoke, VA., married, parents: Nathaniel BURKETT and Polly HARTMAN, death cause: "organic heart disease", informant; Lillie WHITLOCK (Fishdam), died: 26 Nov 1914, record (1914): 285.

Mary Elizabeth BLEVINS, age: illegible, single, parents: father's name illegible and Lucy BLEVINS, death cause: "valvular heart (illegible)", buried: Weaver Cemetery, 21st District, died: 9 Dec 1914, record (1914): 286.

Infant NELSON, male, the remainder of the record is illegible, record (1914): 287.

Eliza GROSS, born: 9 Jan 1842, widow, parents: William GROSS and mother not stated, death cause: "paralysis", buried: New Bethel Cemetery, died at Piney Flats on 7 Nov 1914, record (1914): 288.

Infant GLOOR (?), male, parents: Edward GLOOR and Lillie WATSON, death cause: not known, buried: Chinquipin Grove, born/died: 6 Nov 1914, record (1914): 289.

Infant SHELL, male, parents: Thomas SHELL and Nannie BARR, death cause: "premature", buried: Piney Flats Cemetery, died: 19 Nov 1914, record (1914): 290.

John CRAWFORD, born: 8 Sep 1912, parents: Thomas CRAWFORD and Mary J. CRAWFORD, death cause: "convulsions supposed worms", informant: S.H. CONKIN (Fall Branch), buried: Solomans Temple Cemetery, died: 8 Oct 1914, record (1914): 291.

James Buchanan HAMILTON, born: 15 Nov 1855, married, parents: George HAMILTON and Elizabeth GRAY, death cause: "intestinal hemorrhage, possibly apoplexy", informant: Nancy Hamilton HAWK (Jonesboro), buried: Fordtown Baptist Church, died: 2 Nov 1914, record (1914): 282.

Rosa Bell PHILLIPS, born: 10 Sep 1911, parents: James PHILLIPS and Edna COX, death cause: "croup", informant: father (Fall Branch), buried: Walker Ford Church, died: 14 Nov 1914, record (1914): 293.
Mary HILTON, born: 4 Aug 1838 in Washington Co., TN., married, parents: William CASH (Washington Co.) and Elizabeth WELLS, death cause: "mitral insufficiency", informant: C.F. HILTON (Jonesboro), died in the 15th District on 19 Nov 1914, record (1914): 294.
Annie Lorena EADES, born: 6 Sep 1908, parents: Charles EADES and Mollie BOYD, death cause: "tubercular meningitis", informant: father (Fall Brancy), buried: Easley Cemetery, died: 24 Nov 1914, record: 295.
Lucinda CLARK, born: 31 Aug 1842, married, parents: Alijah TUCKER (Hawkins Co.) and Nancy HUNLEY (Hawkins Co.), death cause: "ovarian ulcer", informant: David CRAWFORD (Church Hill), buried: Blairs Gap Church, died: 24 Nov 1914, record (1914): 296.
Aggie CARTER, age 102 years, widow, born in Virginia, parents: Nathan HOBBS (VA) and Mary SMITH, death cause: "unknown", informant: Jacob HOOVER (Arcadia), buried: on Jacob Hoover farm, died: 17 Nov 1914, record (1914): 297.
Charles Robert COOPER, age 23 years, married, parents: W.F. COOPER and Anna HARTSOCK (VA), death cause: "pneumonia", buried: East Hill Cemetery, died: 28 Nov 1914, record (1914): 298.
Allen P. ROSS, Negro, born: 6 Sep 1914 in Virginia, parents: Neal ROSS (VA) and Ressie WATKINS (VA), death cause: "unknown", died at Bristol on 21 Nov 1914, record (1914): 299.
Thomas HALEY, Negro, born: 27 Dec 1867 in Virginia, married, parents: William HALEY (VA) and mother's name unknown, death cause: "nephritis", informant: William HALEY (Bristol), buried: Jefferson Watts Cemetery, died: 17 Nov 1914, record (1914): 300.
R.P.A. BERRYMAN, born: 31 Oct 1862 in Indiana, married, parents: James A. BERRYMAN (Indians) and Agnes MOORE (Indiana), death cause: "nephritis", informant: Mrs. R.P.A. BERRYMAN (Elizabethton), buried: Elizabethton, died: 5 Nov 1914, record: 301.
John SMITH, Negro, born: 14 Jul 1857, married, parents: David SMITH and mother's name not known, death cause: "mitral insufficiency", informant: Alice SMITH (Bristol), buried: Citizen Cemetery, died: 6 Nov 1914, record (1914): 302.
Infant WOLF, colored, male, parents: Will WOLF (Hawkins Co.) and Francis REYMOND (VA), death cause:

"still born", informant: father (Bristol), died: 4 Nov 1914, record (1914): 303.

Infant COWAN, male, parents: Thomas H. COWAN and Tennessee CARINAS (VA), death cause: "still born", informant: father (Bristol), died: 3 Nov 1914, record (1914): 304.

Columbus MITCHELL, Negro, born: Nov 1872, married, parents: (illegible) MITCHELL (VA) and Ann MOSLY (VA), death cause: "nephritis", informant: Ann MITCHELL (Bristol), buried: Citizen Cemetery, died: 3 Nov 1914, record (1914): 305.

Samuel LAMPKINS, born: 10 Jan 1840 in Tennessee, widower, parents: George LAMPKINS and Eliza MARION, death cause: "cirrhosis liver", informant: Dan DALTON (Kingsport), died: 10 Dec 1914, record (1914): 306.

Missouri Catherine HORN, born: 1 Mar 1845 in Virginia, married, parents: Henry LITZ (VA) and Mary KING (VA), death cause: "cerebral hemorrhage", informant: Mrs. Charles CRUM (Kingsport), buried: Pile Cemetery, died: 19 Dec 1914, record (1914): 307.

John S. CRYSEL, age 85 years, born in North Carolina, widower, parents: not known, death cause: "parcsis", informant: James T. VARGAS (Kingsport), buried: Morrison Chapel, died: 25 Dec 1914, record (1914): 308.

Infant PROFFITT, male, born: 28 Dec 1914, parents: Wade PROFFITT (NC) and Lula WILKES (NC), death cause: "not known", died at Bluff City on 29 Dec 1914, record (1914): 309.

Maria C. DEPEW, born: 8 Oct 1845, widow, parents: Dulaney WILLARD and Caroline CLARK, death cause: "chronic intestinal nephritis", informant: J. Dulaney DEPEW (Fordtown), buried: Rock Springs Church, died: 7 Dec 1914, record (1914): 310.

Ethel FULWILDER, born: 17 Apr 1893, single, parents: Abraham FULWILDER (Washington Co., VA) and Della NELSON, death cause: "pulmonary tuberculosis", informant: T.J. BACHMAN (Fall Branch), buried: Depew Chapel, died: 8 Dec 1914, record (1914): 311.

(Illegible) WEBB, age 69 years and 1 month, death cause: "pneumonia", buried: Webb Cemetery, died: 2 Dec 1914, record (1914): 312.

Robert DAGGS, colored, born: 24 Feb 1913, parents: James DAGGS (VA) and Nora HILL, death cause: "lobar pneumonia", informant: father (Bristol), buried: New Cemetery, died: 2 dec 1914, record (1914): 313.

Infant DEWELL, Negro, male, parents: James DEWELL and Ellie MITCHELL, death cause: "premature birth",

informant: father (Bristol), buried: Citizen Cemetery, died: 3 Dec 1914, record (1914): 314.
William WILSON, born: 25 Jan 1912, parents: Lacy WILSON and Margaret WOOD (Maryville, TN), death cause: "tuberculosis of bowels", died at Bristol on 3 Dec 1914, record (1914): 315.
Infant HEMPHILL, Negro, female, parents: James HEMPHILL (GA) and Mary MAURY (Elizabethton), death cause: "premature", informant: father (Bristol), buried: Citizen Cemetery, born/died: 5 Dec 1914, record (1914): 316.
James DAUGHERTY, Jr., born: 2 Dec 1914, parents: James DAUGHERTY (Pennsylvania) and Nell MCPOLAND (Alabama), death cause: "probably basal hemorrhage", informant: father (Bristol), buried: Catholic Cemetery, died: 5 Dec 1914, record (1914): 317.
Catherine E. MAURY, born: 19 Jun 1829 in Virginia, widow, parents: Berry AMMON (VA) and Neoma CROSS (VA), death cause: "paralysis", informant: M.B. MAURY (Bristol), buried: Marion, VA., died: 6 Dec 1914, record (1914): 318.
Mrs. Alex SMITH, age not stated, married, parents: H.A. CARRIER and Nora COLLINS, death cause: "heart failure", informant: H.A. CARRIER (Bristol), buried: Ordway Cemetery, died: 6 Dec 1914, record (1914): 319.
Infant FRANKLIN, colored, female, born: 4 Dec 1914, parents: Charles FRANKLIN (Chilhowie, VA) and _____ HENDRIX, death cause: "premature birth", informant: father (Bristol), died: 7 Dec 1914, record (1914): 320.
Mrs. R.E. BRISCOL, born: 2 Feb 1852, married, parents: J.H. BRISCOL and Herriel BRISCOL (Washington Co., VA), death cause: illegible, informant: David BRISCOL (Bristol), died: 8 Dec 1914, record (1914): 321.
Merrett Walker BOND, age about 30 years, married, parents: "don't know", death cause: "gunshot wound of abdomen", buried: E. Hill Cemetery, Bristol, died: 8 Dec 1914, record (1914): 322.
John W. PRICE, age 47 years, married, parents: W. PRICE (VA) and Mary K. SHAVER, death cause: illegible, informant: Alex SMITH (Bristol), died: 9 Dec 1914, record (1914): 323.
Mrs. Mary EAST, age 20 years, rest of record illegible, died: 17 Dec 1914, record (1914): 324.
Samuel KEE, born: 29 Mar 1900, parents: W.M. KEE (Washington Co., VA), and Meme SOLS (Washington Co., VA), death cause: "tuberculosis", informant: father

(Bristol), buried: Walnut Grove Cemetery, VA., died: 11 Dec 1914, record (1914): 325.

W.B. BROWN, Negro, born: 11 Aug 1914, parents: E.B. BROWN (VA) and Fannie TURNER, death cause: "broncho pneumonia", buried: Citizen Cemetery, died: 11 Dec 1914, record (1914): 326.

John V. EVERETT, age 48 years, born in Virginia, married, parents: J.H. EVERETT (VA) and ____ VAIL (VA), death cause: "Brights disease", informant: H.E. EVERETT (Bristol), buried: East Hill, died: 23 Dec 1914, record (1914): 327.

Isaac BLEVINS, Negro, age not stated, parents: Richard BLEVINS and mother's name illegible, death cause: "probably froze to death", informant: father (Bristol), buried: Citizens Cemetery, died: 20 Dec 1914, record (1914): 328.

Eralus Harris BOGLE, age 74 years, 4 months and 18 days, born in Virginia, married, parents: not stated, death cause: "chronic Brights", informant: L.P. BOGLE (NC), buried: East Hill, died: 26 Dec 1914, record (1914): 329.

Stella JORDAN, age 3 months and 7 days, parents: Walter JORDAN and Fannie DUGGER, death cause: "croup", informant: A.S. MILLER (Bristol), buried: Weaver Cemetery, died: 26 Jan 1915, record (1915): 210.

Mrs. Jane MILLER, age 83 years, 4 months and 2 days, born in Virginia, widow, parents: James CROW (W. VA) and Mary HAYES (VA), death cause: "pneumonia", buried: Brown's Cemetery, 3rd District, died: 1 Jan 1915, record (1915): 211.

Bery F. WEBB, born: 27 Aug 1831 in Tennessee, married, parents: David WEBB and Sarah J__ (illegible), death cause: "chronic nephritis", informant: Susan WEBB, buried: Crumley Cemetery, Bluff City, died: 5 Jan 1915, record (1915): 212.

Hazel Lynn MOORE, born: 26 Dec 1912, parents; Ray C. MOORE and Maggie ELLER, death cause: "tubercular meningitis", informant: R.C. MOORE (Bristol), buried: East Hill, died: 14 Jan 1915, record (1915): 213.

Mrs. Jane RICHARDS, born: 28 Mar 1842 in Carter Co., married, parents: Henry MORRIS (Carter Co.) and Betsy SCOTT (Carter Co.), death cause: "paralysis", informant: E.H. RICHARDS (Bristol), died: 4 Jan 1915, record (1915): 214.

Margaret NELSON, Negro, born: Apr 1868 in Virginia, married, parents: Rev. Giles COFFER (VA) and Maria THORPE (VA), death cause: "paralysis", buried:

Citizens Cemetery, died: 4 Jan 1915, record (1915): 215.

Lancaster SMITH, Negro, born: 3 Aug 1847 in Virginia, married, parents: Barnet SMITH (VA) and Eliza CATTIDETT (VA), death cause: "uremia", informant: Lillie SMITH (Bristol), buried: Citizens, died: 23 Jan 1915, record (1915): 216.

Grover JONES, born: 20 Aug 1914, parents: George JONES and Ella FELTY (VA), death cause: "pneumonia", informant: J.W. FLEENOR (Indian Springs), buried: Grunnings, TN., died: 13 Jan 1915, record (1915): 217.

Susan Kate BOWRY, born: 14 Jan 1915, parents: John W. BOWRY and Eva CAUFMAN, death cause: "premature birth", died in the 18th District on 15 Jan 1915, record (1915): 218.

Mollie COUSSELL, age 40 years, married, parents: Abe HICKS and mother's name illegible, death cause: "tuberculosis of bowels", died at Blountville, date not stated, buried: 28 Jan 1915, record (1915): 219.

David Wilson CARTWRIGHT, born: 20 Jan 1915, parents: Abija CARTWRIGHT and Lida Ellen CARTWRIGHT, death cause: "birth defect", died at Blountville on 22 Jan 1915, record (1915): 220.

Grover MILLER, born: 15 Jan 1915, parents: Andrew MILLER and Bessie CROW, death cause: "birth defect", informant: Mrs. Lddia ODELL (Emmett), died: 29 Jan 1915, record (1915): 221.

Hiram Parton TOMLINSON, parents: George S. TOMLINSON and Mary E. (surname illegible), death cause: "still born", informant: Dave SMITH (Indian Springs), died: 1 Jan 1915, record (1915): 222.

Mary Jane HESS, born: 2 Aug 1830 in Virginia, widow, parents: Andrew HERVELL and mother unknown, death cause: "chronic intestinal nephritis", informant: Mrs. W.J. YOAKLEY (Kingsport), buried: Bloomingdale, died: 9 Jan 1915, record (1915): 224.

Willie BREWER, born: 7 Dec 1890, single, parents: "unknown", death cause: "sirosis of liver", informant: W.D. NEIL (Kingsport), died; 5 Jan 1915, record (1915): 223.

Edward Harold HAYES, born: 10 Jan 1915, parents: George HAYES (Smith Co., VA) and Lona Mae BOND, death cause: "unknown", buried: Cox Cemetery, died at Indian Springs on 13 Jan 1915, record (1915): 225.

Eva Lee CRAWFORD, born: 26 Nov 1914, parents: Nathan CRAWFORD and Callie HAMMONDS, death cause: "broncho pneumonia", informant: W.W. LEE (Kingsport), buried: Pile Cemetery, died: 15 Jan 1915, record (1915): 226.

Infant PARKER, male, parents: Walker PARKER and Mary BARE, death cause: "still born", buried: Kingsport Cemetery, died: 18 Jan 1915, record (1915): 227.

Mary Cloud NEIL, born: 22 Feb 1833 in Tennessee, widow, parents: Benjamin CLOUD (VA) and Nancy NETHERLAND, death cause: "unknown", informant: W.D. NEIL (Kingsport), died: 29 Jan 1915, record (1915): 228.

Burtie MORREL, age 28 years, parents: not stated, death cause: "(illegible) fever", died at Bluff City on 28 Jan 1915, record (1915): 229.

William McKinley JOBE, parents: Rice JOBE and Sudie ROWLAND, death cause: "premature", buried: Mullins Cemetery, born/died: 13 Jan 1915, record (1915): 230. (twin below)

Francia Ellen JOBE, born: 13 Jan 1915, parents: Rice JOBE and Sudie ROWLAND, death cause: "premature", buried: Mullins Cemetery, died: 20 Jan 1915, record (1915): 231.

Catherine CARRIER, born: 19 Apr 1882, married, parents: William HINKLE and Mary WHITE, death cause: "tuberculosis of lungs", informant: Frank CARRIER (Emmett), buried: Shipley Cemetery, died: 3 Feb 1915, record (1915): 232.

Robert W. EAST, born: 22 May 1851 in Henry Co., VA., married, parents: Thomas EAST (VA) and Jestie CLOUD (VA), death cause: "Brights disease", informant: Mrs. A.E. KETRON (Bloomingdale), buried: Reedy Creek, died: 28 Feb 1915, record (1915): 233.

Margaret Helen HARKLEROAD, born: 25 Feb 1911, parents: Owen HARKLEROAD and Cynthia LEONARD, death cause: "peritonitis", informant: father (Kingsport), buried: Pyle Cemetery, died: 1 Feb 1915, record (1915): 234.

Robert Taylor CARDON, born: 23 Jan 1915, parents: C.C. CARDON and Callie R. HAWKINS (Wilkes Co., NC) death cause: "heart failure", informant: Isaac MINNICK (Indian Springs), buried: Thomas Cemetery, died: 3 Feb 1915, record (1915): 235.

Joseph R. GRAY, born: 1 Sep 1846, married, parents: John GRAY (NC) and Winie RODGERS, death cause: "tuberculosis of lungs", informant: C.H. BARGES (Indian Springs), buried: Bowery Cemetery, died: 19 Feb 1915, record (1915): 236.

David BOWLING, lived 6 days, parents: Butler BOWLING and Susan DUNCAN, death cause: "croup", informant: Mrs. Thomas ODELL (Big Creek), buried: Browns Cemetery, died: 6 Feb 1915, record (1915): 237.

Robert Lee ROSENBAUM, born: 3 Dec 1914, parents: Sam ROSENBAUM and Lissie GODSEY, death cause: "pneumonia", informant: Lizzie SWINNEY, buried: Weaver Cemetery, died: 18 Feb 1915, record (1915): 238.

Mrs. Elizabeth SPEER, age about 74 years, born in Virginia, widow, parents: John T. COLLINS (VA) and Katie NEWMAN (VA), death cause: "carcinoma of uterus", informant: T.C. FLANNERY (Bristol), died: 5 Feb 1915, record (1915): 239.

Mrs. E.W. WOLFE, age 59 years, teacher, married, parents: Nathan JACKSON and Evelyn CHAPMAN, death cause: "cancer of pancreas", informant: E.W. WOLFE (Bristol), died: 7 Feb 1915, record (1915): 240.

Mildred PRICE, born: 24 Aug 1914, parents: B. PRICE and Hattie MURPHEY, death cause: "meningitis and whooping cough", buried: Piney Flats, died: 14 Feb 1915, record (1915): 241.

E.T. JONES, age 63 years, born in Virginia, dentist, married, parents: R.W. JONES (VA) and Cornelia THURMAN (VA), death cause: "perforation of bowel from ulcer", informant: Lindsay BUNTING (Bristol, VA), died: 17 Feb 1915, record (1915): 242.

William Dunn PHIPPS, born: 18 Nov 1914, parents: Guy PHIPPS and Virginia CROSS, death cause: "pneumonia", informant: father (Bristol), buried: East Hill, died: 18 Feb 1915, record (1915): 243.

Martha Irene ARNOLD, born: 9 Mar 1897, single, parents: A.F. ARNOLD (VA) and Irene Huntingdon DAVIS (VA), death cause: "general peritonitis", informant: Mrs. C.R. PEPPER (Bristol, VA), buried: East Hill, died: 24 Feb 1915, record (1915): 244.

Thomas ODELL, age 11 years, 3 months and 7 days, parents: William ODELL and Lydia SHIPLEY, death cause: "injuries sustained in saw mill", informant: Lydia SHIPLEY (Bristol), buried: Shipley Cemetery, died: 27 Feb 1915, record (1915): 245.

Grover W. MILLER, born: 15 Jan 1915, parents: Andrew MILLER (Johnson Co.) and Bessie CROW (VA), death cause: "indigestion", informant: Mrs. Lydia ODELL (Emmett), buried: Shipley Cemetery, died: 22 Feb 1915, record (1915): 246.

Nancy TAYLOR, age 83 years, born in North Carolina, single, parents: Robert SMITH (NC) and Susan (surname illegible)(NC), death cause: "rheumatism", informant: J.L. CAMPBELL (Bluff City), buried: Crumley Cemetery, died: 7 Feb 1915, record (1915): 247.

Alice ANDERSON, born: 25 Mar 1884, single, parents: Watson ANDERSON (Grayson Co., VA) and Mary MILLIOM, death cause: "pulmonary tuberculosis", informant: Dr. F. GRAVES (Piney Flats), buried: New Bethel, died: 28 Feb 1915, record (1915): 248.

Infant WOLF, female, parents: Samuel WOLF and Bessie WEXLER, death cause: "still born", died at Piney Flats on 19 Feb 1915, record (1915): 249.

Jessie Silas POWELL, age 97 years, born in Hawkins County, married, parents: "unknown", death cause: "influenza", informant: J.K.P. CONKIN, buried: Mullins Cemetery, 15th District, died: 28 Feb 1915, record (1915): 250.

Gilbert Everett BOYD, born: 19 May 1871, married, parents: John W. BOYD and Elvira FISH, death cause: "cirrhosis of liver", informant: D.P. DOLEN (Fordtown), buried: Rock Springs Church, died: 6 Feb 1915, record (1915): 251.

Martha COX, born: 11 Apr 1849 in Green County, widow, parents: Isaac TUNNELL (Hawkins Co.) and Pagie BRIGHT (Hawkins Co.), death cause: "pulmonary tuberculosis", informant: G.C. COX (Jonesboro), buried: Double Spring Church, 14th District, died: 2 Mar 1915, record (1915): 252.

Martha Angeline KING, born: 17 Feb 1853, married, parents: Jacob COX and Amanda KING, death cause: "gastro enteritis", informant: John P. KING (Fordtown), buried: King Cemetery, died: 2 Mar 1915, record (1915): 253.

Infant DURHAM, male, parents: Emory L. DURHAM and Bessie L. MITCHELL, death cause: "still born", informant: father (Fordtown), buried: Lebanon Church, died: 22 Mar 1915, record (1915): 254.

Margaret HUDDLE, born: 15 Jun 1836 in Wythe Co., VA., married, parents: Elias FOGLESONG (Wythe Co.) and Annie WILSON (Wythe Co.), death cause: "acute intestinal nephritis", informant: Jacob HUDDLE (Fordtown), buried: Lebanon Church, died: 15 Mar 1915, record (1915): 255.

William SHORT, born: 25 Apr 1860, married, parents: William STEADMAN and Eliza Blakely SHORT, death cause: "acute nephritis", informant: B.F. HOOD (Fall Branch), buried: Depew Chapel, died: 8 Mar 1915, record (1915): 256.

George Henry HILTON, born: 3 Aug 1842, widower, parents: William HILTON and Martha FORD, death cause: "mitral insufficiency, catarrh", informant: C.F. HILTON (Jonesboro), buried: Hilton Cemetery, 13th District, died: 7 Mar 1915, record (1915): 257.

Isaac CLARK, age 85 years, born in Washington Co., TN., married, parents: William CLARK (NC) and Elizabeth CLARKE, death cause: "mitral regurgitation", buried: Soloman's Temple Cemetery, died: 13 Mar 1915, record (1915): 258.

Phoeba DILLON, age about 70 years, born in Hawkins County, widow, parents: Alijah TUCKER (Hawkins Co.) and Nancy HUNLEY (Hawkins Co.), death cause: illegible, informant: David CRAWFORD (Fall Branch), buried: Soloman's Temple Cemetery, died: 21 Mar 1915, record (1915): 259.

Mary Ann BOYD, age 26 years, 7 months and 4 days, single, teacher, parents: George BOYD and Martha ODELL, death cause: "tuberculosis", informant: Thomas ODELL (Emmett), buried: Shipley Cemetery, died: 14 Mar 1915, record (1915): 260.

Eli Preston WARREN, born: 23 May 1885, single, parents: H.C. WARREN and Sarah J. ELLIOTT (VA), death cause: "pulmonary tuberculosis", informant: T.C. WARREN (Bluff City), died: 5 Mar 1915, record (1915): 261.

Evaline FAGANS, age between 80 and 85 years, widow, parents: not stated, death cause: "nephritis", buried: New Bethel Cemetery, died: 20 Mar 1915, record (1915): 262.

Infant BATT (?), male, parents: D.A. BATT and Mollie BUCKLES, death cause: "premature", died at Piney Flats on 28 Mar 1915, record (1915): 263.

George W. CHILDRESS, born: 1 Jan 1841, married, parents: George W. CHILDRESS and Feona HARGIS, death cause: "chronic nephritis", informant: James GIBSON (Kingsport), buried: Pyle Cemetery, died: 5 Mar 1915, record (1915): 264.

Naoh B. DICKSON, born: 27 Mar 1860, married, parents: William B. DICKSON and Sarah A. BROWN, death cause: "broncho pneumonia", informant: R.F. CHILDRESS (Indian Springs), buried: Pyle Cemetery, died: 10 Mar 1915, record (1915): 265.

Mildred MOSELY, parents: A.W. MOSELY (NC) and Adiline HALE (Clinchport, VA), death cause: "cyanosis", informant: J.W. OVERHOLSER (Kingsport), buried: Muddy Creek Cemetery, died: 10 Mar 1915, record (1915): 266.

John K. SHIPLEY, born: 22 Jun 1836 in Washington Co., TN., teacher, married, parents: Asa SHIPLEY and Rosa SHIPLEY, death cause: "double lobar pneumonia", informant: Mrs. J.K. SHIPLEY (Indian Springs), buried: Muddy Creek Cemetery, died: 13 Mar 1915, record (1915): 268.

Levi BEECHBOARD, born: 16 Mar 1852, widower, parents: William BEECHBOARD and Jane JONES, death cause: "organic heart disease", informant: J.D. HICKMAN (Bloomingdale), buried: Reedy Creek, died: 22 Mar 1915, record (1915): 269.

James B. LEEDY, born: 29 Apr 1849, married, parents: Samuel LEEDY and Mary HARGASS, death cause: "la grippe", buried: Pyle Cemetery, died: 29 Mar 1915, record (1915): 270.

Thomas ODELL, age 13 years, parents: William ODELL and Lydia SHIPLEY, death cause: "injuries received in accident", informant: father (Emmett), buried: Shipley Cemetery, died: 1 Mar 1915, record (1915): 271.

Jacob Edward ARNOLD, born: 6 Jun 1866 in Virginia, married, parents: Jaines ARNOLD (NC) and Sarah ARNOLD (NC), death cause: "aortic incom.. (illegible), informant: W.J. ARNOLD (Bristol), buried: Abingdon, VA., died: 6 Mar 1915, record (1918): 272.

E. BURTON, age 66 years, born in Pulaski Co. VA., single, parents: George W. BURTON (NC) and Mary MANUEL (NC), death cause: "organic heart disease", informant: J.P. BURTON (Bristol), buried: Paperville, died: 16 Mar 1915, record (1918): 273.

James C. ROGERS, born: 18 Dec 1853 in Virginia, widower, parents: Robert ROGERS (VA) and Melvina DOBBS (VA), death cause: "carcinoma of stomach and liver", informant: R.D. ROGERS (Bristol), buried: Crumley Cemetery, died: 18 Mar 1915, record (1918): 274.

Emma L. JARRET, Negro, age 23 years, 4 months and 9 days, single, parents: Sanday JARRET (NC) and Caroline COX, death cause: illegible, informant: Caroline COX (Bristol), buried: Citizens Cemetery, died: 18 Mar 1915, record (1918): 275.

Infant DIRAL, Negro, male, parents: Walter DIRAL and Emma HOLT, death cause: "still born", informant: Will HOLT (Bristol, VA), died: 25 Mar 1915, record (1918): 277.

R. Fulton DIXON, Negro, born: 16 mar 1848 in Virginia, single, parents: Reubin DIXON (VA) and mother unknown, death cause: "nephritis", informant: Lizzie THOMPSON, (Bristol), buried: Citizen Cemetery, died: 19 Mar 1915, record (1918): 276.

Lydia Henderson SMITH, born: 10 Mar 1892, married, parents: J.P. HENLEY (W. VA) and Mattie WOLFORD, death cause: "tuberculosis", informant: J.P. HENLEY (Bristol), buried: Blountville, died: 27 Mar 1915, record (1918): 278.

Robert Houston DEFREESE, born: 24 Aug 1849 in Emory, VA,. married, parents: E.Q. DEFREESE (Grayson Co., VA) and Mary VERNON (NC), death cause: "tuberculosis", informant: Jennie DEFREESE (Bristol), buried: E. Hill Cemetery, died: 1 Mar 1915, record (1918): 279.

James C. HENRY, born: 2 Dec 1860, widower, parents: William HENRY and Sarah STONE, death cause: "intestinal nephritis", died at Bluff City on 28 Apr 1915, record (1918): 280.

Isaac A. KENE (?), born: 27 Oct 1828 in Virginia, married, parents: Abraham A. KENE (VA) and Mary PEARLER, death cause: "broncho pneumonia", informant: J.E. RAMEY (Kingsport), died: 1 Apr 1915, record (1918): 281.

Polly Jane HUDSON, born: 21 Mar 1914, parents: Charles R. HUDSON and Polly MYERS, death cause: "broncho pneumonia", informant: Clive PARKER (Kingsport), buried: Liberty, died: 1 Apr 1915, record (1918): 282.

Elbert Alexander GOTT, born: 22 Jun 1846, single, parents: Rolen Perry GOTT and Rachel CHILDRESS, death cause: "chronic intestinal nephritis", informant: C.E. GOTT (Fordtown), buried: Lebanon, died: 2 Apr 1915, record (1918): 283.

William M. LUNONS (?), born: 29 Mar 1871, single, parents: Will LUNONS and Mary SHOEMAKER (VA), death cause: "accidental burn", buried: Emory Cemetery, died: 6 Apr 1915, record (1918): 284.

John BARNES, born: 2 Jan 1838 in Sullivan County, married, parents: William BARNES and Rebecca CROSS, death cause: "carcinoma of face", informant: David BARNES (Indian Springs), buried: Emory, died: 13 Apr 1915, record (1918): 285.

Margaret OVERBAY, born: 17 Sep 1847, widow, parents: James BARE and Besty BARE, death cause: "la grippe", informant: Ed BARE (Kingsport), buried: Martin's Cemetery, died: 17 Apr 1915, record (1918): 286.

Lucinda PERKINS, age 39 years, married, parents: not known (note child's record, below, indicates she was an Akers), death cause: "aortic regurgitation", informant: George PERKINS (Kingsport), buried: Martin's Cemetery, died: 18 Apr 1915, record (1918): 287. (child's record below)

George W. MOODY, born: 18 Sep 1869, married, parents: William H. MOODY and Carrie A. LOYD (VA), death cause: "tuberculosis of lungs", informant: W.H. MOODY (Indian Springs), buried: Emory Cemetery, died: 21 Apr 1915, record (1918): 288.

Lucinda PERKINS, born: 1 Mar 1915, parents: George PERKINS and Lucinda AKERS, death cause: not stated, informant: George PERKINS (Kingsport), buried: Martin Cemetery, died: 30 Apr 1915, record (1918): 289.

Mrs. Eliza Jane PRICE, age about 35 years, born in North Carolina, married, parents: Benjamin ROBERTS (NC) and Eliza ROBERTS (NC) death cause: "..(illegible) poison", informant: James PRICE (W. VA), buried: Bernard, NC., died: 8 Apr 1915, record (1915): 290.

Nannie PATTON, Negro, age about 65 years, born in South Carolina, married, parents: Sam Miller, and mother not stated, death cause: "paralysis due to apoplexy", informant: Barton PATTON (Bristol), buried: Citizen Cemetery, died: 9 Apr 1915, record (1915): 291.

Henry M. MONROE, born: 13 Apr, age 26 years, 11 months and 29 days, born in Hawkins Co., married, parents: W.H. MONROE (Hawkins Co,) and Matilda BELAMY (VA), death cause: "appendicitis", informant: father (Clinchport, VA) buried: Clinchport, VA., died: 12 Apr 1915, record (1915): 292.

Robert MORTON, age 21 years, single, parents: A.O. MORTON and Delia BOUTON, death cause: "pulmonary tuberculosis", informant: J.M. MORTON (Bluff City), buried: Shipley Cemetery, died: 17 Apr 1915, record (1915): 293.

Infant HENEGER, male, parents: J.F. HENEGER Jr., and Pink E. PHIPPS, death cause: "premature", informant: father (Bristol), buried: Paperville, born/died: 17 Apr 1915, record (1915): 294.

Mrs. Martha HORTON, age 70 years, born in North Carolina, widow, parents: ___ BULLOCK (NC) and mother not stated, death cause: "parisis", informant: J.W. COOK (Bristol), died: 20 Apr 1915, record (1915): 295.

Andrew MURRY, Negro, age about 62 years, widower, parents: David EMERSON and mother not stated, death cause: "pellagra", informant: Walter MURRY (Bristol), buried: Citizen Cemetery, died: 12 Apr 1915, record (1915): 296.

W.H. HARRISON, born: 2 Jul 1843 in LaFollette, TN., married, parents: Nathaniel HARRISON and Hanna FORD (Washington Co., TN), death cause: "nephritis", informant: Mrs. W.H. HARRISON (Bristol), buried: Beeler Cemetery, died: 24 Apr 1915, record (1915): 297.

Howard Earl RANGE, parents: W.T. RANGE and Viola PRITCHETT, death cause: "premature birth", informant:

father (Bristol), buried: Johnson City, born/died: 25 Apr 1915, record (1915): 298.
Infant DANCEY, male, parents: Charles DANCEY (NC) and Florrie HUDGENS (NC), death cause: "still born", informant: father (Bristol), buried: Bristol, VA., born/died: 27 Apr 1915, record (1915): 299.
James S. MOORE, born: 15 Apr 1838, widower, parents: James MOORE and Lucy SPROLES, death cause: "Brights disease", informant: Mrs. M.L. HUNT (Bristol), died: 27 Apr 1915, record (1915): 300.
Martha Ellen MILAN, born: 20 Jun 1914 in Kentucky, parents: James MILAN (NC) and Suviller ROSE (VA), death cause: "pneumonia", informant: father (Bristol), buried: East Hill, died: 28 Apr 1915, record (1915): 301.
Jerome CONKIN, born: 15 Jan 1914, parents: Daniel CONKIN and Mary Jane CRAWFORD, death cause: "cerebral abscess", informant: E.P. MORGAN (Fall Branch), died: 4 Apr 1915, record (1915): 302.
Henry BLAKELEY, age 68 years, widower, parents: William BLAKELEY and Polly WHITAKER, death cause: "mitral Insufficiency, tuberculosis", informant: Jackson BLAKELY (Fordtown), buried: Depew Chapel, died: 5 Apr 1915, record (1915): 303.
Ellen Beard LONG, black, age 38 years, born in Hawkins Co., married, parents: George BEARD (VA) and Canzadia MANUEL (Hawkins Co) death cause: "mitral insufficiency", informant: James LONG (Fall Branch), buried: M.E. Church, died: 9 Apr 1915, record (1915): 304.
Rachel PHILIPPS, born: 30 Aug 1858, married, parents: Thomas BRAGG and Rachel BOWSER, death cause: "tuberculosis of muscles of legs followed by tuberculosis of lungs", informant: W.E. PHILLIPS (Fall Branch), buried: Walkers Ford Cemetery, died: 9 Apr 1915, record (1915): 305.
Mary Cleo CRAWFORD, born: 25 Apr 1915, parents: Nathan M. CRAWFORD and Charina CONKIN, death cause: "premature birth", informant: father (Fall Brancy), buried: Depew Chapel, died: 26 Apr 1915, record (1915): 306.
Mrs. Elizabeth BELL, born: 9 Apr 1832, widow, parents: Roland P. CHASE and Catherine BOWSER, death cause: "mitral insufficiency", informant: Roland P. BELL (Fordtown), buried: Rock Springs Church, died: 19 Apr 1915, record (1915): 307.
James P. H. STIDMAN, born: 21 Nov 1839, widower, parents: John STIDMAN and Milvina BURK, death cause:

"broncho pneumonia", informant: George STIDMAN (Fall Branch), buried: Depew Chapel, died: 23 Apr 1915, record (1915): 308.

Linda Alice LUCAS, born: 1 Apr 1896, married, parents: Perry W. POE and Elizabeth HENRY, death cause: "tuberculosis pulmonary", informant: Allie LUCA (Fall Branch), buried: Ball Cemetery, 6th District, died: 3 Apr 1915, record (1915): 309.

Samuel Oscar NEAL, born: 13 Apr 1915, parents; Bee NEAL and Sallie NEAL, death cause: "not known", buried: Muddy Creek, died: 28 May 1915, record (1915): 310.

Norah Pearl FLEENOR, born: 10 Jan 1888, married, parents: J.H. PETTYJOHN (VA) and T.S. ERWIN, death cause: "chronic gastritis", informant: Jacob BARGER (Indian Springs), died: 13 May 1915, record (1915): 311.

Charles HORNE, parents: Simon HORNE and Bertha V. CHILDRESS, death cause: "still born", informant: R.F. CHILDRESS (Indian Springs), buried: Emory, born/died: 15 May 1915, record (1915): 312.

Infant PENIX, male, parents: Preston PENIX and Ethel FRY, death cause: "heart lesion", born/died at Piney Flats on 31 May 1915, record (1915): 313.

Infant CRAWFORD, female, parents: Will CRAWFORD and Tobitha WRIGHT, death cause: "still born", informant: father (Kingsport), buried: Martins Cemetery, died: 7 May 1915, record (1915): 314.

Julius WILSON, black, age: "unknown", born in North Carolina, married, parents: Sam WILSON and mother unknown, death cause: "murdered", informant: Thad WILSON (Kingsport), buried: Martins Cemetery, died: 7 May 1915, record (1915): 315.

Mary WILSON, black, age: "unknown", married, parents: "unknown", death cause: "murdered", informant: Thad WILSON (Kingsport), buried: Martin Cemetery, died: 7 May 1915, record (1915): 316.

Frank ARMSTRONG, black, age: "not known", single, parents: Milt ARMSTRONG and Mary LYONS, death cause: "murdered", informant: Rick ARMSTRONG (Kingsport), buried: Stoney Poing Cemetery, died: 26 May 1915, record (1915): 317.

Noah GALLOWAY, born: 20 Oct 1837, widower, parents: William GALLOWAY and Milly CRUDGINGTON, death cause: "intestinal tuberculosis", informant: S.R. GALLOWAY (Fordtown), buried: Galloway Cemetery, died: 6 May 1915, record (1915): 318.

Elizabeth POORE, born: 15 May 1845, married, parents: David CONKIN and Ruth HALL (Washington Co., TN), death cause: "sudden death, cause unknown", informant: W.M. BACHMAN (Fall Branch), buried: Bowser Cemetery, died: 7 May 1915, record (1915): 319.

Infant COX, male, parents: Grover Cleveland COX and Ida May (surname illegible) (Jefferson Co.), death cause: "cleft palate and double hairlip", informant: father (Jonesboro), buried: Double Springs Church, 14th District, born/died: 17 May 1915, record (1915): 320.

Martha SHIPLEY, born: 29 Oct 1855, married, parents: Thomas DYKES (Hawkins Co.) and Katie LAWSON (Hawkins Co.), death cause: "fibroid tumor of uterus", informant: Diman SHIPLEY (Church Hill), buried: Dykes Cemetery, 6th District, died: 30 May 1915, record (1915): 321.

Infant REED, male, parents: Hardy REED (NC) and Ehtel ADAMS (NC), death cause: "still born", born/died at Bluff City on 5 May 1915, record (1915): 322.

Infant JONES, male, parents: W.T. JONES and Emma ROSENBAUM, death cause: "still born", informant: father (Briston), buried: E. Hill, born/died: 5 May 1915, record (1915): 323.

David B. LILLEY, born: 22 Sep 1865, parents: A.J. LILLEY and Rachel WEBB, death cause: "suicide from drinking chloroform", informant: Mrs. David LILLEY (Bristol), buried: Gunnings, died: 11 May 1915, record (1915): 324.

Mrs. Mary Carter STARNES, born: 17 Dec 1853 in Virginia, married, parents: M.L. CARTER (VA) and Pollie CARTER (VA), death cause: "paralysis", informant: J.S. STARNES (Bristol, VA), buried: East Hill, died: 23 May 1915, record (1915): 325.

Mrs. Vesta BRYANT, born: 1 May 1891 in Mitchell Co., NC., parents; T.J. BRYANT (NC) and Eliza O..(illegible), death cause: "tuberculosis", informant: R.L. BRYANT (Bristol), buried: Susong Cemetery, died: 29 May 1915, record (1915): 326.

Infant MCCANEY, male, parents: Sam MCCANEY and Sallie GROSS, death cause: "not known", buried: New Bethel Cemetery, Piney Flats, born/died: 10 May 1915, record (1915): 327.

J.W. HICKS, age 43 years, 5 months and 10 days, parents: John HICKS (VA) and Jane WEAVER (VA), death cause: "typhoid fever", informant: J.L. CAMPBELL (Bluff City), buried: Cedar Grove, died: 15 Jun 1915, record (1915): 328.

Mrs. S. HENSON, age 57 years, widow, parents: Jake C..(illegible) and __ MILLER, death cause: "heart trouble", died at Bluff City on 7 Jun 1915, record (1915): 329.

__ MILLER, male, age 28 years, single, parents: Alvin MILLER and Lizzie RICHARDS, death cause: "thrown from a horse, concussion brain", died at Bluff City on (day not stated) Jun 1915, record (1915): 330.

David C. EADS, born: 20 Mar 1841, widower, parents: David EADS (VA) and Susan GEISLER, death cause: "dilitation of heart", buried: Bluff City, died: 1 Jun 1915, record (1915): 331.

Miss Corda KING, born: 10 Jun 1874, single, parents: Rutledge KING and Ellie GROSS, death cause: "intestinal nephritis", buried: New Bethel Cemetery, Piney Flats, died: 15 Jun 1915, record (1915): 332.

Zachariah CRAWFORD, born: 20 Aug 1854, married, parents: Edward CRAWFORD and Berbitha CRAWFORD, death cause: "supposed heart failure", informant: G.R. CRAWFORD (Fall Branch), died: 16 Jun 1915, record (1915): 333.

Mollie Pearl MELLON, born: 28 Apr 1915 in Virginia, parents: Horace MELLON and Bettie CARTER (VA), death cause: "cholera", informant: S.P. DEVALUT (Kingsport), buried: Cloud Cemetery, died: 20 Jun 1915, record (1915): 334.

Don HONK, born: 9 Sep 1898, single, parents: father not stated and Barbra HONK (VA), death cause: "accidentally killed by a mule", informant: J.C. NEAL (Kingsport), buried: Pyle Cemetery, died: 9 Jun 1915, record (1915): 335.

Joseph Preston CANOY, born: 31 (?) Nov 1914, parents: R.A. CANOY (VA) and Bessie MOREFIELD, death cause: "cholera", informant: Dan DALTON (Kingsport), buried: Mortin Cemetery, died: 28 Jun 1915, record (1915): 336.

Willie Beatrice MOATS, born: 21 Apr 1915, parents: Thomas B. MOATS (GA) and Ada TRIMBLE (VA), death cause: "meningitis", informant: William TRIMBLE (Kingsport), buried: Martins Cemetery, died: 26 Jun 1915, record (1915): 337.

Mary KYLE, born: 6 Dec 1914, parents: David W. KYLE and Viola HART, death cause: "meningitis", informant: Robert KYLE (Kingsport), buried: Morrison Chapel, died: 10 Jun 1915, record (1915): 338.

John BUELER, age 62 years, 7 months and 3 days, married, parents: Andy BUELER and Mary DAVIS (VA), death cause: "tuberculosis of lungs", buried: Bueler Cemetery, died: 7 Jun 1915, record (1915): 339.

Wade K. KENNEY, born: 27 Mar 1902 in Alabama, parents: Samuel Bruce KENNEY and Ellen R. SNAPP, death cause: "acute leukemia", informant: Dr. SNAPP (Blountville), died: 9 Jun 1915, record (1915): 340.

Jullie MCCANEY, born: 1 Dec 1880, married, parents: David GROSS and mother not stated, death cause: "septic peroninits", buried: New Bethel Cemetery, Piney Flats, died: 5 Jun 1915, record (1915): 341.

Infant PRITCHETT, male, parents: James Henry PRITCHETT (Washington Co., VA) and Virginia Delware MILLIOM, death cause: "premature", buried: Muddy Creek, 20th District, born/died: 16 Jun 1915, record (1915): 342.

Infant PRITCHETT, female, born: 16 Jan 1915, parents: James Henry PRITCHETT (Washington Co., VA) and Virginia Delware MILLIOM, death cause: "premature", buried: Muddy Creek, 20th District, died: 17 Jun 1915, record (1915): 343.

Sarah CASH, age 58 years, born in Grayson Co., VA., widow, parents: Billie ANDERSON (Grayson Co.) and mother not stated, death cause: "tuberculosis", informant: Dr. GRAVES (Piney Flats, buried: Sander Cemetery, died: 3 Jun 1915, record (1915): 344.

Nancy COLE, age 85 years, widow, parents: not stated, death cause: "nephritis", buried: Piney Flats, died: 20 Jun 1915, record (1915): 345.

Glen MARTIN, born: 14 Apr, age 23 years, 2 months and 13 days, married, parents: U.G. MARTIN and Ira DAVIS, death cause: "intestinal obstruction", informant: father (Church Hill), buried: Mt Carmel Cemetery, died: 27 Jun 1915, record (1915): 346.

Mrs. Minnie E. HALL, born: 15 Nov 1859 in Indiana, married, parents: J.W. SHULTZ (Indiana) and mother not stated, death cause: "chronic diarrhoea", informant: S.L. ODELL, (Bristol), buried: East Hill, died: 27 Jun 1915, record (1915): 347.

Hester JORDAN, Negro, born: 17 Feb 1885 in Virginia, married, parents: Samuel GALLOWAY (NC) and Cornelia SMITH (VA), death cause: "pulmonary tuberculosis", informant: Lemon GALLOWAY (Bristol), buried: Jefferson Watt Cemetery, died: 26 Jun 1915, record (1915): 348.

Florence FIELDS, born: 9 Jan 1914 in Virginia, parents: Silas FIELDS (VA) and Mollie BEAVER, death cause: "worm fever", informant: J.W. SMITH (Bristol), buried: East Hill, died: 22 Jun 1915, record (1915): 349.

Frank DICKERSON, Negro, born: 2 Feb 1857 in Virginia, parents: Jessie DICKERSON (VA) and Martha GAINES (VA), death cause: "apoplexy", informant: Walter DICKERSON (Bristol), buried: Kingsport, died: 12 Jun 1915, record (1915): 350.

William Frederick CLARK, born: 5 Oct 1888, married, parents: James CLARK (VA) and Mary E. CROSS, death cause: "pulmonary tuberculosis", informant: Ada PEOPLES (Bristol, VA), buried: Snodgrass Cemetery, died: 10 Jun 1915, record (1915): 351.

William Augustus MASSEY, born: 1 Jan 1844 in Virginia, married, parents: Henderson MASSEY (VA) and Anne MOORE (VA), death cause: "arterio sclerosis", informant: W.E. MASSEY (VA), buried: Clear Branch, VA., died: 8 Jun 1915, record (1915): 352.

Chester CARR, born: Sep 3, age 32 years, 2 months and 8 days, single, parents: Robert CARR and mother not stated, death cause: "drowned", buried: Piney Flats, died: 26 Jun 1915, record (1915): 353.

Virginia COX, born: 2 Oct 1851, widow, parents: James P. WORLEY (VA) and (illegible) SHELL, death cause: "carcinoma liver", buried: Bluff City, died: 3 Jun 1915, record (1915): 354.

Abraham MCCLELLERN, born: Aug 1837 in Virginia, married, parents: John MCCLELLERN (VA) and mother not stated, death cause: "chronic nephritis", buried: Bluff City, died: 20 Jun 1915, record (1915): 355.

Infant SAMS, male, parents: Roof SAMS and Carrie RICHARD, death cause: "still born", died in the 16th District on 16 Jun 1915, record (1915): 356.

Thomas Jefferson DILLOW, born: 8 Aug 1841, married, parents: Peter DILLOW and Parmelia HUNT, death cause: "chronic gastro intestinal catarrh", informant: C.R. BELL (Fordtown), buried: 14th District, died: 7 Jun 1915, record (1915): 357.

David DOLEN, born: 7 Jun 1846, married, parents: Nelson DOLEN and Peggy PAXTON (NC), death cause: "concussion of brain", informant: Ed DOLEN (Fall Branch), buried: Depew Capel, died: 8 Jun 1915, record (1915): 358.

Lillie May TODD, born: 27 Apr 1913, parents: G.F. TODD (NC) and Debora CAMPBELL, death cause: "cerebral meningitis", informant: father (Fordtown), buried: Pactolus Church Cemetery, died: 16 Jun 1915, record (1915): 359.

Mabel Anne LIGHT, born: 8 Jun 1915, parents: George Washington LIGHT and Mary Bessie MOWDY, death cause:

"premature birth", informant: father (Fordtown), died: 9 Jun 1915, record (1915): 360.

Mrs. Lou BERRY, born: 17 Jun 1837 in Washington Co., VA., widow, parents: Jessee HANSHAW (VA) and mother not stated, death cause: "Brights disease", informant: Dr. GRAVES (Piney Flats), buried: New Bethel, died: 17 Jun 1915, record (1915): 361.

Mrs. Susan WEBB, age 60 years, married, parents: not stated, death cause: "carcinoma stomach", died in the 4th District (day not stated) Jul 1915, record (1915): 362.

Mrs. Mattie HICKS, age 54 years, married, parents: Jake CROSS and mother not stated, death cause: "cancer liver", buried: Bluff City, died: 10 Jul 1915, record (1915): 363.

John HENSON, age 30 years, born in North Carolina, parents: Joe HENSON (NC) and Mat LUNCEFORD (NC), death cause: "appendicitis", died in the 3rd District on 26 Jul 1915, record (1915): 364.

John Dulford BEELER, born: 30 Aug 1864, married, parents: Looney BEELER and Gernina PHIPPS, death cause: illegible, informant: T.C. KING (Bristol), buried: Beeler Cemetery, died: 2 Jul 1915, record (1915): 365.

Infant MCKINNEY, male, parents: Nat MCKINNEY and Maud JENKINS, death cause: "still born", informant: Dr. RHEA (Emmett), buried: Crumley Cemetery, died: 13 Jul 1915, record (1915): 366.

Droke HENLEY, age 62 years, married, parents: not stated, death cause: "chronic nephritis", buried: Bluff City, died: 16 Jul 1915, record (1915): 367.

Robert Charles TRIBBLE, born: 7 Jul 1915, parents: John TRIBBLE and Zina LAWSON, death cause: "malnutrition", informant: R.F. CHILDRESS (Indian Springs), buried: Pyle Cemetery, died: 31 Jul 1915, record (1915): 368.

Infant HOLTON, male, parents: J.T. HOLTON and Bertha SMITH, death cause: "still born", died at Piney Flats on 20 Jul 1915, record (1915): 369.

Albert OLINGER, born: 8 May 1915, parents: Isaac OLINGER (VA) and Lilly WILCOX (VA), death cause: "cholera", informant: R.E. NELSON (Kingsport), died: 8 Jul 1915, record (1915): 370.

William CRAWFORD, born: 7 May 1915, parents: William CRAWFORD and Tibitha WRIGHT, death cause: "cholera", informant: Jordan LILLARD (Kingsport), buried: Martin Cemetery, died: 12 Jul 1915, record (1915): 371.

Naoma ALLEN, born: 5 Jul 1915, parents: James Fernanda ALLEN (VA) and Josie Roberts BIRDWELL, death cause: "icterus neonatorium", informant: father (Kingsport), died: 8 Jul 1915, record (1915): 372.

Hellen M. NELMS, born: 6 Dec 1848, married, parents: Aron HOFFMAN and Mary RICHARDSON, death cause: "typhoid fever", informant: Bruce NELMS (Kingsport), died: 17 Jul 1915, record (1915): 373.

Nancy LIGHT, born: 21 Jul 1854, married, parents: Rev. Dutton HOOD (Green Co.) and Sarah STEADMAN, death cause: "acute dysentery", informant: A.G. LIGHT (Fordtown), buried: Depew Chapel, died: 20 Jul 1915, record (1915): 374.

James Buchanan SPEERS, born: 21 Apr 1851, married, parents: John D. SPEERS (Scott Co., VA) and Margaret ALLEN, death cause: "alveolar sarcoma", informant: Cora M. SPEERS (Fall Branch), buried: family cemetery, died: 9 Jul 1915, record (1915): 375.

George W. BRAGG, born: 19 Apr 1837, married, parents: Thomas BRAGG (VA) and Patsy MORRELL (VA), death cause: "chronic heart disease", informant; John LARKINS (Fall Branch), buried: family cemetery, died: 27 Jul 1915, record (1915): 376.

Infant FINK, female, born: 11 Jul 1915, parents: Thomas Bruce FINK and Matilda MORELOCK (Hawkins Co.), death cause: "cleff palate and harelip", informant: W.E. FINK (Fall Branch), died: 27 Jul 1915, record (1915): 377.

Clarence BULLOCK, born: 28 Mar 1915, parents: John BULLOCK and Minie PERRY, death cause: "cholera", died at Bluff City on 27 Jul 1915, record (1915): 378.

Infant JENNINGS, Negro, born: 19 Jul 1915, parents: E.L. JENNINGS (VA) and Emma MERRILL (Ala), death cause: "intestinal obstruction", informant: father (Bristol), buried: Tennessee Cemetery, died: 1 Jul 1915, record (1915): 379.

Charles FELTY, age about 75 years, born in Virginia, widower, parents: not stated, death cause: "heart lesion", informant: G.R. GOODMAN (Bristol), buried: Walnut Grove, died: 5 Jul 1915, record (1915): 380.

Landon ALFORD, age about 60 years, married, parents: not stated, death cause: "Brights and rheumatism", informant: A.F. RAY (Bristol), died: 13 Jul 1915, record (1915): 381.

Infant STARBUCK, female, parents: W.I. STARBUCK and Lizzie MELTZER, death cause: "still born", informant: father (Bristol), buried: East Hill, died: 20 Jul 1915, record (1915): 382.

Mrs. Mary J. ALLSTADT, age 66 years, born in Lexington, VA., widow, parents: William F. KENDOFF (Brooklyn, NY) and Martha E. SMITH (Russellville, KY), death cause: "intestinal nephritis", informant: L. CHAPIN (Bristol), buried: Cincinnati, Ohio, died: 24 Jul 1915, record (1915): 383.
Thomas W. HALL, age 83 years, born in Ohio, U.S. Veteran Soldier, widower, parents: not stated, death cause: "chronic diarrhoea", buried: Bristol, died: 27 Jul 1915, record (1915): 384.
Mrs. Mary J. EPPERSON, age about 83 years, born in Virginia, widow, parents: Joseph STEWARD (VA) and mother not stated, death cause: "old age", informant: Joseph CROWELL (Bristol), died: 29 Jul 1915, record (1915): 385.
Mrs. Mary Holden SHEEN, born: 20 Aug 1839 in Vermont, parents: John HOLDEN (Mass) and Submit D. RICE (Mass), death cause: "uremic poisoning", informant: Will W. SHEEN (Bristol), buried: East Hill, died: 30 Jul 1915, record (1915): 386.
R.R. EARHART, age 47 years, married, parents: J.T. EARHART (VA) and M.P. RHEA, death cause: "suicide by cutting throat", informant; Joseph EARHART (Bristol), buried: Blountville, died: 31 Jul 1915, record (1915): 387.
Samuel LANE, born: 24 May 1881, married, parents: Buck LANE and Elizabeth WEAVER, death cause: "nephritis", informant: William LANE (Fordtown), buried: Gunning Cemetery, died: 17 Jul 1915, record (1915): 388.
Lilburn RHYSTON, age 30 years, 6 months and 3 days, married, parents: John RHYSTON (Johnson Co.) and Nancy FOSTER (VA), death cause: "killed by a falling tree", buried: Bluff City, died: 4 Jul 1915, record (1915): 389.
William R. GOOD, born: 17 Aug 1889 in Scott Co., VA., married, parents: H.P. GOOD (VA) and Mary Jaye MATHERLY, death cause: "toxemia from intestinal parasites", informant: Lola E. GOOD (Fordtown), died: 24 Aug 1915, record (1915): 390.
John W. BATES, born: 25 May 1888 in Washington Co., TN., married, parents: Robert BATES and Ann B. CHILDRESS, death cause: "catarrh of stomach and bowels", informant: James C. BATES (Elizabethton), buried: Morning View Cemetery, died: 31 Aug 1915, record (1915): 391.
Robert Worley SHANKLE, born: 24 Mar 1915, parents: Lafayette SHANKLE (VA) and Laura C. DEFREECE (VA), death cause: "gastritis", informant: R.T. CHILDRESS

(Indian Springs), buried: Gunnings Cemetery, died: 10 Aug 1915, record (1915): 392.

Elizabeth HORNE, age 73 years, widow, parents: Adam BOWERY and mother unknown, death cause: "intestinal tuberculosis", informant: A.P. HORNE (Fordtown), buried: Pactolus Church, died: 9 Aug 1915, record (1915): 393.

William M. SPROLES, born: 5 Dec 1841 in Washington Co., VA., married, parents: Johnathon SPROLES (Washington Co., VA) and Jennie SMITH (Washington Co., VA), death cause: "cerebral hemorrhage", informant: Lizzie SPROLES (Fordtown), buried: Rock Spring Cemetery, died: 9 Aug 1915, record (1915): 394.

Sarah Jane DEPEW, age 70 years, born in Green Co., married, parents: William BLAKELY and Polly WHITAKER (Green Co.), death cause: "chronic muscular (illegible)", informant: George DEPEW (Fall Branch), buried: Depew Chapel, died: 15 Aug 1915, record (1915): 395.

Addie Maxie CHASE, born: 13 Aug 1915, parents: Walter Finley CHASE and Monic Lucinda COX (Green Co.), death cause: "unknown", informant: father (Fordtown), buried: Double Springs Cemetery, died: 29 Aug 1915, record (1915): 396.

John Byrd ROBERTSON, born: 6 Feb 1865 in Bedford Co., VA., married, parents: Byrd Allen ROBERTSON (VA) and Catherine LEONARD (Batetourt Co., VA), death cause: "septicemia from a nail puncture of foot", informant: Miss Fannie ROBERTSON (Fordtown), buried: Fordtown Church Cemetery, died: 30 Aug 1915, record (1915): 397.

Lottie SHELTON, born: 6 Jun 1914, parents: J.H. SHELTON and Carrie STOUT (VA), death cause: "summer diarrhoea", informant: father (Bristol), buried: Ordway Cemetery, died: 1 Aug 1915, record (1915): 398.

M.B. MORELY, age 35 years, born in Virginia, married, parents: E.W. MORELY (VA) and Sarah HARMON, death cause: "anemia", informant: E.L. MORELY (Bristol, VA), buried: Norton, VA., died: 4 Aug 1915, record (1915): 399.

Noah DOWELL, age 34 years, married, parents: Thomas DOWELL and Jennie PATTON, death cause: "hung himself on 10 August 1915", informant: Mrs. Sarah DOWELL (Fish Dam), buried: Bristol, record (1915): 400.

Clarence MAXWELL, colored, born: 17 Sep 1899, parents: Jake MAXWELL (NC) and Bertie WIDLY (NC), death cause: "struck by train, fractured skull", died at Bristol on 11 Aug 1915, record (1915): 401.

E.S. GODSEY, age: about 60 years, widower, parents: not stated, death cause: "apoplexy", informant: E.S. GODSEY (Bristol), buried: East Hill, died: 11 Aug 1915, record (1915): 402.

David SENEKER, age about 47 years, born in Missouri, married, parents: Thomas SENEKER (VA) and Eleanora STAUBUR (VA), death cause: "cancer, informant: Miss Eleanora SENEKER, buried: East Hill, died: 12 Aug 1915, record (1915): 403.

Thomas DICKISON, age about 55 years, born in Virginia, single, parents: not stated, death cause: "Brights disease", informant: C.F. HAGAN (Bristol), buried: Virginia, died: 14 Aug 1915, record (1915): 404.

Benjamin Shipley QUAILES, born: 2 Jul 1842, married, parents: John QUAILES (VA) and Sallie NEWMAN (VA), death cause: "paralysis", informant: R.M. QUAILES (Bristol), buried: East Hill, died: 20 Aug 1915, record (1915): 405.

J.B. CHILDERS, born: 16 Feb in Roanoke, VA., age 70 years, parents: Jonah CHILDERS (VA) and mother not stated, death cause: "intestinal nephritis", informant: William J. CHILDERS (Bristol), buried: East Hill, died: 21 Aug 1915, record (1915): 406.

William G. LOVE, age 40 years, married, parents: Alfred LOVE and mother not stated, death cause: "paralysis", informant: Mrs. W.G. LOVE (Bristol), buried: East Hill, died: 24 Aug 1915, record (1915): 407.

Edward BOY, age 26 years, married, parents: Jacob BOY and Victoria MORRELL, death cause: "typhoid fever", informant: J.L. JONES (Bristol), buried: Beelers Cemetery, died: 24 Aug 1915, record (1915): 408.

Frank COLDWELL, age 32 years, single, parents: H.C. COLDWELL and Sallie TARVER (GA), death cause: "gastritis", informant: J.H. COLDWELL (Bristol), died: 29 Aug 1915, record (1915): 409.

Infant WOOD, male, parents: R.L. WOOD and Nannie GOTT, death cause: not stated, informant: father (Bristol), buried: Lebanon, TN., born/died: 29 Aug 1915, record (1915): 410.

Infant MILLER, male, parents: Godfrey MILLER and Mary ROMINGER (NC), death cause: "still born", informant: Dr. RHEA (Emmett), buried: Stoffle Cemetery, born/died: 10 Aug 1915, record (1915): 411.

Andrew H. BOYD, born: 4 Sep 1845, married, parents: John BOYD and Annie MCGARRY, death cause: "disease of heart", informant: J.L. Campbell (Bluff City), buried:

Shipley Cemetery, died: 5 Aug 1915, record (1915): 412.

Infant WEBB, female, parents: Carl WEBB and Veby WOODS, death cause: "still born", buried: Woods Cemetery, Bluff City, born/died: 3 Aug 1915, record (1915): 413.

Caroline PAINTER, age 73 years, widow, parents: James PAINTER and Mary RAMSEY, death cause: "pneumonia", buried: Cool Springs Cemetery, died: 15 Sep 1915, record (1915): 414.

Eliza Jane KIDD, born: 15 Jan 1860, married, parents: William TATE and Mahalia SMITH, death cause: "carcinoma of uterus", informant: W.J. KIDD (Blountville), buried: Sunrise Cemetery, died: 13 Sep 1915, record (1915): 415.

Sarah Jane STIDMAN, born: 12 Jan 1858 in Wilks Co., VA (?, probably NC), married, parents: W.M. DURHAM (Wilkes Co., NC) and Ellen SHOEMAKER (Wilkes Co., NC), death cause: "angina pectoris", informant: Dr. GRAVES (Piney Flats), buried: Wheeler Cemetery, died: 25 Sep 1915, record (1915): 416.

Eunice BOWERS, born: 19 Aug 1915, parents: William Homer BOWERS (VA) and Viola Vesta PHILLIPS, death cause: "indigestion", informant: father (Bristol), buried: Avoca Cemetery, died: 24 Sep 1915, record (1915): 417.

Infant SOURBEER, male, parents: J.H. SOURBEER (VA) and Irene JETT (VA), death cause: "still born", informant: W.C. GODSEY (Bristol), buried: Jett Cemetery, VA., born/died: 1 Sep 1915, record (1915): 418.

Haynes Glaspey YOUNG, born: 14 Jul 1914, parents: S.J. YOUNG (VA) and Mattie L. RETTER (VA), death cause: "dysentery", informant: father (Bristol), buried: Susong Cemetery, died: 5 Sep 1915, record (1915): 419.

Louise ANDERSON, born: Jul 1915, parents: W.R. ANDERSON and Lydia SMITH, death cause: "tubercular meningitis", informant: father (Bristol), buried: Blountville, died: 9 Sep 1915, record (1915): 420.

Infant GIBSON, male, parents: Neal GIBSON, and Nora HOLLEY, death cause: "born dead", informant: father (Bristol), born/died: 17 Sep 1915, record (1915): 421.

Frank W. ROBINSON, Jr., born: 20 Jan 1907, parents: F.W. ROBINSON and Maud J. KING, death cause: "accidental gunshot", informant: father (Bristol), buried: Knoxville, died: 20 Sep 1915, record (1915): 422.

Mrs. Kate HAMMER, age 79 years and 6 months, widow, parents: Jacob SNAPP and Elenor HUGHES (VA), death

cause: "cancer of liver", informant: J.K. HAMMER (Bristol), died: 26 Sep 1915, record (1915): 423.
William PEAVLER, age 54 years, 7 months and 6 days, married, parents: William PEAVLER and mother not stated, death cause: "typhoid fever", informant: J.R. LADD (Kingsport), buried: Pyle Cemetery, died: 20 Sep 1915, record (1915): 424.
James CAMPBELL, born: 5 Feb 1852, married, parents: James CAMPBELL and mother not stated, death cause: "Brights disease", informant: George W. AKERS (Kingsport), died: 21 Sep 1915, record (1915): 425.
Caroline E. PAINTER, born: 13 Apr 1835, widow, parents: David O. KING and M.W. MCCHESSNEY (Washington Co., VA), death cause: "tuberculosis and cancer of breast", informant: Philip PAINTER (Emmett), buried: Cold Springs, died: 17 Sep 1915, record (1915): 426.
Infant SIMERLY, color (colored ?), male, parents: L.P. SIMERLY (Carter Co.) and Flora FEATHERS, informant: father (Emmett), buried: Weaver Cemetery, died: 26 Sep 1915, record (1915): 427.
Rhoda SMITH, born: 28 Feb 1864, married, parents: Thomas LYON and mother not stated, death cause: "carcinoma of uterus", buried: Chinquipin Grove Cemetery, Bluff City, died: 5 Sep 1915, record (1915): 428.
Quinten Vanburen JONES, born: 20 May 1908, parents: W.H. JONES and Anna CASH (Roane Co., TN), death cause: "croup", informant: Dr. GRAVES (Piney Flats), buried: New Bethel Cemetery, died: 19 Sep 1915, record (1915): 429.
Mary Lou COX, born: 16 Dec 1877, married, parents: Morris COX and Clara MITCHELL (Washington Co., TN), death cause: "anemia", informant: S.P. COX (Jonesboro), buried: Double Spring Cemetery, died: 12 Sep 1915, record (1915): 430.
Gladys Virginia KING, born: 7 Sep 1915, parents: Jacob Leander KING (Scott Co., VA) and Ella Jane PERRY (Scott Co), death cause: "inanition, hare lip and cleft palate", informant: W.A. PERRY (Snow Flake, VA), buried: Rock Spring Cemetery, died: 13 Sep 1915, record (1915): 431.
Jay Fred JONES, born: 11 Aug 1915, parents: Palmer Gialls JONES and Pixie Emma DOLEN, death cause: "acute indigestion", informant: father (Fordtown), buried: Pactolus Church, died: 19 Sep 1915, record: 432.
Mahaley Smith Tate FORD, born: 22 Jan 1839, widow (twice), parents: Casper SMITH, Sr. and Rachel HAMPTON, death cause: "bloody dysentery, informant:

Mary FORD (Fordtown), buried: Wheeler Cemetery, died: 15 Oct 1915, record (1915): 433.

James THOMAS, age 83 years, widower, parents: Jacob THOMAS and Mary PAINTER, death cause: "tuberculosis", buried: Cool Springs Cemetery, died: 15 Oct 1915, record (1915): 434.

Adeline HOPKINS, parents: James HOPKINS and Mary LUNCEFORD, death cause: not stated, informant: father (Bluff City), born/died: 12 Oct 1915, record (1915): 435.

Joseph BARR, born: 20 Feb 1834, married, parents: Samuel BARR and Elizabeth HARR, death cause: "apoplexy, chronic nephritis", informant: E.B. KENNEDY (Blountville), buried at Blountville, died: 20 Oct 1915, record (1915): 436.

George Washington SAMS, born: 18 Dec 1832, married, parents: Wils SAMS and Jane RICHARDS, death cause: "Brights disease", died in the 21st District on 22 Oct 1915, record (1915): 437.

Andy J. CARROLL, age not stated, widower, parents not stated, death cause: "tuberculosis of lungs", informant: J.L. SMITH (Vance, TN), buried: Weaver Cemetery, died: 14 Oct 1915, record (1915): 438.

Sara A. DISHNER, age 58 years, married, parents: James MOORE and mother not stated, death cause: illegible, informant: George H. DISHNER (Bristol), buried: Dishner Cemetery, died: 31 Oct 1915, record: 439.

Mrs. Minnie STERNE, age 58 years, born in Pennsylvania, parents: S.A. GUMP (Germany) and Jearette ELLINGER (Germany), death cause: "mitral regurgitation", informant: Leon STERNE (Bristol), buried: Johnson City, died: 5 Oct 1915, record: 440.

William WHITE, Negro, born: Mar 1863 in Virginia, married, parents: Myers BLACK (VA) and Fannie SHAZER (VA), death cause: "nephritis", informant: Carrie WHITE (Bristol), buried: Chilhowie, VA., died: 17 Oct 1915, record (1915): 441.

Willis LITTLEFORD, age 78 years, born in Albermyrle Co., VA., widower, parents: Richard LITTLEFORD (England) and mother's name not stated (England), death cause: "apoplexy", informant: Sarah HENNESSY (Bristol, VA), buried: Three Springs, VA., died: 27 Oct 1915, record (1915): 442.

Edith L. PHIPPS, born: 1 Jul 1914, parents: J.M. PHIPPS and Maggie SHELL, death cause: "meningitis", informant: father (Bristol), buried: East Hill, died: 28 Oct 1915, record (1915): 443.

Roy TURNER, age 10 years, parents: Alex TURNER and Jennie GLOVER, death cause: "unknown, stomach trouble", informant: O.F. GLOVER (Bristol), buried: Bluff City, died: 6 Oct 1915, record (1915): 444.

Kate GREEN, Negro, age about 40 years, born in Virginia, widow, parents: Bill MERRY (VA) and Kate RAMBO (VA), death cause: "unknown", informant: James HAMMER (Bristol), buried: Citizen Cemetery, died: date not stated, buried: 17 Oct 1915, record (1915): 445.

Mountiful HINA, born: 17 Mar 1851 in Wythe Co., VA., parents: father's name illegible (Ireland) and Miss MOORE (VA), death cause: "pneumonia", informant: Ed FAIDLEY (Bristol), buried: Susong Cemetery, died: 8 Oct 1915, record (1915): 446.

Zolia Edlone HITE, born: 28 Mar 1911, parents: Theodore Hix HITE and Sarah Rebecca BOYD, death cause: "meningitis", informant: Mrs. Rebecca HITE (Fordtown), buried: Rock Springs, died: 4 Oct 1915, record: 447.

Minnie CHURCH, born: 27 May 1886, married, parents: William SHORT and mollie SUMMERS, death cause: "purpural fever", informant: D.B. JONES (Kingsport), died: 22 Oct 1915, record (1915): 448.

James Allen JOHNSON, born: 6 Nov 1859, married, parents: James JOHNSON and Margaret CLEEK, death cause: "pellagra", informant: W.H. JOHNSON (Kingsport), buried: Groseclose Cemetery, died: 21 Oct 1915, record (1915): 449.

Surilla JOHNSON, born: 15 May 1914, parents: James P. JOHNSON and Ada JOHNSON, death cause: "illeo colitis", informant: father (Kingsport), buried: Ketron Cemetery, died: 9 Oct 1915, record (1915): 450.

Nancy MELIOR, age 80 years, widow, parents: David BIRDWELL and Malinda BROWN, death cause: "paralysis", informant: D.R. BIRDWELL (Kingsport), buried: Birdwell Cemetery, died: 8 Oct 1915, record (1915): 451.

J.S. SHIPP, age 72 years, married, parents: not stated, death cause: "heart disease", died in the 11th District, Kingsport on 1 Oct 1915, buried: family cemetery, record (1915): 452.

Infant COATS, male, parents: Dewitt COATS and Margaret SHIPLEY, death cause: "stillborn", buried: Pyle Cemetery, Kingsport, died: 17 Oct 1915, record: 453.

William Pate HICKS, born: 25 Aug 1845, married, parents: Ruben HICKS and Polly MOTTERN, death cause: "carcinoma of stomach", informant: J.E. HICKS (Danville, VA), buried: near Bluff City, died: 24 Oct 1915, record (1915): 454.

Lucinda WASSOM, born: 1854 in Washington Co., TN., widow, parents: Mathern BLAKELY (Washington Co) and Charity CRADAE (Green Co), death cause: illegible, informant: Mrs. W.J. MILAM (Limestone), died at Bluff City on 4 Oct 1915, record (1915): 455.

Lottie Alice PEARLER, born: 11 Jul 1838, widow, parents: William HUES (or HUGHES ?) and Sarah MARKLAND, death cause: "pulmonary tuberculosis", informant: Tiner STILLFE (Kingsport), buried: Reedy Creek, died: 9 Nov 1915, record (1915): 456.

John ALFORD, age 52 years, 4 months and 3 days, married, parents: Claud ALFRED and Minnie SAMS, death cause: "complication of disease", buried: Cedar Grove Cemetery, died: 10 Nov 1915, record (1915): 457.

Dave BRISCO, age 72 years, 7 months and 3 days, widower, parents: Jack BRISCO (VA) and Fanny BANE (VA), death cause: "stomach trouble", buried: Beelers Cemetery, died: 12 Nov 1913, record (1915): 458.

Sallie SAMS, age 18 years, single, parents: A.J. SAMS and Emma CARRIER, death cause: "tuberculosis", buried: Crumley Cemetery, died: 24 Nov 1915, record: 459.

Owen GRUBBS, age 65 years, widower, parents: John GRUBBS and Mary FEATHERS, death cause: "pneumonia", buried: Cool Springs Cemetery, died: 15 Nov 1915, record (1915): 460.

Abe STOFFLE, age: not stated, married, parents: Owen STOFFLE and Mary BLEVINS, death cause: "accident", died in the 1st District on 9 Nov 1915, record: 461.

James FARRETY, age 65 years, married, parents: J.A. FARRETY (VA) and Mary BARR (VA), death cause: "pneumonia", buried: Cool Springs Cemetery, died: 25 Nov 1915, record (1915): 463.

Dr. James MURPHEY, age 91 years, 5 months and 2 days, born in Pennsylvania, widower, parents: Joseph MURPHEY (PA) and mother not stated, death cause: "complication of disease", buried: Weaver Cemetery, died: 8 Nov 1915, record (1915): 464.

David BRISCOE, age 68 years, widower, parents: Richard BRISCOE (VA) and Lyne BRISCOE, death cause: "uremia and typhoid fever", informant: Claud MITCHELL (Bristol), buried: Beelers Cemetery, died: 19 Nov 1915, record (1915): 465.

Nancy Alice WAGNER, born: 5 Oct 1879, married, parents: Wilburn GRINDSTAFF and Nancy ROBINSON, death cause: "cancer of uterus", informant; Wilburn GRINDSTAFF (Doe, Johnson Co., TN), buried: Wagner Cemetery, Johnson Co., died: 21 Nov 1915, record (1915): 466.

Margaret RAMBO, Negro, age about 70 years, born in Virginia, parents: not stated, death cause: "intestinal nephritis", informant: James HAMMER (Bristol), buried: Citizen Cemetery, died: 25 Nov 1915, record (1915): 467.

James K. TILLISON, age 60 years, married, born in Virginia, parents: not stated, death cause: "cerebral hemorrhage", informant: J.T. TILLISON (Bristol), buried: Ordway Cemetery, died: 29 Nov 1915, record (1915): 468.

Edward MCCRARY, born: 2 Sep 1904, parents: Columbus MCCRARY (NC) and Elizabeth CARDEN, death cause: "hydro cleftilelus", informant: Elizabeth CARDEN (Bristol), died: 25 Nov 1915, record (1915): 469.

Chalmas Mack LETHCO, born: Feb 1860 in North Carolina, married, parents: Sandy A. LETHCO (NC) and Margaret CRAIGSON (NC), death cause: "chronic Brights disease", informant: C.L. LETHCO (Abingdon, VA), buried: East Hill, died: 14 Nov 1915, record (1915): 470.

Marquise Benjamin MURRY, born; 7 Jul 1855 in Fincastle, VA., single, parents: Thomas W. MURRY (Staunton, VA) and Catherine E. A..(illegible) (Fincastle, VA), death cause: "chronic bronchitis", informant: Abbie MURRY (Bristol), buried: Marion, VA., died: 6 Dec 1915, record (1915): 471.

Infant HICKS, male, parents: Clen HICKS and Belle HICKS, death cause: "still born", died at Piney Flats on 15 Nov 1915, record (1915): 472.

Clide LILLEY, age 6 years, parents: Andy LILLEY and Nannie MCLANEY, death cause: "myocarditis, diptheria", buried: Lilley Cemetery, Piney Flats, died: 4 Nov 1915, record (1915): 473.

Mary Emma GREGG, born: 9 Sep 1915, parents: Charles GREGG and Louisa Melinda DYKES (Green Co.), death cause: "troumatic pneumonia", informant: father (Fordtown), buried: Gregg family cemetery, 15th District, died: 8 Nov 1915, record (1915): 474.

Florence A. CONKIN, born: 27 Aug 1899, parents; Thomas CONKIN and Sarah BURK, death cause: "pulmonary tuberculosis", informant: J.M. CONKIN (Fall Branch), buried: Fairview Cemetery, 15th District, died: 12 Nov 1915, record (1915): 475.

David Paxton DOLEN, born: 15 Jan 1843, widower, parents: Isaac DOLEN (NC) and Sarah PAXTON, death cause: "paralysis", informant: John N. DOLEN (Fall Branch), buried: Dolen family cemetery, 13th District, died: 15 Nov 1915, record (1915): 476.

David Wesley POORE, age 63 years, born in Botetourt Co., VA., widower, parents: Robert POORE and Lousia SIZEMORE, death cause: "hypertropic cirrhosis of liver", informant: E.S. DILLARD (Fordtown), buried: Vincent family cemetery, died: 15 Nov 1915, record (1915): 477.

Robert William COATES, born: 26 Feb 1911, parents: Robert Nolen COATES and Julia Ann RATLIFF, death cause: "diphtheria", informant: father (Fall Branch), buried: Depew Chapel, died: 27 Nov 1915, record (1915): 478.

Infant CHURCH, female, born: 27 Sep 1914, parents: Jarvis C. CHURCH and Minnie SHORT, death cause: "malnutrition", informant: T. DICKSON (Kingsport), died: 29 Nov 1915, record (1915): 479.

George E. BRALLEY, born: 7 Oct 1915, parents: Jack BRALLEY (VA) and Alice ARNOLD, death cause: "unknown", informant: George ARNOLD (Kingsport), buried: Martin Cemetery, died: 11 Nov 1915, record (1915): 480.

David Allen RUSSELL, born: 7 Jan 1907, parents: James Allen RUSSELL and Bonnie WILES, death cause: "lobar pneumonia", informant: father (Kingsport), buried: Greenville, TN., died: 18 Dec 1915, record (1915): 481.

Walter GRAY, parents: Burleigh C. GRAY (High Point, VA) and Lynn MONGLE (Johnson City), death cause: "still born", buried: Cold Springs, died: 1 Dec 1915, record (1915): 482.

Rufus W. MORRELL, born: 7 Aug 1843, married, parents: Isaac MORRELL and Susan CRUMLEY, death cause: "tuberculosis", informant: Dr. GRAVES (Piney Flats), buried: Drokes Cemetery, died: 6 Dec 1915, record (1915): 483.

Nat MAYS, age 65 years, married, parents: William MAYS and Sarah NICKLES, death cause: "pneumonia", buried: Crumley Cemetery, 3rd District, died: 26 Dec 1915, record (1915): 484.

Florence Williamson BOOHER, age: 25 years, married, parents: James WILLIAMSON and Mollie JONES, death cause: "tuberculosis", informant: James WILLIAMSON (Emmett), buried: Pleasant Grove, died: 25 Dec 1915, record (1915): 485. (duplicate record below)

Flora BOOHER, age 25 years, married, parents: James WILLIAMSON and Mary JONES, death cause: "pulmonary tuberculosis and childbirth", informant: M.D. BOOHER (Bristol), buried: Pleasant Grove, died: 21 Dec 1915, record (1915): 486.

Harold Duane WEBB, born 19 Aug 1912, parents: Mike B. WEBB and Mary CROSS, death cause: "accident, kicked by a horse", informant: Mrs. Mike B. WEBB (Blountville), died: 11 Dec 1915, record (1915): 487.

Mrs. Rebecca SPARR, born: 30 Jan 1836, widow, parents: John DISHNER (VA) and Palsey DISHNER (VA), death cause: "pneumonia", informant: J.B. CLARK (Bristol), buried: Dishner Cemetery, died: 20 Dec 1915, record (1915): 488.

Mrs. T.F. WOOD, born: 22 Mar 1849 in Virginia, widow, parents: John ANDERSON (VA) and mother not stated, death cause: "bronchial asthma", informant: A.P. MOORE (Bristol), buried: East Hill, died: 23 Dec 1915, record (1915): 489.

Noah LEONARD, age 27 years, married, parents: Abram LEONARD and Hattie (surname illegible), death cause: "injury to skull", informant: Mrs. Hattie LEONARD (Blountville), buried: Johnson Cemetery, died: 28 Dec 1915, record (1915): 490.

Lula GAINES, Negro, born: 12 Jan 1878, single, parents: J.H. LEROY and Ella EVANS, death cause: "apoplexy", informant: J.H. LEROY (Bristol), buried: Citizen Cemetery, died: 23 Dec 1915, record (1915): 491.

Infant WOLF, Negro, female, parents: William WOLF and Francis RAMY (VA), death cause: "premature birth", informant: father (Bristol), buried: Citizen Cemetery, died: 22 Dec 1915, record (1915): 492.

Robert Rhea STRAIN, born: 21 Jan 1854, married, parents: James B. STRAIN and Sarah TAYLOR, death cause: illegible, informant: Mrs. R.C. STRAIN (Bristol), buried: East Hill, died: 19 Dec 1915, record (1915): 493.

A.T. BAYLESS, age 76 years, widow, parents: Jackson BAYLESS and Sallie STEPHENSON, death cause: "probably apoplexy", informant: H.C. PERVINE (Bristol), buried: Cleveland, TN., died: 23 Dec 1915, record (1915): 494.

Infant LUTTRELL, male, parents: S.M. LUTTRELL and Callie WHITEHEAD (VA), death cause: "premature birth", informant: father (Bristol), died: 12 Dec 1915, record (1915): 495.

Perry Patton WHITE, Negro, born: 15 Nov 1915, parents: Eugene WHITE (VA) and Elizabeth HARRINGTON, death cause: "marasmus", informant: father (Bristol), buried: Citizen Cemetery, died: 4 Dec 1915, record (1915): 496.

Infant SMITH, male, parents: G.W. SMITH and Essie HENBY, death cause: "still born", informant: father

(Bristol), buried: East Hill, died: 24 Dec 1915, record (1915): 497.

Mrs. Sarah Emma ARNOLD, born: 22 Sep 1867, married, parents: Nichels BARGER and Mary DEVAULT, death cause: "pulmonary tuberculosis", informant: W.T. ARNOLD (Bristol), buried: Preston Cemetery, died: 23 Dec 1915, record (1915): 498.

Maude Helendes BROWN, born: 6 Dec 1915, parents: R.E. BROWN (VA) and Blanch SHOECRAFT, death cause: "found dead in bed", informant: Mrs. E.V. SHOECRAFT (Bristol), buried: Ordway Cemetery, died: 22 Dec 1915, record (1915): 499.

Mrs. Mary COLLINS, age 65 years, married, parents: William CRUSSEL and Ellen MALONE, death cause: "carcinoma, probably liver", informant: J.R. COLLINS (Bristol), buried: Bluff City, died: 21 Dec 1915, record (1915): 500.

Mrs. Lizzie MCCRARY, age 44 years, married, parents: Elbert CARDEN and Emeline HATCHER, death cause: "organic heart disease", informant: John MCCRARY (Bristol), buried: Carden Cemetery, died: 30 Dec 1915, record (1915): 501.

Henry Clay BYINGTON, born: 8 Jan 1914, parents: Carr BYINGTON (Hawkins Co.) and Happyann SETZER (Hawkins Co.), death cause: "croup", informant: Nelson COATS (Fall Branch), buried: Depew Chapel, died: 8 Dec 1915, record (1915): 502.

Bert MONDY, born: 17 Mar 1915, parents: James W. MONDY and M. Ethel OVERBY, death cause: "influenza", informant: father (Fordtown), buried: Pactolus Church, died: 11 Dec 1915, record (1915): 503.

Maggie SHORT, born: 7 Jun 1904, parents: William SHORT and Mary PRATT, death cause: "pulmonary tuberculosis", informant: James HOOD (Fall Branch), buried: Depew Chapel, died: 30 Dec 1915, record (1915): 504.

Noah WILLS, age 35 years, single, parents: not stated, death cause: "pulmonary tuberculosis", buried: Buffalo, 16th District, died: 15 Dec 1915, record (1915): 505.

Hogan SIZEMORE, age 88 years and 6 months, born in Virginia, widower, parents: not stated, death cause: "apoplexy", buried: Chinquipin Grove, Bluff City, died: 12 Dec 1915, record (1915): 506.

Samuel Rhea COX, born: 2 Jun 1845, married, parents: Abram COX and Loucinda BEARD, death cause: "paralysis", informant: Dr. GRAVES (Piney Flats), buried: Muddy Creek, died: 2 Dec 1915, record: 507.

Joseph F. MCPHERSON, born: 10 Aug 1915, parents: Frank MCPHERSON (Columbus, Ohio) and Kittie KING (Russell Co., VA), death cause: "found dead in bed", died at Bristol on 3 Dec 1915, record (1915): 508.

Mrs. Nancy C. COPENHAVER, born: 9 May 1845 in Virginia, widow, parents: James DUNGAN (VA) and Sarah GALLENHON (VA), death cause: "valvular heart disease", informant: J.C. COPENHAVER (Bristol), buried: Seven Mile Ford, VA., died: 9 Dec 1915, record (1915): 509.

Norman P. LONDY, age 17 years, born in Virginia, parents: C.E. LUNDY (NC) and Allie WILLIAMS (VA), death cause: "gunshot wound of thorax", informant: father (Bristol), buried: Wytheville, VA., died: 4 Dec 1915, record (1915): 510.

Mrs. A.M. HATCHER, age 45 years, married, parents: L.W. TIPTON and Clementine HEDRICK, death cause: "cancer of cervix", informant: A.M. HATCHER (Bristol), died: 3 Dec 1915, record (1915): 511.

Mrs. Sallie L. JONES, born: 15 Oct 1844 in Virginia, widow, parents: Martin FLEENOR (VA) and Malinda SHANKLES (VA), death cause: "shock due to fall down stairs, breaking hip", informant: Charles JONES (Bristol), buried: East Hill, died: 3 Dec 1915, record (1915): 512.

Nancy E. MOORE, born: 3 Mar 1843, married, parents: William BORGER and Margaret TAYLOR, death cause: "Brights disease", informant: J.A. MOORE (Blountville), died: 6 Jan 1916, record (1916): 191.

Infant STARBOCK, male, parents: M.C. STARBOCK and Nellie May WOODING (Watauga Co., NC), death cause: "injuries incidental to birth", informant: father (Bristol), buried: East Hill, died: 24 Jan 1916, record (1916): 192.

Daniel ZIMMERMAN, born: 9 Oct 1851, married, parents: Samuel ZIMMERMAN (Washington Co., TN), death cause: "senile gangrene of feet and legs", informant: A.H. WEXLER (Fordtown), buried: Kendrick Creek Church, died: 26 Jan 1916, record (1916): 193.

Joseph Birdwell FINK, born: 27 Jan 1856, married, parents: George Washington FINK and Mary HULSE, death cause: "carcinoma of pancreas", informant: D.P. FINK (Jonesboro), buried: Double Springs Cemetery, 16th District, died: 12 Jan 1916, record (1916): 194.

George W. DARTER, born: 16 Nov 1857 in Virginia, married, parents: John T. DARTER (VA) and Katheryn FLEENOR (VA), death cause: "pancreatic disease, probably cyst or cancerous", informant: Mrs. George W. DARTER (Gate City), buried: Gate City, died: 7 Jan 1916, record (1916): 195.

Marsha Rain ROSE, born: 30 Aug 1828, married, parents: not stated, death cause: "acute indigestion", died at Piney Flats on 12 Jan 1916, buried: New Bethel Cemetery, record (1916): 196.

Mary F. BOWLING, age 75 years, married, parents: not stated, death cause: "lagrippe and pleurisy", died at Piney Flats on 30 Jan 1916, record (1916): 197.

Susan GLOVER, age 40 years, married, parents: David MILLER and mother not stated, death cause: illegible, died at Bluff City on 6 Jan 1916, buried: Peregeray Cemetery, record (1916): 198.

Infant GLOVER, male, parents: Charlie GLOVER and Susan MILLER, death cause: "still born", died at Watauga on 3 Jan 1916, record (1916): 199.

Infant GLOVER, male, parents: Charlie GLOVER and Susan MILLER, death cause: "still born", died at Watauga on 3 Jan 1916, record (1916): 200, buried: Peregoay Cemetery.

Roy GRAY, age 6 years, parents: Mack GRAY and Mary STUMP (VA), death cause: "burns", buried: Cold Springs Cemetery, died: 3 Jan 1916, record (1916): 202.

Mrs. Emaline CLAYMAN, age 73 years, single, parents: J.A. CLAYMAN and Mary JONES, death cause: "rheumatism", buried: Cold Springs, died: 21 Jan 1916, record (1916): 203.

Clarence COLTON, age 25 years, married, parents: James COLTON and Mary ENGLISH, death cause: "killed by a train", buried: Bueler Cemetery, 2nd District, died: 27 Jan 1916, record (1916): 204.

Miss Rebecca MORRELL, age 66 years, single, parents: A.B. MORRELL and Mary SMITH (VA), death cause: "catarrh in head", buried: Shipley Cemetery, died: 5 Jan 1916, record (1916): 205.

Infant PARKER, male, parents: Frank PARKER and Pearl LINKONS, death cause: "still born", informant: Z.W. TIPTON (Kingsport), born/died: 30 Jan 1916, record (1916): 206.

SAlly T. PECKTOL, born: 27 Dec 1836 in Lee Co., VA., widow, parents: ___ NORTON (Lee Co., VA) and Harriett HIKIN (Lee Co., VA), death cause: "Brights disease", informant: F.H. PECKTOL (Bloomingdale), died: 8 Jan 1916, record (1916): 207.

Margareta DIXON, born: 16 Jan 1840, widow, parents: Sam FITSWORTH (VA) and Sarah SMITH (VA), death cause: "catarrhal pneumonia", informant: S.G. FLEENOR

(Kingsport), buried: Preston Cemetery, died: 16 Jan 1916, record (1916): 208.

Thomas M. GALLOWAY, born: 17 Jul 1915, parents: Thomas GALLOWAY and Annie MCKINZIE, death cause: "marasmus", buried: Morrison Chapel, died: 18 Jan 1916, record (1916): 209.

Mattie SHIPLEY, born: 27 Feb 1880, married, parents: Noah CHILDRESS and Nannie COLE, death cause: "lobar pneumonia", informant: Noah SHIPLEY (Kingsport), buried: Preston Cemetery, died: 27 Jan 1916, record (1916): 210.

Julia KISS, born: 28 Feb 1910 in Pennsylvania, parents: John KISS (Austro-Hungary) and Julia PRUSKI (Austro-Hungary), death cause: "burn", informant: father (Kingsport), buried: Preston Cemetery, died: 28 Jan 1916, record (1916): 211.

Martha Fibian MCCORKLE, age 42 years, born at Chuckey, TN., married, parents: W.R. STACEY (Greenville) and Mary BURNETT (Greenville), death cause: "chronic bronchitis", informant: J.J. MCCORKLE (Bristol), buried: Afton, TN., died: 9 Jan 1916, record (1916): 212.

Clara ENGLISH, Negro, age about 70 years, born in North Carolina, single, parents: not stated, death cause: "pneumonia", informant: Eliza ENGLISH (Bristol), buried: Citizens Cemetery, died: 5 Jan 1916, record (1916): 213.

Sarah Virginia GAULDING, born: 20 Mar 1839 in Morristown, TN., widow, parents: John GOLSSIP and ___ CUNNINGHAM, death cause: "Brights disease", informant: Mrs. F.A. BUCHANAN (Fordtown), buried: Emory, VA., died: 31 Jan 1916, record (1916): 214.

Liza C. MCCRARY, born: 18 Dec 1915, parents: Lum MCCRARY and Lizzie CARDEN, death cause: "hemorrhage", died at Bristol on 2 Jan 1916, record (1916): 215.

S.L. MCMILLAN, age 81 years, 2 months and 14 days, born in Virginia, widower, parents: Henry MCMILLAN (VA) and Martha HARRISON (VA), death cause: "Brights disease", informant: G.W. MCMILLAN (Bristol), buried: Ordway Cemetery, died: 14 Jan 1916, record (1916): 216.

Infant HICKMAN, female, born: 24 Dec 1915, parents: C.H. HICKMAN and Lula EDMONSON (VA), death cause: "chronic bronchitis", informant: father (Bristol), buried: East Hill, died: 2 Jan 1916, record (1916): 217.

Flora Alice BOOHER, born: 13 Aug 1881, single, parents: Josiah BOOHER and Tina MARKS, death cause:

"nephritis, cardiac weakness", informant: O.K. BOOHER (Bristol), buried: East Hill, died: 11 Jan 1916, record (1916): 218.

Ira DILAP, Negro, female, age about 68 years, widow, parents: not stated, death cause: "syphilis in last stage", died at Bristol on 16 Jan 1916, record: 219.

W.A. SPARGES, age 72 years, born in North Carolina, married, parents: Merlin SPARGES (NC) and mother not stated, death cause: "cancer of kidney", died at Bristol on 14 Jan 1916, record (1916): 220.

J.N. CARPENTER, age 76 years, 1 month and 15 days, born in North Carolina, married, parents: A.J. CARPENTER (Ashe Co., NC) and Polly CALHOUN (Ashe Co., NC), death cause: "uremia", informant: T.W. CAMPBELL (Bristol), buried: East Hill, died: 10 Jan 1916, record (1916): 221.

J.C. RUTHERFORD, born: 28 May 1855, married, parents: John RUTHERFORD (NC) and Polly CORNETT, death cause: "lobar pneumonia", informant: W.C. SHOEMAKER (Bristol), buried: East Hill, died: 15 Jan 1916, record (1916): 222.

T.P. WATSON, age 37 years, born in Virginia, divorced, parents: M.C. WATSON (VA) and Mollie PEARSON (VA), death cause: "chronic alcoholism and associated problems", informant: A.B. WHITAKER (Bristol), died: 31 Jan 1916, record (1916): 223.

Daniel W. HUGHES, born: 18 Apr 1897, single, parents: J.P. HUGHES (VA) and Sallie STEWART (KY), death cause: "injuries received in coal mines at St. Charles, VA", informant: J.P. HUGHES (St. Charles, VA), buried: Pennington Gap, VA., died: 21 Jan 1916, record: 224.

Isaac DOYLE, age 48 years, born in Virginia, married, parents: not stated, death cause: "pulmonary tuberculosis", died at Bristol on 11 Jan 1916, buried: Walnut Grove, VA., record (1916): 225.

William MUTTER, born: May 1913 in Virginia, parents: Edward MUTTER (VA) and Alice HUDSON (VA), death cause: "diptheria", informant: father (Bristol), buried: East Hill Cemetery, died: 4 Jan 1916, record (1916): 226.

Mary STROTHER, Negro, born: 2 Mar 1882 in Virginia, married, parents: Lewis FARTHER (VA) and Lizzie HARDING (NC), death cause: "pulmonary tuberculosis", informant: Lizzie WATSON (Bristol), buried: Citizens Cemetery, died: 20 Jan 1916, record (1916): 227.

B.S. MCDOWELL, age 82 years, widower, parents: John MCCOWELL and mother's name not stated, death cause: "euramic poison", informant: Miss Irene MCDOWELL (Bristol), died: 8 Jan 1916, record (1916): 228.

David NIALOM, age 60 years, married, parents: not stated, death cause: "nephritis", buried: Bluff City, died: 22 Feb 1916, record (1916): 229.

Paulser WHITSEL, born: 21 Dec 1833 in Virginia, married, parents: Jess WHITSEL (VA) and Betsy COLLARS (VA), death cause: "suppose, influenza", informant: Elbert DYKES (Church Hill), buried: 15th District, died: 3 Feb 1916, record (1916): 230.

William Lynn BOND, Negro, born: 15 Mar 1894, single, parents: Eldridge BOND and (illegible) WILSON (NC), death cause: "lobar pneumonia", informant: father (Fall Branch), buried: Russell School Cemetery, 13th District, died: 5 Feb 1916, record (1916): 231.

Urbana Hite JONES, born: 7 Feb 1871, married, parents: Jackson HITE and Katie CONKIN, death cause: "nephritis", informant: T.D. JONES (Jonesboro), buried: Russell Spring Cemetery, died: 6 Feb 1916, record (1916): 232.

Mrs. Thomas BARRETT, age 56 (?), 8 months and 20 days, born in Washington Co., VA., married, parents: M.J. LINDSEY (Wash. Co., VA) and M.J. MONTGOMERY (Wash, Co., VA), death cause: "pneumonia", informant: Thomas BARRETT (Bristol), buried: East Hill, died: 17 Feb 1916, record (1916): 233.

Ann REYNOLDS, Negro, age approximately 62 years, born in North Carolina, widow, parents: Niles REYNOLDS (NC) and Rhoda REYNOLDS (NC), death cause: "paralysis", informant: Jane COBBS (Bristol), buried: Citizens Cemetery, died: 15 Feb 1916, record (1916): 234.

Revely Avella TOLBERT, female, born: 28 Dec 1915, parents: Charles TOLBERT and Clara VIRES (VA), death cause: "whooping cough", informant: father (Bristol), buried: Oak Grove Cemetery, died: 19 Feb 1916, record (1916): 235.

Mrs. Mollie Magnolia YONCE, born: 12 Mar 1851, married, parents: Samuel JACKSON and Alzenia WAGNER, death cause: "pulmonary ordema", informant: Mrs. Nora STAFFORD (Bristol), buried: East Hill, died: 5 Feb 1916, record (1916): 236.

N.B. FUGATE, born: 10 Sep, age 53 years, born in Scott Co., VA., married, parents: Francis FUGATE (Scott Co.) and Annie ADDINGTON (Scott Co.), death cause: "cancer of pancreas", informant: C.D. FUGATE (Nicklesville, VA), buried: Nicklesville, VA.,. died: 5 Feb 1916, record (1916): 237.

Washington BROYLES, age 78 years, born at Chuckey, TN., married, parents: not stated, death cause: "lobar penumonia", infomant: Miss Nola BAKER

(Bristol), buried: East Hill, died: 4 Feb 1916, record (1916): 239.
Helen Cathlene BAILEY, born; 25 Jan 1916, parents: Oscar BAILEY and Lucille BEDWELL, death cause: "congenital construction of bile duct", informant: Capt. W.H. PHILLIPS (Bristol), buried: East Hill, died: 3 Feb 1916, record (1916): 240.
Earl VANCE, born: Aug 1915, parents: Hugh VANCE and Hattie STINE, death cause: not stated, informant: Bud ROGERS (Bristol), buried: Beelers Cemetery, died: 1 Feb 1916, record (1916): 241.
Infant HEYETT, male, born: 26 Feb 1916, parents; James HEYETT and Polly HEYETT, death cause: "abnormal heart", died at Piney Flats on 28 Feb 1916, record (1916): 242.
Infant WEXLER, female, parents: Henry WEXLER and Lila KING, death cause: "still born", born/died at Piney Flats on 22 Feb 1916, record (1916): 243.
Isaac KAGLE, age 80 years, married, parents: not stated, death cause: "chronic Brights", died at Piney Flats on 1 Feb 1916, record (1916): 244.
A.J. THOMPSON, born: 18 Dec 1838, married, parents: not stated, death cause: "paralysis", died at Piney Flats on 26 Feb 1916, record (1916): 245.
Mrs. Margaret WOODS, born: 17 Sep 1860, married, parents: G.S. LIPPS and Lorina HICKS, death cause: "cancer of liver", informant: F.P. WOODS (Bluff City), buried: Morrell Cemetery, died: 18 Feb 1916, record (1916): 246.
Rufus MORRELL, age 78 years, married, parents: not stated, death cause: "tuberculosis and paralysis", buried: Drokes Cemetery, died at Piney Flats on 6 Feb 1916, record (1916): 247.
Naomi Ruth HENLEY, born: 25 Feb 1914, parents: Samuel G. HENLEY (Washington Co., TN) and Fannie WATTENBERGER (Washington Co., TN), death cause: "whooping cough and broncho penumonia", informant: father (Bluff City), buried: Earnest Chapel Cemetery, died: 9 Feb 1916, record (1916): 248.
William CROSS, born: 2 Sep 1846, widower, parents: George CROSS (VA) and Elizabeth LACY, death cause: "pulmonary tuberculosis", informant: Sam CROSS (Jonesboro), buried: Hilton Cemetery, 15th District, died: 12 Feb 1916, record (1916): 249
George FLEENER, born: 21 Feb 1916, parents: William FLEENER (VA) and Mary CHARLTON, death cause: "premature birth", informant: father (Kingsport), died: 22 Feb 1916, record (1916): 250. (twin below)

Ralph K. MARTIN, born: 27 May 1913, parents: Ed. K. MARTIN and Ollie WEAVER, death cause: "acute nephritis", informant: Dave MILES (Kingsport), buried: Boones Creek, died: 21 Feb 1916, record (1916): 251.

Martha C. WILLS, born: 20 Oct 1845, widow, parents: George HORNE (VA) and Elizabeth WILLARD, death cause: "Brights disease", informant: G.W. HORNE (Kingsport), buried: Wills Cemetery, died: 11 Feb 1916, record (1916): 252.

James MCINTOSH, born: 20 Sep 1837 in Lawrenceville, Georgia, widower, parents: George MCINTOSH (GA) and Eveline WILLIS (GA), death cause: "entenic fever", informant: M.B. MCINTOSH (Kingsport), died: 24 Feb 1916, record (1916): 253.

Ruby FLEENER, born: 21 Feb 1916, parents: William FLEENER (VA) and Mary CHARLTON, death cause: "premature birth", informant: father (Kingsport), died: 22 Feb 1916, record (1916): 254.

Infant RODEFER, male, parents: J.R. RODEFER and Mary TRAUBARGER (VA), death cause: "born dead", informant: father (Blountville), buried: Mill Point, born/died: 20 Feb 1916, record (1916): 255.

James M. PIERCE, born: 22 Mar 1858, widower, parents: Isaac PIERCE and Phoebe GODSY, death cause: "acute [choleyslitis]", informant: H.H. MASSINGILL (Blountville), buried: Weaver Cemetery, died: 4 Feb 1916, record (1916): 256.

Routh Ann WEAVER, age 71 years, 5 months and 2 days, married, parents: Joseph ARENTS (VA) and Maud CLAYMAN, death cause: "tuberculosis of the throat", buried: Weaver Cemetery, died: 4 Feb 1916, record (1916): 257.

Margaret Vader ROYSTON, age illegible (young child), parents Orpha ROYSTON and Loudema TETERS, death cause: "indigestion", buried: Weaver Cemetery, died: 3 Feb 1916, record (1916): 258.

Mary Elizabeth BUCKLES, age 59 years, 3 months and 6 days, born in Virginia, parents: John BUCKLES (VA) and Mandy SMYTHE, death cause: "pneumonia", buried: Green Spring Cemetery, 22nd District, died: 5 Feb 1916, record (1916): 259.

Sousan WEBB, age 75 years, widow, parents: Esy John JONES and mother not stated, death cause: "pneumonia", buried: Crumley Cemetery, died: 16 Feb 1916, record (1916): 260.

Ruby WEBB, age 6 years and 7 months, parents: Mike WEBB and Kate ODELL, death cause: "pneumonia", buried: Crumley Cemetery, died: 28 Feb 1916, record (1916): 261.

Ruby WEBB, age 6 years and 7 months, parents: Mike WEBB and Kate ODELL, death cause: "pneumonia", buried: Crumley Cemetery, died: 28 Feb 1916, record (1916): 261.
J. Hugh CARRIER, age 48 years, married, parents: Jonathan CARRIER and ___ RUSSELL (Ireland), death cause: "cancer of liver", buried: Shipley Cemetery, died: 3 Feb 1916, record (1916): 262.
Gordon SPROLES, age 14 years, born in Virginia, parents: J.K. SPROLES (VA) and Fanny GOBBLE (VA), death cause: "hemorrhage", informant: L.P. KAYLOR (Mendota, VA), buried: Mendota, VA., died: 29 Feb 1916, record (1916): 263.
Maggie SHERMAN, Negro, age 50 years, married, parents: Benjamin JONES and Bertie KING, death cause: "nephritis", informant: James SHERMAN (Bristol), died: 24 Feb 1916, record (1916): 264.
Infant MCNUTT, male, parents: T.A. MCNUTT and Ehtel GLOVER, death cause: "premature birth", informant: father (Bristol), buried: Ordway Cemetery, died: 22 Feb 1916, record (1916): 265.
Sarah T. PICKLE, age 73 years, widow, parents: Andrew CLARK and mother not stated, death cause: "senility", informant: W.L. COMER (Bristol), buried: Atkins, VA., died: 20 Feb 1916, record (1916): 266.
Infant HARRIS, male, born: 10 Feb 1916, parents: Harvey HARRIS (VA) and Belle CHAMBERS, death cause: "intestinal toxemia", informant: William CHAMBERS (Bristol), buried: East Hill, died: 19 Feb 1916, record (1916): 267.
V.W.B. MOODY, age 39 years, married, parents: Thomas MOODY and mother not stated, death cause: "tuberculosis of lungs", informant: J.S. MOODY (Indian Springs), buried: Cooks Valley, died: 22 Mar 1916, record (1916): 268.
Mrs. Loyd HODGES, born: 27 Sep 1873 in North Carolina, married, parents: Evan HODGES (NC) and Sara HODGES (NC), death cause: "pneumonia", informant: R.L. SIMMONS (Big Creek), buried: Shipley Cemetery, died: 22 Mar 1916, record (1916): 269.
Emeline Buckner WILLS, born: 9 Jan 1845, single, parents: William Burton WILLS and Sallie PEOPLES, death cause: "cerebral hemorrhage", informant: John W. WILLS (Fall Branch), buried: Wills Cemetery, 15th District, died: 26 Mar 1916, record (1916): 270.
Chester COLEMAN, black, age: not known, born in Georgia, single, parents: not stated, death cause:

"gun shot in head", informant: John ROSS (Kingsport), died: 13 Mar 1916, record (1916): 271.

Mrs. Julina MONTEITH, born: 10 Jun 1840, widow, parents: George FINK and Sarah FINK, death cause: "angina pectoris", informant: Dr. GRAVES (Piney Flats), died in the 18th District on 21 Mar 1916, buried: Wheeler Cemetery, record (1916): 272.

George Wright BARNES, born: 2 Jan 1901 in Washington Co., TN., parents: Adam Fletcher BARNES and Alice L. WRIGHT (Washington Co.), death cause: "lobar pneumonia", informant: Dr. GRAVES (Piney Flats), buried: Wheeler Cemetery, died: 19 Mar 1916, record (1916): 273.

Mrs. Lillian May CROUCH, born: 28 Jul 1866 in Springfield, Ohio, married, parents: A.B. GILMORE (Juanita Co. PA) and Mary E. TRINNER (PA), death cause: "organic heart lesion", informant: A.G. WAGNER (Bristol), buried: East Hill, died: 18 Mar 1916, record (1916): 274.

Daniel NECESSARY, age 20 years, born in Virginia, single, parents: T.J. NECESSARY (VA) and Mary MOORE (VA), death cause: "internal injuries die to a kick in abdomen", informant: father (Philips, VA), buried: Philips, VA., died: 1 Mar 1916, record (1916): 275.

Clyde WIDNER, born: 31 Dec 1899 in Virginia, parents: P.V. WIDNER (VA) and Cora A. COOK (NC), death cause: "burn", informant: father (Kingsport), buried: Glade Spring, VA., died: 7 Mar 1916, record (1916): 276.

H.V. CRAFT, age 42 years, born in Washington Co., VA., married, parents: Andrew CRAFT (VA) and Mary LOCKETT (VA), death cause: "tuberculosis", informant: Mrs. H.V. CRAFT (Bristol), buried: East Hill, died: 5 Mar 1916, record (1916): 277.

Eva HARRIS, male, age 27 days, parents: Henry HARRIS and Belle CHAMBERS, death cause: "supposed to be intestinal toxemia", informant: William CHAMBERS (Bristol), buried: Keenburg, TN., died: 3 Mar 1916, record (1916): 278.

Nellie BROOKS, born: 1 Mar 1916, parents: Andy BROOKS (Denton Valley, VA) and Rosie THOMAS (Johnson County), death cause: "bold hives", informant: Mrs. Andy BROOKS (Bristol), buried: East Hill, died: 16 Mar 1916, record (1916): 279.

J.H. WILSON, age 32 years, born in Vermont, married, parents: H.K. WILSON (Vermont) and Hattie HALL (Vermont), death cause: "chronic Brights", informant: Mrs. J.H. WILSON (Bristol), died: 6 Mar 1916, record (1916): 280.

Cora Lee GODSEY, born: 17 Nov 1888 in Virginia, single, parents: W.M. GODSEY and Levy HOOVER, death cause: "epilepsy", informant: father (Bristol), buried: East Hill, died: 9 Mar 1916, record (1916): 281.

Thomas COLEY, Negro, born: 27 Jan 1867, married, parents: James COLEY and Eliza HALE, death cause: "intestinal nephritis", informant: Belle COLEY (Bristol), buried: Citizens Cemetery, died: 12 Mar 1916, record (1916): 282.

John CROSS, Jr., born: 14 Mar 1916, parents: John CROSS and Nannie SMITH, death cause: "blue baby", informant: father (Fall Branch), buried: Ordway Cemetery, died: 19 Mar 1916, record (1916): 283.

John A. DOWELL, age about 35 years, married, parents: not stated, death cause: "killed by overturning of railroad locomotive near Church Hill, TN", buried: Big Stone Gap, VA., died: 29 Mar 1916, record (1916): 284.

Mrs. Rhoda RICHARDSON, born: 20 Apr 1854 in Virginia, married, parents: Andrew TARTER (VA) and Alpha HOUSHELL (VA), death cause: "rheumatism", informant: H.G. RICHARDSON (Bristol), buried: Church Hill, TN., died: 26 Mar 1916, record (1916): 285.

Mrs. Ann CRAWFORD, age about 76 years, born in Virginia, widow, parents: not stated, death cause: "..(illegible) of heart", informant: John HAGE (RFD 4), buried: Moore Cemetery, 5th District, died: 25 Mar 1916, record (1916): 286.

George Ringold DOVE, born: 18 Mar 1838, married, parents: Buckner DOVE and Fannie __, death cause: "intestinal nephritis", informant: Charles B. DOVE (Bristol), buried: East Hill, died: 25 Mar 1916, record (1916): 287.

M. Ellen LEROY, Negro, age between 56 and 58 years, married, parents: Ben BRYANT and Barbara BRYANT, death cause: illegible, informant: Rev. J.H. LEROY (Bristol), buried: Citizen Cemetery, died: 8 Mar 1916, record (1916): 288.

Fannie Mae DEPEW, born: 29 Jun 1914, parents: Roby DEPEW and Mary Mahola METCALF, death cause: "spasmodic croup", informant: James DEPEW (Fall Branch), buried: Depew Chapel, died: 11 Mar 1916, record (1916): 289.

Sara SLAUGHTER, born: 11 Mar 1866, married, parents: Harvey CHASE and Mary MURRAY, death cause: "pulmonary tuberculosis", informant: Charlie SLAUGHTER (Fordtown), buried: Fordtown Church Cemetery, died: 12 Mar 1916, record (1916): 290.

Nora May Light HITE, born: 6 Nov 1882, married, parents: Albert G. LIGHT and Nancy HOOD, death cause: "pulmonary tuberculosis", buried: Kendrick Church Cemetery, 14th District, died: 31 Mar 1916, record (1916): 291.

Mrs. Lee HODGES, age 73 years, born in Johnson County, widow, parents: not stated, death cause: "pneumonia", buried: Browns Cemetery, died in the 1st District on 7 Mar 1916, record (1916): 292.

Infant ELLIOTT, male, parents: Montie ELLIOTT (VA) and Hettie GREEN (NC), death cause: "still born", informant: Toben GREEN (Kingsport), buried: Martin Cemetery, born/died: 15 Mar 1916, record (1916): 293.

Woodrow Wilson FOALDEN, born: 21 Dec 1915, parents: Andrew J. FOALDEN (VA) and Dora E. DICKERSON (VA), death cause: "pneumonia", informant: G.W. FOALDEN (Kingsport), buried: Cedar Grove, died: 7 Mar 1916, record (1916): 294.

Margaret V. PILE, parents: W.R. PILE and Eula KETRON, death cause: "still born", informant: father (Kingsport), buried: Morrison Chapel, died: 9 Mar 1916, record (1916): 295.

Catherine SUMMERS, born: 1 Jul 1915, parents: Claude SUMMERS and Maxie COLLINS, death cause: "whooping cough", informant: Maxie COLLINS (Kingsport), buried: Pile Cemetery, died: 12 Mar 1916, record (1916): 296.

Nanie E. VAUGHN, born: 12 May 1910 in Virginia, parents: Cleve VAUGHN (VA) and mother not stated, death cause: "whooping cough", informant: J.W. OVERHOLSER (Kingsport), died: 12 Mar 1916, record (1916): 297.

Thomas PARKER, born: 29 Mar 1852, married, parents: George PARKER and Adeline JOYNER, death cause: "pneumonia", informant: G.A. OVERBAY (Kingsport), buried: Martin Cemetery, died: 29 Mar 1916, record (1916): 299.

Lillie WILSON, colored, born: 17 Aug 1883 in South Carolina, married, parents: Allen KEITH (SC) and Lena KEITH (SC), death cause: "delation of heart", informant: Tom WILSON (Kingsport), buried: Johnson City, died: 18 Mar 1916, record (1916): 298.

Eliza J. HOBBS, born: 3 Jul 1842 in Virginia, married, parents: Lilburn LEONARD (VA) and Sallie LEONARD (VA), death cause: "tuberculosis of lungs", informant: J.A. HOBBS (Bristol), buried: Blountville, died: 1 Mar 1916, record (1916): 300.

David GREEN, born: 8 Aug 1847 in Virginia, married, parents: Joseph GREEN (VA) and Lizzie COLLINS (VA),

death cause: "heart disease", informant: U.H. COX (Blountville), died: 16 Mar 1916, record (1916): 301.
Lucy RHEA, age 80 years, 10 months and 25 days, widow, parents: ___ WILLIAMS and Nancy COPELAND (Albermyrle Sound), death cause: "angina pectoris", informant: Lizzie ENSOR (Bluff City), died: 12 Mar 1916, record (1916): 302.
Rite SMITH, born: 20 Aug 1843, married, parents: Soloman (?) and Elizabeth ARANTS, death cause: "pulrasy and pneumonia", buried: Poplar Ridge Cemetery, Piney Flats, died: 31 Mar 1916, record (1916): 303.
Infant LIPPS, male, parents: Cage LIPPS and Minnie BAINS, death cause: "still born", born/died: Piney Flats on 23 Mar 1916, record (1916): 304.
Adam C. SHIPLEY, born: 2 Nov 1835 in Washington Co., TN., widower, parents: Benjamin SHIPLEY (Washington Co) and Margaret MILLER (Washington Co), death cause: "mitral insufficiency", informant: John L. SHIPLEY (Indian Springs), buried: Shipley Cemetery, died: 20 Apr 1916, record (1916): 305.
William O. HILLIARD, age 48 years, born in Johnson County, TN., married, parents: Silas HILLIARD (NC) and Bettie MUSGROVE (Johnson Co.), death cause: "pellagra", informant: Mrs. William O. HILLIARD (Bristol), buried: Ordway Cemetery, died: 3 Apr 1916, record (1916): 306.
Susannah BLEVINS, age 92 years, born in Virginia, widow, parents: Andrew ARNOLD and Katherine DONNELLY, death cause: "old age", informant: Mrs. Katherine KERIN (Bristol), died: 1 Apr 1916, record (1916): 307.
Hiram KISTNER, born: 14 Aug 1841 in Washington Co., VA., married, parents: John KISTNER (Pennsylvania) and Elizabeth (illegible)(PA), death cause: "cerebral hemorrhage", informant: Charles KISTNER, buried: Kendrick Creek Cemetery, died: 26 Apr 1916, record (1916): 308.
Lucinda SAMS, age about 60 years, single, parents: Wilson SAMS and Martha ___, death cause: "cancer of cervix", informant: W.A. WEAVER (Bristol), buried: Weaver Cemetery, died: 30 Apr 1916, record (1916): 309.
Frank BOLING, age 40 years, 3 months and 2 days, married, parents: John BOLING (VA) and Jane JONCE (VA), death cause: "pneumonia", informant: J.a. MAYSE (Bluff City), buried: Boling Cemetery, died: 26 Apr 1916, record (1916): 310.

Ella SHAFER, age 7 years, 3 months and 2 days, parents: John SHAFER and Minnie SAMS, death cause: "pneumonia", informant: M.A. SOUTH (Bluff City), buried: Shipley Cemetery, died: 4 Apr 1916, record (1916): 311.

Lillie GLOVER, age 26 years, single, parents: Dick GLOVER and Jane MARCE (NC), death cause: "tuberculosis", informant: Dick GLOVER (Bluff City), buried: Crumley Cemetery, died: 15 Apr 1916, record (1916): 312.

George MORTON, age 72 years, 2 months and 2 days, married, parents: G.C. MORTON and Polly MORRELL, death cause: "kidney trouble", informant: R.J. MCGARRY (Emmett), buried: Shipley Cemetery, died: 16 Apr 1916, record (1916): 313.

Infant SMITH, female, parents: Sam E. SMITH and Myrtle DILLOW, death cause: "still born", informant: Sam WALSH (Kingsport), buried: Pile Cemetery, died: 3 Apr 1916, record (1916): 314.

Infant SPAHA, male, lived 4 months, parents: Will SPAHA (NC) and Nannie FRY (NC), death cause: "whooping cough", buried: Chinquipin Grove, Bluff City, died: 7 Apr 1916, record (1916): 315.

Robert HAYETT, age 26 years, married, parents: Albert HAYETT and Mary HUDSON, death cause: "acute nephritis", died at Piney Flats on 22 Apr 1916, record (1916): 316.

Lafayett F. REPOSS, born: 10 May 1851 in Wytheville, VA., parents: Will REPOSS (Wytheville, VA) and Elvese CROSS (Wytheville, VA), death cause: "apoplexy", informant: Mrs. R.F. REPOSS (Piney Flats), died: 24 Apr 1916, record (1916): 317.

Mrs. Mary Wilson ENSOR, born: 4 Aug 1834, married, parents: John SANDERS and Barbara HODGE, death cause: "lagrippe", buried: Sanders Cemetery, died at Piney Flats on 1 Apr 1916, record (1916): 318.

Infant COWAN, female, parents: T.H. COWAN and (illegible) CARMACK (Washington Co. VA), death cause: "still born", informant: George A. COWAN (Bristol), buried: Cowan Cemetery, born/died: 18 Apr 1916, record (1916): 319.

Laura Belle GAULDING, born: 6 Mar 1873 in Virginia, single, parents: Theodore GAULDING (VA) and Sarah LOSSIP, death cause: "growth on left breast, secondary involvement of brain", informant: Ida GAULDING (Bristol), buried: Emory, VA., died: 20 Apr 1916, record (1916): 320.

O.J. SCOTT, age 50 years, single, parents: R.F. SCOTT and Mary HODGE, death cause: "cerebral hemorrhage", informant: J.M. SCOTT (Piney Flats), buried: New Bethel Cemetery, died: 17 Apr 1916, record: 321.
John Elias Lafayette SENEKER, born: 13 May 1848, married, parents: James King SENEKER and Elizabeth BUSHONG, death cause: "uremic poison", informant: O.H. SENEKER (Blountville), died: 17 Apr 1916, record: 322.
Infant HARDY, black, male, parents: father not stated and Strenela HARDY, death cause: "still born", informant: Robert CLARKE (Bristol), buried: Citizen Cemetery, died: 16 Apr 1916, record (1916): 323.
Mrs. Rachel M. GRAY, age about 39 years, married, parents: Andy ROBINSON and Elizabeth HICKS, death cause: "operation, removal of uterus and tubes", informant: Robert GRAY (Indian Springs), died: 13 Apr 1916, record (1916): 324.
Willie Ann FITZGERALD, Negro, born: 13 Mar 1903 (?), age 21 years and 25 days, born in Virginia, parents: William WATKINS (NC) and Agnes WAKE (VA), death cause: illegible, buried: Citizens Cemetery, died: 7 Apr 1916, record (1916): 325.
Alfred POWERS, colored, age 57 years, born in Virginia, parents: not stated, death cause: "intestinal nephritis", informant: Lindsey POWERS (Bristol), buried: Bristol, VA., died: 6 Apr 1916, record (1916): 326.
Fannie R. WEST, Negro, born: 22 Apr 1879 in Virginia, married, parents: Dan HARRINGTON (NC) and Sallie TRIGG (VA), death cause: "abortion", informant: Sallie HARRINGTON (Bristol), buried: Tennessee Cemetery, died: 25 Apr 1916, record (1916): 327.
J.P. RHEA, born: 6 Jan 1872, married, physician, parents: John Preston RHEA and Matilda LONGACRE, death cause: "fall from 2nd story window", informant: Mrs. J.P. RHEA (Bristol), buried: Weaver Cemetery, died: 27 Apr 1916, record (1916): 328. (duplicate record below)
Fannie HINARD, Negro, age about 51 years, married, parents: Ford DELANEY and Maria BLEVINS, death cause: "mitral regurgitation", informant: Stephen BIEDLEMAN (Bristol), buried: Tennessee Cemetery, died: 23 Apr 1916, record (1916): 329.
Burl FRICK, Negro, age about 26 years, born in Virginia, married, parents: Charles FRICK (VA) and Lillie GODSEY (VA), death cause: "pulmonary tuberculosis", informant: Frank GODSEY (Bristol), buried: Citizen Cemetery, died: 7 Apr 1916, record (1916): 330.

Sindy SAMS, age 72 years, single, parents: Owen SAMS and Sarah PETERS, death cause: "cancer", informant: Mrs. George SAMS (Emmett), buried: Weaver Cemetery, died: 10 Apr 1916, record (1916): 331.

Samuel R. RICHARDS, age 68 years, married, parents: Tom RICHARDS and Mary THIER (NC), death cause: "heart trouble", informant: Mrs. Sam RICHARDS (Emmett), buried: Weaver Cemetery, died: 28 Apr 1916, record (1916): 332.

Mrs. Dorcas NEWTON, age 35 years, 3 months and 2 days, married, parents: James CORNETT and Polly CARRIER, death cause: "tuberculosis", informant: J. NEWTON (Bluff City), buried: Shipley Cemetery, died: 7 Apr 1916, record (1916): 333.

Dr. J.P. RHEA, age 43 years, 6 months and 7 days, married, parents: Dr. John P. RHEA and Matilda LONGACRE, death cause: "Brights disease", informant: Mrs. A.T. RHEA, buried: Weaver Cemetery, died: 27 Apr 1916, record (1916): 334. (duplicate of record 328)

W.P. MCCONNELL, age 33 years, born in Virginia, married, parents: W.S. MCCONNELL (VA) and Louisa COMPTON (VA), death cause: illegible, informant: W.S. MCCONNELL (Dungannon, VA), buried: Dungannon, VA., died: 15 May 1916, record (1916): 335.

Haley DEPEW, female, age about 30 years, born in Knox County, married, parents: Allen METCALF and Ann HICKMAN, death cause: "pulmonary tuberculosis", informant: J.E. LIGHT (Fall Branch), died: 21 May 1916, record (1916): 336.

Jessie Lee HARRISON, born: 18 May 1916, parents: Cyrus HARRISON (Washington Co., TN) and Fannie GOODMAN, death cause: "intestinal intoxication", informant: James HODGES (Fordtown), died: 30 May 1916, record (1916): 337.

Infant WHITTAKER, female, parents: Jessee WHITTAKER and Nora HODGE, death cause: "still born", informant: Dr. GRAVES (Piney Flats), buried: New Bethel Cemetery, died: 11 May 1916, record (1916): 338.

Charlie M. ARRANTS, born: 5 Jul 1883, single, parents: James ARRANTS and Bettie HUGHES, death cause: "pulmonary tuberculosis", died at Piney Flats on 14 May 1916, record (1916): 339.

Jess LINCOLNFELT, age 41 years, 6 months and 2 days, born in North Carolina, married, parents: James LINCOLNFELT (NC) and Nancy COLEMAN (NC), death cause: "pneumonia", informant: John COLEMAN (Emmett), buried: Shipley Cemetery, died: 8 May 1916, record: 340.

Beckie MOSS, age 32 years, married, parents: Abe MOSS and Mollie COX (NC), death cause: "tuberculosis", informant: Mike WEBB (Bluff City), buried: Crumley Cemetery, died: 10 May 1916, record (1916): 341.

Bob JENKINS, age 63 years, married, parents: Robert JENKINS and Mary COX (NC), death cause: "kidney trouble", buried: Crumley Cemetery, died: 7 May 1916, record (1916): 342.

Julia GEARY, born: 22 Sep 1855 in North Carolina, widow, parents: James THOMPSON and mother not stated, death cause: "carcinoma", informant: C.D. HOBBS (Bristol), buried: East Hill, died: 5 May 1916, record (1916): 343.

Claude CLARK, age about 21 years, single, parents: James CLARK and mother not stated, death cause: "pneumonia", informant: J.B. CLARK (Bristol), buried: Clear Branch Cemetery, died: 30 May 1916, record (1916): 344.

David DUNCAN, age 73 years, born in Scotland, widower, parents: David DUNCAN (Scotland) and Jean MILLER (Scotland), death cause: "apoplexy", informant: Mrs. G.D. ROSE (Greenville, KY), buried: Rockfort, KY., died: 12 May 1916, record (1916): 345.

Sallie ALFORD, age 50 years, widow, parents: not stated, death cause: "paralysis", informant: George ALFORD (Bristol), died: 26 May 1916, record: 346.

George W. TAYLOR, Negro, age about 72 years, married, parents: George TAYLOR (VA) and Amelia WEEKS (VA), death cause: "mitral insufficiency", informant: Sallie TAYLOR (Bristol), buried: Citizen Cemetery, died: 23 May 1916, record (1916): 347.

Lawrence HART, born: 29 Mar 1906, parents: J.T. (James Tennessee) HART and Harriett FRANCE, death cause: "Peritonitis resulting from injury", informant: S.W. FRANCE (Jonesboro), died at St. Luke Hospital, Bristol on 19 May 1916, buried: Elizabethton, record: 348.

Robert T. JENKINS, born: 4 Apr 1851 in Carter County, married, parents: William JENKINS (Carter Co.) and Fanny WHITE (Carter Co.), death cause: "dropsy", informant: G.E. JENKINS (Bluff City), buried: Chinquipin Grove, died: 8 May 1916, record: 349.

Charles BLEVINS, age 25 years, married, parents: R.L. BLEVINS and Maud BEARD (VA), death cause: "inanition following removal of spleen in 1914", informant: father (Bristol), died: 16 May 1916, record: 350.

Infant PERRY, female, parents: Carson PERRY and Anna SUMMERS (?), death cause: "still born", informant:

William PERRY (Kingsport), buried: Pile Cemetery, died: 18 May 1916, record (1916): 351.

Hal Moore COX, born: 9 Nov 1988, parents: Samuel B. COX and Emma PICKENS, death cause: "toxins absorbed from intestinal tract ....", informant: W.D. PICKENS (Jonesboro), buried: Fordtown Church Cemetery, died: 8 May 1916, record (1916): 352.

Bethel Grace HITE, born: 29 Jan 1916, parents: William Theodore HITE and Nora May LIGHT, death cause: "whooping cough", informant: father (Fordtown), died in the 14th District on 31 May 1916, record: 353.

Marshal B. DURHAM, born: 14 May 1897, single, parents: F.D. DURHAM (NC) and Amanda GILLEY (NC), death cause: "tuberculosis", informant: father (Indian Springs), buried: Emory Cemetery, died: 2 Jun 1916, record (1916): 354.

Clara B. ROGERS, born: 16 Apr 1916, parents: J.D. ROGERS and Ira SMITH, death cause: "spinal meningitis", informant: John SMITH (Indian Springs), buried: Emory Cemetery, died: 16 Jun 1916, record (1916): 355.

Winnie Bell BROWN, born: 1 Jul 1915, parents: Tilden BROWN and Nannie NELSON, death cause: "pertussus", buried: Brown Cemetery, 22nd District, died: 6 Jun 1916, record (1916): 356.

Margaret May FORD, born: 18 May 1916, parents: H. Arthur FORD and Lillie May COX, death cause: "acute indigestion", informant: E.P. ROLLER, buried: Lebanon Church Cemetery, 14th District, died: 13 Jun 1916, record (1916): 357.

Ruby Mae MITCHELL, born: 19 Jun 1915, parents: Floyd MITCHELL and Alice POORE, death cause: "spinal meningitis", informant: father (Fordtown), buried: Pactolus, died: 18 Jun 1916, record (1916): 358.

Frank H. MARION, born: 30 Apr 1916, parents: ___ MARION and Dorthy GOODMAN (Washington Co.), death cause: "intestinal intoxication", informant: Dorth MARION (Fordtown), buried: Goodman Cemetery, died: 20 Jun 1916, record (1916): 359.

Blanch DILLARD, born: 27 Oct 1895, married, parents: James A. JOHNSON and Fannie BARE, death cause: "tuberculosis", informant: Joal MCMURRY (Kingsport), buried: Martin Cemetery, died: 17 Jun 1916, record (1916): 360.

Infant KETRON, female, born: 12 May 1916, parents: O.E. KETRON and (illegible) LONG, death cause: "acute indigestion", informant: S.J. WILLIAMS

(Kingsport), buried: Grosclose Cemetery, died: 5 Jun 1916, record (1916): 361.

Minnie DISHNER, age 1 year, parents: William DISHNER and Fannie COLLINS, death cause: "whooping cough", informant: father (Kingsport), died: 30 Jun 1916, record (1916): 362.

George Author BENNET, born: 12 May 1915 in Virginia, parents: Bert BENNET and Sarah HARRIS, death cause: "entero colitis", informant: father (Kingsport), buried: Pile Cemetery, died: 22 Jun 1916, record (1916): 363.

Lucinda WELCH, age 94 years, born in Virginia, widow, parents: "unknown", death cause: "senility", informant: J.L. COLEY (Kingsport), buried: Reedy Creek Cemetery, died: 21 Jun 1916, record (1916): 364.

Sarah Elizabeth MARTIN, born: 10 Sep 1915, parents: E.K. MARTIN and Ollie WEAVER, death cause: "cholera infantum", informant: Joal MCMURRY (Kingsport), died: 12 Jun 1916, record (1916): 365.

Robert HILTON, age 21 months, born in Virginia, parents: not stated, death cause: "acute gastritis", buried: Dublin, VA., died: 11 Jun 1916, record (1916): 366. (see record 368)

Infant JONES, male, parents: Bob JONES and Blanche BULLOCK, death cause: "still born", informant: Mrs. A.T. BULLOCK (Emmett), buried: Shipley Cemetery, died: 26 Jun 1916, record (1916): 367.

Robert Clark HILTON, age 19 months, parents; John H. HILTON (VA) and Etta HUGHETT (VA), death cause: "acute gastritis", informant: father (Kingsport), buried: Dublin, VA., died: 12 Jun 1916, record (1916): 368. (see record 366)

Charles B. BLANKENSHIP, born: 18 Nov 1915 in Michigan, parents: J.C. BLANKENSHIP and Mary MORRIS, death cause: "cholera infantum", informant: Mrs. J.C. BLANKENSHIP (Bristol), buried: Elizabethton, died: 30 Jun 1916, record (1916): 369.

Mrs. J.T. ALLEY, age 43 years, born in Virginia, married, parents: J.H. ROSS (VA) and Susie LEONARD (VA), death cause: "Brights disease", informant: J.T. ALLEY (Bristol), buried: Norton, VA., died: 20 Jun 1916, record (1916): 370.

Evilen Chaistine JONES, born: 27 May 1916, parents: James K. JONES and Iva Chirstin MAUK, death cause: "infection from the cord", buried: Buckles Cemetery, 17th District, died: 10 Jun 1916, record (1916): 371.

Mildred LANE, age 13 months and 11 days, parents: William LANE and Kate FARRIS, death cause: "gastro intestinal indigestion", informant: Mrs. R.L. BEALER (Bristol), buried: Paperville, died: 8 Jun 1916, record (1916): 372.

Mollie GOBBLE, age 51 years, widow, born in Washington Co., VA., parents: Washington GOBBLE (Washington Co., VA) and Elizabeth HARLESS (Washington Co., VA), death cause: "pellagra", informant: Mary WOOD (Bristol), buried in Virginia, died: 10 Jun 1916, record: 373.

Robert L. HAGY, born: 12 May 1914, parents: Jack HAGY and Ella HOBBS (VA), death cause: "dysentary", informant: father (Bristol), buried: Peterman Cemetery, died: 19 Jun 1916, record (1916): 374.

George Palmer PHIPPS, age 40 years, born in Saltville, VA., married, parents: James PHIPPS (Saltville) and Amanda TAYLOR (Saltville), death cause: "cancer of stomach and liver", informant: Rowena PHIPPS (Bristol), buried: Glade Springs, VA., died: 4 Jun 1916, record (1916): 375.

Mary Jane THOMPSON, Negro, age about 70 years, born in North Carolina, widow, parents: "unknown", death cause: "carcinoma", informant: Lizzie THOMPSON (Bristol), buried: Citizens Cemetery, died: 1 Jun 1916, record (1916): 376.

Thearthur M. LOVE, male, age 17 years, 2 months and 7 days, parents: James LOVE and Amanda CROSS, death cause: "fractured skull", informant: Lola STRASER (Bristol), buried: Ordway Cemetery, died: 4 Jun 1916, record (1916): 377.

Laura Pet GRAY, born: 10 Mar 1900, parents: Elbert GRAY and Ellen GRAY, death cause: "tuberculosis", informant: father (Blountville), buried: Muddy Creek, died: 1 Jun 1916, record (1916): 378.

Mrs. Caroline SHIPLEY, age 58 years, married, parents: Landon LYONS and Lousie GLOVER, death cause: "tuberculosis", informant: Edmond SHIPLEY, died at Bluff City on 6 Jun 1916, record (1916): 379.

Nathan Delaney COWAN, born: 30 May 1896, single, parents: J. Booker COWAN and Ella THOMAS, death cause: "pulmonary tuberculosis", informant: C.M. COWAN (Bristol), buried: East Hill, died: 25 Jul 1916, record (1916): 380.

Juliett Jett WOOD, age 85 years, born in Scott Co., VA., single, parents: James O. WOOD (Scott Co.) and Anna Elizabeth GODSEY (Scott Co.), death cause: "senility", buried: East Hill, died: 29 Jul 1916, record (1916): 381.

Mrs. Martha OLIVER, age 78 years, widow, parents: Bill OLIVER and Jennie GROSS, death cause: "heart failure", buried: Oliver Cemetery, Piney Flats, died: 10 Jul 1916, record (1916): 382.

Oscar JONES, age 40 years, single, parents: John JONES and mother not stated, death cause: "apoplexy and epilepsy", buried: Poplar Ridge, Piney Flats, died: 6 Jul 1916, record (1916): 383.

E.M. WATSON, age 42 years, married, parents: John WATSON and Mollie GLOVER, death cause: "fracture skull, hit on head by limb", buried: Chinquipin Grove, Bluff City, died: 28 Jul 1916, record (1916): 384.

Madison JOHN, age 70 years, married, parents: not stated, death cause: "chronic nephritis", died at Bluff City on 15 Jul 1916, record (1916): 385.

Edward HYETT, age 2 years and 3 months, parents: Sam HYETT (Johnson County) and J. MAYS (Johnson County), death cause: "disentary", informant: father (Emmett), buried: Weaver Cemetery, died: 6 Jul 1916, record (1916): 386.

Lola RUTHERFORD, age 21 years, married, parents: John WEBB and Mary SIMERLY, death cause: "typhoid fever", buried: Bluntville, died: 25 Jul 1916, record (1916): 387.

Sabra Cornet HILLMAN, born: 5 Mar 1916, parents: Walker HILLMAN (VA) and Mary PRTER (VA), death cause: "ileo colitis", buried: Virginia, died: 14 Jul 1916, record (1916): 388.

R. RICHARD, born: 5 Jun 1915, male, parents: ___ RICHARD and Edna LUSTER, death cause: "acute illiocolitis", informant: W.H. WATSON (Kingsport), buried: Pyle Cemetery, died: 13 Jul 1916, record (1916): 389.

Martha PATTEN, age 103 years, born in Virginia, parents: unknown, death cause: "intestinal hemorrhage", buried: Gate City, died in the 13th District on 22 Jul 1916, record (1916): 390.

Henry MURRELL, black, age 92 years, born in Sullivan County, parents: unknown, death cause: not stated, informant: W.M. BACHMAN (Fall Branch), buried: Peoples Cemetery, died: 21 Jul 1916, record (1916): 391.

Loyd ESTEP, age 23 years, born in Virginia, parents: E.M. ESTEP (VA) and Susie BOLING (VA), death cause: "dysentary", informant: G.E. STONE (Emmett), buried: Cold Spring Cemetery, died: 20 Jul 1916, record (1916): 392.

Sarah I. WELSH, parents: John D. WELSH and Ida M. SHIPLEY, death cause: "still born", informant: Dr. A.M. MILLER (Kingsport), buried: Cox Cemetery, died: 15 Jul 1916, record (1916): 393.

Hazel HAYETT, born: 2 Jan 1915, parents: Arthur HAYETT and Rena SHIPLEY, death cause: "dysentary", died at Bluff City on 2 Jul 1916, record (1916): 394.

Norman MASSENGILL, born: 20 May 1915, parents: Sam MASSENGILL and Nettie GREENWAY, death cause: "dysentary", died at Bluff City on 21 Jul 1916, record (1916): 395.

Clarence LILLEY, age 11 months and 11 days, parents: Bill LILLEY and Mollie MCLAURY, death cause: "dysentary", died at Bluff City on 31 Jul 1916, record (1916): 396.

Willie BARE, born: 1 Jul 1915, parents: Doll BARE and Martha BUCKLES, death cause: "indigestion", died at Piney Flats on 5 Jul 1916, record (1916): 397.

Mrs. Will BARRETT, age 65 years, widow, parents: not stated, death cause: "chronic nephritis", died at Piney Flats on 15 Jul 1916, record (1916): 398.

Infant HUGHES, Negro, female, parents: James Preston HUGHES and Beatrice BIRDWELL, death cause: "breach birth", informant: Beatrice BIRDWELL, buried: Citizen Cemetery, died: 18 Jul 1916, record (1916): 399.

Marshall CROSS, born: 30 Apr 1835, widower, parents: David CROSS and Polly HAYNES, death cause: illegible, died in the 5th District on 22 Jul 1916, record (1916): 400.

Rev. Alfred Harrison BURRINGER, born: 18 Mar 1833 in Franklin Co., VA., widower, parents: Thomas BURRINGER (Franklin Co.) and Kitty BOOTH (Franklin Co.), death cause: "heart failure", informant: Mrs. M. DAVENPORT (Bristol), died: 5 Jul 1916, record (1916): 401.

Julia HITE, age about 48 years, married, parents: Robert HUDSON and Fannie ___, death cause: not stated, informant: W.M. DROKE (Blountville), buried: East Hill, died: 8 Jul 1916, record (1916): 402.

Eliza IRVINE, Negro, born: Dec 1870 in Virginia, parents: Bill MURRY (PA) and Frach MURRY (VA), death cause: "pulmonary ..illegible", informant: Lizzie HAMMER (Bristol), buried: Citizen Cemetery, died: 27 Jul 1916, record (1916): 403.

Mamie MONTGOMERY, age 41 years, born in Virginia, married, parents: G.M. KEY (VA) and Evaline HILLARD (VA), death cause: "organic heart disease", informant: C.M. MONTGOMERY (Bristol, VA), buried: Walnut Grove, VA., died: 10 Jul 1916, record (1916): 404.

P.M. BROOKS, age 58 years, born in Washington Co., VA., parents: Sam BROOKS (VA) and Sarah COWAN (VA), death cause: illegible, informant: Mrs. P.M. BROOKS

(Bristol), buried: East Hill, died: 8 Jul 1916, record (1916): 405.
Charlcie Lee JOHNSON, born: 31 Jul 1910, parents; J.E. JOHNSON and Mary SHELL, death cause: "tetanus", informant: father (Bristol), buried: Johnson City, died: 8 Jul 1916, record (1916): 406.
John Allen SCOTT, born: 13 May 1882, single, parents: J.M. SCOTT and Nannie HARRISON (VA), death cause: "railroad accident", informant: father (Bristol), buried: Beelers Cemetery, died: 19 Jul 1916, record (1916): 407.
Joseph Carson JONES, born: Aug 1840, married, parents: Joseph JONES (VA) and (illegible) BURCH (VA), death cause: "senility", informant: George J. JONES (Paperville), died: 17 Jul 1916, record (1916): 408.
Mrs. Sue MCCONNELL, age 68 years, born in Virginia, widow, parents: George MCCONNELL (VA) and Mary GRAY, death cause: "disentary", informant: David MCCONNELL (Emmett), buried: Green Springs, died: 17 Jul 1916, record (1916): 409.
James DEWEY, age 82 years, 6 months and 1 day, widower, parents: James DEWEY (West Virginia) and Margaret (illegible), death cause: "disentary", buried: Shipley Cemetery, died: 17 Jul 1916, record (1916): 410.
Martha BOWERS, age 48 years, 7 months and 2 days, married, parents: James GREEN (VA) and Mary DUGGER, death cause: "kidney trouble", informant: Katherine GREEN (Bluff City), died: 29 Jul 1916, record (1916): 411.
Robert Vernon HAYES, born: 17 Aug 1916, parents: G.C. HAYES (Smith Co., VA) and Lona M. BOND, death cause: "unknown", informant: father (Indian Springs), buried: Emory Cemetery, died: 18 Aug 1916, record (1916): 412.
Mitchell MANESS, age about 25 years, single, parents: "unknown", death cause: "railroad accident, legs cut off and blead to death", buried: Rogersville, TN., died: 22 Aug 1916, record (1916): 413.
Mrs. Elizabeth Gray HAMMER, born: 20 Aug 1832, widow, parents: John GRAY and Maria HARLAND, death cause: "uraemic poisoning", informant: Mrs. George ROBERSON (Bristol), buried: East Hill, died: 23 Aug 1916, record (1916): 414.
Herbert BURKETT, born: Sep 1915, parents: William BURKETT and Ethel BRADLEY, death cause: "unknown", informant: father (Bristol), buried: East Hill, died: 13 Aug 1916, record (1916): 415.

Robert Kyle SMITH, born: 26 Jul 1915, parents: Robert SMITH and Maud SMITH, death cause: "enteritis, pneumonia", informant: C.C. SMITH (Bristol), buried: Ordway Cemetery, died: 8 Aug 1916, record (1916): 416.

Alice MEADOW, born: 23 Jan 1915, parents: father not stated and Wildie MEADOW, death cause: "cholera infantum", informant: W.H. HENLEY (Bristol), died: 6 Aug 1916, record (1916): 417.

Infant MOORE, female, age 1 month and 3 weeks, born in North Carolina, parents: Thomas MOORE and Della PATTON (NC), death cause: "cholera morbus", informant: J.P. PRUETT (Bristol), buried: East Hill, died: 3 Aug 1916, record (1916): 418.

Infant PATTON, female, born: 2 Aug 1916, parents: E.K. PATTON and Bessie B. CARRIER, death cause: "blue disease", informant: Mrs. T.H. CARRIER (Bristol), buried: East Hill, died: 3 Aug 1916, record (1916): 419.

Sallie E. KELSEY, born: 10 Sep 1894, married, parents: J.C. MCHORRIS (Ohio) and Sara BERRY, death cause: "pulmonary tuberculosis", informant: C.M. KELSEY (Bristol), buried: Bulls Gap, died: 9 Aug 1916, record (1916): 420.

Leon JEFFERSON, Negro, born: 31 Jan 1916, parents: Windham JEFFERSON (VA) and Lucile CAMPBELL (VA), death cause: "gastritis", informant: Lucile CAMPBELL (Bristol), buried: Abingdon, VA., died: 9 Aug 1916, record (1916): 421.

James Carlton BOY, age 7 years, 4 months and 13 days, parents: J.C. BOY and Mary (illegible)(Rural Retreat, VA), death cause: "accidental fall", informant: father (Bristol), buried: East Hill, died: 3 Aug 1916, record (1916): 422.

Mattie Lee LEONARD, age 2 years and 10 months, parents: ___ LEONARD (Washington Co., VA) and Mollie KINDRICK (Washington Co., VA), death cause: "cholera infantum", informant: A.C. LEONARD (Bristol), died: 3 Aug 1916, record (1916): 423.

William A. SMITH, age 75 years, born in Kentucky, widower, soldier's home inmate, parents: not stated, death cause: "tuberculosis of bowels", informant: J.M. SMITH (Bristol), buried: East Hill, died: 7 Aug 1916, record (1916): 424.

A. Robert SMITH, born: 18 Apr 1916, parents: C.C. SMITH and Susie SPRAGER (VA), death cause: "gastro intestinal indigestion", informant: father (Bristol), buried: East Hill, died: 19 Aug 1916, record (1916): 425.

Louise PAINTER, age 8 months, born in Virginia, parents: E.S. PAINTER (VA) and Ellen VERRON (MD), death cause: "dysentery", informant: father (Bristol), buried: Rural Retreat, VA., died: 27 Aug 1916, record (1916): 426.

Louise Hyatt PAINTER, age 8 months, parents: E.S. PAINTER and Louise COLE, death cause: "dysentary", buried: Shipley Cemetery, died in the 1st District on 7 Aug 1916, record (1916): 427.

Myrtle Elizabeth GEORGE, age 13 months and 2 days, parents: John GEORGE and Mary GEORGE (VA), death cause: "cholera infantum", informant: Mrs. Clara GEORGE (Emmett), buried: Weaver Cemetery, died: 14 Aug 1916, record (1916): 428.

Sarah Elizabeth SELL, born: 31 Nov 1866 in Virginia, married, parents: S.P. WILLISS (VA) and Nannie BARKER (VA), death cause: "intestinal tuberculosis", informant: G.W. SELL (Kingsport), buried: Ford Cemetery, Fordtown, died: 6 Aug 1916, record: 429.

George OVERBAY, born: 19 Jan 1916, parents: Elijah OVERBAY and Lola INMAN, (VA), death cause: "cholera infantum", informant: William INMAN (Kingsport), buried: Pyle Cemetery, died: 19 Aug 10916, record (1916): 430.

Martha NOAH, born: 14 Aug 1914 in Virginia, parents: Grant NOAH (VA) and Mary HAYNES (VA), death cause: "acute nephritis", informant: R.J. HAYNES (Kingsport), died: 29 Aug 1916, record (1916): 431.

Wilker BARE, born: 5 Aug 1883 in Virginia, single, parents: William BARE (VA) and Ella FOSTER (NC), death cause: "broken back", buried: Piney Flats, died: 5 Aug 1916, record (1916): 432.

Infant SANTIAGO, born: 13 Aug 1916, parents: James J. SANTIAGO (Madrid, Spain) and Maud DOYLE (Abingdon), death cause: "premature", informant: father (Bristol), buried: Walnut Grove, died: 26 Aug 1916, record (1916): 433.

R.M. HAWKS, age 37 years, born in Virginia, married, parents: R.E. HAWKS (VA) and Jane SNOW (VA), death cause: "peritonitis", informant: T.M. HAWKS (Blountville), died: 17 Aug 1916, record (1916): 434.

Mrs. Charles GODSEY, age 36 years, born in Virginia, married, parents: W.S. STRICKLEY (VA) and Mary DICKERSON (VA), death cause: "embolism in heart in childbirth", informant: J.S. GODSEY (Bristol), buried: Ordway Cemetery, died: 13 Aug 1916, record: 435.

Mrs. Henry D. WEBB, age 23 years, married, parents: J.H. RUTHERFORD (Washington Co., VA) and Bettie WHITE, death cause: "typhoid fever", informant: father (Bristol), buried: Bluff City, died: 16 Aug 1916, record (1916): 436.

Nina Virginia FELTY, age 2 years, parents: R.D. FELTY and Mollie MCCAMEY, death cause: "illegible", informant: father (Bristol), buried: Ordway Cemetery, died: 13 Aug 1916, record (1916): 437.

Reesi EYLER, age 14 months and 17 days, parents: C.E. EYLER (Waynesboro, PA) and Myrtle HAUK (Bristol), death cause: "dysentery", informant: Mrs. C.E. EYLER (Bristol), buried: Bluff City, died: 17 Aug 1916, record (1916): 438.

Infant CROSS, female, parents: Jack CROSS and Leashey ROSE, death cause: "still born", buried: Rockey Springs, died: 1 Aug 1916, record (1916): 439.

Roxy Mae MOODY, born: 13 Mar 1912, parents: George MOODY and Lula HILTON, death cause: "spinal meningitis", informant: Lula MOODY (FORDTOWN), buried: Emory Church, died: 3 Aug 1916, record (1916): 440.

Charles Smith ERWIN, born: 23 Mar 1871, married, parents: George Washington IRWIN and Martha E. DEVAULT, death cause: "pulmonary tuberculosis", informant: E.M. HALL (Fordtowon), buried: Fordtown Cemetery, died: 7 Aug 1916, record (1916): 441.

George J. OVERBAY, born: 18 Jan 1916, parents: Elijah OVERBAY and Lee INMAN (VA), death cause: "enterocolitis", informant: father (Fordtown), buried: Pactolus Church Cemetery, died: 18 Aug 1916, record (1916): 442. (duplicate of # 430 ?)

Samuel Rex MULLENS, born: 8 Sep 1905, parents: Lorenzo MULLENS and Alice MULLENS, death cause: "pneumonia", informant: mother (Fall Branch), died: 29 Aug 1916, record (1916): 443.

Infant MURRAY, male, parents: Byrd MURRAY and Samantha SHEPSHIRE, death cause: "still born", informant: Dr. MORGAN (Fall Branch), died: 7 Aug 1916, record: 444.

Isaac ZIMMERMAN, born: 3 Nov 1842, widower, parents: "unknown", death cause: "typhoid fever, chronic intestinal nephritis", informant: J.B. CONKINS (Kingsport), buried: Pyle Cemetery, died: 3 Sep 1916, record (1916): 445.

Calie L.M. CAMPBELL, age 55 years, single, born in Lee County, VA., parents: George W. CAMPBELL (Smythe Co., VA) and Mary Mariah FITZPATRICK, death cause: "tuberculosis", informant: Sallie CAMPBELL (Bristol), buried: East Hill, died: 18 Sep 1916, record: 446.

Emmatin Conkin MINOY (?), born: 15 Dec 1873, married, parents: James CONKIN and Martha Ellen MORRELL, death

cause: "pulmonary tuberculosis", informant: Nobel CONKIN (Fall Branch), buried: Blair Gap Cemetery, died: 3 Sep 1916, record (1916): 447.
Lonzinda DILLARD, born: 3 Jun 1916, parents: Jordan DILLARD and Blanche JOHNSON, death cause: "tuberculosis", informant: Wesley DILLARD (Kingsport), buried: Martins Cemetery, died: 10 Sep 1916, record (1916): 448.
Bertie PIPPIN, age 11 years, born in Virginia, parents: H.G. PIPPIN (VA) and Sarah MARSH (VA), death cause: "typhoid fever", informant: father (Bristol), buried: Pippin Cemetery, died: 26 Sep 1916, record (1916): 449.
Henry HAYES, Negro, age: approximately 61 years, parents: "unknown", death cause: "chronic intestinal nephritis, uremia", informant: Alex HAYES (Bristol), buried: Citizens Cemetery, died: 4 Sep 1916, record (1916): 540.
J.H. MCCLELLAN, age 64 years, born in Virginia, married, parents: Robert MCCLELLAN (VA) and Dolly GREGORY (VA), death cause: "heart disease", informant: J.B. MCCLELLAN (Bluff City), buried: Pleasant Grove, died: 18 Sep 1916, record (1916): 451.
Howard Rutledge CORUM, born: 13 Sep 1915, parents: R.C. CORUM (Johnson County) and Bidy May SHELTON (Washington Co., VA), death cause: "enteritis", informant: Mrs. M.E. SHELTON (Bristol), buried: Walnut Grove, died: 2 Sep 1916, record (1916): 452.
Anna WILLIAMS, Negro, born: 25 Aug 1864 in Virginia, married, parents: Preston HUGHES (VA) and Ruth PENN (VA), death cause: "pulmonary tuberculosis", informant: Robert PENN (Bristol), buried: Citizen Cemetery, died: 5 Sep 1916, record (1916): 453.
Mrs. Mary WAGNER, age 80 years, widow, parents: George WAGNER and Annie MILHORN, death cause: "senility, heart and kidney complication", informant: M.F. WAGNER (Blountville), died: 7 Sep 1916, record (1916): 454.
E.M. LOCKWOOD, born: 2 Dec 1848 in Virginia, married, parents: Zelotis LOCKWOOD (VA) and Mary FAIRBANKS (VA), death cause: "pelvic abscess", informant: E.A. LOCKWOOD (Bristol), buried: Knoxville, died: 24 Sep 1916, record (1916): 455.
Hazel CLOYD, age 19 years, born in Virginia, parents: M.M. CLOYD and Etter MUMPOWER (VA), death cause: "typhoid fever", informant: John CLOYD (Bristol), died: 5 Sep 1916, record (1916): 456.
W.H. HASS, age 21 years, born in North Carolina, married, parents: W.J. HASS (NC) and Jane FOWLER (NC),

death cause: "diabetes", informant: J.C. HASS (Lenoir, NC), buried: East Hill, died: 22 Sep 1916, record (1916): 457.

Joseph GREEN, Negro, age: about 55 years, widower, parents: Richard GREEN and mother's name unknown, death cause: "chronic brights", informant: Violet GREEN (Bristol), buried: Citizens Cemetery, died: 6 Sep 1916, record (1916): 458.

David SPANGLER, age: about 74 years, married, parents: J.R. SPANGLER and mother not stated, death cause: "injury from auto accident", informant: Dr. REESER (Church Hill), buried: Church Hill, died: 12 Sep 1916, record (1916): 459.

Mrs. Minnie Feagins SAULS, born: 28 Jun 1890, widow, parents: J.W. FEAGINS and Lizzie ROSE, death cause: "phthisis", informant: father (Bristol), buried: Bailey Cemetery, died: 4 Sep 1916, record (1916): 460.

Francis CARROLL, age 1 year and 5 months, parents: John CARROLL and Maggie CARRIER, death cause: "spinal neningitis", informant: father (Bristol), died: 7 Sep 1916, record (1916): 461.

Nancy E. GRIMES, age 53 years, widow, parents: John GRIMES and Julia HORTON, death cause: "rheumatism", buried: Weaver Cemetery, died: 27 Sep 1917, record (1916): 462.

Charlie PEAKS, age 6 years, parents: Andrew Peaks and Mary SMITH, death cause: "paralysis", informant: N.S. PETERS (Bristol), buried: Weaver Cemetery, died: 16 Sep 1916, record (1916): 463.

Fransinah WOODS, born: 1 Apr 1842, married, parents: Nathan ARANTS and Mary Ann MOTTERN, death cause: "apoplexy", buried: Poplar Ridge Cemetery, buried: Bluff City, died: 29 Sep 1916, record (1916): 464.

Anna Lee CROSS, born: 2 Jan 1916, parents: Sam CROSS and Nanie FOX, death cause: "dysentery", died at Bluff City on 28 Sep 1916, record (1916): 465.

John E. WALLACE, born: 27 Feb 1875, married, parents: John WALLACE and Amanda BURKHART, death cause: "peritonitis from injury", informant: Mrs. Lanettie WALLACE (Bristol), buried: Chattanooga, died: 7 Sep 1916, record (1916): 466.

Mary Earsel SHEPHERD, born: 13 Jun 1916, parents: L.R. SHEPHERD and Ruth PRICE, death cause: "acute gastritis", informant: J.B. SHEPHERD (Kingsport), buried: Milligan College, TN., died: 7 Sep 1916, record (1916): 467.

John Hoffard BROWN, born: 26 Jul 1916, parents: George BROWN (GA) and Mary DOOLEY (GA), death cause:

"malnutrition", informant: Charley BROWN (Kingsport), buried: Martin Cemetery, died: 8 Sep 1916, record (1916): 468.

Jake COLLINS, age 69 years, widower, parents: father's name not known and Nancy BAINS (VA), death cause: not stated, buried: Loveless Cemetery, died: 9 Sep 1916, record (1916): 469.

Hanibel DULANEY, black, age 49 years, married, parents: father's name not known and Lydia GAINES, death cause: "tuberculosis lungs", informant: John HUMPHREYS (Kingsport), died: 10 Sep 1916, record (1916): 471.

Lucinda UMPHRAS, born: 10 Nov 1876, married, parents: James JOHNSON and Maggie HARKLEROAD, death cause: "typhoid fever", informant: Rich JOHNSON (Johnson City), buried: Pyle Cemetery, died at Bloomingdale on 10 Sep 1916, record (1916): 470.

Wallie ELDRIDGE, age 38 years, place of birth unknown and parents unknown, keeper with Sparks Show, death cause: "killed by elephant", informant: J.M. HAMLETT (Kingsport), died: 15 Sep 1916, record (1916): 472.

Thelma Mae BROWN, born: 15 Mar 1915 in Kentucky, parents: H.C. BROWN (Texas) and Polly BAILEY (KY), death cause: "lobar pneumonia", informant: H.C. BROWN (Kingsport), died: 23 Sep 1916, record (1916): 473.

Kenneth Estell WILLS, born: 9 Aug 1915 in Virginia, parents: C.G. WILLS (KY) and Effie (illegible), death cause: "acute indigestion", informant: John GAINES (Kingsport), died: 17 Sep 1916, record (1916): 474.

Infant WILSON, female, parents: L.S. WILSON and Mamie MCGUFFIE, death cause: "still birth", informant: father (Kingsport), died: 15 Sep 1916, record: 475.

Infant TAYLOR, female, parents: Al TAYLOR and Dora GODWIN, death cause: "born dead", informant: Geroge W. TAYLOR (Bristol), buried: East Hill, died: 4 Sep 1916, record (1916): 476.

Infant BALL, male, parents: D.A. BALL and Mollie BUCKLES, death cause: "still born", buried: Piney Flats, died: 8 Sep 1916, record (1916): 477.

Rachel Dorothy POORE, born: 22 Sep 1914, parents: Floyd POORE and Mamie GRAY, death cause: "diphtheria", informant: Robert GRAY (Indian Springs), buried: Pyle Cemetery, died: 20 Oct 1916, record (1916): 478.

Christine Margaret STOPHEL, born: 20 Apr 1866, widow, parents: James Henry FEATHERS and Christine MYERS, death cause: "brights disease", informant: David STOPHEL (Bristol), buried: Stophel Cemetery, died: 12 Oct 1916, record (1916): 479.

Infant MCMIN, male, parents: O.L. MCMIN and May EDWARDS, death cause: "still born", buried: Bluff City, died: 10 Oct 1916, record (1916): 480.

Infant INMAN, male, parents: Lee INMAN and Carrie PASION (?), death cause: "still born", informant: father (Kingsport), buried: Martin Cemetery, died: 26 Oct 1916, record (1916): 481.

Mrs. Emmie FLEENOR, born: 22 Nov 1856, widow, parents: Thomas P. (illegible) and Mary MORRELL, death cause: "heart disease", informant: T.C. CHILDRESS (Fall Branch), buried: Bachman Family Cemetery, 13th District, died: 2 Oct 1916, record (1916): 482.

Dana MORRELL, born: 15 Feb 1904, parents: Dorsey MORRELL and Ida CLARK, death cause: "pellagra, tuberculosis", informant: father (Fall Branch), buried: Morrell Cemetery, 5th District, died: 5 Oct 1916, record (1916): 483.

Bettie GRILLS, born: 6 Oct 1859, married, parents: Daniel HARGIS (PA) and Nany WHALEY, death cause: "typhoid fever", informant: Henry GRILLS (Fall Branch), buried: Grills Cemetery, 13th District, died: 13 Oct 1916, record (1916): 484.

Cecil Clyde LIGHT, born: 15 Oct 1916, parents: John R. LIGHT and Della C (illegible), death cause: "jaundice, mitral incompetency", died at Fall Branch on 18 Oct 1916, record (1916): 485.

Benjamin Franklin HOOD, born: 23 Sep 1843, married, parents: Dutton HOOD and Nancy LOVE, death cause: "chronic postalitis", informant: Johnathon HOOD (Fordtown), buried: Depew Chapel, died: 16 Oct 1916, record (1916): 486.

Polly Buckeless ZIMMERMAN, born: 21 Jun 1856, widow, parents: George WEXLER and Sarah BUCKELESS, death cause: "rheumatism", informant: A.H. WEXLER (Fordtown), buried: 14th District, died: 10 Oct 1916, record (1916): 487.

Ewell LEONARD, age 75 years, born in Virginia, widower, parents: Mike LEONARD and ___ COLE, death cause: "organic heart disease", informant: W.F. LEONARD (Bristol), buried: Johnson Cemetery, died: 26 Oct 1916, record (1916): 488.

James Henry CHURCH, age 28 years, born in North Carolina, parents: Joseph CHURCH (NC) and Amanda GOODMAN (NC), death cause: "gunshot wound of right arm and chest followed by blood poison", informant: George CHURCH (Shouns, TN), buried: Shouns, TN., died: 21 Oct 1916, record (1916): 487.

Myrtle DAVIS, born: 20 Oct 1871, married, parents: H.C. COLLINS and Susie PRICHARD, death cause: "intestinal tuberculosis", informant: C.E. DAVIS (Bristol), buried: Knoxville, died: 27 Oct 1916, record (1916): 490.

Mrs. Mary SNAPP, age 73 years, born in Virginia, widow, parents: John GRANT (VA) and mother not stated, death cause: illegible, informant: J.W. WEBB (Bristol), buried: Webb Cemetery, died: 15 Oct 1916, record (1916): 491.

Elizabeth Katherine Droke HICKS, born: 12 Mar 1862, married, parents: William DROKE and Agens WEBB, death cause: "Brights disease", buried: Droke Cemetery, died in the 8th District on 13 Oct 1916, record: 492.

Mrs. Fannie MILSAP, born: 19 Oct 1888 in North Carolina, married, parents: Hiram GREEN (NC) and mother not stated, death cause: "acute nephritis", informant: Walter MILSAP (Bluff City), buried: Chinquipin Cem, died: 19 Oct 1916, record (1916): 493.

William I. ISLEY, born: 7 Mar 1849, widower, parents: William ISLEY and Rosana HAWK, death cause: "catarrh stomach", informant; W.H. PERRY (Kingsport), died: 30 Oct 1916, record (1916): 494.

Infant SMITH, female, born: 25 Jul 1916, parents: Isaah SMITH and Kate HOUKE (VA), death cause: "acute indigestion", informant: father (Kingsport), buried: Pyle Cemetery, died: 26 Oct 1916, record (1916): 495.

Edith CHRISTIAN, born: 26 Jan 1916, parents: Landon CHRISTIAN and Odie BLAKELEY, death cause: "pneumonia", informant: father (Kingsport), buried: Liberty Cemetery, died: 23 Oct 1916, record (1916): 496.

Will KELLEY, colored, born: 10 Sep 1890 in Virginia, married, parents: "not known", death cause: "typhoid fever and cerebral meningitis", informant: Jack RUDY (Kingsport), died: 17 Oct 1916, record (1916): 497.

Lida E. BOLTON, born: 14 SEp 1891, single, parents: (illegible) BOLTON, and Nannie JOHNSON, death cause: illegible, informant: Cleve PARKER (Kingsport), buried: Pyle Cemetery, died: 15 Oct 1916, record (1916): 498.

Anna Low BRADLEY, born: 18 Dec 1885 in North Carolina, single, parents: James H. BRADLEY (NC) and Mary E. LEATHERWOOD (NC), death cause: "tuberculosis", informant: father (kingsport), buried: Pyle Cemetery, died: 11 Oct 1916, record (1916): 499.

George William YOAKLEY, born: 4 Jul 1865 in Moresburg, Hawkins County, married, parents: Noah YOAKLEY (Wash Co. VA) and ___ STOFFLE, death cause: "general

peritonitis", informant: Miss M.H. YOAKLEY (Kingsport), died: 7 Oct 1916, record (1916): 500.
Lizzie STOATS, age 51 years, widow, parents: John (illegible) and mother not stated, death cause: "pulmonary tuberculosis", informant: William STOUK (Kingsport), buried: Martin Cemetery, died: 7 Oct 1916, record (1916): 501.
Bradis HORTON, black, born: 2 May 1916, parents: Bradis HORTON and Mamie JONES (NC), death cause: "pneumonia", informant: father (Kingsport), died: 2 Oct 1916, record (1916): 502.
Roy N. HAUN, born: 9 Sep 1888, married, railroad employee, parents: P. HAUN and M.J. CHESTNUT, death cause: "injury, was run over by train", informant: W.E. WILLS (Bristol), buried: Persia, TN., died: 18 Oct 1916, record (1916): 503.
Lillian SCOTT, born: 28 Feb 1916, parents: George SCOTT and Cora HARRISON (Wallace, VA), death cause: "diphtheria", informant: Mrs. Ben SCOTT (Bristol), died: 15 Oct 1916, record (1916): 504.
Fannie CRAWFORD, born: 26 Aug 1906 in Green County, parents: A.L. CRAWFORD and Lidie TAYLOR (Green Co.), death cause: "tetanus", informant: father (Bristol), died: 6 Oct 1916, record (1916): 505.
Elizabeth JACKSON, age not stated, widow, born in Washington Co., VA., parents: John DISHNER (Wash Co., VA) and Martha DISHNER (Wash Co. VA), death cause: "apoplexy", informant: Ms. J.M. LEONARD (Bristol), buried: Three Springs, VA., died: 2 oct 1916, record (1916): 506.
Margaret STOPHLE, age 48 years, widow, parents: William FEATHERS (VA) and Becky BOLING, death cause: "pneumonia", informant: Davy STOPHLE (Bristol), buried; Stophle Cemetery, died: 25 Oct 1916, record (1916): 507.
Davy BERY, age 7 years, parents: Bryan BERY and Lockie WEAVER (VA), death cause: "typhoid fever", buried: Weaver Cemetery, died at Bluff City on 9 Oct 1916, record (1916): 508.
Roy A. COFFMAN, born: 3 Feb 1915, parents: Walter A. COFFMAN and Viola C. COFFMAN, death cause: "diphtheria", informant: Daniel COFFMAN (Fordtown), buried: Wheeler Chapel, died: 7 Oct 1916, record (1916): 509.
Infant VANCE, male, parents: S.J. VANCE and Mattie PHIPPS, death cause: "still born", informant: S.A. BLEVINS (Bristol), buried: Paperville Cemetery, died: 14 Oct 1916, record (1916): 510.

Infant FALK, female, parents: Bordie FALK and Fannie DISHNER, death cause: "born dead", informant: father (Bloomingdale), died: 12 Nov 1916, record (1916): 511.

Almedia Elizabeth ROLLER, born: 29 Mar 1916, parents: William ROLLER and Bessie E. KING, death cause: "broncho pneumonia", informant: G.W. KING (Indian Springs), buried: Emory Cemetery, died: 27 Nov 1916, record (1916): 512.

Amandy HUMPHRIES, age 80 years, separated, parents: Mathey MARION and mother's name not known, death cause: "cancer of lip and cold", informant: James M. HARKLEROAD (Bloomingdale), buried: Reedy Creek, died: 30 Nov 1916, record (1916): 513.

Vernie Murray WARD, age about 20 years, married, parents: Roller MURRAY and Emmaline CONKINS, death cause: "purpual albuminuria", informant: father (Fall Branch), buried: Mullins Cemetery, 15th District, died: 25 Nov 1916, record (1916): 514.

Roy B. SMITH, born: 5 Aug 1901 in Carter County, parents: Henry W. SMITH and Mattie REVESS (NC), death cause: "typhoid fever", informant: Dr. GRAVES (Piney Flats), buried: Muddy Creek, died: 10 Nov 1916, record (1916): 515.

William Ledford ANDERSON, born: 9 Aug 1841, widower, parents: George R. ANDERSON and Eliza LEDFORD, death cause: "diabetes", buried at Bluff City, died: 3 Nov 1916, record (1916): 516.

Amanda HUMPHRIES, born: 30 Nov 1836, widow, parents: not known, death cause: "cancer", informant: S.P. LESSLEY (Bloomingdale), died: 30 Nov 1916, record (1916): 517. (duplicate of # 517)

Lena COLEMAN, black, born: 17 Nov 1910, parents: Albert COLEMAN (GA) and Eva (illegible), death cause: "tuberculosis lungs", informant: George GRIFFIN (Kingsport), died: 17 Nov 1916, record (1916): 518.

Wanita E. JOHNSON, born: 5 Oct 1914 in Virginia, parents: Sam F. JOHNSON (NC) and Nora BEEMAN (VA), death cause: "diphtheria", informant: A.C. JOHNSON (Kingsport), buried: Pyle Cemetery, died: 15 Nov 1916, record (1916): 519.

Nannie COMPTON, born: 9 Jul 1896, married, parents: George A. ARNOLD and Edna MOODY, death cause: "tuberculosis of lungs", informant: Everet COMPTON (Kingsport), buried: Pyle Cemetery, died: 9 Nov 1916, record (1916): 520.

George A. ARNOLD, born: 21 Apr 1861, married, parents: Jack ARNOLD and Edna MOODY, death cause: "cancer of spleen", informant: Everet COMPTON (Kingsport), buried: Pyle Cemetery, died: 5 Nov 1916, record (1916): 521.

Joseph WILKINS, age about 74 years, married, parents: John WILKINS and Mary LANE (VA), death cause: "disease of heart", buried: Weaver Cemetery, 3rd District, died: 28 Nov 1916, record (1916): 522.

Ralph Burton RUBENS, Jr., parents: Ralph B. RUBENS (Ohio) and Lolla ANDERSON (KY), death cause: "premature birth", informant: father (Bristol), born/died: 30 Nov 1916, record (1916): 523.

Infant PRUITT, female, parents: D.F. PRUITT and Addie HENLEY, death cause: "still born", informant: father (Bristol), buried: Ordway Cemetery, died: 9 Nov 1916, record (1916): 524.

Infant HORTON, colored, male, parents: Cecil HORTON (Johnson City) and Viola HARTSEL (Washington Co., VA), death cause: "still born", informant: J.B. MILLARD (Kingsport), died: 9 Nov 1916, record (1916): 525. (twin below)

Infant HORTON, colored, male, parents: Cecil HORTON (Johnson City) and Viola HARTSEL (Washington Co., VA), death cause: "still born", informant: J.B. MILLARD (Kingsport), died: 9 Nov 1916, record (1916): 526. (twin above)

Verrey ROSENBAUM, female, born: 13 Aug 1916, parents: Sam ROSENBAUM (VA) and Lucie GODSEY, death cause: "found dead in bed", informant: father (Bristol), buried: East Hill, died: 21 Nov 1916, record (1916): 527.

Mrs. Nellie DYER, age about 41 years, married, parents: Landon MORELAND and mother not stated, death cause: "tuberculosis (possibly)", informant: J.R. DYER (Bristol), buried: East Hill, died: 19 Nov 1916, record (1916): 528.

Mary Virginia WALLING, born: 16 Jul 1916, parents: Vernon WALLING and Viola JONES, death cause: "found dead in bed", informant: father (Bristol), buried: East Hill, died: 16 Nov 1916, record (1916): 529.

Infant TRINKLE, male, born: 12 Nov 1916, parents: Lee TRINKLE and Annie SHOECRAFT, death cause: "convulsions", informant: father (Bristol), buried: Ordway Cemetery, died: 23 Nov 1916, record (1916): 530.

Charles PERKINS, colored, age about 22 years, born: 22 Feb ___ in Mississippi, single, parents: Charles PERKINS, Sr. (Mississippi) and mother not stated, death cause: "tetanus, wound in right foot", informant: J.R. ALLEN (Bristol), buried: West Point, MS., died: 22 Nov 1916, record (1916): 531.

Edmond Allen TILLY, born; 24 Sep 1864 in Virginia, married, parents: Edmond TILLY (TX) and Belle F. SNAPP (VA), death cause: "hemipligia and acute nephritis", informant: Mrs. E.A. TILLY (Bristol), buried: East Hill, died: 27 Nov 1916, record (1916): 532.

S.C.W. SMITH, age 49 years, born in Virginia, married, parents: A.C. SMITH (VA) and Judith WILKINSON (VA), death cause: "Brights disease", informant: father (Bristol), died: 2 Dec 1916, record (1916): 533.

Mrs. S.E. MUSIC, age 49 years, widow, born in Russell Co., VA., parents: James ARNOLD (VA) and mother not stated, death cause: not stated, informant; Cora MUSIC (Bristol), buried: East Hill, died: 12 Nov 1916, record (1916): 534.

Miss Bula SNYDER, age 40 years, born in Smythe Co., VA., single, parents: P.T. SNYDER (VA) and Emily L. HOOFNAGLE (Smythe Co.), death cause: "chronic lymphatic leukemia", informant: father (Bristol), buried: Marion, VA., died: 13 Nov 1916, record: 535.

William ROGERS, age 4 years, parents: William ROGERS (VA) and Jennie GODSEY, death cause: "carcinoma of bowels", informant: father (Bristol), died: 22 Nov 1916, record (1916): 536.

James LANGLEY, age 69 years, born in Johnson County, widower, parents: John LANGLEY and mother not stated, death cause: not stated, informant: Mrs. Thomas JONES (Bristol), died: 8 Nov 1916, record (1916): 537.

P.H. LEONARD, age 86 years, born in Washington Co., VA., married, parents: Gasper LEONARD (Washington Co., VA) and mother not stated, death cause: "heart failure", informant: J.M. LEONARD (Bristol), buried: Clear Branch, VA., died: 4 Nov 1916, record: 538.

Mrs. Elizabeth SHOUN, age 52 years, married, parents: not stated, death cause: "following operation", informant: Dr. STOUT (Shouns, TN), buried: Shouns, TN., died: 1 Nov 1916, record (1916): 539.

William ANDERSON, born: 6 Jun 1846, married, parents: John ANDERSON, Sr. and mother not stated, death cause: "chronic nephritis", buried: Bluff City, died; 6 Nov 1916, record (1916): 540.

James Russell CARRIER, age 73 years, 3 months and 7 days, married, parents: Johnathon CARRIER and Charlottie RUSSELL, death cause: "bright disease", informant: Sarah CARRIER (Bluff City), buried: Hickory Tree, died: 30 Nov 1916, record (1916): 541.

Rubbie ODELL, female, age 10 months and 21 days, parents: Willia ODELL and Mattie BOWLON, death cause: "pneumonia fever", buried: Crumley Cemetery, 1st District, died: 1 Nov 1916, record (1916): 542.

James David MURRAY, born: 8 Jul 1894, single, parents: James W. MURRAY (Washington Co., TN) and Mary Ann FORD, death cause: "tumor in abdomen following removal of testicle", informant: J.A. MURRAY (Fordtown), buried: Pond Church Cemetery, died: 1 Nov 1916, record (1916): 543.

David Lee COATS, parents: Arthur COATS and Effie GRILLS, death cause: "premature birth", informant: father (Fall Branch), buried: Depew Chapel, born/died: 3 Nov 1916, record (1916): 544.

Henry BRANCH, born: 7 Aug 1912 in Mitchell Co., NC., parents: J.G. BRANCH (Mitchell Co.) and Litha HONECUT (Mitchell Co.), death cause: "tuberculosis lungs, informant: father (Fall Branch), died: 9 Nov 1916, record (1916): 545.

Minnie Leona STEADMAN, born: 10 Dec 1884 in Virginia, married, parents: William KETRON (VA) and Ursula ISAM (VA), death cause: "tubercular meningitis", informant: John STEADMAN (Fall Branch), buried: Depew Chapel, died: 12 Nov 1916, record (1916): 546.

Marry BARNES, age 68 years, widow, parents: Will MINGUS and Mary ROLLER, death cause: "chronic brights", informant: Dr. SNAPP (Blountville), died: 21 Dec 1916, record (1916): 547.

Rebecca Pile YOST, born: 30 Nov 1838, widow, parents: George C. COLE (Lancaster Co., PA) and Prescilla Wheeler SNODGRASS, death cause: "nephritis", informant: Mrs. Dora Y. MCCRARY (Bristol), buried: Bluff City, died: 26 Dec 1916, record (1916): 548.

Samuel Perry GREGG, born: 28 Nov 1916, parents: Charles GREGG and Louisa Melinda DYKES (Green Co., TN), death cause: "acute indigestion", informant: John H. GREGG (Fordtown), died: 25 Dec 1916, record: 549.

Grover A. WILSON, born: 8 Sep 1916, parents: Sam WILSON and Neva CHASE, death cause: "found dead in bed", died at Fall Branch on 9 Dec 1916, buried: Depew Chapel, record (1916): 550.

Ellen CARR, born: 24 Oct 1836, married, parents: John WARD and Hester RATLIFF, death cause: "mitral insufficiency", informant: O.H. CARR (Fall Branch), buried: Carr Cemetery, 15th District, died: 1 Dec 1916, record (1916): 551.

George W. HAYNES, born: 30 Apr 1915 in Virginia, parents: John W. HAYNES (VA) and Ellen DUNCAN (VA), death cause: "rickets", informant: J. HAYNES (Kingsport), died: 1 Dec 1916, record (1916): 552.

Julian MITCHELL, born: 22 Nov 1916, parents: J. Walter MITCHELL (Fairview, NC) and Nina KEENER (Whittier, NC), death cause: "acute indigestion", informant: Dr. MILLARD (Kingsport), died; 11 Dec 1916, record: 553.

Samuel Walker PARKER, born: 15 Oct 1885, married, parents: Joe W. PARKER and Virginia B. JOHNSON, death cause: "hemorrhage of brain, injury by train", informant: W.F. GREEN (Kingsport), died: 18 Dec 1916, record (1916): 554.

Laura STADMAN, born: 28 Nov 1887, married, parents: James OWENS and mother not stated, death cause: "dilatation of heart", informant: W.A. GREEN (Kingsport), buried: Church Hill, TN., died; 24 Dec 1916, record (1916): 555.

Wilber REESE, born: 6 Mar 1914 in Cherokee Co., NC., parents: D.M. REESE (Cherokee Co.) and Nancy (illegible), death cause: "burn", informant: Mrs. D.M. REESE (Kingsport), died: 24 Dec 1916, record: 556.

James BRANDON, born: 3 Dec 1914, parents: S.D. BRANDON and Olie CRAWFORD, death cause: "diphtheria", buried: Fall Branch, died: 25 Dec 1916, record (1916): 557.

Thelma Louise NELMS, born: 7 Nov 1914, parents: Walker NELMS and Josie AKERS (VA), death cause: "drowned by falling in tub of water", informant: Cora MINNICK (Bristol), buried: Kingsport, died: 27 Dec 1916, record (1916): 558.

Mary Lena WOOD, born: 28 Feb 1916 in Virginia, parents: Charles WOODS (VA) and Nancy OAKS (VA), death cause: "premature", informant: Joal MCMURRY (Kingsport), buried: Hilton, VA., died: 28 Dec 1916, record (1916): 559.

Mrs. Reba VENABLE, age 28 years, married, parents: John FAGANS and Mary OLIVER, death cause: "tuberculosis lungs", buried: New Bethel, Piney Flats, died: 25 Dec 1916, record (1916): 560.

Vennie HYATT, born: 10 Aug 1916, parents; Charlie HYATT (Washington Co., TN) and Julia Bell WHITAKER, death cause: "broncho pneumonia", died: Piney Flats on 14 Dec 1916, record (1916): 561.

Alen Monroe TORBETT, born: 3 May 1862, married, parents: John TORBETT and mother not stated, death cause: "carcinoma of stomach and liver", buried: New Bethel, Piney Flats, died: 22 Dec 1916, record: 562.

Charles COX, born: 3 Jan 1868, married, parents: S.R. COX and mother not stated, death cause: "diabetes", buried: New Bethel, Piney Flats, died: 13 Dec 1916, record (1916): 563.

Mrs. Mary DICKERSON, age 60 years, widow, parents: Will DICKERSON and Jane MCCLELLAN, death cause: "pneumonia", buried: Bentley Cemetery, 1st District, died: 11 Dec 1916, record (1916): 564.

Alexander GRAY, age 72 years, 3 months and 13 days, married, parents: Isaac GRAY and Polly SUSONG (VA), death cause: "bright disease", informant: Mrs. Sallie GRAY (Bristol), buried: Paperville, died: 15 Dec 1916, record (1916): 565.

Myrtle TOLBERT, age 5 years, born in Bristol, VA., parents: Joe TOLBERT and Dora COLLINS (Smythe Creek, VA), death cause: "diphtheria", informant: father (Bristol), died: 13 Dec 1916, record (1916): 566.

Infant CARRIER, male, parents: Clarence CARRIER and Ollie M. SOUTH, death cause: "meningitis", informant: father (Bristol), buried: Ordway Cemetery, died: 6 Dec 1916, record (1916): 567.

Mrs. Mary Ann Jenkins TURNER, born: 4 Jul 1846, married, parents: Rollin JENKINS and mother not stated, death cause: "cerebral hemorrhage", informant: T.W. CAMPBELL (Bristol), buried: East Hill, died: 25 Dec 1916, record (1916): 568.

Caroline Virginia FAIR, born: 7 Feb 1842 at Buckley Mill, VA., widow, parents: not stated, death cause: "tubercular peritonitis", informant: Sarah Pet FAIR (Bristol), buried: Blountville, died: 3 Dec 1916, record (1916): 569.

Henry HARRIS, age about 76 years, born in Virginia, widower, parents: Will HARRIS (VA) and mother not stated, death cause: not stated, informant: Miss Fannie HARRIS (Bristol), buried: East Hill, died: 25 Dec 1916, record (1916): 570.

Infant ELAM, female, parents: W.C. ELAM (Washington Co., VA) and Lelia CORNETT (Grayson Co., VA), death cause: "still birth", informant: father (Bristol), died: 27 Dec 1916, record (1916): 571.

Infant VAUGHT, male, parents: G.C. VAUGHT and Mary JONES, death cause: "still born", informant: father (Bristol), buried: Beeler Cemetery, died: 7 Dec 1916, record (1916): 572.

Edna Earl NESTER, born: 18 Dec 1916 in Virginia, parents: John NESTER (VA) and Dove JONES (VA), death cause: "measles", informant: father (Kingsport), buried: Pyle Cemetery, died: 31 Jan 1917, record (1917): 214.

Ralph ODELL, age 15 years, parents: Joseph ODELL and Martha BULLOCK, death cause: "fractured skull, kicked by mule", informant: A.B. ODELL (Bluff City), died: 7 Jan 1917, record (1917): 215.

Mattie GRUBB, age 6 months and 3 days, parents: John GRUBB and Fannie GENTRY, death cause: illegible, buried: Crumley Cemetery, died: 7 Jan 1917, record (1917): 216.

Stachis KITZMILLER (female), age 33 years, single, parents: John KITZMILLER and Lucy GENTRY, death cause: "pneumonia", informant: M.A. KITZMILLER (Bluff City), died: 30 Jan 1917, record (1917): 217 (duplicate ?)

Ruby ODELL, age 12 years, parents: John ODELL and Maud ARANTS, death cause: "measles", buried: Crumley cemetery, died; 9 Jan 1917, record (1917): 218.

Stasha KITZMILLER, born: 4 Apr 1884, parents: Henry MAYNE and Rachel POTTS, death cause: "carcinoma of uterus", informant: J.M. KITZMILLER, died: 30 Jan 1917, record (1917): 219.

Ada MORELOCK, born: 23 Sep 1884, married, parents: James CONKIN and Martha E. MORRELL, death cause: "mitral stenosis", informant: James CONKIN (Fall Branch), buried: Mullins Cemetery, 15th District, died: 18 Jan 1917, record (1917): 220.

Debby JENKINS, age 35 years, married, parents: (illegible) JONES and Jane MASSINGILL, death cause: "tuberculosis of lungs", informant: James HEARTLEY (Bristol), buried: Pleasant Grove, died: 28 Jan 1917, record (1917): 221.

Noah Franklin COLLINS, born: 20 Sep 1913, parents: James E. COLLINS and Martha E. HICKMAN, death cause:: "broncho pneumonia", informant; father (Kingsport), buried: Martin Cemetery, died: 29 Jan 1917, record (1917): 222.

John Pearl SELLS, born: 31 Dec 1904, parents: J.B. SELLS (Washington Co., TN) and Elizabeth MYERS, death cause: "ileo colitis", informant: Elizabeth SELLS (Kingsport), buried: Pyle Cemetery, died: 27 Jan 1917, record (1917): 223.

Lydia JETER, age 33 years, married, parents: "not known", death cause: "acute dilitation of heart", informant: Mike JETER (Kingsport), buried: Martin Cemetery, died: 24 Jan 1917, record (1917): 224. (child below)

Infant JETER, female, parents: Mike JETER and Lydia HOLSCLAW, death cause: "still born", informant: father (Kingsport), buried: Martin Cemetery, died: 24 Jan 1917, record (1917): 225.

Mrs. Martha HORNER, age 78 years, born at Burks Garden, VA., married, parents: William HORNER (VA) and Sallie SWOOPS (VA), death cause: "pelegra", buried: Paperville Cemetery, died: 15 Jan 1917, record: 226.

Richard Dulaney CHASE, born: 11 Nov 1879, married, parents: John T. CHASE and Mary JONES, death cause: "typhoid fever", informant; N.L. LOWE (Jonesboro), buried: Jones Family Cemetery, 14th District, died: 4 Jan 1917, record (1917): 227.

Ollie Simpson MORRISON, age about 35 years, born in Hawkins County, parents: Joseph SIMPSON (Hawkins Co.) and Sarah CARBERRY, death cause: "tuberculosis of lungs and bowels", informant: Riley MORRISON (Fall Branch), buried: Hawkins County, died: 8 Jan 1917, record (1917): 228.

Patton STEADMAN, born: 1 Jul 1830 in Sullivan County, married, parents: John STEADMAN (Sullivan Co) and Melvina BURKE (Sullivan Co), death cause: "influenza", informant; John STEADMAN (Fall Branch), buried: Steadman Cemetery, 13th District, died: 4 Jan 1917, record (1917): 229.

Ruby Chase RICHARDSON, born: 7 Oct 1915, parents: George W. RICHARDSON (VA) and Ottie PERKINS, death cause: "broncho pneumonia", informant: father (Kingsport), buried: Light Cemetery, died: 27 Jan 1917, record (1917): 230.

George S. MILES, born: 16 Mar 1916, parents: Dave MILES and Sallie MCMURRY (VA), death cause: "whooping cough", informant: Jeal MCMURRY (Kingsport), buried: Martin cemetery, died: 16 Jan 1917, record: 231.

Infant OPENMEYER, male, parents: Gerd OPENMEYER (Hoboken, NJ) and Iren EUBANK (Hendersonville, NC), death cause: illegible, informant: father (Kingsport), born/died: 11 Jan 1917, record (1917): 232.

James W. ORNDUFF, age 64 years, born in Virginia, widower, parents: James ORNDUFF (VA) and Nany CHRISTIAN (VA), death cause: "tuberculosis lungs", informant: George JONES (Kingsport), buried: Bristol, died: 9 Jan 1917, record (1917): 233.

Maria VAUGHN, born: 11 Sep 1840 in Virginia, widow, parents: Sam FIELDS (VA) and Sarah RICKETS (VA), death cause: "parisis", informant: C.W. VAUGHN (Kingsport), died: 11 Jan 1917, record (1917): 234.

Beatrice Pearl LAMPKIN, born: 4 Dec 1914, parents: Walker LAMPKIN and Callie MOREFIELD, death cause: "chronic valvulor heart disease", informant: father (Kingsport), buried: Pyle Cemetery, died: 14 Jan 1917, record (1917): 235.

Infant SAMS, female, parents: Bart SAMS (Church Hill) and Pearl LOYD (Rogersville), death cause: "unknown", informant: father (Kingsport), died: 8 Jan 1917, record (1917): 236.

Ray R. CRAWFORD, age 19 years, single, parents: Will CRAWFORD and Rebecca Jane MCCOY, death cause: "met instant death from log rolling over him", informant: G.W. BARRETT (Fall Branch), buried: Blairs Gap, died: 6 Jan 1916, record (1917): 237.

Infant SPIVEY, male, parents: Will SPIVEY and Ida LITE, death cause: "still born", informant: father (Kingsport), died: 16 Jan 1917, record (1917): 238.

Annie SAMS, born: 20 Mar 1912, parents: Bart SAMS and Pearl LOYD, death cause: "diptheria", informant: father (Kingsport), died: 14 Jan 1917, record: 239.

W.M. GLOVER, born: 28 Jun 1849, parents: Richard GLOVER and Pollie BURNETT, death cause: "disease of heart with chronic bronchitis", informant: W.B. SIMERLY, died at Bluff City on 29 Jan 1917, record (1917): 240.

Ethel TESTER, born: ___ Jun 1906, parents: William TESTER (VA) and Janie BRIDGEMAN (VA), death cause: "consumption", informant: Wiley TESTER (Bristol), buried: Walnut Grove, VA., died: 29 Jan 1917, record (1917): 241.

Mrs. W.R. DYKES, born: 7 Jun 1874, parents: Dr. J.P. RHEA (W.VA) and Matilda LANGORNE, death cause: "nephritis", buried: East Hill, died at Bristol on 26 Jan 1917, record (1917): 242.

Ralph ODELL, age 5 years and 3 months, parents: J.D. ODELL and Ella BULLOCK, death cause: "peritonitis", informant: Ed ARANTS, (Bristol), buried: Shipley Cemetery, died: 7 Jan 1917, record (1917): 243.

Stanley BISHOP, born: 20 Mar 1915, parents: William BISHOP and Nannie BURNETT, death cause: illegible, informant: G.H. WHITAKER (Bristol), buried: Ordway Cemetery, died: 6 Jan 1917, record (1917): 244.

Mrs. Eliza DECK, age 37 years, married, parents: John ROLLER and Catherine CROSS, death cause: "general (illegible) following abortion", informant: J.F. ROLLER (Fordtown), buried: Wheeler Cemetery, died: 8 Jan 1917, record (1917): 245.

James Alvin SIMMONS, born: 19 Oct 1880 in Green County, single, parents: James SIMMONS (Green Co.) and Mary PICKING (Green Co.), death cause: "lobar pneumonia", buried: Greenville, TN., died: 7 Jan 1917, record (1917): 246.

Henrietta REYNOLDS, Negro, born: 27 Feb 1874 in Virginia, widow, parents: Peter JOHNSON (VA) and Easter SISSELL (VA), death cause: "lobar pneumonia", informant: Mrs. Helen CROCKETT (Roanoke), buried: Citizens Cemetery, died: 6 Jan 1917, record: 247.
Ed EDWARDS, Negro, born: 23 Dec 1876 in Louisiana, married, parents: (illegible) EDWARDS (LA) and mother not stated, death cause: "mitral insufficiency", informant: Mame EDWARDS (Bristol), buried: Citizens Cemetery, died: 15 Jan 1917, record (1917): 248.
Cynthia C. RICHARDSON, born: 16 Mar 1875, single, parents: John RICHARDSON (VA) and Mary MCGAVOCK (VA), death cause: "cancer of uterus", informant: J.R. RICHARDSON (Bristol), buried: East Hill, died: 15 Jan 1917, record (1917): 249.
Mrs. Sarah A. CHILDRESS, born: 15 Mar 1847, widow, parents: Noah HULL and Lucinda WEBB, death cause: "pneumonia", informant: Charles CHILDRESS (Bristol), buried: East Hill, died: 8 Jan 1917, record: 250.
Virgie Helen WHITE, age 12 years, born in Virginia, parents: T.J. WHITE (VA) and Ella KINCER (VA), death cause: "peritonitis", informant: father (Bristol), buried: Bristol, VA., died: 17 Jan 1917, record (1917): 251.
Mrs. Sophia GRUBBS, age 52 years, born in Russell Co., VA., married, parents: W.E. CAMPBELL (Russell Co.) and L.C. FLETCHER (Russell Co.), death cause: "chronic brights disease", informant: Mrs. George GRUBBS (Southern Pines, NC), buried: East Hill, died: 15 Jan 1917, record (1917): 252.
W.H. ADAMS, age 84 years, born in Virginia, married, parents: not stated, death cause: "nephritis", informant: C.L ADAMS (Bristol), buried: Balto, MD., died: 23 Jan 1917, record (1917): 253.
Clarence Edward REYNOLDS, Negro, age 25 years, born at Jonesboro, parents: Robert REYNOLDS (Winston Salem) and Henrietta REYNOLDS (Tazwell, VA), death cause: "pneumonia", buried: Citizen Cemetery, died: 25 Jan 1917, record (1917): 254.
Myrtle GROGEN, born: 20 Dec 1199 in Virginia, parents: W.W. GROGEN (VA) and Lillie HOLMES (VA), death cause: "pulmonary tuberculosis", informant: Mrs. Lillie GROGEN, buried: Gate City, VA., died: 18 Jan 1917, record (1917): 255.
Mrs. B.D. SPURGEON, age 68 years, widow, parents: Dr. Benjamin F. ZIMMERMAN (Abingdon) and Martha BUCHANAN (Washington Co., VA), death cause: "lobar pneumonia",

informant: Raymond SPURGEON (Bristol), died: 12 Jan 1917, record (1917): 256.

Moses WILSON, age 82 years, widower, parents: Tom WILSON (VA) and Josie (illegible)(VA), death cause: "kidney trouble", buried: Beeler Cemetery, died: 16 Jan 1917, record (1917): 257.

Lucey May KELLER, age 17 years, parents: Martin KELLER (VA) and Jane WHITE, death cause: "pneumonia", buried: Shipley Cemetery, died: 15 Jan 1917, record: 258.

David LATTURE, age 47 years, single, parents: Will LATTURE (W.VA) and Caroline SCOTT (W.VA), death cause: "tuberculosis", died in the 13th District on 17 Jan 1917, record (1917): 259.

Frank G. ROE, born: 19 Feb 1848 in Virginia, married, parents: Auston ROE (VA) and Elizabeth GARRETT (VA), death cause: "chirrosis of liver", informant: Mrs. Roe, buried: Bluff City, died: 2 Feb 1917, record (1917): 260.

Robert WOOD, colored, age 29 years, single, parents: Henry WOOD (W.VA) and Bertie SHRINKLE (VA), death cause: "measles and pneumonia", died in the 22nd District on 3 Feb 1917, record (1917): 261.

Nellie BISHOP, age 3 years, born in Virginia, parents: Henry BISHOP (VA) and Nora KETRON (VA), death cause: "pneumonia", informant: D.C. EDWARDS (Bloomingdale), died: 3 Feb 1917, record (1917): 262.

Hazel A. SMILEY, born: 28 Aug 1916 in Virginia, parents: Pierce SMILEY and Cora ESTEP (VA), death cause: "found dead in bed by parents on awakening", informant: father (Kingsport), buried: Rock Springs, TN., died: 3 Feb 1917, record (1917): 263.

Mary DAVIS, born: 2 Feb 1917, parents: Jefferson DAVIS (PA) and Rena GREER (NC), death cause: "premature birth", informant: father (Kingsport), buried: Old Kingsport Cemetery, died: 3 Feb 1917, record: 267.

Clara Elizabeth POSTON, born: 17 Apr 1914, parents: Tom K. POSTON (VA) and Cora CLOUD (VA), death cause: "diptheria", informant: father (Kingsport), buried: Pyle Cemetery, died: 4 Feb 1917, record (1917): 265.

William BLEVINS, age 68 years, single, parents: Lusian BLEVENS and Pollie CARRIER, death cause: "disease of heart", informant: W.W. CARRIER (Emmett), died: 5 Feb 1917, record (1917): 266.

Will JACKSON, age 43 years, born in Virginia, married, parents: Jim JACKSON (VA) and Sara JACKSON (VA), death cause: "cancer on face", buried: Beeler Cemetery, died: 5 Feb 1917, record (1917): 267.

Jess COOPER, age 35 years, married, parents: James COOPER and Mary COLE (NC), death cause: "accidentally falling from (illegible)", informant: Jack COLE (Bluff City), buried: Shipley Cemetery, died: 5 Feb 1917, record (1917): 268.

Robert L. MILLHORN, age about 65 years, born in Washington Co., TN., married, parents: Harrison MILLHORN and Sarah Ann DYRE, death cause: "tuberculosis of bowels", informant: Dr. GRAVES (Piney Flats), buried: New Bethel, died: 6 Feb 1917, record (1917): 269.

Gordon Isaac PIPPIN, born: 2 Aug 1908 in Virginia, parents: E.H. PIPPIN (VA) and mother not stated, death cause: "meningitis", buried: Pyle Cemetery, died at Kingsport on 6 Feb 1917, record (1917): 270.

Louise FRITTS, age 16 years, parents: Martin FRITTS (NC) and Annie PENSE (VA), death cause: "pneumonia", informant: Julia SPEERS (Bluff City), died: 7 Feb 1917, record (1917): 271.

Mary Robertson WARDEN, born: 19 May 1877 in Saltville, VA., married, parents: Wyndham C. ROBERTSON (Richmond) and Florence HENDERSON (Amhurst Co., VA), death cause: "penumonia and toxemia", informant: J.B. MILLARD (Kingsport), buried: Saltville, VA., died: 7 Feb 1917, record (1917): 272.

George L. JOHNSON, born __ May 1914, parents: John A. JOHNSON and Bessie CROFFORD, death cause: "measles", informant: father (Kingsport), buried: Pyle Cemetery, died: 7 Feb 1917, record (1917): 273.

Mildred Boyd RUMBLEY, born: 18 Dec 1913 in Virginia, parents: Gorden W. RUMBLEY (Glade Springs, VA) and Nydia THOMAS (Meadow View, VA), death cause: "appendicitis", buried: Glade Springs, VA., died: 8 Feb 1917, record (1917): 274.

Carrie Ann MOODY, born: 12 Mar 1842 in Smith Co., VA., married, parents: Stephen W. LOYD (Smith Co.) and Sallie LOYD (Smith Co.), death cause: "chronic gastritis", informant: W.H. MOODY (Indian Springs), buried: Emory Cemetery, died: 8 Feb 1917, record (1917): 275.

Cornelia A. BIEDLEMAN, born: 13 Apr 1836, widow, parents: __ SMITH and __ ROWE, death cause: "hemoplegia", informant: Mrs. J.A. BIEDLEMAN (Emmett), died: 10 Feb 1917, record (1917): 276.

Thomas S. HARDAWAY, age 62 years, born in Virginia, married, parents: father not stated and __ ROBERTSON (VA), death cause: "mitral heart lesion", informant:

E.T. HARDAWAY (Roanoke), buried: East Hill, died: 10 Feb 1917, record (1917): 277.
Flem H. HURST, born: 7 Jul 1914, parents: George W. HURST and Cynthia A. HARKLEROAD, death cause: "pneumonia", informant: H.L. HARKLEROAD (Kingsport), buried: Pyle Cemetery, died: 9 Feb 1917, record (1917): 278.
Susannah STOPHEL, born: 5 Feb 1837 in Tennessee, divorced, parents: Valentine STOPHEL and Jane CLAMON, death cause: "old age", informant: G.W. BOOHER (Bristol), died: 11 Feb 1917, record (1917): 279.
Clarence CALLAHAN, age 11 years, parents: William CALLAHAN (VA) and Fanny GARRETT (VA), death cause: "lobar pneumonia", informant: father (Bristol), buried: East Hill, died: 13 Feb 1917, record: 280.
Modest LEDBETTER, male, born: 16 Feb 1899 in Rutherford Co., NC., parents: Alfred LEDBETTER (Rutherford Co.) and Charlotte MORRIS (Rutherford Co.), death cause: "typhoid fever", informant: Thomas Hamilton (Fagans, NC), buried: Logan, NC., died: 15 Feb 1917, record (1917): 281.
Mattie LENTON, age 7 years, 3 months and 4 days, parents: Fred LENTON and Jane (illegible), death cause: "measles", informant: Jane LENTON (Bluff City), died: 15 Feb 1917, record (1917): 282.
J.A. NICHOLS, age 54 years, born in Ashe County, NC., married, parents: James NICHOLS and Mary MCCOY (Johnson County), death cause: "lobar pneumonia', informant: Mrs. J.A. NICHOLS (Bristol), died: 16 Feb 1917, record (1917): 283.
Gerile Randolph CUNNINGHAM, born: 28 Oct 1909 in Virginia, parents: A.B. CUNNINGHAM (NC) and Fannie GLOVER, death cause: "tomainemia from eating spoiled sweet potatoes", informant: father (Kingsport), buried: Pyle Cemetery, died: 17 Feb 1917, record (1917): 284.
Georgia Mollie BENFIELD, born: 20 Mar 1915, parents: Robert BENFIELD (VA) and Mollie RYAN (Michigan), death cause: "measles", informant: Charles BENFIELD (Kingsport), buried: Pyle Cemetery, died: 18 Feb 1917, record (1917): 285.
Edwin B. ROBERTS, Jr., born: 7 Feb 1914 in Daheloniga, GA., parents: Edwin ROBERTS (GA) and Viola HOUSLEY (GA), "burn, clothes caught on fire at open grate", informant: E.B. ROBERTS (Kingsport), buried: Marion, NC., died: 18 Feb 1917, record (1917): 286.
George MAYS, age 76 years, widower, parents: Jake MAYS and Charlotte COLE, death cause: "pneumonia",

informant: Bill MAYS (Bluff City), died: 18 Feb 1917, record (1917): 287.

Martha KEELING, age 25 years, single, parents: father's name illegible and May SMYTH (VA), death cause: "measles and pneumonia", buried: Paperville, died: 20 Feb 1917, record (1917): 288.

Frank MARSHAL, age 83 years, born in South Carolina, widower, parents: Ben MARSHAL (SC) and Jane FAINE (SC), death cause: "kidney trouble", died in the 1st District on 21 Feb 1917, record (1917): 289.

Jessie RAY, colored, born: 30 Aug 1841, parents: Jessie RAY and mother not stated, death cause: "paralysis", died at Bristol on 22 Feb 1917, record (1917): 290.

Ellen MARTON, age 77 years, 2 months and 1 day, parents: Jonthan MORTON and Marion BULLOCK, death cause: "age and idiotic", buried: Shipley Cemetery, died: 22 Feb 1917, record (1917): 291.

Infant WOLF, Negro, male, parents: William Wolf (VA) and Francis RAMEY (VA), death cause: illegible, informant: father (Bristol), born/died: 23 Feb 1917, record (1917): 292.

Aris COX, born: 8 Apr 1839 in North Carolina, married, parents: not stated, death cause: "pneumonia", informant: M.M. OSBORN (Fish Dam), died in the 19th District on 23 Feb 1917, record (1917): 293.

Mary E.F. TICKLE, born: 4 Apr 1867 in Bland Co., VA., married, parents: J.C. HUTSELL (VA) and Ann THOMPSON (VA), death cause: "typhoid fever", informant: Ira L. TICKLE (Kingsport), buried: Bland, VA., died: 24 Feb 1917, record (1917): 294.

Mollie M. STEADMAN, age 53 years, widow, parents: Payton B. CORNVILLE (Washington Co., TN) and Sabra FORD (Washington Co., TN), death cause: "measles and pneumonia", informant: W.M. CORNWELL (Fordtown), buried: 15th District, died: 25 Feb 1917, record (1917): 296.

Marie L. SPOTTS, colored, born: 26 Oct 1841 in Tazewell, VA., widow, parents: H. TIFFANY (Ireland) and Amey PARRIS (Tazewell, VA), death cause: "nephritis", informant: Helen H. HARPER (Bristol), buried: Tazewell, VA., died: 26 Feb 1917, record (1917): 297.

Ocia MCMURRY, age 22 years, born in Virginia, single, parents: Henry MCMURRY (VA) and Irene HENSLEY (VA), death cause: "puerperal fever", informant: A.G. MCMURRY (Kingsport), died: 26 Feb 1917, record: 298.

John W. EMMETT, age 75 years, married, parents: John EMMETT and Mary WEBB, death cause: "chronic Brights disease", informant: J.C. EMMETT (Bristol), died: 26 Feb 1916, record (1917): 299.

Maxine Neta ROLLER, born: 11 Jan 1917, parents: E. Paul ROLLER and Lona FORD, death cause: "lobar pneumonia", informant: father (Fordtown), buried: Lebanon Church, died: 27 Feb 1917, record (1917): 300.

Joe WILKINS, age 89 years, married, parents: Joe WILKINS (VA) and Martha WEBB, death cause: "dropsy", died in the 22nd District on 28 Feb 1917, record (1917): 301.

Ellen GRANT, age 27 years, born in Virginia, single, parents: Jackson GRANT (VA) and Mary TRIVETT (VA), death cause: "tuberculosis", informant: father (Bluff City), buried: Bluff City Cemetery, died: 29 Feb 1917, record (1917): 302.

Infant CRUM, male, parents: R.K. CRUM and Pet LADY, death cause: "still birth", informant: C.D. STONE (Kingsport), buried: Old Kingsport Cemetery, died: 28 Feb 1917, record (1917): 303.

Infant HUDSON, male, parents: Jim HUDSON and Eva LIGHT, death cause: "stillborn", informant: father (Kingsport), buried: Old Kingsport Cemetery, born/died: 13 Feb 1917, record (1917): 304.

Infant DISHNER, male, parents: Kyle D. DISHNER and Bertie May COLE (VA), death cause: "still birth", informant: George BAILEY (Kingsport), died: 16 Feb 1917, record (1917): 305.

Montie Floyd MYRES, born: 18 Feb 1917, parents: Claude MYRES (VA) and Okie HARDIN (VA), death cause: "found dead in bed", informant: Madison GREEN (Kingsport), buried: Cranberry, NC., died: 1 Mar 1917, record (1917): 306.

James DAGGETT, age 13 years, parents: Joseph DAGGETT (VA) and Jane HENSON (VA), death cause: "tree fell cross his body", buried: Cool Springs Cemetery, died: 1 Mar 1917, record (1917): 307.

Pearl HILL, colored, born: 2 Mar 1892 at New Market, TN., single, parents: father not stated and Carrie BOWERS (New Market), death cause: illegible, informant: Jerry CHAMBERS (Kingsport), buried: New Market, TN., died: 2 Mar 1917, record (1917): 308.

Mrs. Neoma A. COLE, age 73 years, born in Smythe Co., VA., widow, parents: William SMITH and Lidia LESTER (Washington Co.), death cause: "chronic brights disease", informant: Linnie DROKE (Bristol), buried: Salem Cemetery, died: 2 Mar 1917, record (1917): 309.

Earl J. LONG, born: 24 Jul 1917 (?) in Reebuck, VA., parents: Frank J. LONG (Holston, VA) and Pearl PELPORT (VA), death cause: "pneumonia", informant: father (Kingsport), buried: Glade Springs, VA., died: 2 Mar 1917, record (1917): 310.
Edna SPEARS, born: 14 Oct 1915, parents: Ross Alexander SPEARS (Rogersville) and Canie Cecil SAMS, death cause: "pneumonia", informant: Dr. JORDAN (Kingsport), buried: Persia, TN., died: 3 Mar 1917, record (1917): 311.
Mary POORE, age 54 years, 2 months and 7 days, married, parents: John POORE and Jane STEWART (Washington Co., VA), death cause: "pneumonia and measles", informant: Mrs. Hattie PETERS (Bristol), buried: Rosedale Cemetery, died: 4 Mar 1917, record (1917): 312.
Mary Lee Oma FISH, born: 16 Nov 1891, single, parents: Isaac P. FISH and Ruth OWENS, death cause: "pulmonary tuberculosis", informant: father (Fall Branch), buried: family cemetery, 13th District, died: 6 Mar 1917, record (1917): 313.
Mack DALTON, age 8 years, born in Virginia, parents: C.A. DALTON and Alice COLIER (VA), death cause: "tuberculosis of bowels", informant: father (Kingsport), died: 7 Mar 1917, record (1917): 314.
Hazel E. ROBBINS, born: 16 Feb 1916 in North Carolina, parents: M.C. ROBBINS (NC) and Maude AUSTIN (NC), death cause: illegible, informant: father (Kingsport), buried: North Carolina, died: 8 Mar 1917, record (1917): 315.
Penelopia LEONARD, age 32 years, single, parents: M.B. LEONARD and Agnes GIBSON, death cause: "peretonitis following operation", informant: B.B. LEONARD (Bristol), buried: Shankle Cemetery, died: 8 Mar 1917, record (1917): 316.
Tracy WOODS, born: 16 Feb 1916 in Virginia, parents: Robert WOODS (VA) and Mary Idela EPERSON (VA), death cause: "broncho pneumonia", informant: father (Kingsport), died: 9 Mar 1917, record (1917): 317.
Joseph J. MCFERRIS, born: 18 Aug 1846 in Green County, TN., parents: Samuel MCFERRIS (VA) and Catherine DROKE, death cause: "myocarditis", informant: M.M. MCFERRIS (Augusta, GA), buried: Morristown, died: 10 Mar 1917, record (1917): 318.
Minnie JOBE, born: 2 Dec 1895, married, parents: Joseph HICKMAN and Sina BRAGG, death cause: "tuberculosis", informant: Will JOBE (Kingsport),

buried: 15th District, died: 10 Mar 1917, record (1917): 319.

Infant HENSLEY, female, born: 7 Mar 1917, parents: A.D. HENSLEY (VA) and (illegible) TORBET (VA), death cause: "jaundice", died in the 1st District on 11 Mar 1917, record (1917): 320.

Lucy COMES, age 51 years, 9 months and 28 days, widow, parents: ___ SMITH (VA) and Martha ROWE, death cause: "hemophegria", informant: Robert ROWE (Bluff City), died: 11 Mar 1917, record (1917): 321.

Elizabeth PAGE, Negro, born: 5 Sep 1915, parents: Claud PAGE and Hattie SKAGGS (VA), death cause: "croup", informant: father (Bristol), buried: Citizen Cemetery, died: 11 Mar 1917, record (1917): 322.

James E. FOUST, age 33 years, married, parents: David V. FOUST and Susan SUSONG, death cause: "measles and pneumonia", informant: Mrs. J.E. FOUST (Bristol), died: 12 Mar 1917, record (1917): 323.

K.A. LEONARD, age 30 years, married, parents: Ed LEONARD and Nancy LEONARD, death cause: "mitral insufficiency", informant: Bert LEONARD (Bristol), buried: Zions Cemetery, died: 12 Mar 1917, record (1917): 324.

Artie ROBINSON, male, age: 7 years, 2 months and 3 days, parents: Howard ROBINSON (VA) and Harriet GRAY (VA), death cause: "spinal trouble", buried: Pleasant GROVE, died: 12 Mar 1917, record (1917): 325.

James E. WORKMAN, Sr., age 77 years, born in Davidson County, NC., married, parents: William WORKMAN (NC) and Nancy ELLIS (Elliston, VA), death cause: "pulmonary oedema", buried: Lexington, NC., died: 13 Mar 1917, record (1917): 326.

Lucy HODGE, age 33 years, born in North Carolina, married, parents: Jim HODGE (NC) and Anis CROW, death cause: "kidney trouble", informant: Jim CROW (Bluff City), buried: Crumley Cemetery, died: 15 Mar 1917, record (1917): 327.

Mrs. Guss BIEDLEMAN, age 54 years, 3 months and 4 days, married, parents: Joseph SMYTH and Emeline HOYT, death cause: "pneumonia", buried in Biedleman Cemetery, 21st District, died: 15 Mar 1917, record (1917): 328.

Steve KIBLER, Negro, age: not stated, parents: not stated, death cause: "heart lesion", buried: Knoxville, died: 17 Mar 1917, record (1917): 329.

J.C. FLEMMING, age 43 years, 2 months and 8 days, widower, parents: Isaac FLEMMING (NC) and Maggie ROSE

(VA), death cause: "measles", buried: Hickory Tree Cemetery, died: 19 Mar 1917, record (1917): 330.

Millard TILLEY, age 43 years, born in North Carolina, parents: Emory TILLEY (NC) and Elizabeth LEWIS (NC), death cause: "pneumonia and measles", informant: F.L. LEWIS (Ashland, NC) buried: Shouns, TN., died: 23 Mar 1917, record (1917): 331.

Mrs. Will HALE, age 37 years, 6 months and 2 days, married, parents: Mose HALE (VA) and Lucy MCGENTRY, death cause: "from a fall", buried: Bluff City Cemetery, died: 20 Mar 1917, dred 332.

Mrs. Charlotte MILLER, age 62 years, married, parents: J.R. JONES and Elizabeth NEWTON, death cause: "tuberculosis", informant: W.H. MILLER (Bristol), buried: Crumley Cemetery, died: 25 Mar 1917, record (1917): 337.

Bettie HALE, born: 26 mar __, age 33 years, married, parents: Leander CARRIER and Nancy MORRELL, death cause: "tuberuclosis of lungs", informant: Will HALE (Bluff City), buried: Crumley Cemetery, died: 26 Mar 1917, record (1917): 334.

Charlie HUTSON, born: 16 Mar 1916, parents: Claude HUTSON (Hawkins Co.) and Mary SIMS (Hawkins Co.), death cause: "diptheria", buried: Solitiude Cemetery, died at Kingsport on 27 Mar 1917, record (1917): 335.

Wilson GROSS, born: 27 Apr 1864, married, parents: Jacob GROSS and Eliza A. GROSS, death cause: "tuberculosis", informant: Dr. GRAVES (Piney Flats), died: 27 Mar 1917, record (1917): 336.

Ruby H. OLINGER, male, born: 24 Mar 1917, parents: Thomas OLINGER (Scott Co., VA) and Sallie OLINGER (Scott Co., VA), death cause: "spinal meningitis", informant: Maude SMALLWOOD (Kingsport), buried: Bachman Cemetery, died: 27 Mar 1917, record: 337.

George M. COLEMAN, born: 8 Aug __, age 47 years, 6 months and 20 days, single, parents: Frank COLEMAN (VA) and Sarah HARKLEROAD, death cause: "pulmonary tuberculosis", informant: Lina STOFFLE (Kingsport), died: 28 Mar 1917, record (1917): 338.

Larry Elain STEADMAN, born: 24 Dec 1916, parents: C.J. STEADMAN and Laura L. OWEN, death cause: "found dead in bed", informant: Joe SENEBOUGH (Kingsport), buried: Hawkins, County, died: 29 Mar 1917, record: 339.

Jim CARRIER, age 17 years, 7 months and 3 days, married, parents: Will CARRIER and Mariah SOUTH, death cause: "tuberculosis of lungs", died in the 22nd District on 30 Mar 1917, record (1917): 340.

Mary Magdaline HALE, born: 15 Nov 1891, single, parents: J. Melvin HALE and Phoebe Jane FERGUSON, death cause: "whooping cough", informant: Phoebe J. HALE (Jonesboro), buried: Copass Family Cemetery, 14th District, died: 30 Mar 1917, record (1917): 341.

Fannie Myrtle SMITH, born: 4 May 1916, parents: L.C. SMITH (VA) and Cora SMITH (KY), death cause: "pneumonia", informant: father (Kingsport), buried: Zuma Cemetery, died: 31 Mar 1917, record (1917): 342.

Mary CARROLL, born: 7 Oct 1880, married, parents: Albert G. LIGHT and Nancy HOOD, death cause: "pulmonary tuberculosis", informant: D.F. CARROLL (Fall Branch), buried: Depew Chapel, died: 31 Mar 1917, record (1917): 343.

Infant WALKER, male, parents: Charles R. WALKER (VA) and Margaret MULHOLTZ (Pennsylvania), death cause: "still born", informant: father (Kingsport), born/died: 18 Mar 1917, record (1917): 344.

Infant BULLOCK, male, parents: Joseph BULLOCK and M__ (illegible) SHIPLEY, death cause: "still born", buried: Carr Cemetery, Bluff City, died: 2 Mar 1917, record (1917): 345.

James Orville CRAWFORD, parents: Thomas M. CRAWFORD and Mary K. ROBERTS (Washington Co., TN), death cause: "still born", informant: father (Fall Branch), buried: Depew Chapel, died: 26 Mar 1917, record (1917): 346.

William Riley STONE, born: 31 Dec 1837 in Virginia, married, parents: William STONE (VA) and Louisa LUNDY (VA), death cause: "carcinoma of prostate", informant: Joseph A. STONE (Bristol), buried: Maple Grove Cemetery, Washington Co., VA, died: 20 Apr 1917, record (1917): 347.

James SMITH, born: 28 Mar 1917, parents: Lee SMITH and Annie ADAMS, death cause: "found dead in bed", informant: father (Bristol), buried: Bristol, VA., died: 1 Apr 1917, record (1917): 348.

Omega COMPTON, female, born: 29 Jul 1916, parents: Everet COMPTON and Nannie ARNOLD, death cause: "whooping cough", informant: E.M. COMPTON (Kingsport), buried: Pyle Cemetery, died: 1 Apr 1917, record (1917): 349.

John ALFRED, age 53 years, widower, parents: Peter ALFRED (VA) and Sarah SAWYERS (VA), death cause: "heart trouble", buried: Shipley Cemetery, died: 1 Apr 1917, record (1917): 350.

Kiziah VANCE, born: 28 Dec 1843, single, parents: James H. VANCE and Jane SEVIER, death cause:

"apoplexy", informant: J.S. VANCE (Kingsport), buried: Pyle Cemetery, died: 5 Apr 1917, record (1917): 351.
Harry E. THRALL, age unknown, born in Pennsylvania, parents: "unknown", death cause: "Brights Disease and heart failure", informant: H.A. PARROTT (Blountville), buried: County Farm, Blountville, died: 5 Apr 1917, record (1917): 352.
Cora Dale DISHNER, born: 28 Aug 1870 in Virginia, married, parents: J.J. LEONARD (VA) and __ SMITH (VA), death cause: "measles and heart failure", informant: J.L. DISHNER (Blountville), buried: Dishner Cemetery, died: 5 Apr 1917, record (1917): 353.
Dora Myrtle CLAY, parents: Henry Lee CLAY and Nellie (illegible), death cause: "unknown", informant: father: (Piney Flats), died: 5 Apr 1917, record (1917): 354.
Ralph Graden COATS, born: 4 Jul 1915, parents: Blain COATS and Dora ARNOLD, death cause: "measles", informant: Walter SMITH (Kingsport), buried: Bachman Cemetery, died: 6 apr 1917, record (1917): 355.
Abraham MASS, age 70 years, widower, parents: Ananias MASS and Minnie JONES, death cause: "rhumatism", died in the 21st District on 6 Apr 1917, record: 356.
Amanda K. CARR, born: 18 Apr 1884, married, parents: Wesley OFFIELD and Fannie HAMILTON, death cause: "asthma and gastritis", informant: Robert CARR (Fordtown), buried: Pyle Cemetery, died: 13 Apr 1917, record (1917): 357.
A.W. BOYD, age 54 years, widower, parents: Andrew BOYD (VA) and Sallie (illegible), death cause: "kidney trouble", died in the 21st District on 6 Apr 1917, record (1917): 358.
Ben SIMMONS, Negro, age: "unknown", born in Georgia, parents: "unknown", death cause: "sypleletic anerism", informant: Joe PRICE (Kingsport), died: 7 Apr 1917, record (1917): 359.
Bonnie Alison MILLER, born: 31 Dec 1893, married, parents: Robert ALISON and Catherine Elizabeth SAWYERS (Buncumb Co., NC), death cause: "tuberculosos of lungs", informant: Dr. GRAVES (Piney Flats), buried: New Bethel Cemetery, died: 8 Apr 1917, record: 360.
Peter ASHBY, age 71 years, born in North Carolina, parents: not stated, death cause: "cancer of rectum", informant: Marth ASHBY (Bristol), buried: Susong Cemetery, Bristol, died: 8 Apr 1917, record: 361.
Henry Lee CECIL, born: 8 Mar 1866 in Virginia, married, parents; Witten CECIL (VA) and Elizabeth SHUFFLEBARGER (VA), death cause: "pneumonia",

informant: W.T. CECIL (Dublin, VA), buried: Sweetwater, VA., died: 9 Apr 1917, record (1917): 362.
T.H. ANDERSON, age 72 years, married, parents: George ANDERSON and Routh ANDERSON, death cause: "chronic brights, bronchitis", informant: J.H. ANDERSON (Blountville), buried: Mill Point Cemetery, died: 10 Apr 1917, record (1917): 363.
George Edward HENDERLITE, Jr., born: __ Feb, age: 20 years and 1 month, born in Virginia, parents: George E. HENDERLITE (VA) and __ KILLINGER (MOSLEY), death cause: not recorded, informant: J.H. HENDERLITE (Gastonia, NC), buried: Virginia, died: 18 Apr 1917, record (1917): 264.
Montie KERIN, age 30 years, married, born in Virginia, parents: George LAYNE (VA) and Mary OWENS (VA), death cause: "acute indigestion", informant: George ANDERSON (Bloomingdale), buried: Reedy Creek, died: 10 Apr 1917, record (1917): 365.
Mrs. Sallie C. CRIDLEN, born: 17 apr 1876 in Virginia, parents: J.L.C. SMITH (VA) and Sallie CAMPBELL (VA), death cause: "pneumonia, asthma", informant: G.P. CRIDLEN (Jonesville, VA), buried: Jonesville, Va., died: 11 Apr 1917, record (1917): 366.
Billy GLOVER, age 77 years, married, parents: Jim GLOVER and Nancy CRAIG, death cause: "pneumonia", informant; Hebert GLOVER (Emmett), died: 12 Apr 1917, record (1917): 367.
Laura Jane HATCHER, born: 6 Oct 1885 in Virginia, married, parents: Will DAVIS (VA) and mother's name illegible, death cause: "mitral insufficiency", informant: Alf HATCHER (Kingsport), buried: Elizabethton Cemetery, died: 12 Apr 1917, record (1917): 368.
Luther Calvin MARSH, born: 14 Feb 1896, single, parents: John MARSH and Mandie (illegible), death cause: "acute cardiac dilation", informant: E.P. GRAY (Church Hill), buried: Church Hill, died: 13 Apr 1917, record (1917): 369.
J.W. CROSS, age 35 years, married, parents: John F. CROSS and Sarah BOOHER, death cause: "tuberculosis", informant: Wesley BOOHER (Blountville), buried: Gunning Cemetery, died: 13 Apr 1917, record: 370.
George OLIVER, age 77 years, married, parents: William OLIVER (Carter County) and Betsy GENTRY (Johnson County), death cause: "diabetes", buried: East Hill, died: 14 Apr 1917, record (1917): 371.
Kyle Z. PHIPPS, age 2 years and 4 months, parents: J.Z. PHIPPS and Mary HUNTINGTON (VA), death cause:

"measles", informant: father (Bristol), buried: Paperville, died: 14 Apr 1917, record (1917): 372.

F.L. WHITE, age 51 years, born in Scott Co., VA., married, parents: Jacob WHITE (VA) and Elizabeth QUAILS (VA), death cause: not stated, informant: Mrs. F.L. WHITE (Bristol), buried: Weaver Cemetery, died: 15 Apr 1917, record (1917): 373.

Lizzie VICKERS, age 63 years, born in Virginia, widow, parents: George JONES (VA) and Nancy HAYS (VA), death cause: "not known", informant: Carter CLOUD (Kingsport), died: 15 Apr 1917, record (1917): 374.

Allice M. SENEKER, born: 27 Jul 1854, parents: W.R. SENEKER and __ BOOHER (VA), death cause: "tuberculosis with pneumonia", informant: W.T. SMITH (Blountville), buried: Seneker Cemetery, died: 16 Apr 1917, record (1917): 375.

Edna MARTIN, age: 18 months, parents: Aleck MORTIN and Emma SCOTT, death cause: "whooping cough", informant: A. MITCHELL (Bristol), buried: Beeler Cemetery, died: 16 Apr 1917, record (1917): 376.

Ota BOWERS, male, born: 19 Apr 1890, married, parents: Isaac BOWERS and Emma OLIVER (NC), death cause: "tuberculosis", died at Bluff City on 16 apr 1917, record (1917): 377.

Wilburn Eugene MARTIN, born: 24 Apr 1913, parents: J.A. MARTIN and Emma SCOTT, death cause: "whooping cough", informant: father (Bristol), buried: Beeler Cemetery, died: 18 Apr 1917, record (1917): 378.

Sarah A. MORTON, age 74 years, parents: Henry BULLOCK and mother not stated, death cause: "senility", informant: R.L. MORTON (Bristol), buried: Weaver cemetery, died: 18 Apr 1917, record (1917): 379.

Henry SHUMAN, born: 15 Mar 1868 in Russia, married, parents: Hershel SHUMAN (Russia) and Hannah SOLOMAN (Russia), death cause: not stated, informant: Isaac SHUMAN (Bristol), buried: Jewish Cemetery, Bristol, died: 18 Apr 1917, record (1917): 380.

Julia HODGE, age 7 years, parents: Hubert HODGE and Martha PICKLE, death cause: "measles", buried: Sinking Spring Cemetery, died in the 21st District on 19 Apr 1917, record (1917): 381.

C.D. BURKHART, age 64 years, born in Rogersville, married, parents: James W. BURKHART and Mary DELANEY, death cause: "Brights disease", informant: Mrs. J.R. ROBINSON (Glade Springs, VA), buried: Paperville, died: 19 Apr 1917, record (1917): 382.

Danid Alice STONE, age 52 years and 2 days, married, parents: C.W. DAILY (VA) and __ SENEKER (VA), death cause: "cancer of bowels", informant: Mrs. J.T. STONE (Blountville), buried: Seneker Cemetery, died: 19 Apr 1917, record (1917): 383.

Mrs. Addie PRUETT, age 55 years, widow, parents: not stated, death cause: "nephritis", informant: D.F. PRUETT (Bristol, VA), died: 20 Apr 1917, record (1917): 384.

Mrs. Hannah FOUCH, age 59 years, married, parents: Henry FITCH and mother not stated, death cause: "pulmonary tuberculosis", informant: A.C. KETRON (Bloomingdale), buried: Arcadia, died: 22 Apr 1917, record (1917): 385.

Mary Melvina FLEENOR, born: 12 Sep 1878, married, parents: Jacob HOOVER and Martha CARTER, death cause: "acute dilatation of heart", informant: Jacob HOOVER (Bloomingdale), buried: Fleenor Cemetery, died: 22 Apr 1917, record (1917): 386.

Paul J. RIGGS, born: 19 Jun 1916, parents: Jack C. RIGGS and Louriene SMITH, death cause: "tubercular peritonitis", informant: H.L. RIGGS (Fall Branch), buried: Double Springs, died: 23 Apr 1917, record (1917): 387.

Elbert Sener DOUGLAS, born: 9 Nov 1852, married, parents: Jacob DOUGLAS and Mollie BACON (Washington Co., TN), death cause: "carcinoma of bladder", informant: J.A. DOUGLAS (Fordtown), died: 23 Apr 1917, record (1917): 388.

Simpson B. DILLOW Jr., born: 10 Jan 1917, parents: Simpson B. DILLOW (Carter County) and Hannah EDWARDS (NC), death cause: "acute intestinal indigestion", informant: father (Fordtown), buried: Johnson City, died: 25 Apr 1917, record (1917): 389.

Mrs. Carrie Dulaney ST JOHN, born: 24 Mar 1839, widow, parents: Dr. William R. DULANEY and Mary TAYLOR (Carter County), death cause: "lobar pneumonia", informant: William B. ST JOHN (Bristol), died: 26 Apr 1917, record (1917): 390.

William Calvin HINES, age 84 years, born in Virginia, parents: not stated, death cause: illegible, informant: J.J. HINES (Blackwood, VA), buried: Avoca Cemetery, died: 28 Apr 1917, record (1917): 391.

Cart AKERS, born: 2 Sep 1901 in Virginia, parents: Tom AKERS (VA) and Francis WHITE (VA), death cause: "measles", informant: father (Fall Branch), buried: Walker Cemetery, 14th District, died: 29 Apr 1917, record (1917): 392.

Charles Henry KYLE, age 28 years, born in Pennsylvania, single, parents: J.W. KYLE (VA) and

Margaret ETTOR (PA), death cause: "dropsy", informant: J.W. KYLE (Chambersburg, PA), buried: Chambersburg, PA., died: 29 Apr 1917, record (1917): 393.

Infant BISHOP, male, parents: James BISHOP (Scott Co., VA) and Sarah LAMBERT (Scott Co., VA), death cause: "premature birth", informant: father (Kingsport), buried: Herman Cemetery, born/died: 30 Apr 1917, record (1917): 394.

Groover BOWER, age 22 years, parents: Ned BOWER (NC) and Jane ADAMS (NC), death cause: "bronchitis", buried: Rosedale Cemetery, died in the 3rd District on 30 Apr 1917, record (1917): 395.

Margaret LEONARD, born: 30 Nov 1830, widow, parents: Jake MINNICK and Katy SOURBUR (VA), death cause: "old age, fractured hip", buried: Harr cemetery, died in the 1st District on 30 Apr 1917, record (1917): 396.

Roy S. NORMAN, Negro, born: 4 Feb 1917, parents: William NORMAN (VA) and Emma JONES (VA), death cause: "unknown", informant: father (Bristol), buried: Citizen Cemetery, died: 30 Apr 1917, record (1917): 397.

Ethel LAMBERT, born: 8 Mar 1915 in West Virginia, parents: W.M. BROWN (VA) and Alice CATRON (VA), death cause: "ilio colitis", informant: T.A. COLEY (Kingsport), buried: Pyle Cemetery, died: 30 Apr 1917, record (1917): 398.

Infant GREEN, male, parents: Jack GREEN and Visa HENRY, death cause: "still born", died at Piney Flats on 10 Apr 1917, record (1917): 399.

Infant TOLBERT, male, parents: Charles TOLBERT and Clary VOWERS (VA), death cause: not stated, informant: father (Bristol), buried: Paperville, born/died: 4 Apr 1917, record (1917): 400.

Infant BEBBER, female, parents: John BEBBER (NC) and Bettie WIDNER (VA), death cause: "still born", died in the 17th District on 1 Apr 1917, record (1917): 401.

Mary Amanda POORE, age 89 years, 20 (?) months and 17 days, widow, parents: Hiram POORE (W.VA) and Rachel PEWLER (VA), death cause: "kidney trouble", informant: Bob POORE (Emmett), buried: Crumley Cemetery, died: 4 May 1917, record (1917): 402.

Nellie B. CROSS, born: 25 Nov 1896, widow, parents: Simon BURNETT and Elizabeth BOYD, death cause: "dropsy of bowels", informant: Tishie BURNETT (Bristol), buried: Gunning Cemetery, died: 1 May 1917, record (1917): 401.

Sealey Emiline MILHORN, age 72 years, single, parents: Henry MILHORN and Sarah DYRE, death cause: "angina pectoris and Brights disease", informant: Dr. GRAVES (Piney Flats), buried: New Bethel, died: 1 May 1917, record (1917): 404.

Annie L.M. PARKER, born: 4 Mar 1887, single, parents: Thomas PARKER and Mollie PARKER, death cause: "tuberculosis of lungs and ulcerated stomach", informant: W.E. WODS (Kingsport), buried: Bachman Cemetery, died: 1 May 1917, record (1917): 405.

Lydia ODELL, age 75 years, married, parents: Abe MORRELL and Jane BOOHER, death cause: "rheumatism", informant: Will ODELL (Bluff City), buried: Shipley Cemetery, died: 1 May 1917, record (1917): 406.

Robert CROSSWHITE, age 38 years, married, parents: Flemings CROSSWHITE and Julie CARR, death cause: "tuberculosis of lungs", informant: John MASS (Bluff City), buried: Shipley Cemetery, died: 3 May 1917, record (1917): 407.

Carl J. SCOTT, born: 5 Jun 1914, parents: Benjamin H. SCOTT and Esther HARRISON (VA), death cause: "measles", informant: J.C. HARRISON (Bristol), buried: Beeler Cemetery, died: 4 May 1917, record (1917): 408.

Mike HALE, age 16 years, born in North Carolina, parents: Alexander HALE (NC) and Beck HALE, death cause: "accidentally shot himself in the abdomen", died in the 1st District on 5 May 1917, record (1917): 409.

Mrs. Annie E. FAIRFAX, age 80 years, widow, parents: Sylvester BURFORD (VA) and Annie E. COX (VA), death cause: "cerebral hemorrhage", informant: R.R. FAIRFAX (Roanoke, VA), buried: East Hill, died: 7 May 1917, record (1917): 410.

Annie E. FORD, born: 20 Mr 1841, widow, parents: Will B. CHILDRESS and Annis GREGG, death cause: "acute pyetitis", informant: A.O. FORD (Kingsport), buried: Childress Cemetery, died: 9 May 1917, record (1917): 411.

Walter PARKER, age about 36 years, born in Georgia, married, parents: Albert PARKER (NC) and Margaret BRYSON (NC), death cause: "injured in explosion", informant: Mrs. Henry PARKER (Kingsport), buried: Americus, GA., died: 9 May 1917, record (1917): 412.

Nathan Thomas MOORE, born: 7 Dec 1856, married, parents: William MOORE (Washington Co, VA) and Mary L. GILES (Washington Co., VA), death cause: "diabetes", informant: R.C. MOORE (Bristol), buried: East Hill, died: 10 May 1917, record (1917): 413.

Mrs. Sarah HOWELL, age 55 years, born in North Carolina, widow, parents: ___ HUDGENS and Polly STANLEY

(NC), death cause: "chronic intestinal nephritis", informant: Charles DANCY (Bristol), died: 10 May 1917, record (1917): 414.

Arther REYNOLDS, Negro, born: 2 Feb 1895, widower, parents: Frank REYNOLDS (VA) and Lucy PENN (VA), death cause: "intestinal nephritis", informant: Mrs. Lucy THURSTON (Bristol), buried: Citizen cemetery, died: 11 May 1917, record (1917): 415.

John Rubin CARTER, born: 14 Aug 1892, single, parents: Enoch CARTER (VA) and Finnie FITCH, death cause: "tuberculosis of lungs", informant: J.S. ISLEY (Indian Springs), buried: Emory Cemetery, died: 12 May 1917, record (1917): 416.

Mrs. J.B. YOUNG, age 24 years, born in Virginia, married, parents: Henry MUMPOWER (VA) and Malissa HARTSOCK (VA), death cause: "gangrenous appendix", informant: J.B. YOUNG (Appalachia, VA), buried: Oak Grove, VA., died: 13 May 1917, record (1917): 417.

Elizabeth WITCHER, age 9 years, 4 months and 12 days, parents: Joe WITCHER and Adeh HELTON (NC), death cause: "pendicitus", informant: Mary WITCHER (Bluff City), buried: Hickory Tree, died: 11 May 1917, record (1917): 418.

Rebecca CAMPBELL, age 30 years, married, parents: Enoch CARTER and Polly CARTER, death cause: "tuberculosis", informant: Will MCCOY (Kingsport), buried: Martin cemetery, died: 16 May 1917, record (1917): 419.

Worley PERSINGER, born: 18 May 1901, parents: J.P. PERSINGER and Molly DYKES (VA), death cause: "tuberculosis lungs", informant: Newt COMPTON (Kingsport), buried: Fall Branch, died: 18 May 1917, record (1917): 420.

Susan Rebecca BLIZZARD, born: 13 Nov 1850, married, parents: Elkanah POE and __ COX, death cause: "tubercular peritonitis", informant: G.C. BLIZZART (Kingsport), buried: Muddy Creek Cemetery, died: 20 May 1917, record (1917): 421.

Leonard SEXTON, age 14 years, parents: W.P. SEXTON (White Pine, TN) and Lula CUTSHAW, death cause: "hit by train, died in 6 hours", informant: John G. GUINN (Kingsport), buried: Pactolus, died: 20 May 1917, record (1917): 422.

Walter Cecil HERREN, born: 4 Jan 1916, parents: R.D. HERREN (NC) and Ethel COX, death cause: "measles", buried: Henderson Cemetery, died at Kingsport on 22 May 1917, record (1917): 423.

B. Ballard UMBARGER, age 35 years, born in Wythe Co., VA, single, parents: M. Lafayett UMBARGER (Wythe Co.) and Luce UMBARGER (Wythe Co.), death cause: "homicide, meningitis from fractured skull", informant: D.L. UMBARGER (Wytheville, VA), died at Bristol on 24 May 1917, record (1917): 424.

Elizabeth VANCE, born: 12 Jan 1830, parents: Joshua HAMILTON and Sallie HOEBAUCH (PA), death cause: "old age", informant: R.B. RUTTER (Blountville), died: 26 May 1917, record (1917): 425.

Kennith Monroe BULLION, born: 26 Mar 1916, parents: James BULLION (Liverpool, England) and Victoria HARMON (W.VA), death cause: "measles and pneumonia", informant: father (Indian Springs), buried: Emory Cemetery, died: 26 May 1917, record (1917): 426.

Infant JENKINS, male, parents: William JENKINS and Amanda SIMERLY, death cause: "still born", informant: father (Bluff City), died: 26 May 1917, record (1917): 427.

William B. WILDER, born: 1 Feb 1844 in Virginia, parents: Palser WILDER (VA) and Kate RUTLEDGE (VA), death cause: "shock due to fall", informant: Kate WILDER (Bristol), buried: Wilder Valley, VA., died: 27 May 1917, record (1917): 428.

Harnie Clifford WHITE, born: 15 Jan 1875, married, parents: J.J. WHITE and mother not stated, death cause: "pneumonia", informant: Mrs. Lula WHITE (Bristol), buried: East Hill, died: 29 May 1917, record (1917): 429.

Anna Lee SHIPLEY, born: 25 Apr 1917, parents: Faustine SHIPLEY and Jola GOODMAN, death cause: "spina bifida", informant: Dr. GRAVES (Piney Flats), buried: Goodman Cemetery, died: 28 May 1917, record (1917): 430.

Connie Rhea Lee BULLION, born: 29 Apr 1913, parents: James BULLION (Liverpool, England) and Victoria HARMON (W.VA), death cause: "measles and pneumonia", informant: father (Indian Springs), buried: Emory Cemetery, died: 28 May 1917, record (1917): 431.

John Ross MCKENZIE, age 63 years, born at Halifax, Nova Scotia, widower, parents: John M. MCKENZIE and mother not stated, death cause: "malignant disease of stomach", informant: J.C. MCKENZIE (Appalachia, VA), buried: Mendota, VA., died: 31 May 1917, record (1917): 432.

Infant COX, male, parents: Virgil Thomas COX and Elizabeth BOYD, death cause: "died 3 or 4 days before delivery", informant: father (Fordtown), buried: Double Springs, died: 30 May 1917, record (1917): 433.

Infant RIVERS, male, parents: W.D. RIVERS (KY) and Fannie Lee JOHNSON (KY), death cause: "still born", informant: W.M. RIVERS (Kingsport), buried: Martin cemetery, died: 25 May 1917, record (1917): 434.

Infant GRAY, female, parents: Burley GRAY and Mary M.. (illegible), death cause: "still born", informant: father (Emmett), buried: Sinking Springs, died: 12 May 1917, record (1917): 435.

Infant GREEN, male, parents: Jack GREEN and Vice HARVEY, death cause: "still born", died at Piney Flats on 8 May 1917, record (1917): 436.

Infant GODSEY, male, parents: John T. GODSEY and Molly RICHARDS, death cause: "died at birth (twin), informant: father (Bluff City), buried: Vance, TN., died: 9 May 1917, record (1917): 437.

Infant GODSEY, male, parents: John T. GODSEY and Molly RICHARDS, death cause: "died at birth (twin), informant: father (Bluff City), buried: Vance, TN., died: 9 May 1917, record (1917): 438. (next two records duplicates of # 437 and 438)

Roxie ROSENBALM, born: 14 Oct 1869 in Russell Co., VA., widow, parents: William LOCKHART (VA) and Elizabeth SPEAR (VA), death cause: "carcinoma of uterus", informant: Mrs. Jack MARKS (Alvarado, VA), buried: Greenwood, VA., died: 16 Jun 1917, record (1917): 441.

Elbert SHARP, age 43 years, 9 months and 8 days, married, parents: Jasper SHARP (VA) and Sarah HARROPP (Missouri), death cause: "tuberculosis of lungs", informant: A.M. SHARP (Bluff City), died: 28 Jun 1917, record (1917): 442.

Everett MAHATHA, age 21 years, born in Wythe Co., VA., parents: James MAHATHA (NC) and (illegible) WARICK (NC), death cause: "fracture spine due to fall from building", informant: S.S. KRIGER, buried: Wytheville, VA., died: 1 Jun 1917, record (1917): 443.

George Wilson FELTY, born: __ Mar 1915, parents: G.F. FELTY (VA) and __ JESSIE (VA), death cause: "measles, pneumonia", informant: father (Bristol), buried: East Hill, died: 1 Jun 1917, record (1917): 444.

Zebulon Vance SPARGER, born: 17 Feb 1844 in Mt. Airy, NC., married, parents: William SPARGER (Mt. Airy, NC) and Mary E. FULTON (Mt. Airy, NC), death cause: "carrigans disease", informant: W.H. SPARGER (Bristol), died: 1 Jun 1917, record (1917): 445.

Daris THOMAS, age 1 month, parents: Charles O. THOMAS (Roxboro, NC) and Lillie WOODY (Boxville, KY), death cause: "cholera infantum", informant: G.W. WOODY

(Kingsport), buried: Pyle cemetery, died: 2 Jun 1917, record (1917): 336.

Charles Herbert CROSS, age 8 years, 11 months and 21 days, parents: George CROSS and __ SMITH, death cause: "suspect strychining poisoning", informant: father (Bristol), buried: Ordway cemetery, died: 4 Jun 1917, record (1917): 447.

O.S. BROWN, age 66 years, born in Virginia, married, parents: Z. BROWN (VA) and Martha EARLY (VA), death cause: "paralysis", informant: F.E. BROWN (Bristol), buried: Ordway Cemetery, died: 4 Jun 1917, record (1917): 448.

Bonnie Laura JENKINS, born: 11 May 1915 in Virginia, parents: Elbert JENKINS (VA) and Ludie FALIN (VA), death cause: "entero colitis", informant: father (Kingsport), died: 8 Jun 1917, record (1917): 449.

Ester BERNETT, age 45 years, born in Virginia, married, parents: William AKERS (VA) and mother not stated, death cause: "tuberculosis", informant: D.H. BERNETT (Bristol), buried: Ordway Cemetery, died: 9 Jun 1917, record (1917): 450.

N.C. ST JOHN, born: 3 Apr 1844 in Smyth County, VA., married, parents: Berry ST JOHN (Smyth Co., VA) and Hannah DUNCAN (Smyth Co., VA), death cause: "Brights Disease", informant: Mrs. Robert L. TAYLOR (Bristol), buried: Chilhowie, VA., died: 12 Jun 1917, record (1917): 451.

Susie COX, born: 30 Mar 1899, single, parents: Thomas Walker COX and Loula ELSOM (Washington Co, VA), death cause: "epilepsy", informant: T.W. COX (Jonesboro), died in the 14th District on 13 Jun 1917, record (1917): 452.

Zola MCKINNEY, born: 2 Oct 1900, parents: Benjamin H. MCKINNEY and Mollie C. MILLS, death cause: "tuberculosis", informant: father (Piney Flats), died: 14 Jun 1917, record (1917): 453.

Ora Estella JACKSON, born: 10 Oct 1902 in North Carolina, parents: J.W. JACKSON (NC) and Laura TRULL (NC), death cause: "dysentery", informant: Leonard LITTLE (Kingsport), buried: Old Kingsport Cemetery, died: 15 Jun 1917, record (1917): 454.

John Nelson DOLEN, born 26 Jul 1837, married, parents: Nelson DOLEN and Peggie PARTON, death cause: "tuberculosis", informant: A. DOLEN (Fall Branch), buried: Dolen Cemetery, died: 16 Jun 1917, record (1917): 455.

Alice HARDY, born: 28 Dec 1867, widow, parents: James CHAPMAN and Matilda HITE, death cause: "cardiac hypertrophy", informant: Roy HARDY (Indian Springs), buried: Kingsport, died: 17 Jun 1917, record (1917): 456.

Ebonezer Mikin Patton MOORE, born: 6 Jun 1833 in Washington Co., TN., parents: James MOORE (VA) and Sallie COLLONS (Washington Co., TN), death cause: "organic heart lesion", informant: J.R. DELANEY (Bristol), buried: Holston Valley, died: 18 Jun 1917, record (1917): 457.

Infant BARGER, male, parents: R.L. BARGER and ___ LADY, death cause: "child not developed", born/died: Indian Springs on 19 Jun 1917, record (1917): 458.

Maude HALL, born: 22 May 1892 in North Carolina, married, parents: William R. ANDERSON (NC) and Nancy J. TRULL (NC), death cause: illegible, informant: Blanche ANDERSON (Kingsport), buried: North Carolina, died: 20 Jun 1917, record (1917): 459.

Woodrow COLLINS, born: 2 Jan 1916, parents: Sullins COLLINS and Lettie CARTWRIGHT, death cause: "severe burn", buried" Pyle Cemetery, died at Kingsport on 21 Jun 1917, record (1917): 460.

Olena LEONARD, born: 14 Apr 1917, parents: Benjamin F. LEONARD (Washington Co., VA) and Mary MESSICK (Washington Co., VA), death cause: "cholera", informant: B.F. LEONARD (Kingsport), died: 21 Jun 1917, record (1917): 461.

Fannie PERRY, born: 30 May 1917, parents: father not stated and Nannie PERRY, death cause: "malnutrition", informant: John PERRY (Kingsport), died: 4 Jun 1917, record (1917): 462.

Joe DAVIS, age about 55 years, married, parents: William R. DAVIS and Jane SLAGLE, death cause: "valvulor heart disease", informant: Hariet DAVIS (Bristol), buried: Weaver Cemetery, died: 21 Jun 1917, record (1917): 463.

Infant BUMGARDNER, male, parents: J.D. BUMGARDNER (NC) and Bessie G. KEGLEY (VA), death cause: "premature birth", informant: father (Bristol), died: 22 Jun 1917, record (1917): 464.

Robert WOODY, Jr., born: 21 Apr 1917, parents: Robert WOODY (NC) and Mary MANN (PA), death cause: "enteritis", informant: father (Kingsport), buried: Methodist Cemetery, Kingsport, died: 23 Jun 1917, record (1917): 465.

Georgie WARREN, age 33 years, 5 months and 6 days, married, parents: J.W. BOOHER and Louisa FLETCHER, death cause: "complication of disease", died in the 3rd District on 23 Jun 1917, record (1917): 466.

Wanna CASE, born: 29 Apr 1914, parents: Walter CASE and Magie KAGLE, death cause: "dysentery", buried: Lilley Cemetery, Bluff City, died: 23 Jun 1917, record (1917): 467.

Lawrence SIMPSON, born: 4 Nov 1893 in West Virginia, single, parents: J.W. SIMPSON (VA) and Cora Lee SMITH (VA), death cause: "drowned in Holston River", informant: R. Floyd SMITH (Kingsport), buried: Bluefield, W. VA., died: 23 Jun 1917, record: 468.

Adrian Alva LOYD, born: 18 Jul 1895 in Johnson County, parents: J.L. LOYD (Johnson Co.) and Sarah BERRY, death cause: "drowned in Holston River", informant: J.C. STONE (Kingsport), buried: Johnson City, died: 23 Jun 1917, record (1917): 469.

D.N. SHEPARD, age 21 years, single, parents: not stated, death cause: "acute (illegible) and paralysis", buried: Bluff City, died at Kingsport on 26 Jun 1917, record (1917): 470.

Mary Emma GILMORE, born: 17 Oct 1847 in Newport, PA., widow, parents: Joseph TRIMMER and mother not stated, death cause: "chronic intestinal nephritis", informant: J.W. HOUCK (Bristol), died: 26 Jun 1917, record (1917): 471.

Clarence Herman MOODY, born: 28 Dec 1915, parents: D.C. MOODY and Patsy FLEENER, death cause: "dysentery", informant: father (Kingsport), buried: Rock Springs, died: 28 Jun 1917, record (1917): 472.

Ralph Vernon OVERBAY, born: 20 Nov 1917, parents: G. OVERBAY and Allie PARKER, death cause: "whooping cough", informant: S.P. PARKER (Kingsport), buried: Bachman Cemetery, died: 29 Jun 1917, record: 473.

Vestal CARR, born: 9 Apr 1910, parents: Walter CARR and Mary KAGLE, death cause: "dysentery", died at Bluff City on 30 Jun 1917, record (1917): 474.

Infant JONES, male, parents: Raughleigh JONES and Maggie Etta FERGUSON, death cause: "still born", informant: father (Fordtown), buried: Rock Springs, born/died: 5 Jun 1917, record (1917): 475.

Infant FULLER, male, parents: Erwin FULLER and Eliza STARNES, death cause: "still born", informant: father (Kingsport), buried: Martin Cemetery, died: 22 Jun 1917, record (1917): 476.

Flick ROUSE, age 19 years, married, parents: John ROUSE (Washington Co., VA) and Rosy FLICK, death cause: "drowning", informant: N.E. ROGERS (Fish Dam), died: 27 Jul 1917, record (1917): 477.

Mary Lynn STITT, born: 26 Jun 1917, parents: J.A. STITT (NC) and Lizzie ROYSTON, death cause:

"premature", informant: father (Kingsport), buried: Reedy Creek Cemetery, died: 2 Jul 1917, record: 478.

Robert Franklin CLAYMAN, born: 31 Jul 1915, parents: R.F. CLAYMAN and __ KING, death cause: "ileo colitis", informant: father (Bristol), buried: East Hill, died: 2 Jul 1917, record (1917): 479.

Harry WILLIAMS, born: 28 Nov 1916 in Richmond, Virginia, parents: "not known", death cause: "ileo colitis", informant: Tate WILLIAMS (Kingsport), buried: Vermont Cemetery, died: 5 Jul 1917, record (1917): 480.

Gladys MCCRACKEN, born: 8 Oct 1916, parents: George MCCRACKEN and Geneva WILLS, death cause: "ileo colitis", informant: John MCCRACKEN (Kingsport), died: 6 Jul 1917, record (1917): 481.

Ruth Autance CARTER, age 3 years and 4 months, born in Virginia, parents: R.B. CARTER (VA) and Lillie FRITZ, death cause: "tuberculosis", informant: father (St Charles, VA), buried: Scott Co., VA., died: 6 Jul 1917, record (1917): 482.

James TAYLOR, age about 58 years, widower, born in Scott County, VA., parents: "not known", death cause: "tuberculosis", informant: Jacob ROLLER (Indian Springs), buried: Childress Cemetery, died: 7 Jul 1917, record (1917): 483.

James TAYLOR, age 68 years, married, parents: Manuel TAYLOR and mother not stated, death cause: "pneumonia", informant: William H. TAYLOR (Blountville), buried: Gunnings Cemetery, died: 8 Jul 1917, record (1917): 484.

James Richard OWENS, born: 29 Jul 1868 in Virginia, married, parents: John Henry OWENS (VA) and Mary (illegible)(VA), death cause: "pulmonary tuberculosis", informant: Mrs. Hender Etta OWENS (Bristol), buried: East Hill, died: 8 Jul 1917, record (1917): 485.

Andrew DAVIS, born: 12 Oct 1849 in Virginia, married, parents: Duncan DAVIS (Grayson Co., VA) and Jane SEXTON (Grayson Co., VA), death cause: "pellegra", informant: S.J. PYLE (Kingsport), buried: Pyle Cemetery, died: 9 Jul 1917, record (1917): 486.

Wilkey Kenneth MOWDY, born: 2 Dec 1916, parents: William MOWDY and Ethel OVERBAY, death cause: "pertusans, broncho pneumonia", informant: J.W. MOWDY (Fordtown), buried: Pactolus Cemetery, died: 10 Jul 1917, record (1917): 487.

Thomas Walker COX, born: 27 Mar 1872, married, parents: William F. COX and Jane CLARK, death cause:

"intestinal parasite, probably hook worm", informant: O.M. CHASE (Fordtown), buried: Presbyterian Church Cemetery, died: 10 Jul 1917, record (1917): 488.

Prince Eugennes HORTON, born: 7 May 1910, parents: Eugenens HORTON (VA) and Claissa C. GOAD (VA), death cause: "ileo colitis", informant: father (Kingsport), buried: Pyle Cemetery, died: 11 Jul 1917, record (1917): 489.

Elizabeth GRAY, born: 12 Nov 1845, widow, parents: Mark MONTIETH and Jane PAGE, death cause: "tumor of stomach", informant: Sallie GRAY (Fordtown), died: 11 Jul 1917, record (1917): 490.

Mildred Abbey SHOWALTER, born: 11 Oct 1912, parents: W.N. SHOWALTER and ___ PARKER, death cause: "ileo colitis", informant: father (Kingsport), died: 11 Jul 1917, record (1917): 491.

Anderson HODGE, age 70 years, single, parents: John HODGE and ___ GRASS, death cause: "chronic nephritis", buried: New Bethel Cemetery, died at Piney Flats on 12 Jul 1917, record (1917): 492.

Bettie BROOKS, Negro, born: 2 Jul 1853 in Virginia, widow, parents: Winfield WRIGHT (VA) and Parthena BANKS (VA), death cause: "nephritis", informant: Cora EDWARDS (Bristol), buried: Citizen Cemetery, died: 13 Jul 1917, record (1917): 493.

Ruth HOLDSCLAW, Negro, born: May 1911 in North Carolina, parents: West HOLDSCLAW (NC) and Mary HOLDSCLAW (Hawkins County), death cause: "ileo colitis", informant: father (Kingsport), buried: Kingsport Colored Cemetery, died: 15 Jul 1917, record (1917): 494.

Bessie PRITCHARD, born: 27 Mar 1880, widow, parents: J.H. OWEN and ___ SETLES, death cause: "tuberculosis", informant: A.A. OWENS (Johnson City), buried: East Hill, died: 15 Jul 1917.

Elizabeth SOUTH, age 18 years and 3 months, single, parents: Mose SOUTH (VA) and Julia SOURBEER (W. VA), death cause: "typhoid fever", informant: Jane WEBB (Bristol), buried: Paperville, died: 15 Jul 1917, record (1917): 496.

Dave BOOHER, age 18 years, single, parents: Walter BOOHER and Lillie GRAY, death cause: "blood poison from a mashed foot", informant: Mrs. Lillie BOOHER (Emmett), buried: Hickory Tree, died: 16 Jul 1917, record (1917): 497.

Saphrona BARE, age 50 years, married, parents: (illegible) BARE (VA) and Nancy BARE, death cause: "mitral regurgitation of heart", buried: Rumbley

Cemetery, died at Piney Flats on 18 Jul 1917, record (1917): 498.

George ROADS, age 55 years, 3 months and 10 days, born in Virginia, married, parents: father not stated and Sallie ROADS (VA), death cause: "heart failure", buried: Shipley Cemetery, died: 13 Jul 1917, record (1917): 499.

Lola Lavinia BROYLES, born: 16 Jul 1917, parents: R.L. BROYLES and May MOORE, death cause: "premature birth", died at Fall Branch on 20 Jul 1917, record: 500.

Ora Anna Lee JOYCE, born: 30 Apr 1916 in Virginia, parents: W.H. JOYCE (VA) and Rosa E. HOMMEL (VA), death cause: "acute dysentery", informant: father (Kingsport), buried: Woods Cemetery, died: 21 Jul 1917, record (1917): 501.

Ernie Carr TRIPLETT, born: 21 Feb 1917, parents: Ernest TRIPLETT (NC) and Martha (illegible)(NC), death cause: "ileo colitis", informant: father (Kingsport), buried: Oak Grove, died: 21 Jul 1917, record: 502

Infant CLAYMAN, male, born: 20 Jul 1917, parents: F.S. CLAYMAN and __ HARKER, death cause: "premature birth", informant: father (Bristol), buried: Morrison Chapel, died: 21 Jul 1917, record (1917): 503.

Vernon Lindville REPOSS, born: 18 Jul 1917, parents: John REPOSS (Washington Co., VA) and Carrie (illegible), death cause: "unknown", informant: father (Piney Flats), died: 22 Jul 1917, record (1917): 504.

Ellen WISDOM, Negro, born: 18 Apr 1832, widow, parents: "unknown", death cause: "mitral insufficiency of heart", informant: Shadrack WISDOM (Bristol), buried: Tennessee Cemetery, died: 23 Jul 1917, record (1917): 505.

M. STEADMAN, female, age 50 years, single, parents: Patton STEADMAN and Mary DOLEN, death cause: "pulmonary tuberculosis", informant: R. SHIPP (Kingsport), died in the 13th District on 24 Jul 1917, record (1917): 506.

Eula Dale HUMPHREYS, born: 25 Jul 1914, parents: William T. HUMPHREYS and Mary Ellen JOHNSTON, death cause: "typhoid fever", informant: father (Kingsport), buried: Pyle Cemetery, died: 24 Jul 1917, record (1917): 507.

Joseph NELMS, born: 23 Dec 1843, widower, parents: William NELMS and Elizabeth CHILDRESS, death cause: "dysentery", informant: L.L. NELMS (Kingsport), buried: Presbyterian Cemetery, died: 25 Jul 1917, record (1917): 508.

George W. HICKS, age: 29 years, 11 months and 13 days, single, parents: John W. HICKS and Marinda MINGEA, death cause: "typhoid fever", informant: father (Bristol), buried: Arcadia, died: 25 Jul 1917, record (1917): 509.

Nathaniel Green KITTS, born: 24 Feb 1855 in Virginia, married, parents: Ganim KITTS (VA) and Abigal STEELE (VA), death cause: "chronic brights disease", informant: Mrs. Cora K. KITTS (Bristol), buried: East Hill, died: 25 Jul 1917, record (1917): 510.

Annie Dickerson SMITH, black, born: 6 Aug 1894, married, parents: Hugh DICKERSON and Eva NETHERLAND, death cause: "tuberculosis", informant: Sam PATTON (Kingsport), died: 26 Jul 1917, record (1917): 511.

Felick ROUSE, age 19 years, born in Virginia, married, parents: John C. ROUSE and Nancy FELICK, death cause: "drowned", buried: Holston Valley, died: 27 Jul 1917, record (1917): 512.

Maggie SMITH, age 12 years, parents: David SMITH and Ruth CHILDRESS, death cause: "flux", informant: D.J. BLALOCK (Blountville), buried: Childress Cemetery, died: 27 Jul 1917, record (1917): 513.

Robert Carrier HENDERSON, born: 3 Jul 1917, parents: W.M. HENDERSON (VA) and Mandy CRUSENBERRY (VA), death cause: "indigestion and malnutrition, informant: mother (Bristol), buried: East Hill, died: 27 Jul 1917, record (1917): 514.

William DOUGLAS, born: 20 Sep 1860, married, parents: George W. DOUGLAS and Mary LAY, death cause: "dysentery", informant: T.J. DOUGLAS (Kingsport), died: 28 Jul 1917, record (1917): 515.

George Rhodes HUGHS, age 55 years, 3 months and 2 days, born in Virginia, married, parents: George RHODES (VA) and Martha S. (illegible)(VA), death cause: "heart failure", buried: Sinking Spring Cemetery, died: 28 Jul 1917, record (1917): 516.

Selvia May FLEENOR, born: Feb 1916 in Ohio, parents: James FLEENOR (VA) and Vergie EATON (VA), death cause: "ileo colitis", informant: father (Kingsport), died: 30 Jul 1917, record (1917): 517.

Enon Harrison BROWN, colored, born: 3 Jul 1917, parents: Will BROWN (GA) and Effie HARRISON (Ala), death cause: "malnutrition", buried: Kingsport Colored Cemetery, died: 31 Jul 1917, record (1917): 518.

Infant SPEARS, female, parents: James E. SPEARS (Hawkins County) and Lillie S. MORROW (NC), death cause: "still born", informant: father (Kingsport), died: 11 Jul 1917, record (1917): 519.

Infant VANCE, female, parents: R.H. VANCE and Maude PHIPPS, death cause: "still born", informant: J.M. PHIPPS (Bristol), buried: Paperville, died: 10 Jul 1917, record (1917): 520.

Mrs. Julia A. MALONE, born: 17 Jul 1867 in Washington Co., VA., widow, parents: James HOLLEY and Martha HUSTON (Washington Co., VA), death cause: "gallstone", informant: F.B. MALONE (Blountville), buried: Buffalo Cemetery, died: 1 Aug 1917, record (1917): 521.

Mary Jane ROYSTON, age 4 months, parents: T.B. ROYSTON and mother not stated, death cause: "acute dysentery", informant: S.H. PETERS (Emmett), buried: Warren Cemetery, died: 1 Aug 1917, record (1917): 522.

Gladys JOYCE, born: 29 May 1914 in Virginia, parents: W.H. JOYCE (VA) and Rosa HOMMEL (VA), death cause: "dysentery", informant: father (Kingsport), buried: Wood Cemetery, died: 3 Aug 1917, record (1917): 523.

Mrs. Elmira WALKER, born: 24 Feb 1831, widow, parents: John LESLIE and Sarah ___, death cause: "senility", informant: Charles N. KELSEY (Bristol), buried: Limestone, died: 3 Aug 1917, record (1917): 524.

Johnathan MCKINNEY, age 79 years, widower, parents: James MCKINNEY (VA) and Jane LOVE, death cause: "heart trouble", died in the 1st District on 4 Aug 1917, record (1917): 525.

Myrtle COATS, born: 4 Jun 1913, parents: John COATS and Daisey WHITE (VA), death cause: "dysentery", informant: Walt SMITH (Kingsport), buried: Pyle Cemetery, died: 8 Aug 1917, record (1917): 526.

Margaret VANCE, born: 19 May 1915, parents: Nick VANCE (Washington Co., VA) and Martha KEITH (Washington Co., VA), death cause: "stomatitis and malnutrition", informant: father (Bristol), died: 10 Aug 1917, record (1917): 527.

Lucian BROWN, age 6 years, parents: Albert BROWN and Mollie ARNOLD, death cause: "tuberculosis of lungs", informant: Charles SAMS (Kingsport), buried: Cameron Cemetery, died: 10 Aug 1917, record (1917): 528.

Edwin ROBERTS, age 28 years, born in Mohawk, TN., single, parents: M.C. ROBERTS (NC) and Mary L. MARSHALL (Mohawk, TN), death cause: "tuberculosis", buried: East Hill, died: 11 Aug 1917, record: 529.

Mrs. E. H. WHITE, age 40 years, married, parents: J.E. ESTEP and mother not stated, death cause: "tuberculor meningitis", informant: E.H. WHITE (Bristol), died: 12 Aug 1917, record (1917): 530.

Katie GAMBILL, born: 1 Nov 1895 in Hawkins County, single, parents: W.W. GAMBILL (Hawkins Co.) and Mary MATHEWS (Hawkins Co.), death cause: "pulmonary tuberculosis", informant: Hal HAYNES (Kingsport), buried: Rogersville, TN., died: 13 Aug 1917, record (1917): 531.

John M. MILLIOM, age 70 years, married, parents: father not stated and Sarah DYRE, death cause: "mitral regurgitation of heart", informant: Dr. GRAVES (Piney Flats), buried: New Bethel, died: 13 Aug 1917, record (1917): 532.

Nathan DeWitt BACHMAN, born: 26 Dec 1844, married, parents: E.K. BACHMAN and __ POWELL, death cause: not stated, informant: E.K. BACHMAN, Jr. (Bristol), buried: East Hill, died: 13 Aug 1917, record: 533.

Emaline MOSS, born: 14 Apr 1917, parents: John MOSS and Leland RICHARD, death cause: "meningitis", informant: James HAWK (Indian Springs), died: 13 Aug 1917, record (1917): 534.

Irene V. KING, born: 18 May 1916, parents: Elisha KING and Bertha WOODY, death cause: "meningitis", informant: G.W. KING (Indian Springs), buried: Emory Cemetery, died: 14 Aug 1917, record (1917): 535.

G.R. SHIPLEY, age 78 years, widower, parents: Park SHIPLEY and mother not stated, death cause: "chronic dysentery", informant: H.H. SHIPLEY (Indian Springs), buried: Emory cemetery, died: 15 Aug 1917, record (1917): 536.

Blanche A. KETRON, born: 12 Jun 1891, married, parents: John D. ROGERS and Elizabeth BEARD, death cause: "typhoid fever", informant: S.G. KETRON (Kingsport), buried: Vermont, TN., died: 17 Aug 1917, record (1917): 537.

Sarah A. DICKSON, age 65 years, widow, parents: George DICKSON and mother not stated, death cause: "pellagra", buried: Pyle Cemetery, died at Indian Springs on 17 Aug 1917, record (1917): 538.

Andrew Thomas MOFFIT, born: 4 Mar 1829 in North Carolina, married, parents: Dan MOFFIT (Ireland) and Nancy CARROWELL (Ireland), death cause: "paralysis", informant: George MOFFIT (Kingsport), buried: Morrison Chapel, died: 18 Aug 1917, record (1917): 539.

James Ambros Wallace CRAWFORD, born: 25 Jun 1916, parents: William CRAWFORD and Birthy WRIGHT, death cause: "dysentery", informant: father (Kingsport), buried: Pyle Cemetery, died: 18 Aug 1917, record (1917): 540.

Joel LITZ, born: 8 Aug 1827 in Virginia, widower, parents: John H. LITZ (VA) and Barbara KING (VA), death cause: "acute dysentery", informant: J.W. LITZ (Kingsport), buried: Pyle cemetery, died: 20 Aug 1917, record (1917): 541.

James C. KETRON, born: 12 May 1857, married, parents: Joseph KETRON and Betsy COOKENHOUR, death cause: "cancer of stomach", informant: L.B. MCCRARY (Bloomingdale), buried: Arcadia, died: 20 Aug 1917, record (1917): 542.

Infant LAMPKINS, female, born: 21 Aug 1917, parents: Walker LAMPKINS and Callie MOREFIELD, death cause: "hemorrhage", informant: father (Kingsport), buried: Pyle Cemetery, died: 21 Aug 1917, record (1917): 543.

Wade Edward HOLLEY, born: 23 Dec 1916, parents: Wade HOLLEY (VA) and Anna Belle HOLLEY (VA), death cause: "meningitis", buried: Pyle Cemetery, died at Kingsport on 21 Aug 1917, record (1917): 544.

Mrs. Elizabeth S. COOK, age 75 years, married, parents: George MORRIS (NC) and __ CHRTCHER (NC), death cause: "diarrhea", informant: J.O. COOK, died at Bluff City on 22 Aug 1917, record (1917): 545.

Mable STEPHENSON, colored, born: 15 Dec 1916, born at Big Stone Gap, VA., parents: Jessie STEPHENSON (Chicago) and Nellie MITCHELL, death cause: "broncho pneumonia", informant: Alice MITCHELL (Bristol), buried: Big Stone Gap, VA., died: 23 Aug 1917, record (1917): 546.

McKinley COATS, born: 1 Jan 1917, parents: Blain COATS and Dora ARNOLD, death cause: "ileo colitis", informant: John COATS (Kingsport), buried: Martin Cemetery, died: 23 Aug 1917, record (1917): 547.

Cecil JOHNSON, born: 30 May 1896, divorced, parents: James JOHNSON and Feornil CARROLL, death cause: "pellegra", informant: Walter JOHNSON (Kingsport), buried: Pyle Cemetery, died: 25 Aug 1917, record (1917): 548.

Nancy EASLEY, born: 25 May 1830, widow, parents: Samuel CRABTREE (NC) and Bersheba GLENN (NC), death cause: "hemiplegia", informant: S.P. STEADMAN (Fall Branch), buried: Rock Springs, died: 26 Aug 1917, record (1917): 549.

R.M. ANDERSON, Jr., born: 27 Jan 1916, parents: R.M. ANDERSON and Mattie ADAMS, death cause: "indigestion", died at Piney Flats on 27 Aug 1917, record (1917): 550.

Cora STOUT, born: 6 Aug 1888, married, parents: Bill JONES and Corda COLLINS, death cause: "mio carditis,

nephritis", informant: Clide JONES (Bluff City), buried: Jones Cemetery, died: 28 Aug 1917, record (1917): 551.
Mary A. SHIPLEY, born: 10 Mar 1916, parents: Maurice SHIPLEY and Alice TAYLOR, death cause: "dysentery and meningitis", informant: Enoch SHIPLEY (Kingsport), buried: Pyle Cemetery, died: 31 Aug 1917, record (1917): 552.
Jott BARKER, born: 5 Mar 1883, divorced, parents: William BARKER (VA) and Lonisa FIELDS (VA), death cause: "typhoid fever", informant: Clint BARKER (Kingsport), died: 31 Aug 1917, record (1917): 553.
Toy Alden SMITH, born: 23 Jun 1913, parents: G.E. SMITH and Alice SHIPLEY, death cause: "throat infection", informant: father (Bristol), buried: Pleasant Hill, Blountville, died: 31 Aug 1917, record (1917): 554.
Julia CAMPBELL, parents: E.L. CAMPBELL and Grace BUCKLES, death cause: "seven month child", buried: Paperville, born/died: 7 Aug 1917, record (1917): 555.
Infant MORRELL, female, parents: Dosie MORRELL and Lillie HARBOUR, death cause: "premature", buried: Morrell Cemetery, died in the 15th District on 4 Aug 1917, record (1917): 556.
Infant DOUGHERTY, female, parents: father not stated and Grace DOUGHERTY (Gate City), death cause: "still born", informant: J.C. DOUGHERTY (Bristol), born/died: 11 Aug 1917, record (1917): 557.
Infant DOUGHERTY, male, parents: father not stated and Grace DOUGHERTY (Gate City), death cause: "premature", informant: J.C. DOUGHERTY (Bristol), buried: Bristol Cemetery, born/died: 11 Aug 1917, record (1917): 558.
Infant BOOHER, male, parents: Elbert BOOHER and Mattie BRACE, death cause: "still born", buried: Hickory Tree Cemetery, died: 18 Aug 1917, record (1917): 559.
Infant GRAHAM, female, parents: D.F. GRAHAM and mother's name illegible, death cause: "still born", informant: father (Emmett), died: 14 Sep 1917, record (1917): 560.
Andy GODSEY, Negro, age about 70 years, widower, parents: Alex GODSEY and mother's name illegible, death cause: "mitral regurgitation", died: 1 Sep 1917, record (1917): 561.
Sallie Golloway GRILLS, born: 4 Jan 1840, widow, parents: William GOLLOWAY and Millie CRUDGINGTON, death cause: "paralysis", informant: I.P. FISH (Fall Branch), buried: Galloway Cemetery, 13th District, died: 2 Sep 1917, record (1917): 562.

John Logan WOODS, born: 17 Jul 1889, married, parents: Thomas G. WOODS and ___ HENRY, death cause: "abscess of liver", informant: Mrs. J.L. WOODS (Bristol), buried: Ordway Cemetery, died: 2 Sep 1917, record (1917): 563.

Freddie WHITE, born: 3 Mar 1915, colored, born in Alabama, parents: Henry WHITE (Florida) and Ollie MITCHELL (Alabama), death cause: "dysentery", informant: father (Kingsport), died: 3 Sep 1917, record (1917): 564.

Martin WELCH, age 41 years, born in Virginia, married, parents: Mart WELCH (VA) and Ora MAYS, death cause: "scalded at a steam engine", buried: Abingdon, died: 3 Sep 1917, record (1917): 565.

James Nathaniel FAIR, born: 29 Jun 1874, married, parents: Harmon FAIR (NC) and Carolina BUNDER (NC), death cause: "tuberculosis of kidneys", informant: Gussie FAIR (Jonesboro), buried: Hite Family Cemetery, 13th District, died: 3 Sep 1917, record (1917): 566.

Charles Edward DICKSON, born: 8 Nov 1915, parents: Edgar DICKSON and Ethel CHILDRESS, death cause: "dysentery and diptheria", informant: I.T. CHILDRESS (Indian Springs), buried: Gunnings Cemetery, died: 5 Sep 1917, record (1917): 567.

Johnson Paul HUTSON, born: 23 Jun 1917, parents: Claud HUTSON and Mary SAMS, death cause: "spinal meningitis", informant: Charles HUTSON (Kingsport), buried: Liberty Hill, died: 5 Sep 1917, record: 568.

Geneva GREEN, born: 12 May 1912 in North Carolina, parents: Tabor GREEN (NC) and Annie HARRISON (NC), death cause: "acute dysentery", informant: father (Kingsport), buried: Pyle Cemetery, died: 5 Sep 1917, record (1917): 569.

Paul JETER, age 17 years and 5 months, parents: John JETER (VA) and Lucy CARRIER, death cause: "typhoid fever", buried at Bluff City, died: 7 Sep 1917, record (1917): 570.

J.P. HARLESS, born: 2 Apr 1917 in Oklahoma, parents: W.M. HARLESS (VA) and Matilda ROBINS (VA), death cause: "found dead in bed", informant: father (Pattonfield, VA), buried: Duffield, died: 7 Sep 1917, record (1917): 571.

Mrs. Ella KETRON, born: Feb 1886 in Virginia, married, parents: Rev. George BYRD (VA) and (illegible) Jane CARTER (VA), death cause: "hemorrhage", buried: Pyle Cemetery, died at Kingsport on 9 Sep 1917, record (1917): 572.

Nathan DULANEY, Negro, age 46 years, married, parents: George DULANEY and Julia GAMMON, death cause:

"cirrhosis", informant: Janie DULANEY (Blountville), died: 9 Sep 1917, record (1917): 573.
Benjamin RAMEY, born: 28 Aug 1915, parents: Johnathon RAMEY (VA) and Eliza BLAIR (VA), death cause: "typhoid fever", informant: mother (Kingsport), died: 10 Sep 1917, record (1917): 574.
Isaac COLE, age 75 years, born in Virginia, married, parents: not stated, death cause: "tuberculosis of bowels", died at Piney Flats on 10 Sep 1917, record (1917): 575.
Willie B.R. HALL, born: 19 Jun 1917, parents: B.B. HALL (NC) and Maude ANDERSON (NC), death cause: "cholera infantum", informant: father (Kingsport), buried: North Carolina, died: 11 Sep 1917, record (1917): 576.
Willie Gray WAYMAN, female, born: 14 Feb 1917, parents: J.W. WAYMAN (NC) and Martha OSBORNE (NC), death cause: "dysentery", informant: father (Kingsport), buried: Bachman Cemetery, died: 13 Sep 1917, record (1917): 577.
Bessie JOHNSON, age 27 years, married, parents: Sam HENLEY and mother not stated, death cause: "pulmonary tuberculosis", informant: John JOHNSON (Kingsport), buried: Pyle Cemetery, died: 13 Sep 1917, record (1917): 578.
Johnie Fred GODSEY, born: 10 Apr 1916, parents: W.R. GODSEY and Lucy JONES, death cause: "ileo colitis and pneumonia", informant: father (Kingsport), buried: Roller Cemetery, died: 15 Sep 1917, record: 579.
Nannie Willes DAVIS, born: 20 Aug 1917, parents: John D. DAVIS and Maud SHOECRAFT, death cause: "found dead in bed", buried: Ordway, died: 17 Sep 1917, record (1917): 580.
Cliff MORE, age 3 months and 15 days, parents: Jonathan MORE and Susie (illegible) (VA), death cause: "croup", buried: Crumley Cemetery, died at Bluff City on 17 Sep 1917, record (1917): 581.
Infant REPOSS, male, parents: Will REPOSS and Annie MORRELL, death cause: "still born", died in the 21st District on 11 Sep 1917, record (1917): 582.
Elbert EPPERSON, age 15 years and 3 months, born in South Carolina, parents: Jake EPPERSON (SC) and mother's name illegible, death cause: "pneumonia", buried: Walnut Grove, VA., died in the 4th District on 17 Sep 1917, record (1917): 583.
Emma Taylor BROWN, colored, born: 5 Jul 1917, parents: William BROWN (GA) and Effie HARRISON (Alabama), death

cause: "malnutrition", buried: Kingsport Cemetery, died: 18 Sep 1917, record (1917): 584.

Eliza Ann COATS, born: 19 Feb 1858, married, parents: John HOMEL and Susan SMITH (VA), death cause: "tuberculosis of lungs", informant: Dan COATS (Kingsport), buried: Martin Cemetery, died: 18 Sep 1917, record (1917): 585.

Mary HUTSON, born: 28 Dec 1896, married, parents: Henry SAMS and Katherine LOYD, death cause: "typhoid fever", informant: Ross SPEARS (Kingsport), buried: Liberty Hill, died: 18 Sep 1917, record (1917): 586.

Jennie CHAMBERS, born: 17 Jul 1879 in Virginia, housewife, parents: not stated, death cause: "pulmonary tuberculosis", informant: W.M. CHAMBERS (Bristol), died: 20 Sep 1917, record (1917): 587.

Octar MCCLELLEN, born: 17 Jul 1894, married, parents: A.B. MCCLELLEN and mother not stated, death cause: "automobile accident", informant: Mrs. Octar MCCLELLEN (Bristol), buried: East Hill, died: 24 Sep 1917, record (1917): 588.

David MITCHELL, Negro, born: 30 Aug 1866 in Virginia, married, parents: James MITCHELL and Perlina (illegible), death cause: "heart lesion", informant: Alice MITCHELL (Bristol), buried: Big Stone Gap, VA., died: 25 Sep 1917, record (1917): 589.

William PEMBERTON, age 23 years, single, parents: W.B. PEMBERTON and mother not stated, death cause: "automobile accident", informant: William OSBORN (Bristol), died: 25 Sep 1917, record (1917): 590.

Plese Henderson PETTERES, born: 17 Sep 1862, married, parents: Roubin PETTERES and __ BERRY, death cause: "paralysis", informant: Mrs. P.H. PETTERES (Bristol), buried: Shipley Cemetery, died: 26 Sep 1917, record (1917): 591.

Leila Ethel JONES, born: 21 Jul 1902, married, parents: James HOSS and Alice WEXLER, death cause: "puerperal eclampsia", informant: Haskell JONES (Fordtown), buried: Pactalus Church Cemetery, died: 27 Sep 1917, record (1917): 592.

Lenna Jane CLICK, born: 10 Jun 1910, parents: J.J. CLICK (VA) and Lillie HARKLEROAD, death cause: "summer diarrhea", informant: father (Kingsport), died: 27 Sep 1917, record (1917): 593.

Infant TOLLEY, female, parents: M.L. TOLLEY and Pearl LESTER (VA), death cause: "still born", informant: father (Bristol), buried: East Hill, died: 5 Sep 1917, record (1917): 595.

Monerie PENLEY, female, born: 15 May 1907 in Virginia, parents: Sam PENLEY (VA) and Priscilla PRICE (VA), death cause: "acute dysentery", informant: father (Kingsport), buried: Gate City, died: 29 Sep 1917, record (1917): 594.

Josie LILLY, parents: M.L. LILLY and Pearl LESTER (VA), death cause: "three month child", buried: Weaver Cemetery, born/died: 4 Sep 1917, record (1917): 596.

Infant GRAHAM, female, parents: D.F. GRAHAM (VA) and Magie SELLS, death cause: "still born", informant: father (Emmett), died: 14 Sep 1917, record: 597.

Infant JONES, female, parents: Haskell JONES and Lelia Ethel HORNE, death cause: "maternal convulsions, still born", informant: father (Fordtown), buried: Pactolus Church, died: 26 Sep 1917, record (1917): 598.

Infant WOLF, male, parents: Walter WOLF and Maggie BAINS, death cause: "still born", died at Piney Flats on 25 Sep 1917, record (1917): 599.

George W. TILTSWORTH, born: 28 Jun 1830, single, parents: Thomas TILTSWORTH, Jr. and Sarah ROLLER, death cause: "age", informant: A.B. KETRON (Bloomingdale), buried: Reedy Creek Cemetery, died: 18 Oct 1917, record (1917): 600.

Rose WALLACE, born: 11 Feb 1877, single, parents: J.A. WALLACE and Mollie TADLOCK, death cause: "carcinoma uterus", informant: James WALLACE (Bristol), died: 1 Oct 1917, record (1917): 601.

Maxel DIXON, born: 16 Dec 1916, parents: John DIXON and Eliza OWENS, death cause: "ileo colitis", informant: Jthan DIXON (Kingsport), buried: Childress Cemetery, died: 2 Oct 1917, record (1917): 602.

James Nelson CRAWFORD, born: May 1916, parents: John CRAWFORD and Ollie FRAZIER, death cause: "ileo colitis", informant: Bersty CRAWFORD (Kingsport), buried: Blairs Gap, died: 7 Oct 1917, record: 603.

Preston HAYETT, age 26 years, married, parents: Alphard HAYATT and Mary HUDSON, death cause: "mitral regurgitation of heart", died at Piney Flats on 7 Oct 1917, record (1917): 605.

Rhoda AGER, age 37 years, 10 months and 2 days, born in Virginia, widow, parents: Charles AGER and Mariah RUBEN (VA), death cause: "tuberculosis of lungs", buried: Rumley Cemetery, died in the 1st District on 3 Oct 1917, record (1917): 604.

Rashel H. NEFF, born: 6 Feb 1837 in Virginia, widow, parents: John SCOTT (VA) and Peggy PORTER (VA), death cause: "injury from fall", informant: Mrs. E.P. SCOTT

(Bristol), buried: Rural Retreat, VA., died: 7 Oct 1917, record (1917): 606.

Brooks McCowell MORRELL, born: 3 Oct 1891 in Carter County, parents: M.J. MORRELL and Magge B. BEIDLEMAN, informant: father (Big Creek), buried: Beidleman Cemetery, died: 7 Oct 1917, record (1917): 607.

Hezia GOHEEN, female, born: 8 Oct 1834 in Illinois, single, parents: John Wesley GOHEEN and Rebecca HOUCK, death cause: "pellagra", informant: Laura B. HOUCK (Bristol), buried: Springfield, Ohio, died: 8 Oct 1917, record (1917): 608.

James MCGEE, born: 10 May 1891, married, parents: George MCGEE and Ella HARKLEROAD, death cause: "typhoid fever", informant: W.M. MOORE (Kingsport), buried: Vermont Cemetery, died: 9 Oct 1917, record (1917): 609.

Mrs. D.C. BOWERS, age 60 years, born in Virginia, married, parents: D.W. MAIDEN (VA) and Lizzie LOGAN (VA), death cause: "chronic nephritis", informant: D.C. BOWERS (Bristol), buried: Abingdon, VA., died: 2 Oct 1917, record (1917): 610.

Oscar J. KERN, age 24 years, born in Virginia, married, parents: James F. KERN (VA) and Lucy JOHNSON (VA), death cause: illegible, informant: father (Dungennon, VA), died: 11 Oct 1917, record: 611.

Katheryn WILLIAMS, born: 1 Mar 1916 in Wise County, VA., parents: C.H. WILLIAMS (VA) and Mary D. NICHOLS (KY), death cause: "dysentery", informant: father (Kingsport), buried: Corbin, Ky., died: 11 Oct 1917, record (1917): 612.

Bonnie CRAWFORD, born: 29 Jan 1916, parents: Oliver CRAWFORD and Mary MORRELL, death cause: "entero colitis", informant: Dorsey MORRELL (Fall Branch), buried: Blairs Gap, died: 12 Oct 1917, record: 613.

Nancy HIX, born: 27 Apr 1909, parents: George HIX and Mollie HIX, death cause: "acute dysentery", informant: father (Kingsport), buried: Morrison Chapel, died: 14 Oct 1917, record (1917): 614.

Phoeba Eva Gray DALTON, born: 12 Oct 1911 in North Carolina, parents: Charles A. DALTON and Alice COLLIER (VA), death cause: "hook worm and pellagra", informant: father (Kingsport), died: 14 Oct 1917, record (1917): 615.

Marion Lofton FORD, born: 8 Sep 1914, parents: Ernest FORD and Ida KETRON (Scott Co.), death cause: "diphtheria", informant: father (Kingsport), buried: Emory, died: 14 Oct 1917, record (1917): 616.

Pleas G. PETERS, born: Sep 1855, married, parents: Abe PETERS and Hannah POE, death cause: "cancer of stomach", informant: A.P. PETERS (Bristol), buried: Hickory Tree, died: 15 Oct 1917, record (1917): 617.

Conrad BOOHER, age 63 years, born in Virginia, widower, parents: David BOOHER (VA) and Martha BEELOR, death cause: "heart trouble", buried: Beelor Cemetery, died in the 21st District on 15 Oct 1917, record (1917): 618.

Thomas H. CARRIER, born: 17 Jan 1869 in Pennsylvania, parents: Isaac CARRIER (PA) and __ HARRIS, death cause: "lobar pneumonia", informant: Mrs. Thomas CARRIER (Bristol), buried: East Hill, died: 15 Oct 1917, record (1917): 619.

Hallie Lee LEWIS, age 3 years, 5 months and 8 days, born in Virginia, parents: Tom LEWIS (KY) and Lula HAMMER, death cause: "croup", informant: A.P. LEWIS (Bristol), buried: Sinking Spring Cemetery, died: 15 Oct 1917, record (1917): 620.

Infant HOLT, female, parents: Tom HOLT (VA) and Mina HOUSER, death cause: "premature", died in the 3rd District on 18 Oct 1917, record (1917): 621.

Infant HARKLEROAD, female, parents: Jess J. HARKLEROAD and Mary Alice RUTLEDGE, death cause: not stated, informant: father (Bluff City), born/died: 31 Oct 1917, record (1917): 622.

Elmo BLIZZARD, born: 17 Oct 1917, parents: N.C. BLIZZARD and Dorothy KING, death cause: illegible, informant: C.C. BLIZZARD (Kingsport), buried: Gunnings Cemetery, died: 18 Oct 1917, record (1917): 623.

Edith WATSON, colored, born: 18 Oct 1917, parents: Ernest WATSON (GA) and Edith KEITH (SC), death cause: "premature", informant: father (Kingsport), died: 19 Oct 1917, record (1917):624.

John HITCHENS, born: 14 Jan 1859 in Cornwell, England, married, parents: Sevanius HITCHENS (England) and Eliza HICKS (England), death cause: "weak heart and acute indigestion", informant: Mrs. John HITCHENS (Kingsport), buried: Bristol, VA., died: 18 Oct 1917, record (1917): 625.

Maxie DIXON, born: Feb 1916, parents: John DIXON and Eliza OWENS, death cause: "ileo colitis", informant: W.D. ARNBUSTER (Kingsport), buried: Horse Creek, died: 20 Oct 1917, record (1917): 626.

Mrs. Mattie Oliver KING, age 38 years, married, parents: David OLIVER and Fannie SCOTT, death cause: "chronic valvular heart disease", buried: New Bethel, died at Piney Flats on 20 Oct 1917, record: 627.

Bertie Hillen RAMEY, born: 22 Jun 1916 in Hawkins County, parents: Jack RAMEY (Scott Co.) and Myrtle BUTLER, death cause: "ileo colitis", died at Kingsport on 22 Oct 1917, record (1917): 628.
Debbie Jean GREGG, born: 24 Mar 1915 in Washington Co., TN., parents: Joseph G. GREGG (Cocke Co.) and Josephine GREGG, death cause: "rickets", informant: father (Jonesboro), buried: Kendrick Creek, died: 26 Oct 1917, record (1917): 629.
Benjamin Andrew ARNOLD, born: 28 Mar 1916, parents: Steve ARNOLD and Oakley COLE (VA), death cause: "ileo colitis", informant: Tom BUCK (Kingsport), died: 26 Oct 1917, record (1917): 630.
Georgia CASTLE, born: 26 Sep 1917, parents: John CASTLE (VA) and Nannie HAYNES (VA), death cause: "found dead in bed", informant: father (Kingsport), buried: Vermont Cemetery, died: 26 Oct 1917, record (1917): 631.
Joseph Elmer GROW, born: 8 Jan 1873 in Ohio, married, parents: James W. GROW and Mary MCCONNELL, death cause: "syphilis of brain", informant: Lucy GROW (Kingsport), buried: Buena Vista, VA., died: 27 Oct 1917, record (1917): 632.
Charles Alexander LYNN, born: 18 Feb 1862, married, parents: James LYNN and mother not stated, death cause: "sarcoma of stomach", informant: S.B. LYNN (Indian Springs), buried: Blountville, died: 27 Oct 1917, record (1917): 633.
Mary Ruth GALYON, born: 5 Jun 1905, parents: J.R. GALYON (VA) and Ida HALL (Knoxville), death cause: illegible, informant: mother (Bristol), buried: East Hill, died: 31 Oct 1917, record (1917): 634.
Jacob Isaac ISENBERG, born: 1 Oct 1850 in Washington Co., TN., married, parents: Nicholas ISENBERG and Elizabeth ADAMS (Washington Co., TN), death cause: "cancer of stomach", informant: A.J. ISENBERG (Jonesboro), buried: Liberty Church, died: 31 Oct 1917, record (1917): 636.
William A. MOORE, age 56 years, married, parents: not stated, death cause: "mitral incompancy", informant: W.A. MOORE (Bristol), buried: Ordway Cemetery, died: 31 Oct 1917, record (1917): 635.
Ethel WYSONG, born: 23 Mar 1915 in Virginia, parents: Charles R. WYSONG (VA) and Addie ROCK (VA), death cause: "purpura from eating chestnuts", informant: father (Kingsport), died: 31 Oct 1917, record: 637.
Marion Ross CRESS, born: 9 Jun 1894, single, parents: W.A. CRESS and Emma CRESS, death cause: "perforated

ulcer", informant: father (Mountain City, TN), buried: Mountain City, TN., died: 22 Nov 1917, record: 638.
Nannie J. SCOTT, age 60 years, married, parents: J.J. HARRISON and ___ COMBES, death cause: "paralysis", informant: J.M. SCOTT (Bristol), buried: Beelor Cemetery, died: 3 Nov 1917, record (1917): 639.
Robert Steve TAYLOR, born: 17 Feb 1917 in West Virginia, parents: W.C. TAYLOR and Martha E. DUFF, death cause: "tuberculosis of glands of neck", informant: father (Kingsport), buried: Emory Cemetery, died: 3 Nov 1917, record (1917): 640.
James B. PORTER, born: 1 Jul 1867 in Kentucky, widower, parents: not stated, death cause: "lagrippe followed by kidney complications", informant: J.C. MCMILLON (Bristol), buried: East Hill, died: 4 Nov 1917, record (1917): 641.
John B. NALL, Jr., born: 29 Oct 1915, parents: John B. NALL (KY) and Zellie WILLIAMS, death cause: "ileo colitis", informant: Mrs. E.W. TIPTON (Kingsport), buried: Blountville, died: 6 Nov 1917, record: 642.
Eliza Kathern WARREN, born: 26 Feb 1872, parents: C.C. OLLIVER and ___ RILEY, death cause: "apoplexy", informant: S.K. WARREN (Piney Flats), buried: New Bethel, died: 5 Nov 1917, record (1917): 643.
Nancy C. BRAGG, age 73 years, born in North Carolina, widow, parents: Joseph DAVIS (NC) and Winny LOUIS (NC), death cause: "pneumonia", informant: T.L. BRAGG (Fall Branch), buried: family cemetery, 15th District, died: 9 Nov 1917, record (1917): 644.
Cromwell H. HALL, born: 21 Mar 1900 in North Carolina, single, parents: Frank B. HALL (NC) and Hester MCAFEE (NC), death cause: "typhoid fever", informant: O.M. HALL (Kingsport), buried: Hominy, NC., died: 10 Nov 1917, record (1917): 645.
Bessie RICHARDSON, age 20 years and 15 days, married, parents: F.S. MISE and Geniza BLEVINS, death cause: "tuberculosis of lungs", informant: W.D. PETERS (Emmett), died: 10 Nov 1917, record (1917): 646.
Nora MILHORN, age 17 years, single, parents: G.W. MILHORN and Lucy CARTER, death cause: "typhoid fever", informant: R.W. GRIFFITH (Bluff City), buried: Buffalo Cemetery, died: 27 Nov 1917, record (1917): 647.
Lucyann BOTT, born: 10 Jan 1857, married, parents: Abram BOTT and Sallie SMITH, death cause: "chronic brights", informant: J.T. BOTT (Kingsport), died: 9 Nov 1917, record (1917): 648.
Homer FLETCHER, age 13 years 8 months and 7 days, parents: Elbert FLETCHER and Roberta CRACEY, death

cause: "pneumonia", buried: Paperville Cemetery, died: 12 Nov 1917, record (1917): 649.

Mrs. Elizabeth THOMAS, age 72 years, parents: not stated, death cause: "heart trouble", buried: Pleasant Grove Cemetery, died at Bluff City on 21 Nov 1917, record (1917): 650.

William Hix FORD, age about 48 years, married, parents: William FORD and Loucinda JONES, death cause: "typhoid fever", informant: Dana FORD (Fall Branch), buried: Hite Cemetery, died: 12 Nov 1917, record (1917): 651.

Shelby SHAW, male, age 22 years, single, parents: not stated, death cause: "perforated typhoid ulcer", informant: Thomas TEASTER (Bristol, VA), buried: Bristol, VA., died: 13 Nov 1917, record (1917): 652.

Wilma Etta HICKMAN, born: 30 Jul 1915 in Green County, parents: S.E. HICKMAN and Susanna DYKES, death cause: "ileo colitis", informant: Mrs. John CRUM (Kingsport), buried: Depew Chapel, died: 14 Nov 1917, record (1917): 653.

Brooks MORRELL, age 23 years, 6 months and 12 days, married, parents: John MORRELL and Pet BEIDLEMAN, death cause: "pneumonia", buried: Hickory Tree, died: 14 Nov 1917, record (1917): 654.

William T. DRAPER, born: 10 Dec 1839, single, parents: John DRAPER and Elizabeth DRAPER, death cause: "general break down from age", informant: F.H. BOTOL (Kingsport), buried: 5 miles East of Kingsport, died: 15 Nov 1917, record (1917): 655.

Benjamin Franklin CRABTREE, born: 7 Apr 1857, married, parents: not stated, death cause: "strangulated hernia", informant: Catherine CRABTREE, died at Bluff City on 15 Nov 1917, record (1917): 656.

Mary Ann SHELLEY, age 45 years in Virginia, married, parents: Jesse VESTAL (NC) and Elizabeth JAYN, death cause: "typhoid fever", informant: D.M. SHELLEY (Kingsport), buried: Pyle Cemetery, died: 16 Nov 1917, record (1917): 657.

Jake BOWMAN, age 69 years, 3 months and 2 days, single, born in Virginia, parents: Earl BOWMAN (W. VA) and May BROWN (VA), death cause: "dropsy and rheumatism", died in the 3rd District on 16 Nov 1917, record (1917): 658.

Lula OWENS, age 12 years, born in Virginia, parents: John OWENS (VA) and Mary JETER (SC), death cause: "pneumonia", informant: father (Bristol), buried: Weaver Cemetery, died: 16 Nov 1917, record: 659.

Ruth DENTON, born: 17 Jun 1916, parents: Robert DENTON (Washington Co., VA) and Lutissia SMITH (Johnson County), death cause: "broncho pneumonia", informant: R.C. DENTON (Alvorado, VA), buried: Denton Valley, died: 17 Nov 1917, record (1917): 660.

Earnest HICKS, born: 17 Feb 1901, parents: John HICKS and Sallie SMALLING, death cause: "apoplexy", buried: Poplar Ridge, died at Piney Flats on 17 Nov 1917, record (1917): 661.

Varginer SWEET, age 16 years, 11 months and 7 days, parents: Abe SWEET (Texas) and Martha OWENS (Texas), death cause: "pneumonia and measles", buried: Walnut Grove, VA., died: 18 Nov 1917, record (1917): 662.

Henry A. FORD, age 51 years, 7 months and 27 days, born: 22 March, married, parents: Henry FORD and Mary SHIPLEY, death cause: "pulmonary tuberculosis", informant: F.M. FORD (Kingsport), buried: Gunnings Cemetery, died: 19 Nov 1917, record (1917): 663.

Lina R. BURKETT, born: 9 Sep 1890, married, parents: W.H. DICKINSON and ___ HARRISON, death cause: "septicemia following abortion", informant: Lee BURKETT (Bristol), buried: East Hill, died: 20 Nov 1917, record (1917): 664.

Sendia CARROLL, age 62 years, married, parents: William BEAR and Susan CARTMAN, death cause: "tuberculosis", informant: Jim LUSTER (Kingsport), died: 22 Nov 1917, record (1917): 665.

Charlie HORTON, black, born: 20 Nov 1917, parents: Arthur HORTON and Lannie KELLEY, death cause: "broncho pneumonia", informant: father (Kingsport), died: 24 Nov 1917, record (1917): 666.

Ossel FINK, born: 10 Oct 1916, parents: T.C. FINK and Ida M. HORN, death cause: "diabetes and cerebral tumor", informant: father (Jonesboro), buried: Fink Cemetery, died: 24 Nov 1917, record (1917): 667.

Delia Pearce LIGHT, born: 2 Jul 1914, parents: Pearce LIGHT and Pearl HENLEY, death cause: "diphtheria", buried: Vermont Cemetery, died: 26 Nov 1917, record (1917): 668.

Evalyn Marie JENKINS, born: 7 Sep 1913 in North Carolina, parents: Nathaniel JENKINS (NC) and Ethel MOODY (NC)_, death cause: "bronchial pneumonia", informant: father (Kingsport), died: 28 Nov 1917, record (1917): 669.

Jessie COLLINS, born: 17 Aug 1850, widower, parents: Lark COLLINS and mother not stated, death cause: "Brights disease", informant: C.C. SMITH (Bristol), buried: Bluff City, died: 29 Nov 1917, record: 670.

Elizabeth ASHEY, born: 1 May 1848 in North Carolina, widow, parents: ___ SMITH (NC) and mother not stated, death cause: "old age", informant: Martha ASHEY (Bristol), buried: Susong Cemetery, died: 30 Nov 1917, record (1917): 671.

Infant MOODY, male, parents: J.R. MOODY and Sallie MOODY, death cause: "still born", informant: father (Kingsport), buried: Emory Cemetery, died: 2 Nov 1917, record (1917): 672.

Infant STROLS, male, parents: Luther STROLS and Madeline CROSS, death cause: "still born", died in the 3rd District on 14 Nov 1917, record (1917): 673.

Infant JONES, female, parents: Joseph Tully JONES and Mary Etta SLAUGHTER, death cause: "premature birth", informant: father (Jonesboro), buried: Presbyterian Church Cemetery, died: 3 Nov 1917, record (1917): 674.

Infant POE, female, parents: Will L. POE and Laura MURRAY, death cause: "still born", informant: James SHAFFER (Kingsport), buried: Mount Carmel, died: 28 Nov 1917, record (1917): 675.

Infant DOWELL, male, parents: Will DOWELL and ___ ODELL, death cause: "unknown", informant: father (Emmett), born/died: 30 Dec 1917, record (1917): 676.

Dorothy Virginia SMITH, born: 21 Dec 1917, parents: John SMITH and Mary E. BROWN (VA), death cause: "premature birth", informant: father (Kingsport), buried: Gunning Cemetery, died: 26 Dec 1917, record (1917): 677.

Sinora Francis HOOD, born: 3 Mar 1848, widow, parents: Thomas COLEY (VA) and Emmaline (illegible)(VA), death cause: "organic heart disease", informant: J.D. HOOD (Fall Branch), died: 11 Dec 1917, record (1917): 678.

Annie Beatris JONES, age 3 years and 9 months, parents: Tom JONES and Martha HOPKINS, death cause: "diphtheria", informant: Mrs. Tom JONES (Bristol), buried: East Hill, died: 23 Dec 1917, record: 679.

James Allen SMITH, age 2 months and 12 days, parents: G.W. SMITH and Essie HENRY (Limestone), death cause: "broncho pneumonia", informant: mother (Bristol), buried: Bloomingdale, died: 13 Dec 1917, record (1917): 680.

Emma Virginia WILBORN, born: 1 Jun 1874 in Washington Co., VA., married, parents: Valentine HOOVER (VA) and Feubia LINDSEY (VA), death cause: "paralysis", informant: Sam WILBORN, buried: East Hill, died: 17 Dec 1917, record (1917): 681.

Sara M. JONES, born: 17 Dec 1835, widow, parents: David O'BRIEN (NC) and Louisa GODSEY, death cause:

"senility", informant: J.H. JONES (Emmett), buried: Paperville, died: 18 Dec 1917, record (1917): 682.
Norris Allen PAYNE, born: 23 Dec 1917, parents: J.D. PAYNE and Lillie GRIFFIN (Springfield, MO), death cause: "bronchitis", informant: father (Bristol), buried: Gunnings, died: 29 Dec 1917, record: 683.
Fannie P. DOLEN, born: 13 Oct 1890, widow, parents: George A. TIPTON and Annie BACHMAN, death cause: "cancer of breast", informant: E.W. TIPTON (Kingsport), buried: Dolen Cemetery, died: 31 Dec 1917, record (1917): 684.
Infant VAUGHT, female, parents: S.N. VAUGHT and Ada VANCE, death cause: "still born", informant: father (Bristol), died: 18 Dec 1917, record (1917): 685.
Nellie Ellen GODSEY, born: 4 Jun 1867, married, parents: Thornton HENRY (VA) and Mollie HARRIS, death cause: "pellagra", informant: W.J. GODSEY (Bristol), buried: East Hill, died: 3 Dec 1917, record: 686.
Georgia Alice SPEARS, born: 29 Nov 1917, parents: Charles H. SPEARS and Della Lee SANDERS, death cause: "erysipelas", informant: father (Kingsport), buried: Oak Grove Cemetery, died: 3 Dec 1917, record: 687.
Maynard BROOKS, age 5 years, born in Virginia, parents: William BROOKS (VA) and Julia ELLIOTT (VA), death cause: "broncho pneumonia", informant: J.N. BROOKS (Kingsport), buried: Pyle Cemetery, died: 4 Dec 1917, record (1917): 688.
Worley DALTON, born: 25 Jun 1914, parents: Charles A. DALTON (Hawkins County) and Alice COLLINS (Wise Co., VA), death cause: "hook worm with heart and kidney complications", informant: father (Kingsport), buried: Roller Cemetery, died: 4 Dec 1917, record (1917): 689.
Infant LEONARD, male, parents: Carl LEONARD (VA) and Jetta BURCHETT (VA), death cause: "still born", informant: father (Bristol), buried: Shaffer Cemetery, died: 7 Dec 1917, record (1917): 690.
Mattie C. BREEDING, born: 23 Nov 1917, parents: I.T. BREEDING (VA) and Lora V. PYLE, death cause: "spina bifida", informant: D.A. PYLE (Kingsport), buried: Vermont Cemetery, died: 7 Dec 1917, record: 691.
Emeline GARLAND, age 90 years, widow, born in West Virginia, parents: Joe GARLAND (VA) and Mary (illegible)(VA), death cause: "age and rheumatism", informant: Mrs. Martin MILLER (Bristol), buried: Paperville, died: 9 Dec 1917, record (1917): 692.
Mose CARRIER, age 70 years, born in Virginia, married, parents: Cain CARRIER (W. VA) and Fannie KEETON (VA), death cause: "dropsy", informant: May CARRIER

(Bristol), buried: Crumley Cemetery, died: 10 Dec 1917, record (1917): 693.
Martha MCMURRAY, born: 20 Apr 1856, born in Scott Co., VA., married, parents: William HENSLEY (Scott Co.) and Jane YOUOUS, death cause: "pellagra and dysentery", informant: Joel MCMURRAY (Kingsport), buried: Pyle Cemetery, died: 10 Dec 1917, record (1917): 694.
Thomas Henry JONES, born: 16 Nov 1916, parents: Tom JONES and Mattie HOPKINS (Smythe Co.), death cause: illegible, informant: Mrs. Thomas JONES (Bristol), buried: East Hill, died: 11 Dec 1917, record: 695.
Gertrude VAN HOESEN, born: 3 Jul 1830 in New York, parents: Isaac VAN HOESEN (NY) and __ FRANNELL (NY), death cause: "senile debility", informant: A. VAN MILLER (Bristol), died: 12 Dec 1917, record: 696.
George ALFRED, born: 17 Nov 1865 in Ohio, married, parents: Landon ALFRED (Carter County) and Sallie MCCRACKEN (Carter County), death cause: "ruptured ulcer", informant: Mrs. George ALFRED (Bristol), buried: East Hill, died: 15 Dec 1917, record: 697.
Starlin CARROLL, age 77 years, widower, parents: David CARROLL and Charlotty EASTMAN, death cause: "parlaysis", informant: James LUSTER (Kingsport), buried: Childress Cemetery, died: 15 Dec 1917, record (1917): 698.
G.W. WOODS, age 69 years, born in Virginia, married, parents: John Henry WOODS (VA) and mother not stated, death cause: "pellagra", informant: A.E. DOTSON (Kingsport), buried: Pyle Cemetery, died: 15 Dec 1917, record (1917): 699.
Claud WRIGHT, age 5 years, 7 months and 11 days, born in Virginia, parents: Alfred WRIGHT and Mollie PLEASANT (VA), death cause: "measles and pneumonia", informant: father (Bluff City), buried: Crumley Cemetery, died: 18 Dec 1917, record (1917): 700.
James Lynwood HEMPHILL, Negro, born: 24 Dec 1916, parents: James HEMPHILL and Mary MURRY, death cause: "lobar pneumonia", informant: mother (Bristol), buried: Citizens Cemetery, died: 20 Dec 1917, record (1917): 701.
Eva Caster MORLEY, born: 9 Sep 1877, single, parents: P. CASTER and mother not stated, death cause: "(illegible) of lungs", informant: Joe WORLEY (Bristol), buried: East Hill, died: 23 Dec 1917, record (1917): 702.
James TOLLEY, age 26 years, single, parents: John TOLLEY and Elizabeth TOLLEY (NC), death cause: "burn",

informant: father (Damascus, VA), buried: Damascus, VA., died: 25 Dec 1917, record (1917): 703.

Nannie CROSS, born: 7 Jun 1864, single, parents: Benjamin SMITH and Sarah JONES, death cause: "puperal", informant: John CROSS (Bristol), buried: Ordway Cemetery, died: 27 Dec 1917, record: 704.

Nannie E. DOAN, born: 20 Jan 1868, married, parents: Robert HAWK and __ SUSONG, death cause: "pneumonia", informant: A.B. DOAN (Blountville), buried: Gunnings Cemetery, died: 27 Dec 1917, record (1917): 705.

Florence A. ANDERSON, born: 4 May 1873, single, parents: J.C. ANDERSON and mother not stated, death cause: "pellagra", informant: King ANDERSON (Bristol), buried: East Hill, died: 28 Dec 1917, record: 706.

Infant WAMPLER, female, parents: J.W. WAMPLER and Mary MEADOWS (VA), death cause: "puerperal convulsions", informant: father (Bristol), buried: East Hill, born/died: 4 Dec 1917, record (1917): 707.

Infant VAUGHT, male, parents: George VAUGHT and Ethel VANCE, death cause: "still born", informant: Peter VANCE (Bristol), buried: Paperville, died: 18 Dec 1917, record (1917): 708.

Infant BARKER, female, parents: Hat BARKER and Julie MAYS, death cause: "malformation", informant: father (Kingsport), died: 3 Dec 1917, record (1917): 709.

Decatur BURNETT, age 79 years, six months and 12 days, born in Sullivan Co., widower, parents: Greenbury BURNETT (TN) and Lectisue GODSEY (TN), death cause: "dysentery", informant: Roy Burnett (Bristol), buried: Ordway Cemetery, died: 2 Jan 1918, record (1918): 226.

George PETERS, born: Nov 1846, married, parents: Roy PETERS and mother not stated, death cause: "cerebral applexy, died at Piney Flats on 3 Jan 1918, record (1918): 227.

Mary Lee WITCHER, age 18 years, 5 months and 8 days, single, parents: Hubert WITCHER and Jennie BROOKS (NC), death cause: illegible, informant: Mrs. Sallie WITCHER (Bluff City), died: 3 Jan 1918, record: 228.

Mrs. Ann CHILDRESS, born: 4 Jul 1851, widow, parents: John HARGIS (VA) and Nancy L. WHALEY, death cause: "chronic nephritis", informant: Mrs. Maude POTTS (Kingsport), died: 6 Jan 1918, record (1918): 229.

Clyzil AUSTIN, born: 4 Oct 1913 in Virginia, parents: Lee AUSTIN (VA) and Nettie POWELL (VA), death cause: "dysentery", informant: father (Kingsport), buried: Martin Cemetery, died: 6 Jan 1918, record (1918): 230.

Mrs. Fannie CARRIER, age 30 years, married, parents: John WAMPLER and Mattie VANCE, death cause:

"tuberculosis of the lungs", informant: Frank CARRIER (Bristol), buried: Paperville, died: 8 Jan 1918, record (1918): 231.

Infant ROYSTON, male, born: 1915, parents: Frank ROYSTON and Belle ELY, death cause: "acute indigestion", informant: Joe RICHARDS (Bristol), buried: Chinquipin Grove, died: 8 Jan 1918, record (1918): 232.

David S. BOND, born: 14 May 1863, married, parents: Andrew J. BOND and Eliza CARTWRIGHT, death cause: "acute dilitation of heart", informant: Mrs. Frank NELMS (Kingsport), died: 9 Jan 1918, record: 233.

Hollis WILSON, born: 12 May 1915, parents: Jack WILSON and Irene FULKERSON, death cause: "convulsions from indigestion", informant: Mrs. Irene WILSON (Bristol), buried: East Hill, died: 9 Jan 1918, record: 234.

Jessie AUSTIN, Negro, born: 2 May 1875 in North Carolina, married, parents: "unknown", death cause: "heart failure", informant: William AUSTIN (Bristol), buried: Citizens Cemetery, died: 10 Jan 1918, record (1918): 235.

Selina P. FULKERSON, born: 9 Sep 1832 in Clarksville, TN., widow, parents: Allen JOHNSON (Clarksville) and Selina HUNTER (Campell Co., VA), death cause: "accidental fall, senility", informant: S.V. FULKERSON (Bristol), died: 11 Jan 1918, record (1918): 236.

Mrs. Susan ROSE, born: 8 Nov 1880, married, parents: Adam MOODY and Eliza Bishop MOODY, death cause: "chronic gastritis", informant: Dr. F. WEAVER (Piney Flats), buried: New Bethel, died: 12 Jan 1918, record (1918): 237.

Joe MORRELL, age 63 years and 5 months, born in Virginia, widower, parents: Jack MORRELL (VA) and Fannie (surname illegible), death cause: "bronchial trouble", informant: Lucy MORRELL (Bristol), buried: Shipley Cemetery, died: 12 Jan 1918, record: 238.

Vernon Dillon BELL, born: 9 Jan 1918, parents: John Rush BELL (Montgomery Co., VA) and Alice Velmer DILLON, death cause: "acute indigestion", informant: father (Fordtown), died: 13 Jan 1918, record: 239.

Ethel LETHCO, age 22 years, single, parents: E.F. LETHCO (VA) and Tenny SMITH, death cause: "abscess of brain", informant: father (Bristol), buried: Jonesboro, died: 13 Jan 1914, record (1918): 240.

Perry HARDY, Negro, age 38 years, born in Virginia, married, parents: Niles HARDY (VA) and mother's name unknown, death cause: "lobar pneumonia", informant:

Eliza HARDY (Bristol), buried: Virginia, died: 15 Jan 1918, record (1918): 241.

Elizabeth STARBUCK, born: 8 Mar 1831 in North Carolina, widow, parents: not stated, death cause: "apoplexy", informant: W.I. STARBUCK (Bristol), buried: East Hill, died: 16 Jan 1918, record: 242.

Vera Mae CARRIER, born: 3 May 1890, married, parents: S.S. CROCKETT and Mag PETERS, death cause: illegible, informant: James CARRIER (Bluff City), died: 17 Jan 1918, record (1918): 243.

Sallie LETHCO, age 22 years, 5 months and 6 days, single, parents: John LETHCO and Fannie St..(illegible), death cause: "brain trouble", informant: mother (Bristol), buried: Weaver Cemetery, died: 19 Jan 1918, record (1918): 244.

Alice Belle HORNE, born: 24 Feb 1884, married, parents: Joseph R. WEXLER and Sarah ZIMMERMAN, death cause: "uterine hemorrhage from incomplete abortion", informant: J.H. HORNE (Fordtown), buried: Pactolus Church, died: 19 Jan 1918, record (1918): 245.

Daniel JONES, Negro, born: 7 Aug 1870 in Virginia, married, parents: Walter JONES (VA) and mother's name unknown, death cause: "Brights disease", informant: Lucy JONES (Bristol), buried: Meadow View Cemetery, died: 18 Jan 1918, record (1918): 246.

Clide FOUCH, born: 6 Oct 1917, parents: John D. FOUCH and Cora (Illegible), death cause: "acute indigestion", informant: George ANDERSON (Kingsport), buried: Reedy Creek, died: 20 Jan 1918, record: 247.

Beechie HOUK, female, born: 19 Feb 1913 in Virginia, parents: C.A. HOUK (VA) and Ida BENNETT, death cause: "dysentery", informant: A.A. WYATT (Kingsport), died: 20 Jan 1918, record (1918): 248.

Cynthia Margruite HOOD, born: 20 Oct 1850 in Wythe Co., VA., married, parents: Thomas Coley (Wythe Co) and Emaline ARNEY (Wythe Co), death cause: "cerebral hemorrhage", informant: Thomas M. HOOD (Fall Branch), buried: Depew Chapel, died: 21 Jan 1918, record (1918): 249.

Gracie SPEARS, born: 4 Oct 1916, parents: Ross A. SPEARS and Carrie SAMS, death cause: "bronco pneumonia, meningitis", informant: father (Kingsport), died: 22 Jan 1918, record (1918): 250.

Francis PIERCY, born: 25 Dec 1865 in Scott Co., VA., married, parents: N. WILLIAMS (Scott Co) and Polly C.. (illegible), death cause: "paralysis", informant: Wesley PIERCY (Kingsport), buried: Spears Ferry, VA., died: 23 Jan 1918, record (1918): 251.

Miss Sallie HUNT, born: 29 Aug 1851 in Lynchburg, VA., single, parents: James C. HUNT (Pittsylvania Co., VA) and Elizabeth LANGHORNE (Lynchburg), death cause: "brights disease", informant: Kate M. HUNT (Bristol), buried: Richmond, VA., died: 25 Jan 1918, record (1918): 252.

Arlie Lee LIGHT, born: 3 Jul 1913, parents: George Washington LIGHT and Mary Bessie MONDY, death cause: "bronco pneumonia", informant: C.C. OVERBAY (Fordtown), died: 25 Jan 1918, record (1918): 253.

Ed. CRAWFORD, age 56 years, married, parents: Edmon CRAWFORD and Birtha P..(illegible), death cause: "acute indigestion from eating cake", informant: E.W. TIPTON (Kingsport), buried: Blairs Gap, died: 26 Jan 1918, record (1918): 254.

John Joseph SHARP, born: 22 Jul 1912, parents: James A. SHARP and Mildred (illegible), death cause: "measles", informant: father (Bluff City), buried: Weaver Cemetery, died: 26 Jan 1918, record: 255.

Wesley HAZZARD, Jr., Negro, born: Nov 1886 in Virginia, married, parents: Wesley HAZZARD and Bettie WATSON (VA), death cause: "pneumonia", informant: Harrison HAZZARD (Bristol), buried: Citizens Cemetery, died: 27 Jan 1918, record (1918): 256.

Mrs. W.M. BURROW, born: 23 Sep 1853 in Virginia, married, parents: Alexander WHITEAKER (VA) and Nancy ST JOHN (VA), death cause: "nephritis", informant: W.M. BURROW (Bristol), buried: East Hill, died: 29 Jan 1918, record (1918): 257.

Annie Melissa HALL, born: 30 Nov 1856, married, parents: Jacob COX and Eleanor KING, death cause: "lobar pneumonia", informant: J.A. HAMILTON (Jonesboro), buried: Fordtown Baptist Church, died: 3 Feb 1918, record (1918): 258.

Mildred Ruth RICHARDSON, born: 9 Jun 1917, parents: F.N. RICHARDSON (VA) and Ossie MONK (VA), death cause: "malnutrition", died at Kingsport, buried: Martin Cemetery, died: 3 Feb 1918, record (1918): 259.

Gracie Lee AUSTIN, born: 17 Feb 1914, parents: Lee AUSTIN and Nettie (illegible) (Wise Co., VA), death cause: "malnutrition", informant: father (Kingsport), died: 3 Feb 1918, record (1918): 260.

Emerson NEAL, born: 12 Jan 1852, married, parents: not stated, death cause: "pulmonary tuberculosis", died in the 17th District on 4 Feb 1918, buried: Greenville, record (1918): 261.

Della Lee SPEARS, born: 14 Jan 1895, married, parents: Joseph SANDERS and Cora KELLER, death cause:

"nephritis", informant: father (Kingsport), buried: Oak Grove Cemetery, died: 4 Feb 1918, record: 262.
Andrew Jackson DISHNER, born: 19 Sep 1840 in Virginia, married, parents: John DISHNER (VA) and ___ COLEMAN (VA), death cause: "Brights", informant: J.L. DISHNER (Bristol), buried: Dishner Cemetery, died: 5 Feb 1918, record (1918): 263.
William Preston DENAUFF, age 10 years, parents: R.H. DENAUFF and ___ HALL, death cause: "unknown", informant: R.H. DENAUFF (Bristol), buried: Johnson City, died: 5 Feb 1918, record (1918): 264.
Margaret FULKERSON, born: 12 Dec 1885, married, parents: G.A. ARNOLD and mother's name unknown, death cause: "pulmonary tuberculosis", buried: Pyle Cemetery, Kingsport, died: 5 Feb 1918, record: 265.
Lucy Ann PARKER, born: 21 Dec 1841, widow, parents: George W. VAUGHN and Elizabeth K.. (illegible), death cause: "chronic dysentery", informant: Jim CHURCH (Kingsport), died: 6 Feb 1918, record (1918): 266.
Cornelia Hardin CLOYD, born: 5 Jul 1915, parents: M.M. CLOYD and Etta MUMPOWER, death cause: "acute indigestion", informant: J.C. CLOYD (Bristol), buried: East Hill, died: 7 Feb 1918, record (1918): 276.
Jane FICKLE, age 43 years and 5 months, born in Texas, widow, parents: William FICKLE (Texas) and Lula WELCH (VA), death cause: "accidentally thrown from a buggy", informant: William FICKLE (Emmett), buried: Shipley Cemetery, died: 7 Feb 1918, record (1918): 268.
Cecil Mae CARDON, born: 6 Apr 1917, parents: C.C. CARDON and Callie R. HAWKINS (Wilkes Co., NC), death cause: "meningitis", informant: father (Kingsport), buried: Snodgrass Cemetery, died: 7 Feb 1918, record (1918): 269.
Mrs. Bernita JONES, born: 3 Mar 1878 in Kentucky, married, parents: William RODGERS and Bernita RODGERS (KY), death cause: "diabetes", informant: W.W. JONES (Bristol), buried: East Hill, died: 8 Feb 1918, record (1918): 270.
Webb BROWN, age 28 years, born in West Virginia, widower, parents: William BROWN (W. VA) and Margaret NEWLAN (W.VA), death cause: "cancer on face", informant: Luther BROWN (Bluff City), died: 9 Feb 1918, record (1918): 271.
Sarah Jane LISENBEY, born: 25 Feb 1864 in Washington Co., VA., widow, parents: John Quincy FLEENOR (Washington Co., VA) and Sarah A. GOBBLE (Washington Co., VA), death cause: "mitral insufficiency",

informant: G.W. JONES (Fordtown), buried: Rock Springs, died: 10 Feb 1918, record (1918): 272.

Jacob BARLOW, age 49 years, 8 months and 12 days, born in Virginia, single, parents: Jacob BARLOW (VA) and Mary FEATHERS (NC), death cause: "dropsy and kidney trouble", informant: Mrs. John WORLEY (Bluff City), died: 10 Feb 1918, record (1918): 273.

Mrs. Mary WAGNER, born: 17 Mar 1874 in Mountain City, TN., married, parents: Kemp MURPHEY and Susan WILLS, death cause: "tubercular (illegible)", informant: Charles M. WAGNER (Mountain City), buried: Mountain City, TN., died: 12 Feb 1918, record (1918): 274.

Mrs. M.K. TAYLOR, born: 7 Jul 1841 in Virginia, widow, parents: Dr. C.P. JONES (VA) and Mary WINGFIELD (VA), death cause: "Brights disease", informant: Mrs. C.C. ENGLISH (Bristol), died: 14 Feb 1918, record: 275.

Mrs. Mary A. ROUTH, born: 2 Feb 1841 in Virginia, widow, parents: William TIPTON (VA) and mother not stated, death cause: "cancer of stomach", informant: J.H. ROUTH (Bristol), buried: Bluff City, died: 14 Feb 1918, record (1918): 276.

Elnora MARTIN, colored, born: 15 Sep 1902, parents: Conias MARTIN (Mascot, TN) and Rosa MARTIN (Mascot, TN), death cause: "tuberculosis", informant: M. COLDWELL (Kingsport), buried: Kingsport Colored Cemetery, died: 14 Feb 1918, record (1918): 277.

Mrs. Phronia ALFRED, born: 6 Jul 1877 in Carter County, widow, parents: John L. BOWERS (MO) and Polly CANNON (Siam, TN), death cause: "cancer of womb", buried: East Hill Cemetery, died: 15 Feb 1918, record (1918): 278.

Susie JONES, age 15 years, 3 months and 2 days, parents: Johnathon JONES (NC) and Pearl MADON, death cause: "pneumonia", informant: father (Bristol), buried: Beeler Cemetery, died: 15 Feb 1918, record (1918): 279.

Mary RITCHIE, age 70 years and 2 months, born in North Carolina, married, parents: Samuel BISHOFF (NC) and SUMERLIN (NC), death cause: "hyperattis of heart", buried: Bluff City, died: 16 Feb 1918, record: 280.

Haskel GREEN, age 1 year and 7 months, parents: Clide GREEN and Bessie BOY, death cause: "pneumonia and measles", informant: father (Bluff City), buried: Shipley Cemetery, died: 17 Feb 1918, record: 281.

Charlie BUTLER, born: Jan 1844 in Ohio, married, parents: Charles BUTLER and Elizabeth FILON, death cause: "pellagra", informant: Lelia BUTLER

(Kingsport), buried: Pyle Cemetery, died: 17 Feb 1918, record (1918): 282.

Edna A. SHIPLEY, born: 9 Jun 1829, widow, parents: Andy MAUK and Sarah MAUK, death cause: "euremic poisoning", informant: J.M. SHIPLEY (Indian Springs), buried: Shipley Cemetery, died: 18 Feb 1918, record (1918): 283.

Mary C. Caroline LOMAX, Negro, born: 28 Mar 1891, single, parents: George LOMAX (NC) and Lizzie DOBBINS (NC), death cause: "ecopic gestation appendicitis", informant: Lizzie LOMAX (Mountain City), buried: Mountain City, TN., died: 19 Feb 1918, record: 284.

Permelia BLEVINS, Negro, born: Feb 1853, married, parents: Soloman BEARD and mother not stated, death cause: "nephritis", informant: Augustus BLEVINS (Bristol), buried: Citizens Cemetery, died: 20 Feb 1918, record (1918): 285.

Ivin Gene DEMPSEY, female, born: 5 Aug 1917, parents: W.P. DEMPSEY and Josie MALONE, death cause: "croup, cold", informant: father (Bluff City), buried: Morning View Cemetery, died: 21 Feb 1918, record (1918): 286.

James BARNETT, age 67 years, married, parents: not stated, death cause: "unknown", informant: Mrs. J.A. BLEVINS, buried: Scott Count, VA., died: 21 Feb 1918, record (1918): 287.

Samuel ROYSTON, born: 24 Jul 1876, married, parents: George K. ROYSTON and Rebecca A. GLOVER, death cause: "intestinal obstruction", informant: John ROYSTON (Kingsport), buried: Boyd Cemetery, died: 23 Feb 1918, record (1918): 288.

Robert L. MITCHELL, race: "dark", born: 14 Aug 1915 in Alabama, parents: Isiah MITCHELL (Ala) and Lela ROSS (Ala), death cause: "marasmus", informant: M.M. CLOUD (Kingsport), died: 23 Feb 1918, record (1918): 289.

James Larmon MCCORMICK, born: 18 Dec ___ in Virginia, age 26 years, 2 months and 8 days, married, parents: R.B. MCCORMICK (VA) and ___ FULTON, death cause: "pulmonary tuberculosis", informant: Mrs. J.L. MCCORMICK (Bristol), buried: East Hill, died: 26 Feb 1918, record (1918): 290.

Octavia WASHINGTON, black, born: 29 Dec 1917, parents: Jim WASHINGTON (Abingdon) and Nellie WASHINGTON (VA), death cause: "pneumonia fever", informant: father (Bristol), buried: Tennessee Cemetery, died: 27 Feb 1918, record (1918): 291.

Ruby Irene GALLOWAY, born: 19 Feb 1918, parents: Jacob GALLOWAY and Dora DUNCAN, death cause: "found dead in bed", informant: father (Fall Branch), buried: family

cemetery, 15th District, died: 1 Mar 1918, record (1918): 292.
Calvin A. BREWER, Negro, born: 7 Sep 1886, married, parents: R.D. PENN (VA) and Lizzie BREWER, death cause: "gunshot wound in base of brain, by policeman", informant: Mrs. Nettie BREWER (Bristol), buried: Tennessee Cemetery, died: 1 Mar 1918, record: 293.
William CONTY, black, born: 6 Sep 1893 in South Carolina, married, parents: R.J. CONTY (SC) and Pauline MURRELL (SC), death cause: "pulmonary tuberculosis", informant: M.M. CLOUD (Kingsport), died: 1 Mar 1918, record (1918): 294.
Martha Nell CROSS, age 5 years, born in North Carolina, parents: Jean CROSS (NC) and Fannie HICKS, death cause: "measles", informant: Mrs. John CROSS (Bluff City), buried: Pleasant Grove, died: 2 Mar 1918, record (1918): 295.
Mrs. Andrew COWAN, born: 6 Jul 1892 in Virginia, married, parents: J. FLEENOR (VA) and Lola ADAMS, death cause: "pelvic peritonitis", informant: Andrew COWAN (Landron, SC), buried: Stophel Cemetery, died: 3 Mar 1918, record (1918): 296.
Cyris M. ODELL, born: 9 Dec 1844, widower, parents: William ODELL and Mary CRUMLEY, death cause: "paralysis", informant: D.T. ODELL (Bristol), buried: Shipley Cemetery, died: 5 Mar 1918, record: 297.
Mrs. Serenal GARLAND, born: 28 Jan 1851 in Virginia, married, parents: Stephen COLE (VA) and Winnie COLE (VA), death cause: "carcinoma of (illegible)", informant: G.H. HODGE (Carter, TN), buried: Hunter, TN., died: 3 Mar 1918, record (1918): 298.
William WINEGAR, born: 6 Mar 1851, married, parents: Joe WILLS and Anie WINEGAR (VA), death cause: "nephritis", informant: Robert HUDSON (Kingsport), buried: Morrison Chapel, died: 3 Mar 1918, record (1918): 299.
Lula SHOEMAKER, age 24 years, 5 months and 2 days, single, parents: Jonathan SHOEMAKER and Laura JENKINS (VA), death cause: "thrown from a horse, injuries to the head", informant: Lola SHOEMAKER (Emmett), buried: Crumley Cemetery, died: 7 Mar 1918, record: 300.
Mrs. J.M. CHESTER, born: 7 May 1892, married, parents: W.H. JONES and Cordie COLLINS, death cause: "intestinal obstruction", informant: J.W. CHESTER (Bristol, VA), buried: Elkana, TN., died: 9 Mar 1918, record (1918): 301.
Adam COLLINS, born: 6 Feb 1848 in Grayson, VA., married, parents: Don COLLINS (VA) and mother not

stated, death cause: "meningitis", informant: S. COLLINS (Kingsport), buried: Valley View, died: 10 Mar 1918, record (1918): 302.

Polly MILLER, age 69 years, widow, parents: Joshua MILLER and Amanda GREEN (VA), death cause: "pneumonia fever", informant: Willie CHILDRESS (Bristol), buried: Paperville, died: 12 Mar 1918, record (1918): 303.

Annie Francis PEAVER, born: 4 Jul 1892, married, parents: Rollie P. MURRAY and Mary E. FLEENOR (VA), death cause: "pulmonary tuberculosis", informant: Mrs. W.H. MURRAY (Bloomingdale), died: 12 Mar 1918, record (1918): 304.

Leonard Cecil HARKERODE, born: 2 Jan 1914 in Virginia, parents: Lee HARKERODE and ___ PHIPPS, death cause: "scarlet fever", informant: father (Bristol), buried: Bluff City, died: 13 Mar 1918, record (1918): 305.

Mattie WILLIAMS, age 35 years, married, parents: John AKERS (VA) and Jane WILEY (NC), death cause: "dropsy", informant: Mose AKERS (Bristol), buried: Paperville, died: 15 Mar 1918, record (1918): 306.

Infant ODELL, male, born: 19 Mar 1918, parents: Andy ODELL and Stella WOODS, death cause: "not known", buried: Poplar Ridge, died at Piney Flats on 20 Mar 1918, record (1918): 307.

James A. SMITH, born: 1833, married, parents: John SMITH and Gensie TAYLOR, death cause: "tuberculosis of lungs", buried: Shipley Cemetery, died in the 21st District on 20 Mar 1918, record (1918): 308.

John H. SANDERS, age 70 years, 9 months and 4 days, widower, parents: William SANDERS and Jane YOKLEY, death cause: "apoplexy", buried: New Bethel, died at Piney Flats on 21 Mar 1918, record (1918): 309.

Earling Monroe GODSEY, born: 3 Mar 1902, parents: Frank GODSEY and Ella HARRIGAN, death cause: "anemia", buried: Weaver Cemetery, died in the 17th District on 21 Mar 1918, record (1918): 310.

Ira A. ROGERS, female, age 39 years, married, parents: W.T. SMITH and Julia A. SMITH, death cause: "extra uterine hemorrhage", informant: W.T. SMITH (Kingsport), died: 21 Mar 1918, record (1918): 311.

Mrs. Rena Alice MOSES, born: 14 Jun 1850 in Virginia, married, parents: Thomas BURROUGHS (VA) and Kittie BOOTH (VA), death cause: "apoplexy", informant: R.A. MOSES (Bristol), buried: East Hill, died: 21 Mar 1918, record (1918): 312.

Martha E. COATES, born: 13 Sep 1845, married, parents: Dutton HOOD and Nancy LANE, death cause: "cerebral hemorrhage", informant: T.J. BACHMAN (Kingsport), buried: Depew Chapel, died: 22 Mar 1918, record (1918): 313.

Robert CARROLL, Negro, born: 24 Aug 1860 in Virginia, married, parents: Bill CARROLL (VA) and mother not stated, death cause: "tuberculosis", informant: Rev. S.P. GIBSON (Gate City), buried: Kingsport, died: 23 Mar 1918, record (1918): 314.

Helon REESE, female, born: 11 Aug 1917, parents: D.M. REESE (NC) and Nancy ALLEN, death cause: "pneumonia", informant: father (Kingsport), buried: Martin Cemetery, died: 24 Mar 1918, record (1918): 315.

John BRAGG, age about 39 years, married, parents: Noble BRAGG and Elizabeth FINCHER, death cause: "mitral insufficiency, nephritis", informant: T.J. PHILLIPS (Fall Branch), died: 25 Mar 1918, record (1918): 316.

Fora BUDGMAN, born: 2 Aug 1898, parents: A.J. BUDGMAN (VA) and ___ WOODWARD (VA), death cause: "pulmonary tuberculosis", informant: Gordie BUDGEMAN (Bristol), buried: East Hill, died: 27 Mar 1918, record: 317.

Annie May GALLOWAY, born: 5 Jul 1892 in Cocke County, married, parents: H.W. MCKENZIE and mother's name illegible, death cause: "tuberculosis", buried: Morrison Chapel, died at Kingsport on 27 Mar 1918, record (1918): 318.

P.H. LOGINS, born: 6 Aug 1868 in Virginia, married, parents: father not stated and Orpha VANDERPOOL, death cause: "yellow atrophy of liver", informant: Mrs. P.H. LOGINS (Bristol), buried: Holston Institute, died: 27 Mar 1918, record (1918): 319.

Marion HODGES, age 59 years, married, parents: John C. HODGES and Priscilla KING, death cause: "jaundice", informant: Dr. GRAVES (Piney Flats), buried: New Bethel, died: 28 Mar 1918, record (1918): 320.

Edd GEARHART, born: 4 Jun 1893 in Virginia, single, parents: Johnston GEARHART (VA) and ___ KING (VA), death cause: "accidental fractured skull", informant: W.E. GEARHART, died in the 15th District on 29 Mar 1918, record (1918): 321

Caroline HICKOK, age 86 years, widow, parents: Henry BAIR and Hannah STOFFLE, death cause: "dropsy", informant: Mrs. David NAVE (Bristol), buried: East Hill, died: 30 Mar 1918, record (1918): 323.

Sallie T. COLDWELL, born: 8 Sep 1859 in Georgia, married, parents: Augustus TOWER (?)(GA) and mother not stated, death cause: illegible, informant: H.C. COLDWELL (Bristol), buried: East Hill, died: 31 Mar 1918, record (1918): 324.

Infant HAYATT, male, parents: (illegible) HAYATT and Rena SHIPLEY, death cause: "still born", died at Bluff City on 14 Mar 1918, record (1918): 325.
Infant CARR, female, parents: N.F. CARR and Tina LILLEY, death cause: "still born", buried: Carr Cemetery, died at Bluff City on 22 Mar 1918, record (1918): 326.
Infant MCCORMICK, male, parents: C.M. MCCORMICK (Washington Co., TN) and Dorcen HAYS (KY), death cause: "still born", informant: father (Kingsport), died: 24 Mar 1918, record (1918): 327.
Infant PARKER, female, parents: Frank PARKER and Pearl (illegible), death cause: "still born", buried: Cloud Cemetery, died at Kingsport on 9 Mar 1918, record (1918): 328.
Infant DURHAM, female, parents: William Leonard DURHAM (Ashe Co., NC) and Wilmer Anna CRETSINGER (Washington Co., TN), death cause: "still born", informant: W.L. DURHAM (Fordtown), died: 29 Mar 1918, record: 329.
W.H. GRAY, born: 3 Jun 1835, parents: Jack GRAY and Sarah HARLAND, death cause: "uremia", informant: Joe GRAY (Bristol), buried: Weaver Cemetery, died: 1 Apr 1918, record (1918): 330.
George SHIPLEY, born: 10 Dec 1874, married, parents: George SHIPLEY and Margaret FITZGERALD, death cause: "ulcerated stomach", informant: Ida SHIPLEY (Kingsport), buried: Pyle Cemetery, died: 1 Apr 1918, record (1918): 331.
Mrs. Minnie WEAVER, born: 22 Mar 1883 (age shown as 95 ?), married, parents: Rob RADER and ___ RADER, death cause: "lobar pneumonia", informant: J.E. WEAVER, Jr. (Bristol), buried: Weaver Cemetery, died: 3 Apr 1918, record (1918): 332.
Thomas Logan NELMS, Jr., born: 3 Mar 1916, parents: Walker NELMS and Josie AKERS (VA), death cause: "bronco pneumonia", informant: father (Kingsport), died: 3 Apr 1918, record (1918): 333.
Ray CRAWFORD, born: 13 Dec 1919 in Alabama, parents: John CRAWFORD and Ollie FRAZIER (Ala), death cause: "pneumonia", informant: father (Kingsport), buried: Blairs Gap, died: 4 Apr 1918, record (1918): 334.
Sallie MAWK, age 47 years, single, parents: Gilbert MAWK and Susan LOWERY (Mississippi), death cause: "dropsy", informant: Bessie MAWK (Bristol), buried in Virginia, died: 5 Apr 1918, record (1918): 335.
Leonda F. MOORE, born: 9 Jun ___, age 39 years, 10 months and 1 day, single, parents: J.T. MOORE and ___

___ GIBSON, death cause: "struck by a log, fractured skull", died at Bristol on 5 Apr 1918, record: 336.

Lizzie CHAPMAN, age about 80 years, single, parents: J. CHAPMAN and mother not stated, death cause: "paralyzed", informant: W.H. PHILLIPS (Bristol), buried: East Hill, died: 6 Apr 1918.

Sarah Ford SHIPLEY, born: 8 Sep 1858, married, parents: Ezekiel FORD and Winnie FORD, death cause: "organic heart disease", informant: J.T. SHIPLEY (Fordtown), died: 6 Apr 1918, record (1918): 338.

Harve PERKINS, born: 15 Sep 1917, parents: Abe PERKINS and Cora HOOD, death cause: "bronco pneumonia", informant: father (Kingsport), buried: Fordtown, died: 7 Apr 1918, record (1918): 339.

Carl D. JOHNSON, born: 5 Feb 1918, parents: Sam JOHNSON (NC) and Nora BEAMAN (VA), death cause: "bronco pneumonia", informant: S.R. JOHNSON (Kingsport), buried: Pyle Cemetery, died: 7 Apr 1918, record (1918): 340.

Banjamin H. SCOTT, born: 6 Apr 1899, married, parents: J.M. SCOTT and Nannie J. HARRISON, death cause: "dynamite explosion", informant: J.C. HARRISON (Bristol), buried: Beeler Cemetery, died: 8 Apr 1918, record (1918): 341.

Sallie A. MITCHELL, born: 22 Nov 1841, widow, parents: Elija KIDWELL and Mary HAWKINS, death cause: "senile debility", informant: J.J. MITCHELL (Greenville), buried: Greenville, died: 8 Apr 1918, record: 342.

J.L. LANE, age 70 years, born in Louden County, TN., married, parents: not stated, death cause: "nephritis", informant: Mrs. W.T. DOOLEY (Bristol), buried: Maryville, TN., died: 8 Apr 1918, record (1918): 343.

Mary HALE, Negro, age about 52 years, born in Virginia, widow, parents: Calvin NEWTIN (VA) and mother not stated, death cause: "nephritis", informant: Maude BRANCH (Bristol), buried: Citizen Cemetery, died: 13 Apr 1918, record (1918): 344.

Herbert Lee JOHNSON, born: 12 Apr 1918, parents: C.E. JOHNSON and mother not stated, death cause: "premature", informant: father (Bristol), buried: Ordway Cemetery, died: 13 Apr 1918, record: 345.

Mary C. BAYLESS, born: 1 Mar 1918, parents: H.E. BAYLESS (Limestone, TN) and Flora E. JOHNSON (Lee Co., VA), death cause: "pneumonia fever", informant: father (Kingsport), died: 14 Apr 1918, record (1918): 346.

Lucy HAYS, age 13 years and 4 months, parents: Frank HAYS and Julia HAYS, death cause: "tuberculosis of

lungs", buried: Shipley Cemetery, died in the 1st District on 15 Apr 1918, record (1918): 347.
Matthew J. BROWN, age 17 years, single, parents: Matthew L. BROWN and Maria BLAIR, death cause: "pneumonia and measles, informant: Lucy BROWN (Bluff City), buried: Crumley Cemetery, died: 15 Apr 1918, record (1918): 348.
Lizzie Macklin LONGLEY, Negro, born: 22 Feb 1886 in Virginia, divorced, parents: Samuel LONGLEY (VA) and Sallie TRIGG (VA), death cause: "tuberculosis", informant: Annie L. BROWN (Bluefield, VA), buried: Citizen Cem., died: 16 Apr 1918, record (1918): 349.
James PORTER, born: 5 Aug 1916 in Roanoke, VA., parents: Henry PORTER (Pikeville, KY) and Callie HOLOMAN (Clinchport, VA), death cause: "broncho penumonia", informant: Mrs. M.E. HOLOMAN (Kingsport), buried: Roanoke, VA., died: 16 Apr 1918, record (1918): 350.
Mrs. G.H. GALLOWAY, age 53 years, married, parents: George (illegible)(VA) and Virgie SOUTH (W. VA), death cause: "measles", buried: Weaver Cemetery, died in the 1st District on 17 Apr 1918, record (1918): 351.
Harold C. RITCHIE, born: 2 Jan 1912 in Illinois, parents: I.K. RITCHIE and ___ SALTS, death cause: "convulsions", buried: Bluff City, died: 17 Apr 1918, record (1918): 352.
James THOMAS, age 49 years, widower, parents: Lee THOMAS (VA) and Josephine PENITER (VA), death cause: "spinal meningitis", informant: Mattie THOMAS (Bluff City), died: 18 Apr 1918, record (1918): 353.
Lizzie RUTLEDGE, Negro, born: 5 Jun (year illegible), age 62 years, widow, parents: not stated, death cause: "pulmonary tuberculosis", informant: Nettie HARRINGTON (Bristol), died: 20 Apr 1918, record (1918): 354.
Isabeller HAWK, age 36 years, single, parents: J.A. HAWK and Sarah HARLEROAD, death cause: illegible, informant: John A. HAWK (Bristol), buried: Weaver Cemetery, died: 20 Apr 1918, record (1918): 355.
Nancey CHASE, born: Dec 1840 in Washington Co., TN., single, parents: Jary CHASE and mother not stated, death cause: "dropsy and heart disease", buried: Muddy Creek Cemetery, died at Piney Flats on 20 Apr 1918, record (1918): 356.
Frank SCOTT, age 34 years, born in Johnson County, married, parents: Pete SCOTT and Mary Ann BOOHER, death cause: "killed by dynamite explosion", informant: Josie SCOTT (Bristol), buried: Beeler Cemtery, died: 28 Apr 1918, record (1918): 357.

Robert PENN, Negro, born: 18 Mar 1851 in Virginia, married, parents: father not stated and Ruth PENN (VA), death cause: "nephritis", informant: Susan T. PENN (Bristol), buried: Citizen Cemetery, died: 21 Apr 1918, record (1918): 358.

Daniel Hayden TUELL, age 18 years, born in Virginia, parents: A.W. TUELL (VA) and Ellen S (illegible), death cause: "accidental gun shot", informant: J.W. TUELL (Bristol, VA), buried: Chilhowie, VA., died: 22 Apr 1918, record (1918): 359.

William WHITEHEAD, Negro, age about 50 years, married, parents: not stated, death cause: "dynamite explosion", informant: Belle WHITEHEAD (Bristol), died: 23 Apr 1918, record (1918): 360.

Ruth Bethel SMITH, born: 15 Sep 1917, parents: P.O. SMITH (VA) and Mary K. MILHORN, death cause: "spinal meningitis", informant: father (Kingsport), buried: Weaver Cem., died: 24 Apr 1918, record (1918): 361.

Mary Etta ROGERS, born: 21 Mar 1918, parents: Abe ROGERS (VA) and Amanda WEBB (VA), death cause: "unknown", informant: Logan ROGERS (Kingsport), died: 24 Apr 1918, record (1918): 362.

Frank CARRIER, age 47 years, widower, parents: John CARRIER and Jane SMYTH (W. VA), death cause: "tuberculosis of lungs", informant: Mrs. REPOSS, buried: Weaver cemetery, died: 24 Apr 1918, record (1918): 363.

Theona PHILIPS, born: 17 Apr 1908, parents: James PHILIPS and Ada NELMS, death cause: "meningitis", informant: Arch WATKINS (Kingsport), buried: Presbyterian cemetery, died: 25 Apr 1918, record (1918): 364.

Frank CARRIER, born: 12 Aug 1886, parents: Matt CARRIER and mother not stated, death cause: "tuberculosis", informant: father (Bristol), buried: Ordway Cem., died: 25 Apr 1918, record (1918): 365.

Ludy Andy DAVIS, age 13 years, 11 months and 7 days, parents: Andy DAVIS and Sharlotte WOOD (W.VA), death cause: "pneumonia", informant: father (Emmett), buried: Beeler Cemetery, died: 16 Apr 1918, record (1918): 366.

Ell GRAY, age 75 years, married, parents: Jack GRAY and Fannie BEIDLEMAN, death cause: "paralysis", informant: Mrs. Joe GRAY (Emmett), buried: Weaver cemetery, died: 26 Apr 1918, record (1918): 367.

Infant HOOVER, male, parents: Claud HOOVER and Wilrie CARROLL, death cause: "premature", informant: father (Kingsport), born/died: 26 Apr 1918, record: 368.

Eva SHOECRAFT, age 10 months, parents: Clyde SHOECRAFT and ___ EAST, death cause: "croup, pneumonia", informant: J.D. DAVIS (Bristol), buried: Ordway Cemetery, died: 27 Apr 1918, record (1918): 369.

Charlie DEAKENS, born: 1 Jul 1850, widower, parents: Jim DEAKENS and mother not stated, death cause: "pelegra", buried: Poplar Ridge, died at Piney Flats on 28 Apr 1918, record (1918): 370.

Loura Mae Pearl GOODWIN, age 4 months, parents: B.F. GOODWIN and ___ CORNETT, death cause: "found dead in bed", informant: father (Bristol), buried: Susong Cemetery, died: 28 Apr 1918, record (1918): 371.

Ruth Ann Poe DILLARD, born: 15 Nov 1879, married, parents: Wesley POE (Hawkins County) and Lizzie (illegible), death cause: illegible (miscarriage ?), informant: Elbert DILLARD (Fordtown), buried: Poe Cemetery, died: 30 Apr 1918, record (1918): 373.

Infant GOODMAN, female, parents: A.H. GOODMAN and Hazy RANDOLPH (NC), death cause: "still born", informant: father, buried: Ordway Cemetery, died: 19 Apr 1918, record (1918): 373.

Infant BROWN, colored, parents: Lee BROWN (VA) and Lula CARTER (SC), death cause: "still born", buried: Old Kingsport Cemetery, died: 10 Apr 1918, record (1918): 374.

Infant SPIVEY, male, parents: William SPIVEY (VA) and Mollie LITE, death cause: "still born", informant: father (Kingsport), died: 6 Apr 1918, record: 375.

Amanda Esther SHIPLEY, born: 20 Mar 1859, single, parents: Joshua SHIPLEY and Melvina MCCOLLEY (Scott Co. VA), death cause: "tuberculosis", informant: E.L. SHIPLEY (Fordtown), buried: Shipley Cemetery, died: 5 May 1918, record (1918): 376.

Sallie HATCHER, age 3 years, 11 months and 2 days, parents: Tom HATCHER (VA) and Vernie HULL, death cause: "croup", informant: Mrs. Tom HATCHER (Bluff City), buried: Weaver Cemetery, died: 5 May 1918, record (1918): 377.

Mamie Ruth SMITH, born: 20 Mar 1917, parents: Robert SMITH and mother not stated, death cause: "broncho pneumonia", informant: father (Bristol), buried: Ordway Cemetery, died: 6 May 1918, record (1918): 378.

Sam Alfred PETERS, born: 22 Mar 1918, parents: W.J. PETERS and Beattie BLEVINS, death cause: "pneumonia", informant: Henry PETERS (Bristol), buried: Weaver Cemetery, died: 6 May 1918, record (1918): 379.

Elsie PETERS, age 5 months and 7 days, parents: Will PETERS and Martha Vada BLEVINS, death cause:

"dysentery", informant: Mrs. May PETERS (Emmett), buried: Weaver cemetery, died: 7 May 1918, record (1918): 380.

James C. BLEVINS, age 30 years, single, parents: W.C. BLEVINS and Lousy BLEVINS, death cause: "pulmonary tuberculosis", informant: father (Bristol), died in the 17th District on 11 May 1918, record (1918): 381.

Emma OWENS, black, age not stated, married, parents: Bob CARROLL (VA) and mother not stated, death cause: "tuberculosis", informant: Sam OWENS (Kingsport), buried: Martin Cemetery, died: 12 May 1918, record (1918): 382.

John H. HENIGER, born: 7 Jun 1876, married, parents: John L. HENGIER and mother not stated, death cause: "percicious anemia", informant: John MAUK (Bristol), buried: East Hill, died: 12 May 1918, record: 383.

Mary L. FIELDS, born: 21 May 1917, parents: Steve FIELDS (NC) and Ella HUDSON, death cause: "measles and penumonia", informant: father (Kingsport), buried: Mt. Carmel Cem., died: 13 May 1918, record (1918): 384.

Thomas Johnson TURNER, born: 13 Apr 1841, parents: Jacob TURNER and __ JOHNSON, death cause: "paralysis", informant: Mrs. Samuel MUSGRAVE (Bristol), buried: East Hill, died: 14 May 1918, record (1918): 385.

Emmert SAMS, age 36 years, born in Virginia, single, parents: Montroe SAMS (VA) and Maggie (illegible)(NC), death cause: "heart trouble", informant: Carrie SAMS (Bluff City), buried: Weaver Cemetery, died: 15 May 1918, record (1918): 386.

Viola REPOSS, born: 2 Nov 1900, parents: Henry REPOSS (Knox County) and Cordelia RIGSBY, death cause: "pulmonary tuberculosis", informant: Mary Jane FORD (Jonesboro), buried: Fordtown, died: 17 May 1918, record (1918): 387.

David W. HULL, born: 2 Sep 1880 in Wytheville, VA., married, parents: Rolland HULL (VA) and Amelia HULL (VA), death cause: "tuberculosis", informant: Mrs. D.H. HULL (Bristol), buried: East Hill, died: 19 May 1918, record (1918): 388.

Miss Elizabeth SPURGEON, born: 7 Sep 1832, single, parents: Joseph SPURGEON and Ann CRAFT, death cause: "senility", informant: C.B. CROSS (Bristol), buried: Muddy Creek, died: 19 May 1918, record (1918): 389.

Claud W. WARREN, Jr., born: 31 Nov 1917, parents: Claud W. WARREN (NC) and Sallie BUMGARDNER (Jackson Co., NC), death cause: "bronchial penumonia", informant: F.W. BUMGARDNER (Kingsport), died: 19 May 1918, record (1918): 390.

Lucile GUDGER, Negro, born: 19 Feb 1917, parents: William BOWEN and Katie GUDGER, death cause: "pulmonary tuberculosis", informant: mother (Bristol), buried: Citizen Cemetery, died: 19 May 1918, record (1918): 391.

Fred ROBBINETT, age 1 year and 8 months, parents: T.B. ROBBINETT and ___ FORD, death cause: "pneumonia", informant: father (Bristol), buried: Church Hill, died: 20 May 1918, record (1918): 392.

Harry Anderson TEVIS, age 66 years, born in Germany, parents: H.A. TEVIS (Germany) and mother not stated, death cause: "emphasema", informant: Ernest TEVIS (Bristol), buried: East Hill, died: 20 May 1918, record (1918): 393.

Katie GOFF, age 42 years, born in Virginia, married, parents: Mike REARDEN (Ireland) and Janie WISE (VA), death cause: "lagrippe and pneumonia", informant: W.L. GOFF (Bristol), buried: Catholic Cemetery, died: 23 May 1918, record (1918): 394.

Miss Virginia ROE, born: 2 May ___, age 36 years, single, parents: Frank ROE and ___ GARRETT, death cause: "heart disease", informant: Oscar ROE (Bluff City), died: 24 May 1918, record (1918): 395.

Mariah COLE, age 43 years, born in South Carolina, widow, parents: Mark COLE (SC) and Sarah (illegible), death cause: "side pleurisy", informant: Mark COLE (Emmett), buried: Beelors Cemetery, died: 27 May 1918, record (1918): 396.

Mary SHOEMAKER, black, age 35 years, single, parents: Soloman SHOEMAKER (VA) and May Hill (VA), death cause: "tuberculosis of lungs", informant: May SHOEMAKER (Emmett), buried: Crumley Cemetery, died: 28 May 1918, record (1918): 397.

Mary Sue STEGALL, born: 7 Jul 1898 in Virginia, single, parents: Henry STEGALL (VA) and Nettie BROWN (VA), death cause: "abscess of lungs", buried: East Hill, died: 29 May 1918, record (1918): 398.

James HICKS, born: 7 Jul 1857, married, parents: Isaac HICKS and ___ HULL, death cause: "organic heart disease", informant: Mrs. Kattie B. HICKS (Blountville), buried: Gunnings Cemetery, died: 30 May 1918, record (1918): 399.

Clyde E. HUDSON, born: 19 May 1918, parents: James HUDSON and Eva LITE, death cause: "inherited syphilis", informant: John LITE (Kingsport), died: 30 May 1918, record (1918): 400.

Infant JOYCE, female, parents: W.H. JOYCE (VA) and Rosa HOMEL (VA), death cause: "still born", informant:

father (Kingsport), buried: Martin Cemetery, died: 23 May 1918, record (1918): 401.

Infant STAFFORD, female, parents: Charles STAFFORD (NC) and Lila CHAPPELL (NC), death cause: "still born", informant: father (Kingsport), buried: Martin Cemetery, died: 28 May 1918, record (1918): 402.

Daisey CRAWFORD, born: 29 Apr 1917, parents: Ed CRAWFORD and Berdie DYKES, death cause: "bronchial pneumonia", informant: Mrs. Ed CRAWFORD (Kingsport), buried: Lovelace Cemetery (Green County), died: 1 Jun 1918, record (1918): 403.

Charles Evans BENNET, born: 17 Dec 1916, parents: Burke BENNET and Sarah HARRIS, death cause: "diptheria and measles", buried: Pyle Cemetery, died at Kingsport on 4 Jun 1918, record (1918): 404.

Ollie MAYS, age 6 years, 6 months and 3 days, born in Virginia, parents: Jim MAYS and Bettie LITTLE (VA), death cause: "spinal meningitis", informant: father (Emmett), buried: Shipley Cemetery, died: 5 Jun 1918, record (1918): 405.

Fred Millard BROUT, born: 8 Jan 1918, parents: John BROUT (KY) and Lola FITZGERALD (TX), death cause: "ileo colitis", informant: father (Kingsport), buried: Pactolus, died: 7 Jun 1918, record (1918): 406.

Bob P. LECE, born: 9 May __, age 16 years, 1 month and 2 days, born in Kentucky, parents: W.M. LECE (KY) and ___ MASON, death cause: "brick fell from high building, fractured skull", informant: father (Kingsport), died: 7 Jun 1918, record (1918): 407.

Isaac CHASE, born: 8 Jun 1852, married, parents: Thomas Jefferson CHASE and Jane ARTEBURN (Washington Co., TN), death cause: "chronic intestinal nephritis", informant: G.C. CHASE (Jonesboro), buried: Chase Cemetery, 14th District, died: 8 Jun 1918, record (1918): 408.

Mrs. Minnie BEIDLEMAN, Negro, born: 11 May 1898, married, parents: Frank DICKINSON and Mary NETHERLAND, death cause: "child birth", informant: Wesley BEIDLEMAN (Bristol), buried: Tennessee Cemetery, died: 10 Jun 1918, record (1918): 409.

J. Milton CRUMLEY, age 65 years, born in Virginia, widower, parents: Luther CRUMLEY (VA) and Mary SHIPLEY, death cause: "paralyzed", informant: May SHIPLEY (Emmett), buried: family cemetery, 21st District, died: 12 Jun 1918, record (1918): 410.

Callie MALONE, born: 19 Aug 1916, born in Oklahoma, parents: Robert MALONE (TX) and Mattie BOWMAN, death cause: "dysentery", informant: father (Kingsport), buried: Pyle Cemetery, died: 12 Jun 1918, record (1918): 411.

M.V. BASS, age 82 years, married, parents: Henry BASS and (illegible) STOFFEL, death cause: "apoplexy of brain", informant: H.B. BASS (Bristol) died: 13 Jun 1918, record (1918): 412.

Zora CLARK, Negro, born: 10 Jun 1899 in North Carolina, single, parents: James CLARK (NC) and Laura WOOD (NC), death cause: "tuberculosis of lungs", informant: Harrison CLARK (Bristol), buried: Tennessee Cemetery, died: 15 Jun 1918, record (1918): 413.

W.M. FLANIGAN, born: 5 Aug 1894, single, parents: C.M. FLANIGAN (VA) and Margaret FERGUSON, death cause: "sarcoma of neck", informant: Mrs. W.L. GODSEY (Bristol), buried: Susong Cemetery, died: 15 Jun 1918, record (1918): 414.

Ossie MUMPOWER, age 4 years, 4 months and 12 days, parents: Will MUMPOWER (VA) and Dora ROUSE (VA), death cause: "whooping cough and measles", informant: Jane ROUSE (Emmett), buried: Shipley Cemetery, died: 15 Jun 1918, record (1918): 415.

Nellie Mae PERRY, born: 20 Mar 1918 in Harlan, Kentucky, parents: Thomas PERRY and Stella BRYANT (VA), death cause: "meningitis", informant: father (Kingsport), buried: Pyle Cemetery, died: 15 Jun 1918, record (1918): 416.

Tennie SWINNEY, age 13 years, 3 months and 5 days, parents: Jacob SWINNEY (VA) and Iva CAMPBELL, death cause: "blood poison from scald on hand", informant: Katy CAMPBELL (Emmett), buried: Weaver Cemetery, died: 16 Jun 1918, record (1918): 417.

James L. ROE, born: 12 Nov 1869 in Virginia, married, parents: F.G. ROE (VA) and Nannie GRANT (VA), death cause: "gastritis and mitral regurgitation", buried: Bluff City Cemetery, died: 17 Jun 1918, record: 418.

James Henry ANDERSON, age 4 years, parents: W.G. ANDERSON and ___ WILSON, death cause: "ileo colitis", informant: J.F. ANDERSON (Blountville), buried: Mill Point Cemetery, died: 17 Jun 1918, record (1918): 419.

Loura D. NEWLAND, age 36 years, 6 months and 2 days, married, parents: Henry A. PARETT and ___ SELLS, death cause: "sarcoma of thyroid", informant: W.H. NEWLAND (Blountville), died: 18 Jun 1918, record (1918): 420.

Mary E. HARRIS, born: 18 Jun 1917, parents: Joe HARRIS (Washington Co., VA) and Sallie BLEVINS, death cause: "ileo colitis", informant: father (Bristol), buried: near Blountville, died: 20 Jun 1918, record: 421.

Wanda K. ANDERSON, age 1 year and 6 months, parents: W.G. ANDERSON and ___ WILSON, death cause: "colitis", buried: Mill Point Cemetery, died at Blountville on 20 Jun 1918, record (1918): 422.

Susan ROBERTS, born: 22 May 1918, parents: W.E. ROBERTS and Martha HUTSON, death cause: not stated, informant: father (Kingsport), buried: Old Kingsport Cemetery, died: 20 Jun 1918, record (1918): 423.

Margaret BOWMAN, born: 24 Mar 1837, widow, parents: Henry LINEWEAVER (Rockingham Co., VA) and Catherine (illegible)(VA), death cause: "delitation of heart", informant: Mrs. T.D. PEMBERTON (Emmett), buried: Boones Creek, died: 21 Jun 1918, record (1918): 424.

John E. SEAHREST, born: 24 Sep 1860, married, parents: not stated, death cause: "suicide, gun shot through head", informant: Mrs. John SEAHREST (Bristol), buried: East Hill, died: 22 Jun 1918, record: 425.

Hazel FORD, born: 3 Jun 1916, parents: G.H. FORD and Lula GEAVINS, death cause: "ileo colitis", informant: Fred KEENER (Kingsport), died: 22 Jun 1918, record (1918): 426.

Jessie ROBERTS, born: 22 Jun 1915, parents: J.M. ROBERTS and mother not stated, death cause: "colitis", informant: father (Blountville), buried: Johnson Cemetery, died: 22 Jun 1918, record (1918): 427.

Robert A. DEMPSEY, age 17 years, parents: W.P. DEMPSEY and Sarah E. LITTLE, death cause: "tuberculor pertonitis", informant: father (Bluff City), died: 24 Jun 1918, record (1918): 428.

Mary Nettie DECK, age 10 years, parents: W.B. DECK and ___ BARNES, death cause: "rhumatism with delation of heart", informant: father (Fordtown), buried: Wheeler Chapel, died: 24 Jun 1918, record (1918): 429.

Sam AVRIA, colored, born: 18 May 1873 in Georgia, parents: Sam AVRIA (GA) and Cora JENNINGS (GA) death cause: not stated, died at Kingsport on 24 Jun 1918, record (1918): 430.

Mary C. KETRON, born: 30 Apr 1861 in Washington Co., VA., single, parentws: Philip KETRON (Washington Co., VA) and Sarah KEYS (Washington Co., VA), death cause: "dysentery and malnutrition", informant: Joe KETRON (Bluff City), died: 29 Jun 1918, record (1918): 431.

Gordon CAMPIE, age 19 months and 13 days, born in Bristol, VA., parents: F.M. CAMPIE (VA) and Pearl GALEY (Washington Co., VA), death cause: "ileo colitis", informant: father (Bristol), buried: Shafer Cemetery, died: 30 Jun 1918, record (1918): 432.

Infant FULLER, male, parents: I.N. FULLER (VA) and Elizabeth STARNES, death cause: "intra cranial hemorrhage", informant: father (Kingsport), born/died: 21 Jun 1918, record (1918): 433.

Eugene SWEENEY, age 23 years, single, parents: James SWEENEY and Nannie VANDEVENTER, death cause: "dysentery", informant: Willis WIDENER (Watauga), buried: Watauga, TN, died: 2 Jul 1918, record: 434.

John M. RILEY, born: 18 Dec 1857, married, parents: James RILEY and Sarah MORRELL, death cause: "lobar pneumonia", buried: Chinquipin Grove, died at Bluff City on 2 Jul 1918, record (1918): 435.

Irma EGGERS, born: 2 Jul 1895 (age 13 ?) in North Carolina, parents: W.D. EGGERS and Callie SHOUN, death cause: "peritonitis from operation", informant: father (Mountain City), buried: Mountain City, died: 2 Jul 1918, record (1918): 436.

Willie SHARROTT, age 16 years, 8 months and 12 days, born in Virginia, parents: Earl SHARROTT (VA) and Ottie WILLS (VA), death cause: "blood poison from mashed foot", informant: father (Bristol), buried: Paperville Cem., died: 2 Jul 1918, record (1918): 437.

Joseph Randall WILLIAMS, age 1 year and 9 months, parents: D.J. WILLIAMS (VA) and Lester HICKS, death cause: "ileo colitis", informant: Mrs. J.T. WILLIAMS (Bristol), buried: Three Springs Cemetery, died: 3 Jul 1918, record (1918): 438.

Arther G. MCCONNELL, born: 7 Dec 1916, parents: Arthur Grant MCCONNELL (Maryville, TN) and Lillie Bell (illegible)(Blount County), death cause: "ileo colitis", informant: father (Kingsport), died: 4 Jul 1918, record (1918): 439.

Hiram ROLLER, age 46 years, 3 months and 5 days, born in South Carolina, married, parents: Amos ROLLER (VA) and Sinde SENTER (W. VA), death cause: "blood poison from nail injury on hand", informant: Effie WEST (Bluff City), buried: Weaver cemetery, died: 5 Jul 1918, record (1918): 440.

Eugene Aaron WHITE, colored, born: 26 Nov 1916, parents: Eugene WHITE (Abingdon, VA) and Lizzie HARRINGTON, death cause: "rickets", informant: father (Bristol), buried: Citizens Cemetery, died: 5 Jul 1918, record (1918): 441.

J.B. Clinton GRUBB, born: 4 Jan 1917, parents: David GRUBB (VA) and ___ HOBBS (VA), death cause: "ileo colitis", informant: father (Bristol), died: 5 Jul 1918, record (1918): 442.

Zola HARPER, age 12 years, 7 months and 5 days, parents: Will HARPER and Josa ROAR (VA), death cause: "hook worm", informant: father (Emmett), buried: Paperville, died: 9 Jul 1918, record (1918): 443.

Sindy BEAR, age 49 years, born in Virginia, parents: Wroller BEAR (VA) and Mollie CROSS, death cause: "cancer in the mouth", informant: Maggie RAMSEY (Bluff City), buried: Paperville, died: 7 Jul 1918, record (1918): 444.

Hazel TRINKLE, age 9 months, parents: J.E. TRINKLE (VA) and Bertha MOORE, death cause: "dysentery", informant: father (Bristol), buried: Susong Cemetery, died: 7 Jul 1918, record (1918): 445.

J.R. GALYON, age 71 years, married, parents: Hamilton GALYON and mother not stated, death cause: "uremic coma", informant: Mrs. J.R. GALYON (Bristol), buried: East Hill, died: 8 Jul 1918, record (1918): 446.

John FAGANS, born: 10 Jul 1915, parents: Charlie FAGANS and Magie FOX, death cause: "cholera infantum", buried: Rumbley Cemetery, died at Piney Flats on 10 Jul 1918, record (1918): 447.

Lucy BOOHER, age 72 years, 8 months and 12 days, born in West Virginia, married, parents: Jack BOOHER (VA) and Mary CROSS (VA), death cause: "paralysis", informant: Martin BOOHER (Emmett), buried: Shipley Cem., died: 10 Jul 1918, record (1918): 448.

Rachel DOLLS, age 51 years, born in Kentucky, married, parents: Elbert DOLLS (KY) and Rosanah SMYTH (KY), death cause: "pandemic cholera", buried: Widner Cemetery, died: 12 Jul 1918, record (1918): 449.

Junior MOORE, born: 27 Mar 1916, parents: Fuller MOORE and Voley May STEWARD, death cause: "ileo colitis", informant: S.T. STEWARD (Bristol), buried: Snodgrass Cem., died: 10 Jul 1918, record (1918): 450.

Mrs. Alice St John DULANEY, born: 6 Nov 1875 in Chilhowie, VA., married, parents: A.C. ST JOHN (VA) and ___ HAYNES, death cause: "valvular heart lesion", informant: E.K. BACHMAN (Bristol), died: 12 Jul 1918, record (1918): 451.

Sarah Jane SPURGEON, born: 7 Dec 1832, married, parents: James COX and ___ EVANS, death cause: "senility", informant: S.W. MILLER (Blountville), died: 12 Jul 1918, record (1918): 452.

Lynn G. ROGAN, born: 20 Jul 1849, widower, parents: David ROGAN and Annie GAMBLE, death cause: "seirrhosis of liver", informant: Charlie ROGAN (Kingsport), buried: Old Kingsport Cem., died: 12 Jul 1918, record (1918): 453.

John Ervin PETERS, born: 21 Feb 1883 in Hawkins County, married, parents: Samuel E. PETERS and Sarah DICKINSON (VA), death cause: "homicide, was shot by Jessie CANTRELL", informant: Mrs. Sarah PETERS (Emmett), buried: Cold Springs Cemetery, died: 14 Jul 1918, record (1918): 454.

Ben RAMBO, Negro, born: 1 Jun 1894 in Virginia, single, parents: William SAGI (VA) and Catherine MURRAY (VA), death cause: "heart and kindey disease", informant: Kizzie HAMMER (Bristol), buried: Citizen Cemetery, died: 14 Jul 1918, record (1918): 455.

Samuel K. BARGER, born: 13 May __, age 70 years, 2 months and 4 days, married, parents: Nicholas BARGER and ___ TAYLOR, death cause: "gangrene", informant: S.K. LEONARD (VA), buried: Blountville, died: 16 Jul 1918, record (1918): 456.

L.B. MCCURRY, born: 16 May 1854, married, parents: John MCCURRY and Hannah MORELOCK, death cause: "typhoid fever", informant: George MCCURRY (Kingsport), buried: Greenville, TN., died: 16 Jul 1918, record (1918): 457.

Mary E. SINON, born: 27 Apr 1852 in Abingdon, VA., single, parents: Henry SINON (Ireland) and Mary E. SHOEMAKER, death cause: "mitral insufficiency", buried: East Hill, died: 17 Jul 1918, record (1918): 458.

Infant STEEL, born: 15 Jul 1918, parents: John STEEL and ___ ESTEP, death cause: "acute indigestion", informant: J.H. STEEL (Bristol), buried: Seneker Cemetery, died: 17 Jul 1918, record (1918): 459.

Mrs. Ferdinand POTTS, age 78 years, 3 months and 12 days, born in England, widow, parents: Jack ROWE (England) and Fannie WHIFLER, death cause: "leakage of heart", informant: Mrs. James CRUMLEY (Emmett), buried: Shipley Cem., died: 18 Jul 1918, record (1918): 460.

Ronle COOPER, age 16 years, 8 months and 2 days, parents: Landon COOPER and Sarah GRUBBS, death cause: "typhoid fever", informant: Landa COOPER (Emmett), buried: Hickory Tree, died: 18 Jul 1918, record (1918): 461.

Mrs. Bessie PENNINGTON, age 36 years, born in Virginia, married, parents: F.P. BARLOW (VA) and mother not stated, death cause: "pulmonary tuberculosis", informant: J.R. PENNINGTON (Bristol), buried: Abingdon, VA., died: 18 Jul 1918, record (1918): 462.

Emmett Clay BISHOP, born: 23 Aug 1917, parents: Bob BISHOP (VA) and Della KETRON (VA), death cause: "illeo colitis", informant: father (Kingsport), died: 20 Jul 1918, record (1918): 463.

James B. SOUTHERLAND, age 46 years, born in North Carolina, married, parents: T.H. SOUTHERLAND (NC) and Mary GRANT, death cause: "carcinoma of prostate", informant: C.C. SOUTHERLAND (Ashland, NC), buried: NC., died: 28 Jul 1918, record (1918): 464.

Martha MCGUINN, age 83 years, born in Ohio, widow, parents: father not stated and Harriott SPEERS, death cause: "age mostly", informant: John SPEERS (Bristol), buried: Ohio, record (1918): 28 Jul 1918, record (1918): 465.

Gladys PENLEY, born: 14 May 1916, parents: English PENLEY (Green County) and __ COLLINS (Green County), death cause: "illeo colitis", informant: L.M. PENLEY (Kingsport), died: 28 Jul 1918, record (1918): 466.

Cicero E. EVERETT, age 57 years, born in North Carolina, parents: John H. EVERETT (Bristol, VA) and Mary KING (NC), death cause: "anerism", informant: W. EVERETT (Bristol, VA), buried: East Hill, died: 28 Jul 1918, record (1918): 467.

Albert STATEN, parents: John STATEN (MO) and Lena SMITH, death cause: "still born", informant: father (Kingsport), died: 1 Aug 1918, record (1918): 468.

Infant HOOPER, male, parents: Mat HOOPER and Julia CRANE (NC), death cause: "still born", informant: father (Emmett), buried: Weaver Cem., died: 13 Jul 1918, record (1918): 469.

Infant HALL, female, parents: C.F. HALL (NC) and Francis STONE (VA), death cause: "still born", informant: father (VA), buried: Wallace, VA., died: 17 Jul 1918, record (1918): 470.

Infant ARNOLD, female, parents: Gale ARNOLD and Virgie SAMS, death cause: "premature birth, still born", informant: Joe ARNOLD (Kingsport), died: 14 Jul 1918, record (1918): 471.

Infant LADY, male, parents: Richard Carl LADY and Effie Pearl JACKSON (Washington Co., TN), death cause: "still born", informant: father (Jonesboro), buried: Double Springs Cemetery, died: 28 Jul 1918, record (1918): 472.

Matilda BRUNER, born: 28 Mar 1850, widow, parents: Charles JONES and Elizabeth CRAWFORD, death cause: "gastric catarrh", informant: Oma BRUNER (Jonesboro), died: 1 Aug 1918, record (1918): 473.

Charles William STATEN, born: 1 Aug 1918, parents: John STATEN (MO) and Lena SMITH, death cause: "intra cranial hemorrhage", informant: father (Kingsport), buried: Martin Cemetery, died: 2 Aug 1918, record (1918): 474.
Lillian May CHAMBERS, born: 26 Feb 1916, parents: John CHAMBERS and __ GREEN (VA), death cause: "meningitis", informant: father (Bristol), buried: East Hill, died: 2 Aug 1918, record (1918): 475.
Pattie Rose PITTS, born: 26 Jan 1917, parents: Guy D. PITTS and Samina Kate WILLIAMS, death cause: "ileo colitis", informant: J.G. PITTS (Kingsport), buried: Johnson City, died: 6 Aug 1918, record (1918): 476.
James S. BRISCO, age 76 years, born in Germany, widower, parents: not stated, death cause: "cancer of stomach", informant: Mrs. J.S. BRISCO, died in the 22nd District on 7 Aug 1918, record (1918): 477.
Anna L. COOPER, born: 1 Aug 1846 in Virginia, widow, parents: William HARTSOCK (VA) and Margaret E. SHUTTLE (VA), death cause: "asthma", informant: John COOPER (Bristol), buried: East Hill, died: 7 Aug 1918, record (1918): 478.
Lena Mae HODGE, born: 25 Dec 1917, parents: Landon HODGE and Anna Mae JONES, death cause: "brain fever", informant: Dr. GRAVES (Piney Flats), buried: New Bethel Cemetery, died: 10 Aug 1918, record (1918): 479.
Samuel P. DEVAULT, born: 19 Jun 1868, married, parents: J.M. DEVAULT and mother not stated, death cause: "peritonitis following appendicitis abscess", informant: Guy E. DEVAULT (Kingsport), died: 10 Aug 1918, record (1918): 480.
Polly W. GALLAHER, age 1 year and 7 months, parents: William GALLAHER and Josephine WILLIAMS, death cause: "ileo colitis", informant: father (Bristol), died: 10 Aug 1918, record (1918): 481.
Clarence FLENCHER, age 6 years, born in Virginia, parents: William FLENCHER (VA) and Lizzie BOWMAN (VA), death cause: "dysentery", informant: W.E. BOWMAN (Bristol), buried: Greendale Cemetery, VA., died: 10 Aug 1918, record (1918): 482.
Mrs. E.J. COOK, born: 22 Jan 1872, married, parents: William KING and E.. (illegible) HODGE, death cause: "cancer of stomach", informant: E.W. KING (Bristol), died: 11 Aug 1918, record (1918): 483.
Johnie SMOTHERS, age 4 years, 3 months and 7 days, born in Virginia, parents: John M. SMOTHERS (VA) and Mattie PHIPS, death cause: "whooping cough",

informant: father (Bristol), buried: Shipley Cemetery, died: 12 Aug 1918, record (1918): 484.

N.B. REMIUL, born: 7 Jul 1876, married, parents: H.C. REMIUL (VA) and Sarah FALLS, death cause: "pernicious (illegible)", informant: Mrs. N.B. REMIUL (Bristol), buried: East Hill, died: 13 Aug 1918, record (1918): 485.

Mary K. Armena HAYS, age 18 years, single, parents: W.H. HAYS and Allie SHIPLEY, death cause: "tuberculosis of lungs", informant: father (Bluff City), buried: Shipley Cem., died: 13 Aug 1918, record (1918): 486.

Mrs. Millie SCOTT, age 70 years, born in Virginia, widow, parents: not stated, death cause: "asthma and heart failure", informant: C.J. VERNON (Bristol), died: 13 Aug 1918, record (1918): 487.

Ella CARTER, born: 17 Jul 1879 in Virginia, married, parents: Henry M. STUART (VA) and Sylvinia PENDLETON (VA), death cause: "shock following operation", informant: J.E. CARTER (Clinchport, VA), buried in Virginia, died: 14 Aug 1918, record (1918): 488.

Robert L. FARTHING, born: 18 Oct 1846 in North Carolina, married, parents: William Young FARTHING (NC) and mother not stated, death cause: "dysentery", informant: R.B. FARTHING (Blountville), died: 15 Aug 1918, record (1918): 489.

Nancie Caroline JONES, born: 18 May 1879 in Virginia, married, parents: father not stated and ___ DEBOARD (VA), death cause: illegible, informant: C.H. JONES (Bristol), buried: VA., died: 18 Aug 1918, record (1918): 490.

Charles Marion HAMILTON, born: 19 Jul 1890, single, parents: James Buchanan HAMILTON (Washington Co., TN) and Elizabeth SLAUGHTER, death cause: not stated, informant: W.A. HAMILTON (Jonesboro), buried: Fordtown, died: 18 Aug 1918, record (1918): 491.

Mrs. Anna HARR, age 40 years, born in Virginia, widow, parents: J.A. WHISMAN and Mary HARR (VA), death cause: illegible, informant: J.R. WHISMAN (Bloomingdale), died: 20 Aug 1918, record (1918): 492.

Mollie HENSON, age 45 years, 3 months and 15 days, born in North Carolina, married, parents: Luther HENSON (NC) and Martha GRUBBS, death cause: "cancer of stomach", informant: Joe HENSON (Bluff City), buried: Shipley Cemetery, died: 21 Aug 1918, record (1918): 493.

Saphia JONES, colored, age 75 years, married, parents: father not stated and Saphia DAKE, death cause:

"dysentery", died in the 15th District on 22 Aug 1918, record (1918): 494.

George VAUGHN, age 5 years, parents: George VAUGHN and Matilda DEPEW, death cause: "colitis", died at Kingsport on 25 Aug 1918, record (1918): 495.

Marjorie E. BYRD, born: 3 Sep 1915, parents: G.T. BYRD (GA) and Bertie E. MCMAHON, death cause: "dysentery", informant: father (Bristol), buried: Sevierville, TN., died: 25 Aug 1918, record (1918): 496.

John MALONE, age 68 years, widower, parents: not stated, death cause: "lung abscess", informant: J.L. DISHNER (Bristol), died in the 5th District on 26 Aug 1918, record (1918): 497.

William Henry BARNETT, born: 14 Apr 1914, parents: Henderson BARNETT and Cora WILLIAMS, death cause: "typhoid fever", informant: father (Kingsport), died: 27 Aug 1918, record (1918): 498.

John MARTIN, black, age 64 years, born in Virginia, single, parents: Alfred MARTIN (VA) and Dinah PRESTON, death cause: "rheumatism", died in the 3rd District on 28 Aug 1918, record (1918): 499.

Tom OLLIVER, born: 7 May 1916, parents: Pete OLLIVER and mother not stated, death cause: "dysentery", buried: East Hill, died: 29 Aug 1918, record (1918): 500.

Walter E. GALLAHER, Jr., born: 2 Aug 1915, parents: Walter E. GALLAHER and Lena WHITE, death cause: "dysentery", informant: father (Bristol), buried: Weaver Cemetery, died: 29 Aug 1918, record (1918): 501.

Infant MILHORN, female, born: 21 Jul 1918, parents: William MILHORN and Lula E. FORD, death cause: "gastritis", informant: Dr. GRAVES (Piney Flats), buried: Wheeler Cem., died: 30 Aug 1918, record (1918): 502.

Infant CONKIN, female, parents: John CONKIN, Jr., and Bertie FEAGONS, death cause: "still born", informant: Dr. WHITE (Fall Branch), buried: Blairs Gap, died: 23 Aug 1918, record (1918): 503.

G.W. SMITH, male, parents: G.W. SMITH and __ HENRY, death cause: "still born", informant: Mrs. D.K. PRUETT (Bristol), buried: Bloomingdale, died: 31 Aug 1918, record (1918): 504.

Mary CALDWELL, black, parents: Cicero CALDWELL (NC) and Zollie COLLINS (VA), death cause: "still born", informant: father (Kingsport), died: 4 Aug 1918, record: 505.

Infant KEESLING, male, parents: J.A. KEESLING (VA) and Bessie DETHRIDGE (VA), death cause: "still born", informant: father (Bristol), died: 9 Aug 1918, record (1918): 506.

Infant HUNTER, male, parents: Hudson HUNTER (MO) and Hazel Clara YOAKLEY, death cause: "still born", informant: father (Kingsport), died: 20 Aug 1918, record (1918): 507.

Infant GRAY, sex: not stated, parents: J.S. GRAY (VA) and Peral MORRIS, death cause: "still born", informant: father (Bristol), buried: East Hill, died: 24 Aug 1918, record (1918): 508.

Jesse Lee HICKS, born: 17 Aug 1918, parents: Marshall HICKS and Eva DUNN, death cause: "acute indigestion", informant: M. HICKS (Fordtown), buried: Pactolus Cemetery, died: 1 Sep 1918, record (1918): 509.

Mary Lucille CARROLL, born: 26 Feb 1918, parents: John E. CARROLL and Sarah A. WISNER (Washington Co., VA), death cause: "ileo colitis", informant: father (Fordtown), died: 1 Sep 1918, record (1918): 510.

David T. TAYLOR, born: 5 Oct 1859, married, parents: John P. TAYLOR and Maria RUTHERFORD, death cause: "pneumonia", informant: J.W. TAYLOR (Kingsport), buried: Pyle Cemetery, died: 2 Sep 1918, record (1918): 511.

William Lloyd HUDSON, born: 18 Oct 1917, parents: W.J. HUDSON and Cyniha FREEMAN (VA), death cause: " .. (illegible) stomatitis", informant: father (Kingsport), died: 2 Sep 1918, record (1918): 512.

Sam STEWART, Negro, age approximately 35 years, parents: not stated, death cause: "heart failure", buried: Chattanooga, died at Kingsport on 3 Sep 1918, record (1918): 513.

Annie Mae BALDWIN, born: 3 Jun 1916 in Virginia, parents: Emmet BALDWIN (VA) and Alice REED (VA), death cause: "ileo colitis", informant: father (Kingsport), buried: Clinchport, VA., died: 6 Sep 1918, record (1918): 514.

Charlotte Elizabeth MURRAY, born: 2 Feb 1918, parents: John Anderson MURRAY and Grace Elizabeth MILLHORN, death cause: "disease of liver", informant: father (Fordtown), buried: Fordtown, died: 11 Sep 1918, record: 515.

Arthor P. BUCKLES, age 60 ?, divorced, parents: Robert BUCKLES and Winnie BERRY, death cause: "intestinal nephritis", informant: S.L. BUCKLES (Bristol), buried: Shipley Cemetery, died: 7 Sep 1918, record (1918): 516.

Robert CRAWFORD, born: Sep 1916, parents: Mat CRAWFORD and Ida ARNOLD, death cause: "broncho pneumonia", informant: D. CRAWFORD (Kingsport), died: 7 Sep 1918, record: 517.

Sallie COPENHAVER, age 52 years, born in South Carolina, married, parents: Jonathan COPENHAVER (SC) and Gretchen HAYNES (W.VA), death cause: "tuberculosis of lymph glands", buried: Weaver Cemetery, died: 8 Sep 1918, record (1918): 518.

J.W. HARTSOCK, born: 1 Sep 1917, parents: R.E. HARTSOCK (VA) and Julia JOHNSON (VA), death cause: "dysentery", informant: father (Kingsport), died: 8 Sep 1918, record: 519.

Elizabeth HICKMAN, born: 7 Mar 1908, parents: Simon HICKMAN (VA) and ___ LEONARD, death cause: "pertussis and pneumonia", informant: J.J. HICKMAN (Bristol), buried: Johnson Chapel, died: 5 Sep 1918, record (1918): 520.

Charles Henry BALL, born: 20 Sep 1916, parents: George BALL (VA) and mother's name illegible, death cause: "dysentery", informant: father (Bristol), buried: Ordway Cem., died: 8 Sep 1918, record (1918): 521.

Etta SAMS, age 3 months and 8 days, parents: Landon SAMS (VA) and Clendie AKERS (VA), death cause: "acute stomititis", informant: father (Bristol), buried: Shipley Cemetery, died: 10 Sep 1918, record (1918): 522.

James BRISCOE, age 82 years, married, parents: Matthew BRISCOE (VA) and Susan WHITE (Michigan), death cause: "Brights disease", informant: Mrs. BRISCOE (Emmett), buried: Crumley Cemetery, died: 11 Sep 1918, record (1918): 523.

Mollie VAUGHN, age approximately 65 years, parents: not stated, death cause: "pellagra", died at Kingsport on 11 Sep 1918, record (1918): 524.

Elia Virginia FLETCHER, born: 25 May 1903 in Virginia, parents: Stacy FLETCHER and Mattie CRESS, death cause: "appendicitis", informant: Mrs. Stacy FLETCHER (Mountain City), buried: Mountain City, died: 11 Sep 1918, record (1918): 525.

Ed HAMILTON, age 65 ? years, born in West Virginia, widower, parents: John HAMILTON (VA) and Hannah FOX (VA), death cause: "chronic rheumatism", informant: Mrs. HAMILTON (Bristol), buried: Beelors Cemetery, died: 11 Sep 1918, record (1918): 526.

Charlie DICKERSON, born: 15 May ___, age 31 years, married, parents: Hugh DICKERSON and Eva DICKERSON, death cause: "tuberculosis", died at Kingsport on 11 Sep 1918, record (1918): 527.

Elizabeth TROBAUGH, age 46 years, married, parents: not stated, death cause: "lobar pneumonia", informant: Brady VERNON (Bristol), buried: East Hill, died: 12 Sep 1918, record (1918): 528.

Ethel TESTER, born: 6 Aug 1896 in North Carolina, single, parents: Smith TESTER (NC) and Elizabeth YORK (NC), death cause: "gangrenous stomititis", informant: Fred TESTER (Kingsport), buried: Pyle Cemetery, died: 12 Sep 1918, record (1918): 529.

Dorothy Francis PYLE, born: 28 Apr 1917, parents: W.R. PYLE and Eula B. KETRON, death cause: "meningitis", informant: father (Kingsport), buried: Morrison Chapel, died: 12 Sep 1918, record (1918): 530.

Emerson LITTON, colored, age approximately 21 years, born in Virginia, single, parents: Oliver LITTON (Scott Co.) and Loura LITTON (Lee Co., VA), death cause: "uremia", informant: Margie LITTON (VA), died at Kingsport on 12 Sep 1918, record (1918): 531.

Jane BUCKLES, age 35 years, married, parents: Jake BUCKLES and Viola BRAM (VA), death cause: "blood poison from mashed hand", informant: Rube BUCKLES (Emmett), buried: Crumley Cemetery, died: 15 Sep 1918, record (1918): 532.

William REESE, age 33 years, 5 months, born: 25 Apr ___, married, parents: W.F. REESE and Malissa SMITH, death cause: "appendicitis", buried: Reese, NC., died: 17 Sep 1918, record (1918): 533.

Eddie FORD, born: 4 Jul 1897, single, parents: John FORD and Mariah HITE, death cause: "septicemia, typhoid", informant: mother (Jonesboro), buried: Hite Cemetery, died: 18 Sep 1918, record (1918): 534.

Robert Henry STINNETTE, born: 5 Nov 1876 in Amherst, Co., VA., married, parents: R. Nicholas STINNETTE (VA) and Mary Ellen HARRISON (VA), death cause: "accident in Columbia paper mill", informant: E.B. WHITE (Bristol), buried: Bristol, VA., died: 18 Sep 1918, record (1918): 535.

Thomas WALLING, age 12 years, parents: Joe WALLING (VA) and Sue BOUTAIN (VA), death cause: "pneumonia", informant: Sue WALLING (Bluff City), buried: Bluff City Cemetery, died: 18 Sep 1918, record (1918): 536.

Clarence CRAINFORD, age 3 years, parents: John CRAINFORD and Lucille CARROLL, death cause: "ileo colitis", informant: father (Kingsport), died: 18 Sep 1918, record (1918): 537.

R.J. DODD, Negro, born: 17 Sep 1870 in South Carolina, parents: father's name illegible and mother not stated, death cause: "dysentery and rheumatism", informant: L.C. DODD (New Jersey), died at Kingsport on 19 Sep 1918, record (1918): 538.

Oron Robert AKERS, age 9 years, born in Champaign, Illinois, parents: William AKERS and mother not stated, death cause: "tonsillitis", informant: G.W. STEELE (Kingsport), died: 18 Sep 1918, record (1918): 539.

J.M. HENLEY, born: 7 Nov 1835, widower, parents; Sam HENLEY (VA) and mother not stated, death cause: "lobar pneumonia", informant: Sam HENLEY (Bristol), died: 20 Sep 1918, record (1918): 540.

James W. BROWN, age 16 months, parents: illegible, death cause: "pneumonia", died in the 17th District on 30 Sep 1918, record (1918): 541.

J.H. BERRY, born: 7 Jul 1848, married, parents: Sam BERRY and ___ HEATHERLY, death cause: not stated, informant: L. BERRY (Bristol), buried: Ordway Cemetery, died: 21 Sep 1918, record (1918): 542.

V. MALONE, female, age 1 month and 3 days, parents: F.O. MALONE and mother's name illegible, death cause: "meningitis", died in the 17th District on 20 Sep 1918, record (1918): 543.

Mary E. COLE, age 1 year, 4 months and 16 days, born in Virginia, parents: W.J. COLE (Iowa) and Laura DEREY (VA), death cause: "influenza", informant: father (Bristol), buried: Paperville, died: 23 Sep 1918, record (1918): 544.

John Thomas (illegible), born: 1 Apr 1868, married, parents: John (illegible)(VA) and Mary HAGY (VA), death cause: "tuberculosis", buried: Cold Spring Cemetery, died: 23 Sep 1918, record (1918): 545.

Florence Ora SMALLING born: 23 Jun 1865, married, parents: Jackson M. SMITH and Catherine WEBB, death cause: "pneumonia", informant: J.E. SMALLING (Bristol), buried: Piney Flats, died: 23 Sep 1918, record (1918): 546.

Infant MARSHALL, female, born: Apr 1918, parents; E.L. MARSHALL (VA) and ___ TAYLOR (NC), death cause: "ileo colitis", informant: father (Bristol), buried: Snodgrass Cemetery, died: 23 Sep 1918, record (1918): 547.

Mrs. A.E. BARGER, age 36 years, married, parents: Cress INMAN and mother not stated, death cause: "intestinal obstruction", informant: A.E. BARGER

(Bristol), buried: North Carolina, died: 26 Sep 1918, record (1918): 549.

Rockett Verlan HIXSON, born: 5 Oct 1917, parents: Thomas HICKMAN and Carrie Bell BLACK, death cause: "deptheria", informant: father (Kingsport), buried: Pyle Cemetery, died: 24 Sep 1918, record (1918): 548.

Mrs. John N. STEVENS, born: 22 May 1870 in Virginia, parents: Jessie F. GILES (VA) and Sallie SPROLES (VA), death cause: "paralysis", informant: Mrs. E. HARDAWAY (Bristol), buried: Ordway Cemetery, died: 26 Sep 1918, record (1918): 550.

Ollie CRAWFORD, born: 14 May 1884 in Alabama, married, parents: James FRAZIER and Belle POE (Alabama), death cause: "typhoid fever", informant: Ealey CRAWFORD (Kingsport), died: 26 Sep 1918, record (1918): 551.

Frank SMITH, age 18 years, 7 months and 5 days, single, parents: Elbert SMITH and Elizabeth YOKLEY, death cause: "Spanish influenza", informant: Mrs. Elbert SMITH (Bristol), buried: Weaver Cemetery, died: 27 Sep 1918, record (1918): 552.

Susan A. BARR, born: 3 Oct 1827 in Virginia, widow, parents: George CRUSSELL (VA) and Katherine CARAWAY (VA), death cause: "senility", informant: Will BARR (Blountville), buried: Blountville, died: 27 Sep 1918, record (1918): 553.

Charles Andrew ENGLISH, age 1 year and 11 months, parents: J.A. ENGLISH (Washington Co., VA) and Daisy HARKLEROAD, death cause: "deptheria", informant: father (Kingsport), died: 27 Sep 1918, record (1918): 554.

Hattie REPOSS, age 18 years, single, parents: Elic REPOSS (VA) and Alace HENRY (VA), death cause: "influenza", informant: Mrs. Alace REPOSS (Bristol), buried: Shipley Cemetery, died: 28 Sep 1918, record (1918): 555.

Magie E. HAWLEY, born: 28 Feb 1856, single, parents: John HAWLEY and Susan ROLLER, death cause: "nephritis", informant: A.C. ROLLER (Blountville), died: 28 Sep 1918, record (1918): 556.

Emeline LIGHT, age approximately 64 years, parents: not stated, death cause: "disease of heart", buried: Kingsport, died in the 12th District on 30 Sep 1918, record (1918): 557.

R.W. GOSS, born: 17 May 1873 in North Carolina, married, parents: Robert GOSS (NC) and mother not stated, death cause: "perforated ulcer", informant: J.E. THOMAS (Bristol), buried: Tuckerville, NC., died: 30 Sep 1918, record (1918): 558.

Infant DELANEY, male, parents: William DELANEY and Lue KING, death cause: "still born", died in the 3rd District on 6 Sep 1918, record (1918): 559.

Infant OFFIELD, male, parents: Jake OFFIELS and Julia MAGEE, death cause: "still born", informant: Mrs. MAGEE (Bluff City), buried: Bluff City Cemetery, died: 8 Sep 1918, record (1918): 560.

Infant RICHARDSON, female, parents: C.A. RICHARDSON and Elsie HUTSON, death cause: "still born", informant: father (Kingsport), died: 28 Sep 1918, record (1918): 561.

Infant HICKMAN, female, parents: Simon HICKMAN and mother not stated, death cause: "still born", informant: father (Bristol), buried: Johnson Chapel, died: 14 Sep 1918, record (1918): 562.

Clide SHOECRAFT, born: 9 Mar 1891, parents: M.B. SHOECRAFT and ___ TURNER, death cause: "penumonia", informant: Mrs. Nanie SHOECRAFT (Bristol), buried: Ordway Cemetery, died: 2 Oct 1918, record (1918): 563.

Hiram MITCHELL, Negro, age approximately 64 years, born in Virginia, married, parents: not stated, death cause: "paralysis", informant: Mrs. Lucy MCINTOSH (Bristol), buried: Citizen Cemetery, died: 3 Oct 1918, record (1918): 564.

Ollie OFFIELD, age 28 years, 4 months and 15 days, married, parents: King OFFIELD and Jane MILLER, death cause: "influenza and pneumonia", informant; Mrs. Ollie OFFIELD (Emmett), buried: Paperville Cemetery, died: 3 Oct 1918, record (1918): 565.

Hester ANDERSON, Negro, age 26 years, married, parents: Ike ANDERSON and mother not stated, death cause: "penumonia", informant: Dennie SMITH (Kingsport), died: 3 Oct 1918, record (1918): 566.

Eralin POE, born: 13 Jun 1907, parents: Evert POE and ___ MCCANNIS, death cause: "meningitis following measles", informant: G. WARREN (Piney Flats), buried: New Bethel, died: 4 Oct 1918, record (1918): 567.

John BUCHANAN, age 43 years, born in North Carolina, married, parents: Abe BUCHANAN (NC) and Adah BENTLY (NC), death cause: "side plurasy", informant: Mrs. John BUCHANAN (Emmett), buried: Crumley Cemetery, died: 4 Oct 1918, record (1918): 568.

Rebecca E. HOUPT, age 37 years, single, parents: George HOUPT and Margaret LANE, death cause: "uterine carcinoma", informant: I.V. SMITH (Kingsport), died: 5 Oct 1918, record (1918): 569.

Annis Byrd SHUPE, born: 26 May 1900, married, parents: William E. BUTLER and Maggie WHITE (VA), death cause:

"pneumonia", informant: Mrs. W.E. BUTLER (Kingsport), died: 6 Oct 1918, record (1918): 570.
Ray Herbert DEPEW, born: 5 Sep 1844, single, parents: Elbert S. DEPEW and Mariah C. WILLARD, death cause: "influenza and lobar pneumonia", informant: E. Orville DEPEW (Fordtown), buried: Rock Springs Cemetery, 13th District, died: 7 Oct 1918, record (1918): 571.
Blanche JESSIE, age 18 years, 6 months and 14 days, single, parents: Jess JESSIE (VA) and Jane CRABTREE, death cause: "typhoid fever", informant: Mrs. Jess JESSIE (Bristol), buried: Paperville, died: 7 Oct 1918, record (1918): 572.
Walter CARROLL, age 20 years, parents: David CARROLL and ___ COLEY, death cause: "influenza", informant: G.W. CARROLL (Knox County), buried: Ordway Cemetery, died: 7 Oct 1918, record (1918): 573.
Clarence SIMERLY, age 17 years, 7 months and 2 days, parents: Daniel SIMERLY and Mollie JENKINS, death cause: "pneumonia", informant: father (Bluff City), buried: Crumley Cem., died: 8 Oct 1918, record (1918): 574.
Gladys FOY, Negro, born: 28 Mar 1917, parents: William FOY (NC) and Sallie TAYLOR, death cause: "influenza", informant: father (Bristol), buried: Citizen Cemetery, died: 8 Oct 1918, record (1918): 575.
Jacob K. FINK, age about 72 years, single, Civil War soldier, Union Army, parents: George Washington FINK and Sarah PICKENS, death cause: "paralysis", informant: W.E. FINK (Fall Branch), buried: Pickens School House Cemetery, 14th District, died: 8 Oct 1918, record (1918): 576.
Robert LEEPER, born: 15 Sep 1905 in Alabama, parents: L.F. LEEPER and Sallie M. LEEPER, death cause: "pneumonia", buried: Morristown, died at Kingsport on 9 Oct 1918, record (1918): 577.
Henry CLICK, black, age approximately 30 years, single, born in North Carolina, parents: illegible, death cause: "pneumonia", informant: Arthur HOBSON (Kingsport), died: 9 Oct 1918, record (1918): 578.
Lucille McGowen ALLISON, born: 17 Jun 1890 in Fayetteville, TN., parents: G.V. MCGOWEN and Mary Lou CATHEY, death cause: "influenza", buried: Johnson City, died at Kingsport on 9 Oct 1918, record (1918): 579.
Jake STOPHEL, age 12 years, 6 months and 13 days, parents: Joseph STOPHEL and (illegible) MUMPOWER, death cause: "bronchitis", informant: father (Emmett),

buried: Shipley Cem., died: 9 Oct 1918, record (1918): 580.
Margeurite Lyons PAYNE, Negro, born: 24 Dec 1913, parents: Hugh Lyons PAYNE and Maggie DAGGS (VA), death cause: "influenza", informant: Mrs. Ida PAYNE (Bristol), buried: Tennessee Cemetery, died: 9 Oct 1918, record (1918): 581.
Henry HARRIS, Negro, born: 1 Aug 1917 in North Carolina, parents: Lonnie HARRIS (NC) and Delia WILLIAMS (NC), death cause: "influenza and pneumonia", informant: Nelie HARRIS (Bristol), buried: Citizen Cemetery, died: 9 Oct 1918, record (1918): 582.
Janie E. Bradley GUTHRIE, Negro, born: 16 Feb 1892 in Virginia, married, parents: P.B. BRADLEY and Mary SMITH (VA), death cause: "influenza and pneumonia", informant: father (Bristol), buried: Gate City, died: 9 Oct 1918, record (1918): 583.
Frank B. MORRELL, age 34 years, 7 months and 5 days, parents: B.W. MORRELL and ___ RAY, death cause: "influenza", informant: father (Bristol), buried: East Hill, died: 10 Oct 1918, record (1918): 584.
Warren BLAKELY, age 25 years, married, parents: Taylor BLAKELY and Evalin HITE, death cause: "Spanish influenza", informant: S.J. BLAKELY (Kingsport), buried: Rock Springs, died: 10 Oct 1918, record: 585.
Nellie WEXLER, born: 18 Aug 1883, married, parents: J.W. DEVALUL and mother not stated, death cause: "deabetes", informant: father (Kingsport), buried: Kendrick Creek, died: 10 Oct 1918, record (1918): 586.
Lue Ray TAYLOR, age 4 years, parents: Dan TAYLOR and Blanch CROSS, death cause: "pneumonia", informant: Landon COLE (Kingsport), died: 10 Oct 1918, record (1918): 587.
Jane BOND, age 58 years, married, parents: David ROLLER and ___ JOHNSON, death cause: "cancer of stomach", informant: B.L. BOND (Blountville), buried: Gunnings Cemetery, died: 11 Oct 1918, record (1918): 588.
Ray B. SHIPLEY, age 15 years, 5 months and 17 days, parents: Martin SHIPLEY and Julia SHARP, death cause: "plurisy", informant: father (Emmett), buried: Paperville Cemetery, died: 11 Oct 1918, record (1918): 589.
George CHATEMAN, age 24 years, born in Virginia, married, parents: Sam CHATEMAN and mother not stated, death cause: "influenza", informant: Mrs. May CHATEMAN (Bristol), buried: Greenville, died: 11 Oct 1918, record (1918): 590.

Margaret CONKIN, born: 15 Apr 1889, married, parents: William MULLINS and Maryan HENSLEY, death cause: "pneumonia", informant: Laura CONKIN (Kingsport), buried: Fordtown, died: 12 Oct 1918, record (1918): 591.

Gale ARNOLD, male, born: 25 Sep 1897, married, parents: Show ARNOLD and Annie CLEMMONS, death cause: "pneumonia", informant: Mrs. Gale ARNOLD (Kingsport), died: 12 Oct 1918, record (1918): 592.

Ruby WHITT, colored, born: 10 Apr 1912 in Georgia, parents: ___ WHITT and Nellie CRAWFORD (GA), death cause: "influenza", informant: Rauley KEATON (Kingsport), died: 12 Oct 1918, record (1918): 593.

Callie LAMPKINS, age 37 years, married, parents: Jack MOREFIELD and mother not stated, death cause: "influenza", informant: John SMITH (Kingsport), buried: Pyle Cem., died: 13 Oct 1918, record (1918): 594.

Katie HATCHER, age 9 years, 11 months and 18 days, parents: John P. HATCHER and Maggie BULLOCK, death cause: "influenza", informant: George HATCHER (Bluff City), buried: Weaver Cem., died: 13 Oct 1918, record (1918): 595.

Ellen WASHINGTON, Negro, born: May 1886 in Virginia, married, parents: Andrew GODSEY (KY) and Maria HUGHES (VA), death cause: "pneumonia", informant: Frank GODSEY (Bristol), buried: Tennessee Cemetery, died: 13 Oct 1918, record (1918): 596.

Bertha May WASHINGTON, Negro, born: 17 Aug 1910, parents: Dink WASHINGTON and Ellen GODSEY (VA), death cause: "influenza and pneumonia", informant: father (Bristol), buried: Tennessee Cemetery, died: 14 Oct 1918, record (1918): 597.

Bessie WINGFORD, age: illegible, single, parents: W.T. WINGFORD and Maggie TELLWOODY, death cause: "influenza and pneumonia", informant: mother (Bristol), buried: East Hill, died: 14 Oct 1918, record (1918): 598.

Mrs. Viola BEIDLEMAN, Negro, age 25 years, married, parents: George SUSONG and mother not stated, death cause: "influenza and pneumonia", buried: Tennessee Cem., died at Bristol on 14 Oct 1918, record (1918): 599.

M. (illegible) AUSTIN, female, born: 3 Apr 1917, parents: Lee AUSTIN (VA) and Nettie PAUEL (VA), death cause: "pneumonia", informant: father (Kingsport), buried: Pyle Cem., died: 14 Oct 1918, record (1918): 600.

Blanche Elizabeth SHAFFER, age 1 year and 10 months, parents: J.H. SHAFFER (VA) and Gertrude BRIDWELL, death cause: "pneumonia", informant: father (Kingsport), buried: Gunnins Cemetery, died: 14 Oct 1918, record (1918): 601.

Fred HARMON, age 22 years, 11 months and 12 days, single, parents: Luther HARMON (VA) and Dora SOUTH (W.VA), death cause: "tuberculosis of spinal cord", informant: father (Emmett), buried: Pleasant Grove Cemetery, died: 15 Oct 1918, record (1918): 602.

Lee Sebastion FITZGERALD, born: 17 Jul 1893, single, parents: not stated, death cause: "influenza and pneumonia", buried: Catholic Cemetery, died at Bristol on 15 Oct 1918, record (1918): 603.

Samuel Neil HUTSON, born: 11 Feb 1915, parents: Jim HUTSON and Evie LIGHT, death cause: "pneumonia", informant: father (Kingsport), buried: Old Kingsport Cemetery, died: 16 Oct 1918, record (1918): 605.

Maggie JOHNSON, born: 11 Feb 1887 in Virginia, married, parents: Walter F. THOMPSON (VA) and ___ HIGHT (VA), death cause: "influenza", informant: father (Bristol), buried: East Hill, died: 15 Oct 1918, record (1918): 604.

Stella HICKS, born: 12 Aug 1915 in Virginia, parents: Henry HICKS and Rose GOINS, death cause: "pneumonia", informant: father (Kingsport), buried: Pyle Cemetery, died: 16 Oct 1918, record (1918): 606.

Minnie NELMS, born: 3 Jan 1887, married, parents: William PRESSLEY and Tennie PRESSLEY, death cause: "pneumonia", informant: Trigg NELMS (Kingsport), buried: Old Kingsport Cemetery, died: 16 Oct 1918, record (1918): 607.

Thomas MAYO, born: 4 Sep 1916, parents: Walter MAYO and Anna MAYO, death cause: "pneumonia", informant: father (Kingsport), died: 16 Oct 1918, record (1918): 608.

Joe HARRINGTON, age 32 years, married, parents: William HARRINGTON and Precilla MASSINGALE, death cause: "Spanish influenza", informant: father (Emmett), buried: Weaver Cem., died: 16 Oct 1918, record (1918): 609.

Mary Lucille EMMETT, age 4 years, 9 months and 9 days, born in Appalachia, VA., parents: J.W. EMMETT (Washington Co., VA) and Gertrude MOFFITT (NC), death cause: "pneumonia", informant: father (Bristol), buried: Bluff City, died: 16 Oct 1918, record (1918): 610.

Charlie WASHINGTON, Negro, born: 1 Dec 1908, parents: Dink WASHINGTON and Ellen GODSEY (VA), death cause: "influenza", informant: father (Bristol), buried: Tennessee Cemetery, died: 17 Oct 1918, record (1918): 611.

Earnest VANCE, age 27 years, 6 months and 17 days, married, parents: E.G. VANCE and Martha GOLF, death cause: "pneumonia", informant: father (Bristol), buried: Paperville, died: 17 Oct 1918, record (1918): 612.

Jackson C. RIGGS, born: 25 Dec 1888, married, parents: Jackson C. RIGGS and Evaline CHILDRESS, death cause: "influenza and tuberculosis", informant: H.L. RIGGS (Kingsport), buried: Double Springs Cemetery, died: 17 Oct 1918, record (1918): 613.

Eliza Anna Shipley DAVIDSON, born: 20 Nov 1842, parents: Tolbert SHIPLEY (Washington Co., TN) and Jennie DYRE (Washington Co., TN), death cause: "pulmonary hemorrhage", informant: Dr. GRAVES (Piney Flats), buried: New Bethel, died: 17 Oct 1918, record: 614.

Joe HAWKINS, age 27 years, single, parents: Will HAWKINS and Mary WILLOUGHBY (Mountain City, TN), death cause: "pneumonia", informant: father (Emmett), buried: Shipley Cem., died: 18 Oct 1918, record (1918): 615.

Mrs. Arthur MOCK, age 24 years, born in New York, married, parents: William WILHERIN (NY) and mother not stated, death cause: "influenza and pneumonia", informant: Arthur MOCK (Bristol), died: 18 Oct 1918, record (1918): 616.

Hattie TRENT, age 1 year, born at Austin Springs, parents: George TRENT and Liddie TAYLOR, death cause: "influenza", informant: W.E. TRENT (Bristol), buried: Austin Springs, died: 18 Oct 1918, record (1918): 617.

Howard WASHINGTON, Negro, born: 22 Feb 1917, parents: Dink WASHINGTON and Ellen GODSEY, death cause: "influenza", informant: father (Bristol), buried: Tennessee Cemetery, died: 18 Oct 1918, record (1918): 618.

James PICKLE, age 18 years, single, parents: Tom PICKLE and Laura LUNCEFORD (NC), death cause: not stated, informant: L.T. TRIVETT (Fish Dam), died in the 19th District on 18 Oct 1918, record (1918): 619.

Dolly NEWMAN, born: 24 Jul 1916, parents: John NEWMAN and Lula PENDIGRASS, death cause: "pneumonia", informant: J.W. NEWMAN (Kingsport), died: 19 Oct 1918, record (1918): 620.

Mary TRENT, born: 17 Mar __, age 12 years, parents: William TRENT and mother not stated, death cause: "influenza", informant: father (Bristol), buried: Austin Springs, died: 19 Oct 1918, record (1918): 621.

Blanch JESSIE, born: 19 Mar __, age 14 years, parents: Will JESSIE and Angie JESSIE, death cause: "influenza", buried: Ordway Cemetery, died: 19 Oct 1918, record (1918): 622.

Mildred DIXON, Negro, born: 24 Mar 1918, parents: Calvin DIXON (NC) and Matilda JOHNSON (NC), death cause: "influenza", informant: father (Bristol), buried: Tennessee Cemetery, died: 20 Oct 1918, record (1918): 623.

Harnin JENKINS, age 4 years, 5 months and 6 days, born in Virginia, parents: Ed JENKINS and Mary Ellen SIMERLY, death cause: "pneumonia", informant: mother (Emmett), buried: Crumley Cemetery, died: 20 Oct 1918, record (1918): 624.

James OLIVER, born: 4 Jun 1919, parents: Sam OLIVER and Lula POWERS, death cause: "influenza, meningitis", informant: J.S. POWERS (Bristol), died: 20 Oct 1918, record (1918): 625.

Thomas Richards RUTHERFORD, born: 20 May 1856, single, parents: William RUTHERFORD (Green County) and Maria PERRY, death cause: "gastro enteritis", informant: J.M. OLER (Fordtown), buried: Kendrick Church Cemetery, died: 20 Oct 1918, record (1918): 626.

Edd THOMAS, age 33 years, married, parents: W.D. THOMAS (VA) and mother's name illegible, death cause: "influenza", informant: S.L. THOMAS (Bristol), buried: East Hill, died: 21 Oct 1918, record (1918): 627.

Samuel K. MYERS, born: 22 Sep 1916, parents: Thomas MYERS and Georgie DEVAULT, death cause: "pneumonia", informant: J.R. LADD (Kingsport), died: 21 Oct 1918, record (1918): 628.

Dave CHRISTIAN, born: 4 May __, age 36 years, married, parents: John CHRISTIAN and Florence SMITH, death cause: "pneumonia", informant: J.C. CHRISTIAN (Kingsport), died: 21 Oct 1918, record (1918): 629.

James C. QUAILS, age 78 years, widower, parents: John QUAILS and mother not stated, death cause: "old age", informant: Cora KIDD (Kingsport), buried: East Hill, Bristol, died: 23 Oct 1918, record (1918): 630.

Sarah M. MILLER, age illegible, born in Virginia, parents: M.J. COLLINS and Mary VANCE, death cause: "influenza", informant: E.J. VANCE (Bristol), buried: Susong Cem., died: 22 Oct 1918, record (1918): 631.

Charlie HOUSTON, born: 15 Feb 1888, single, parents: Alex HOUSTON and Sarah HOUSTON, death cause: "influenza and pneumonia", informant: George HICKS (Kingsport), died: 23 Oct 1915, record (1918): 632.

Clarence MARTIN, age 38 years, single, parents: not stated, death cause: "pneumonia", informant: W.D. ARMBUSTER (Kingsport), buried: Old Kingsport Cemetery, died: 24 Oct 1918, record (1918): 633.

John BEAR, born: Jul 1841, parents: James BEAR and Bettie MYERS, death cause: "valvulor heart disease", informant: J.H. CALHOUN (Kinggsport), died: 24 Oct 1918, record (1918): 634.

William Ernest SAMS, born: 1 Aug 1887 in Unicoi County, married, parents: William T. SAMS (Unicoi Co.) and Mary M. REMMION (Unicoi Co.), death cause: "influenza and pneumonia", informant: Robert T. SAMS (Bristol), buried: East Hill, died: 24 Oct 1918, record: 635.

Basil Fred LIGHT, born: 24 Sep 1918, parents: George Washington LIGHT and Mary Bessie MOWDY, death cause: "premature birth", informant: G.W. LIGHT (Fordtown), buried: Kendrick Cemetery, died: 24 Oct 1918, record (1918): 636.

Mike B. WEBB, age 29 years, married, parents: James D. WEBB and Elizabeth DEVAULT, death cause: "typhoid fever", informant: H.C. WEBB (Bluff City), buried: Holston Grove Cemetery, died: 25 Oct 1918, record (1918): 637.

Julia Rachel ARNOLD, born: 3 Jul 1916, parents: William ARNOLD and Callie LAWSON, death cause: "influenza", informant: Steve ARNOLD (Kingsport), buried: Pyle Cemetery, died: 25 Oct 1918, record (1918): 638.

Frank M. HILTON, born: 23 Dec 1917 in Virginia, parents: A.S. HILTON (VA) and Flora FREEMAN (VA), death cause: not stated, informant: father (Kingsport), buried in Virginia, died: 25 Oct 1918, record: 639

Susan ESTEP, born: 7 Jul 1886 in Virginia, married, parents: A.J. BOLLING and Sallie MCCULLOUGH, death cause: "influenza", informant: E.M. ESTEP (Bristol), buried: Holston Valley, died: 25 Oct 1918, record (1918): 640.

Blanche COLLINS, age 24 years, married, parents: J.J. CROSS (VA) and ___ TRINKLE (VA) death cause: "Spanish influenza and pneumonia", informant: John CROSS (Bristol), buried: Ordway Cemetery, died: 23 Oct 1918, record (1918): 640a.

Rauster LEONARD, age 2 years and 1 month, parents: David LEONARD and ___ SAMPSON, death cause: "influenza", informant: father (Bristol), buried: Leonard Cemetery, died: 25 Oct 1918, record (1918): 641.

Hue WYATT, age 25 years, married, born in Washington Co., VA., parents: C. Jim WYATT and Sue WARREN (Washington Co., TN), death cause: "influenza", died in the 19th District on 26 Oct 1918, record (1918): 642.

Mrs. E. PAINTER, born: 27 Jan 1876 at Peach Orchard, KY., married, parents: John TOLBERT (VA) and Jennie SALIERS (KY), death cause: "locked bowels", informant: C.S. PAINTER (Kingsport), buried: Pyle Cemetery, died: 26 Oct 1918, record (1918): 643.

G. Wayne OVERSTREET, age 37 years, 6 months and 1 day, born in Kentucky, married, parents: G.W. OVERSTREET (KY) and Mattie WILLIAMS (KY), death cause: "typhoid fever", informant: H.B. BROWN (Radford, VA), buried: East Hill, died: 27 Oct 1918, record: 644.

Flora A. RICHARDS, age 11 months, parents: illegible, death cause: "lobar pneumonia", buried: Susong Cemetery, died in the 17th District on 27 Oct 1918, record (1918): 645.

L.M. SCIFRES, male, age 47 years, born in Indiana, married, parents: G.M. SCIFRES (Ind) and mother illegible, death cause: "influenza and pneumonia", died in the 17th District on 27 Oct 1918, record (1918): 646.

Elizabeth J. SLAUGHTER, born: 11 Apr 1829 in Washington Co., TN., widow, parents: James JACKSON and Elizabeth CHANDLER, death cause: "apoplexy", informant: Elizabeth HAMILTON (Fordtown), buried: Jackson Cemetery, died: 27 Oct 1918, record (1918): 647.

Silas G. DYKES, born: 30 Oct 1874 in Virginia, married, parents: father not stated and Sallie DYKES (VA), death cause: "influenza", informant: C.W. VAUGHN (Kingsport), buried: Groseclose Cemetery, died: 28 Oct 1918, record (1918): 648.

Isaac H. MORROW, age 73 years, born in North Carolina, married, parents: J.C. MORROW (NC) and Lou CARVER (NC), death cause: "influenza", died at Bristol on 29 Oct 1918, record (1918): 649.

Mrs. Mary E. BROWN, age 67 years, born in Virginia, widow, parents: E.E. EARLY (VA) and mother not stated, death cause: "influenza", informant: Fred BROWN

(Bristol), buried: Ordway Cemetery, died: 29 Oct 1918, record (1918): 650.

Horace DICKSON, age 4 years, 1 month and 10 days, born in Maryland, parents: father not stated and Della DICKSON, death cause: "tonsilitis", informant: Tom LUSTER (Kingsport), buried: Cloud Cemetery, died: 29 Oct 1918, record (1918): 651.

Allen BURNER, born: 19 Dec 1838, widower, parents: Arthur N. BRUNER (Germany) and Mahala JONES, death cause: "lobar pneumonia", informant: Mrs. Belle MCCURRY (Kingsport), died: 29 Oct 1918, record (1918): 652.

Clarence Fleenor STUFFLE, born: 21 Mar 1915, parents: M.R. STUFFLE and Mary Myrtle VANCE, death cause: "influenza", informant: Mack STUFFLE (Bristol), died: 29 Oct 1918, record (1918): 653.

Orville BROWN, age illegible, single, parents: O.S. BROWN (NC) and mother's name illegible, death cause: "influenza", informant: Fred BROWN (Bristol), buried: Ordway Cemetery, died: 31 Oct 1918, record (1918): 654.

Infant PRESCOTT, male, parents: C.S. PRESCOTT (NC) and Ella HOLDER (NC), death cause: "still born", informant: father (Bristol), buried: East Hill, died: 4 Oct 1918, record (1918): 655.

Infant MORELOCK, female, parents: C.H. MORELOCK and Yetava MITCHELL, death cause: "still born", died at Kingsport on 14 Oct 1918, record (1918): 656.

Helen LEONARD, parents: C.A. LEONARD and Jetta BURSHELL (VA), death cause: "still born", informant: O.E. LEONARD (Bristol), buried: Three Springs Cemetery, died: 19 Oct 1918, record (1918): 657.

Andrew PARTRUM, dark ?, age 38 years, parents: not stated, death cause: "influenza and pneumonia", informant: Will MOSS (Kingsport), buried: Old Fort, NC., died: 2 Nov 1918, record (1918): 658.

Ruby Lee BULLIS, born: 11 Mar 1917 at Bristol, VA., parents: Andrew BULLIS and Virginia PICKENS (Washington Co., TN), death cause: "deptheria", informant: father (Kingsport), buried at Bristol, VA., died: 2 Nov 1918, record (1918): 659.

Alice VESTAL age 24 years, married, parents: Badger MCELYEA and Dena ALLEN, death cause: "influenza", informant: Wade VESTAL (Bristol), buried: Mountain City, TN., died: 3 Nov 1918, record (1918): 660.

Hugh Fortune SHOWALTER, born: 15 Sep 1914, parents: Charles SHOWALTER and Lula ROGAN, death cause: "dyptheria", informant: C.P. SHOWALTER (Kingsport),

buried: Liberty Cemetery, died: 4 Nov 1918, record (1918): 661.
David E. READ, age 22 years, married, born in Green County, parents: James READ and Rebecca LEONARD (VA), death cause: "influenza and pneumonia", informant: Mrs. Rebecca READ (Bristol), died: 5 Nov 1918, record (1918): 662.
Ida Ethel DONAHUE, born: 24 Jun 1918, parents: J. Kyle DONAHUE (VA) and Ollie QUILLEN (VA), death cause: "influneza and pneumonia", informant: father (Kingsport), buried: Hilton, VA., died: 6 Nov 1918, record (1918): 663.
Helen LAMPKINS, born: 21 Sep 1918, parents: Walker LAMPKINS and Callie MOREFIELD, death cause: "indigestion", informant: Floyd LAMPKINS (Kingsport), buried: Pyle Cemetery, died: 7 Nov 1918, record (1918): 664.
Ethel HICKS, age 15 years, parents: George HICKS and Carrie WILLIAMS, death cause: "influenza", died at Piney Flats on 8 Nov 1918, record (1918): 665.
Arthur BROWN, age 22 years, single, parents: Will BROWN and Amanda CLAY (SC), death cause: "rock crusher accident", informant: father (Emmett), buried: Beeler Cemetery, died: 9 Nov 1918, record (1918): 666.
Caroline PENLEY, age 53 years, born in Virginia, widow, parents: John PRICE and Fannie ALDRIGE (VA), death cause: "pellagra", informant: F.M. PENLEY (Kingsport), buried: Gate City, VA., died: 10 Nov 1918, record (1918): 667.
Elizabeth P. Janes ST JOHN, born: 28 Feb 1855 in Wales, parents: Robert JANES and Elizabeth (illegible), death cause: "nephritis", informant: Mrs. R.L. TAYLOR (Bristol), buried: Chilhowie, VA., died: 10 Nov 1918, record (1918): 668.
Floyd MITCHELL, born: 7 Feb 1895, married, parents: Charles MITCHELL (Hawkins Co.) and Fannie PARKER, death cause: "skull crushed in automobile accident", informant: father (Kingsport), buried: Pactolus Church Cemetery, died: 12 Nov 1918, record (1918): 669.
George VESTAL, age 1 year and 3 months, parents: Wade VESTAL (VA) and Alice MCELYEA, death cause: "influenza and pneumonia", informant: father, buried: Laurel Bloomery, Johnson Co., TN., died: 12 Nov 1918, record (1918): 670.
James W. CRAWFORD, Jr., Negro, born: 31 Jan 1897, single, parents: James W. CRAWFORD, Sr. (Alabama) and Lucy CARTER, death cause: "accidental gun shot wound",

informant: father (Bristol), buried: Citizen Cemetery, died: 13 Nov 1918, record (1918): 671.

John N. STEADMAN, born: 5 Oct 1855, married, parents: Patton STEADMAN and Mary DOLEN, death cause: "intestinal tuberculosis", informant: Edna M. STEADMAN (Kingsport), buried: Depew Chapel, died: 14 Nov 1918, record (1918): 672.

Moses HENDRICKS, Negro, age about 73 years, born in Virginia, widower, parents: Green HENDRICKS (VA) and Malinda HOPKINS (VA), death cause: "nephritis", informant: Johnson HENDRICKS (Bristol), buried: Citizen Cemetery, died: 15 Nov 1918, record (1918): 673.

Mattie CROSS, age 12 years, parents: John CROSS and Hattie BROSE, death cause: "influenza and pneumonia", informant: Joe CROSS (Emmett), buried: Crumley Cemetery, died: 15 Nov 1918, record (1918): 674.

James MILLER, born: 9 Mar 1887, married, parents: Thomas MILLER and Pattie LARGE, death cause: "tuberculosis of lungs", buried: Ruthton Cemetery, Bristol, died: 16 Nov 1918, record (1918): 675.

Eugene REED, born: 14 Nov 1914 in Virginia, parents: Ben H. REED (VA) and Nancy HUSLEY (VA), death cause: "marasmus", buried: Clinchfort, VA., died at Kingsport on 16 Nov 1918, record (1918): 676.

Ellen BROWN, age 8 years, parents: L. BROWN and Elizabeth CARRIER, death cause: "typhoid fever", informant: father (Emmett), buried: Crumley Cemetery, died: 16 Nov 1918, record (1918): 677.

Luther A. WALLACE, born: 12 Jan 1890 in Johnson County, married, parents: G.W. WALLACE (Johnson Co.) and Emma VANOVER (Ashe Co., NC), death cause: "tuberculosis of lungs", informant: father (Fish Dam), died: 20 Nov 1918, record (1918): 678.

Helen FRANCIS, born: 20 Nov 1918, parents: T.A. FRANCIS (VA) and Venita DUNN (VA), death cause: "premature", informant: father (Kingsport), buried: Abingdon, VA., died: 20 Nov 1918, record (1918): 679.

Hersel Carl BRAY, age 6 years, 8 months and 25 days, parents: Alvin BRAY and Addie WHITAKER, death cause: illegible, informant: Addie S. BRAY (Bristol), buried: Ordway Cemetery, died: 22 Nov 1918, record (1918): 680.

Hershel BRAY, age 6 years and 9 months, parents: Alvin BRAY and Addie WHITAKER, death cause: "influenza", informant: G.H. WHITAKER (Bristol), buried: Ordway Cemetery, died: 22 Nov 1918, record (1918): 681.

D.C. MCKENZIE, born: 29 Nov 1897 in Virginia, single, parents: John MCKENZIE (VA) and Clara BELLAMY, death cause: "influenza and pneumonia", informant: father (Yuma, VA), buried: Bellamy Cemetery, died at Kingsport on 23 Nov 1918, record (1918): 682.

Oscar WHITSEL, age 24 years, single, parents: Nathan W. WHITSEL and Rowena CARR, death cause: "influenza and typhoid fever", informant: N.W. WHITSEL (Kingsport), died: 24 Nov 1918, record (1918): 683.

Ellen HICKS, born: 18 Jun 1915, parents: H.B. HICKS and Nelie SANDERS (VA), death cause: "whooping cough", informant: George ANDERSON (Kingsport), buried: Reedy Creek, died: 26 Nov 1918, record (1918): 684.

Mary HAMILTON, born: 6 Sep 1878, single, parents: James B. HAMILTON (Washington Co., TN) and Elizabeth SLAUGHTER, death cause: "influenza and pneumonia", informant: J.A. HAMILTON (Jonesboro), buried: Fordtown Cemetery, died: 29 Nov 1918, record (1918): 685.

James NORDYKE, Negro, age about 65 years, born in Virginia, married, parents: not stated, death cause: "heart disease", informant: Annie NORDYKE (Bristol), died: 30 Nov 1918, record (1918): 686.

Infant BRADLEY, Negro, parents: William M. BRADLEY and Cynthia HAZZARD (VA), death cause: "still born", informant: P.B. BRADLEY (Bristol), buried: Citizen Cemetery, died: 6 Nov 1918, record (1918): 687.

Infant COOK, male, parents: Elbert COOK and Laura GARLAND, death cause: "still born", informant: H.F. PHIPPS (Bristol), buried: Paperville, died: 10 Nov 1918, record: 688.

Infant WARREN, male, parents: John WARREN and Eliza SHANKLE, death cause: "still born", informant: father (Emmett), buried: Bluff City, died: 11 Nov 1918, record (1918): 689.

Infant VANCE, female, parents: Elbert VANCE and Sallie BOOHER, death cause: "still born", informant: father (Emmett), died: 18 Nov 1918, record (1918): 690.

William Paul HENNINGER, age 1 month and 15 days, parents: J.T. HENNINGER and Ruby PHIPPS, death cause: "found dead in bed", informant: S.L. HENNINGER (Bristol), buried: Paperville, died: 3 Dec 1918, record: 691.

Infant DENNEY, male, age 3 days, parents: B.R. DENNEY (VA) and ___ SMALLING, death cause: "jaundice", informant: father (Bristol), buried: Poplar Grove Cemetery, died: 2 Dec 1918, record (1918): 692.

Infant SMITH, female, born: 2 Dec 1918, parents: J. Millard SMITH and Fannie PEPPIN, death cause:

"premature birth", informant: father (Bristol), buried: East Hill, died: 3 Dec 1918, record (1918): 693.

Bessie SIMERLY, age 15 years, 7 months and 3 days, parents: L.P. SIMERLY (NC) and Flora FEATHERS, death cause: "pneumonia", informant: father (Bluff City), buried: Weaver Cemetery, died: 4 Dec 1918, record (1918): 694.

John W. WILCOX, born; 7 Jul 1856, married, parents: Joseph WILCOX (VA) and Mary CROCKETT (VA), death cause: "multiple sarcoma", informant: Mrs. W.D. KEESLING (Bristol), buried: East Hill, died: 4 Dec 1918, record (1918): 695.

Avery JOHNSON, Negro, female, born: 3 Oct 1885 in Virginia, parents: Patrick NUSHBORNE (VA) and Jenny DINGUS (VA), death cause: "heart and kidney disease", informant: Mrs. Jennie WILSON (Bristol, VA), buried: Gate City, VA., died: 5 Dec 1918, record (1918): 696.

William McClellan HUNT, born: 22 Apr 1855, married, parents: John HUNT and Sallie COX, death cause: "Spanish influenza", informant: J.R. COX (Fordtown), buried: Washington College Cemetery, died: 5 Dec 1918, record (1918): 697.

James Rhea WITCHER, born: 15 Oct 1901, single, parents: D.A. WITCHER and Myra RHEA, death cause: "influenza and pneumonia", informant: John RHEA (Piney Flats), buried: Blountville, died: 6 Dec 1918, record: 698.

Lucile CRAWFORD, age 35 years, married, parents: Tom CARROLL and Janett HICKMAN, death cause: "pellagra", informant: John CRAWFORD (Kingsport), died: 7 Dec 1918, record (1918): 699.

Bessie B. Rhea GLOVER, born: 18 Feb 1883, married, parents: S.W. RHEA and Sarah H. (illegible), death cause: not recorded, informant: S.W. RHEA (Piney Flats), buried; Blountville, died: 8 Dec 1918, record: 700.

Paul CHEEK, born: 9 Feb 1917, parents: J.E. CHEEK and Sether BERRY, death cause: "illio colitis", informant: father (Kingsport), buried: Pyle Cemetery, died: 10 dec 1918, record (1918): 701.

Sarah Fidella GREEN, born: 20 Feb 1852 in Watauga County, NC., parents: Elijah TRIVETT (Coldwell Co., NC) and Becka DAVIS (NC), death cause: "Brights disease", informant: Jack GREEN (Bluff City), buried: Crumley Cemetery, died: 11 Dec 1918, record: 702.

Jonathan SHUMAKER, age 83 years, born in North Carolina, widower, parents: Elbert SHUMAKER (NC) and

Rachel HANSOR (NC), death cause: "heart disease", buried: Shipley Cemetery, died in the 2nd District on 12 Dec 1918, record (1918): 703.

Susa H. HOGAN, Negro, born: 1 Jan 1886 in Virginia, married, parents: Frank DEAN (VA) and mother not stated, death cause: "pulmonary hemorrhage", informant: William R. HOGAN (Bristol), buried: Citizen Cemetery, died: 13 Dec 1918, record (1918): 704.

W.H. NAVE, age 69 years, born in Washington Co., TN., married, parents: Henry W. NAVE (Carter County) and Susan DUNKIN (Washington Co., TN), death cause: "mitral aortic regurgitation", informant: David NAVE (Bristol), buried: East Hill, died: 14 Dec 1918, record (1918): 705.

Ella Kate MASSY, age 4 months and 3 days, born in North Carolina, parents: John MASSY (NC) and Jane CLOUD (NC), death cause: "pneumonia", informant: father (Emmett), buried: Crumley Cemetery, died: 13 Dec 1918, record (1918): 706.

Clyde OWENS, born: 28 May 1916, born in Virginia, parents: Elish OWENS (VA) and Eliza BABB (VA), death cause: "tuberculosis of bowels", informant: Elish OWENS (Kingsport), died: 13 Dec 1918, record (1918): 707.

George Washington MATHERLY, born: 1 Jun 1847 in Carter County, parents: father not stated and Fannie MATHERLY (Carter Co.), death cause: "Hodgkins disease", informant: Garfield MATHERLY (Jonesboro), buried: Double Spring Cemetery, died in the 15th District on 13 Dec 1918, record (1918): 708.

James Albert CARROLL, born: 25 Jun 1909, parents: John E. CARROLL and Sarah A. KISTNER (Washington Co., VA), death cause: "pressure on brain, tumor or hemorrhage", informant: J.E. CARROLL (Fordtown), died: 15 Dec 1918, record (1918): 709.

Hattie ISELY, age 5 years and 3 months, parents: Clarence ISLEY (NC) and Dottie KING, death cause: "croup", informant: father (Emmett), buried: Shipley Cemetery, died: 15 Dec 1918, record (1918): 710.

Francis OLIVER, born: 4 Jun 1846 in Grayson County, VA., widow, parents: John W. WELSH (Grayson Co.) and Lucinda LONG (Grayson Co.), death cause: "Brights disease", informant: Walter Oliver (Kingsport), buried: Arcadia Cemetery, died: 15 Dec 1918, record: 711.

James CLARKSON, Colored, born: 24 Nov 1912, parents: Edd CLARKSON and Tennie FUGATE, death cause:

"influenza and pneumonia", informant: father (Kingsport), died: 19 Dec 1918, record (1918): 712.
Infant THOMPSON, male, born: 16 Dec 1918, parents: Patton THOMPSON (VA) and Nettie CLOUD, death cause: "meningitis", informant: father (Kingsport), buried: Cloud Cemetery, died: 21 Dec 1918, record (1918): 713.
John MCCLELLAN, age 70 years, born in Virginia, married, parents: Robert W. MCCLELLAN (VA) and mother not stated, death cause: "tuberculor abscess in lung", informant: C.T. MCCLELLAN (Bristol), died: 21 Dec 1918, record (1918): 714.
Allice SMITH, born: 26 Nov 1895 in Hawkins County, TN., married, parents: Rutledge PATTERSON (Hawkins Co.) and Ella WEBSTER (Hawkins Co.), death cause: "accidental gun shot wound, husband cleaning pistol", informant: J.A. SMITH (Kingsport), buried: Greenville, TN., died: 21 Dec 1918, record (1918): 715.
Infant FLEENOR, male, parents: William Whitfield FLEENOR (VA) and Jennie JONES (VA), death cause: "premature birth", informant: father (Bristol), buried: Walnut Grove Cemetery, born/died: 22 Dec 1918, record (1918): 716.
Samuel Henry FAGINS, born: 1 Aug 1908, parents: Andrew FEAGINS and Alpha MORELOCK (VA), death cause: "influenza and pneumonia", informant: T.J. DOUGLAS (Kingsport), died: 23 Dec 1918, record (1918): 717.
Harold P. HUNT, born: 5 Nov 1868, married, parents: John HUNT and mother's name illegible, death cause: "pulmonary tuberculosis", informant: Charlie HUNT (Kingsport), buried: Pactolus, died: 23 Dec 1918, record (1918): 718.
Valina SNODGRASS, age 21 years and 2 months, born in Virginia, married, parents: W.F. WYATT (VA) and Mollie EMMETT, death cause: "pneumonia", informant: father (Bristol), buried: Ordway Cemetery, died: 24 Ded 1918, record (1918): 719.
Charles Quillen GODSEY, Jr., born: 20 Apr 1912, parents: C.Q. GODSEY (VA) and Susan LATTURE, death cause: "auto accident", informant: J.L. GODSEY (Bristol), buried: Ordway Cemetery, died: 25 Dec 1918, record (1918): 720.
James Carter GODSEY, born: 16 Apr 1917, parents: C.J. GODSEY and Addie Strukley (VA), death cause: "auto accident", informant: J.L. GODSEY (Bristol), buried: Ordway Cemetery, died: 25 Dec 1918, record (1918): 721.
Jessie May GODSEY, born: 1 Aug 1909, parents: C.J. GODSEY (VA) and Susan LATTURE (VA), death cause: "auto

accident", informant: J.L. GODSEY (Bristol), buried: Ordway Cemetery, died: 25 Dec 1918, record (1918): 722.
Charles Quillen GODSEY, born: 23 Feb 1877 in Snowflake, VA., married, parents: Drury S. GODSEY (Crabtree Branch, VA) and Susan LATTURE, death cause: "auto accident", informant: J.L. GODSEY (Bristol), buried: Ordway Cemtery, died: 25 Dec 1918, record (1918): 723.
James COOK, age 56 years, married, parents: Alex COOK and Nancy RAMBO (VA), death cause: "paralysis", informant: M.H. COOK (Bristol), buried: Beelor Cemetery, died: 25 Dec 1918, record (1918): 724.
Mrs. Ala May SHEPHERD, age 33 years and 7 months, born: 2 May ___ in Virginia, parents: E.K. Kanah (VA) and mother not stated, death cause: illegible, died in the 17th District on 25 Dec 1918, record (1918): 725.
Herbert HAUK, age 13 years and 9 months, parents: Dr. O.S. HAUK and Allie G.. (illegible), buried: Gunnings Cemetery, 2nd District, died: 26 Dec 1918, record: 726.
Donald Bernard JONES, born: 13 Apr 1918, parents: Walter JONES and Cordelia WATKINS (Washington Co., TN), death cause: "weak heart", informant: father (Jonesboro), died in the 14th District on 28 Dec 1918, record (1918): 727.
Grace Virginia K. FIELDS, born: 2 Dec 1871, married, parents: Thomas A. ARNOLD and Mary E. REYNOLDS (VA), death cause: "goitre", informant: Thomas FIELDS (Kingsport), died: 28 Dec 1918, record (1918): 728.
Mary Alice DIXON, born: 9 Dec 1918, parents: John DIXON and Eliza OWENS, death cause: "spina bifida", informant: father (Kingsport), buried: Childress Cemetery, died: 29 Dec 1918, record (1918): 729.
Jane Cox MILLER, born: 3 Mar 1858, single, parents: Jesse MILLER and Elizabeth MORGAN, death cause: "organic heart disease", informant: Mrs. J.E. ARRANTS (Bristol), buried: Pleasant Grove, died: 29 Dec 1918, record (1918): 730.
John Preston KING, born: 18 apr 1852, widower, parents: William Harvey KING and Mahola Jane CHASE (Washington Co., TN), death cause: "catarral dysentery", informant: John L. KING (Fordtown), buried: King Cemetery 14th District, died: 29 Dec 1918, record (1918): 731.
Mary C. PHIPPS, age 28 years, married, parents: James WEBB and Caroline GEISLER, death cause: "influenza and

pneumonia", buried: East Hill, died at Bristol on 30 Dec 1918, record (1918): 732.

Amanda SHARRETT, age 61 years, married, parents: not stated, death cause: "Brights disease", buried: Browns Cemetery, 1st District, died: 30 Dec 1918, record: 733.

Mrs. Christa Bell LAWSON, born: 3 May 1889 in Hawkins County, TN., married, parents: James CARUNCHAEL (illegible) (Hawkins Co.) and Mary SPRIGGS (Hawkins Co.), death cause: "flue, abortion, pneumonia", informant: C.W. LAWSON (Kingsport), died: 30 Dec 1918, record (1918): 734.

William R. MILLER, age 78 years, married, parents: not stated, death cause: "mitral regurgitation of heart", died at Piney Flats on 31 Dec 1918, record (1918): 735.

S. WOLFE, male, born: 20 Sep 1889, married, parents: John B. WOLFE and (illegible) HUGHES, death cause: "tuberculosis of kidneys", died at Piney Flats on 31 Dec 1918, record (1918): 736.

Infant EASLEY, male, parents: William W. EASLEY and Ida Jane LISENBY, death cause: "still born", informant: father (Kingsport), died: 2 Dec 1918, record (1918): 737.

Infant HOLTON, male, parents: J.T. HOLTON and Bertha SMITH, death cause: "still born", died at Piney Flats on 2 Dec 1918, record: 738.

William HALL, parents: B.H. HALL (GA) and S. PEREGOY, death cause: "premature", informant: father (Kingsport), buried: Pyle Cemetery, born/died: 4 Dec 1918, record (1918): 739.

Edkert BELLAMY, born: 15 Dec 1918, parents; John BELLAMY (VA) and Venia LOYD, death cause: "premature", informant: father (Kingsport), buried: Liberty Hill, died: 15 Dec 1918, record (1918): 740.

Edna BELLAMY, born: 15 Dec 1918, parents; John BELLAMY (VA) and Venia LOYD, death cause: "premature", informant: father (Kingsport), buried: Liberty Hill, died: 15 Dec 1918, record (1918): 741.

Infant CHURCHWELL, male, parents: William H. CHURCHWELL and Nannie VILES, death cause: "mother had influenza", informant: father (Kingsport), buried: Cloud Cemetery, born/died: 26 Dec 1918, record (1918): 742.

Index

Adams, Annie 177 Charles 58 C.L. 168 Elizabeth 58 204 Ethel 110 Gernia 25 Infant 12 Jake 56 Jane 182 Lola 218 Margaret 79 Mary 80 Mattie 196 M.E. 80 W.H. 168
Addington, Annie 132
Agee, Addie 88 C.W. 74 88
Ager, Charles 201 Rhoda 201
Akard, David 1 Rebecca E 80
Akers, Cart 181 Clendie 239 George W. 120 John 219 Josie 163 221 Lucinda 107 Margaret 66 Mose 219 Oron Robert 241 Susan 79 Tom 181 William 187 241
Aldrige, Fannie 253
Alexander, J.L. 52
Alford, Flancey 17 George 143 John 123 Landon 115 Sallie 143
Alfred, Claud 123 George 210 George (Mrs) 210 John 177 Landon 210 Peter 177 Phronia 216
Alison, Elizabeth 19 Robert 178
Allen, Dena 252 James F. 115 J.R. 161 Margaret 115 Nancy 220 Naoma 115
Alley, J.T. (Mrs) 145
Allison, Joe M. 48 John 19 Joseph 72 Lucille M. 244 Rob 72 Robert 72
Allstadt, Mary J. 116
Almaroad, Fannie 29
Alsgue, Sarah 88
Ammon, Berry 98
Anderson, Alice 102 Billie 112 Blanche 188 Buster 1 C. 91 Eli 42 Florence A. 211 George

Anderson (continued) 179 213 255 George R. 159 Hester 243 Ike 243 Infant 91 James H. 229 John 126 John, Sr. 161 J.C. 211 J.F. 229 J.H. 179 King 211 Lolla 160 Louise 119 Maude 199 Rebecca 78 Routh 179 R.M. 196 R.M. Jr. 196 R.R. (Mrs) 92 T.H. 179 Wanda K. 230 Watson 92 102 William 161 William L. 159 William R. 188 William S. 11 W.G. 229 230 W.R. 119
Arants, Ed 167 Elizabeth 139 Maud 165 Nathan 154
Archer, G.M. 83 Infant 83
Arcut, Paul 42
Arents, Joseph 134
Armbuster, W.D. 250
Armstrong, Annie 59 Frank 109 Milt 109 Rick 109
Arnbuster, W.D. 203
Arney, Emaline 213
Arnold, Alice 125 Andrew 139 A.F. 102 A.J. 74 Benjamin A. 204 Carl H. 2 Dora 178 196 Emmert 38 Gale 234 246 George 125 George A. 159 G.A. 215 Ida 239 Infant 234 Jack 159 Jacob E. 105 Janies 105 James 161 James A. 74 Joe 234 Julia R. 250 Lula 40 Martha E. 72 74 Martha I. 102 Mollie 194 Nannie 177 Newton 66 Sarah 105 Sarah E. 127 Show 246 Steve 204 250 Thomas A. 259 William 250 W.J. 105 W.T. 127
Arrants, Charlie M. 142 James 142 J.E. (Mrs) 259

Arteburn, Jane 228
Arwood, Maggie 25 Thomas 82
Ashby, Marth 178 Peter 178
Ashley, Elizabeth 208 Martha 208
Ashly, Mary 81
Austin, Annie 85 Clyzil 211 Gracie L. 214 Jessie 212 Lee 211 214 246 Maude 174 M. 246 Nettie 214 William 212
Avria, Sam 230
Babb, Eliza 257
Bachman, Anna 44 Annie 209 E.K. 195 232 E.K., Jr. 195 Nathan D. 195 T.J. 97 219 W.M. 110 147
Bacon, Lydia 74 Mollie 181
Bailey, Annie 26 George 173 173 Helen C. 133 Oscar 133 Perry 27 44 Polly 155 S.S. (Mrs) 69
Bains, Maggie 201 Minnie 139 Nancy 155
Bair, Henry 220
Baker, Harriet 76 Infant 4 Nola 132 Sallie 83 53
Baldwin, Annie Mae 238 Emmet 238
Ball, Charles H. 239 D.A. 155 Francis 19 50 George 19 85 87 239 Grac May 87 Infant 155 Lela Kate 85
Bane, Fanny 123
Banks, Parthena 191
Barbe, Mary 69
Bare, Besty 106 Doll 148 Ed 106 Fannie 144 James 106 Jess 23 Lucy 90 Mary 101 Nancy 191 Nellie 91 R. Wiley 29 Saphrona 191 Susan 90 Wilker 151 William 90 Willie 148

Bare (continued) 191
Barger, A.E. 241 A.E. (Mrs) 241 G.S. 79 Infant 188 Jacob 109 Nicholas 233 Nickels 127 R.L. 188 Samuel K. 233 Will Rhea 32
Barges, C.H. 101 Willie 54
Bargus, Lula 51
Barken, Carrie 51
Barker, Clint 197 Hat 211 Infant 211 Jott 197 Nannie 151 William 197
Barlow, F.P. 233 Jacob 216
Barnd, Guy 10
Barnes, Adam F. 136 David 106 George W. 136 Infant 30 Isabella 68 John 70 106 J.R. 36 Lee 43 Lonie L. 21 L.R. 36 Marry 162 Mary Ellen 70 Mildred L. 43 Nettie F. 93 Oliver 36 Robert W. 93 William 106 W.D. 93 230
Barnett, Bettie 82 Henderson 237 James 217 William H. 237
Barr, Earl 94 Infant 20 Joseph 121 J.S. 94 Mary 123 Nannie 95 Norman 39 Samuel 121 Susan A. 242 Will 242
Barrett, G.W. 167 Thomas 132 Thomas (Mrs) 132 Will (Mrs) 148
Barrs, John 14
Bass, Henry 229 H.B. 229 M.V. 229 Patey 82
Bates, James C. 116 John W. 116 Robert 116
Batt, D.A. 104 Infant 104
Bautan, Martha 28

Baxter, Mary Ann 93
Bayless, A.T. 126 H.E.
   222 Jackson 126
   Mary C. 222
Bays, Clarence H. 40
Bealer, R.L. (Mrs) 146
Beaman, Nora 222
Bear, James 250 John 250
   Sindy 232 William 207
   Wroller 232
Beard, Elizabeth 195
   George 74 108 Loucinda
   127 Maud 143 Soloman 217
   William 32 __ 76
Beaver, Mollie 112
Bebber, Infant 182
   John 182
Beckett, Percy 52
Bedwell, Lucille 133
Beechboard, Levi 105
   William 105
Beeler, John D. 114
   Looney 114
Beelor, Martha 203
Beeman, Nora 159
Beidleman, Fannie 224
   Magge B. 202 Minnie 228
   Pet 206 Viola 246
   Wesley 228
Belamy, Matilda 107
Bell, C.R. 93 113
   C.R. (Mrs) 23 Elizabeth
   108 John R. 212 Mary E.
   83 Vernon D. 212
Bellamy, Clara 255 Edna
   260 Elkert 260 John 260
Beller, Elsie Mae 93
Benfield, Charles 171
   Georgia M. 171
   Robert 171
Bennet, Burke 228
   Charles E. 228
Bennett, Bert 145
   George A. 145 Ida 213
   Nellie V. 58
Bently, Adah 243

Bernett, D.H. 187
   Ester 187
Berry, J.H. 241 Lou 114
   L. 241 Sam 241 Sara 150
   Sarah 189 Sether 256
   Winnie 238 __ 200
Berryman, James A. 96
   R.P.A. 96
Bery, Bryan 158 Davy 158
Bibber, Bascom 16
Biedleman, Cornelia A. 170
   Guss (Mrs) 175 J.A. 18
   J.A. (Mrs) 170
   Stephen 141
Binhang, Mary C. 71
Birch, Milly 75
Birdwell, Beatrice 148
   Benjamin 74 David 122
   Dora E. 46 D.R. 122
   Josie R. 115 Matilda 49
   Tommy 46
Bishoff, Samuel 216
Bishop, Bob 234 Emmett C.
   234 Henry 169 Infant 182
   James 182 Nancy N. 68
   Nellie 169 Stanley 167
   Virginia May 26
   William 167
Black, Carrie B. 242
   Myers 121
Blackman, Hubert H. 13
Blair, Eliza 199
   Maria 223
Blake, Freddie 85
   George 85
Blakeley, Henry 108 Odie
   157 William 108
Blakely, Jackson 108
   Mathern 123 Retta 12
   Sallie 58 S.J. 245
   Taylor 245 Warren 245
   William 117
Blalock, Billie 70
   D.J. 193
Blankenship, Charles 145
   J.C. 145 Walter 39

Blevins, Alfred 75
  Alfred W. 67 Augustus
  217 Beattie 225
  Bettie E. 40 Charles 143
  E.M. 56 Geniza 205
  George A. 65 Georgie 18
  Isaac 99 Jackson 4
  James C. 226 Jane 92
  John Sanford 32
  J.A. (Mrs) 217 Larulu 84
  Lousy 226 Lucy 95 Lusian
  169 Maggie 6 Maria 141
  Martha V. 225 Mary 123
  Mary E. 95 Permelia 217
  Rena 81 82 Richard 99
  Roda E. 9 R.L. 143
  Sallie 229 Susannah 139
  S.A. 158 William 169
  W.C. 226 W.P. 87
Blizzard, C.C. 203 Elmo
  203 G.C. 184 N.C. 203
  Susan R. 184
Bogle, Eralus H. 99
  L.P. 99
Boling, Becky 158
  Betsy 70 C.P. 70 Frank
  139 John 139 Luther 32
  Rebecca 32 Susie 147
Bolling, A.J. 250
Bolton, George 91 Kate E.
  91 Lida E. 157 Margaret
  76 Robert 91 __ 157
Bond, Andrew J. 212 B.L.
  245 David S. 212
  Elbert Gibson 82
  Eldridge 132 Fannie 23
  James 82 Jane 245
  Lena M. 149 Lona Mae
  100 Merrett W. 98
  William L. 132
Booher, Andrew 61 Carson
  66 Conrad 203 Daniel 39
  Dave 191 David 203
  Elbert 197 Fannie C. 20
  Flora A. 130 Florence
  77 Florence W. 125

Booher (continued)
  Golda A. 37 G.W. 171
  Infant 197 Jack 232 Jane
  183 John M. 37 Joseph
  130 Josiah 67 J.W. 188
  Lillie 191 Lucy 232
  Martin 232 Mary Ann 223
  Myrtle 77 M.D. 125 O.K.
  131 Sallie 255 Sarah 179
  Walter 179 Wesley 179
  __ 180
Booker, Johnnie 12
Booth, Kittie 219
  Kitty 148
Borger, William 128
Bostic, Emaline P. 80
Botol, F.H. 206
Bott, Abram 205 J.T. 205
  Lucyann 205
Boutain, Sue 240
Boutin, Ada 69 Belle 26
  J.M. 69
Bouton, Delia 107
  Fannie 67
Boweary, John 54
Bowen, William 227
Bower, Groover 182 Ned 182
Bowers, Beatrice 61 Carrie
  173 D.C. 95 202 D.C.
  (Mrs) 202 Eunice 119
  Isaac 180 John L. 216
  Martha 149 Ota 180
  Virgil 95 William H. 119
Bowery, Adam 117 Conrad
  71 Infant 60 J.R. 70
  Mary Mosie 70 Thomas 60
  W.M. 8
Bowland, Sudie 101
Bowling, Alf 77 Butler
  101 David 101 J.W. 77
  Larkin 77 Mary F. 129
Bowlon, Mattie 162
  William 77
Bowman, Earl 206 Jake 206
  Lizzie 235 Margaret 230
  Mattie 228 Thomas 74

Bowman (continued)
 W.E. 235
Bowon, James 77
Bowry, John W. 100
 Susan Kate 100
Bowser, Catherine 108
 Melvin C. 2 Rachel 108
Boy, Andrew 92 Bessie 216
 Edward 118 Francis M.
 35 Jacob 118 James C.
 150 J.C. 150 Mary 150
 Phil J. 92
Boyd, Andrew 178 Andrew H.
 118 A.W. 178 Charles 44
 Elizabeth 182 185
 George 104 Gilbert E.
 103 G.W. 13 Infant 44
 John 118 John W. 103
 Mary Ann 104 Mollie 96
 Nathan M. 64 Rachel 73
 Robert William 18 Sallie
 178 Sarah R. 122
Brabson, Kittie 90 Noah
 90 Patsy 90
Brace, Mattie 197
Brach, Nathan 9
Bradley, Anna L. 157
 Ethel 149 Infant 255
 James H. 157 Mary E. 71
 P.B. 245 255
 William M. 255
Bragg, George W. 115 John
 220 Nancy C. 205 Noble
 220 Sina 174 Thomas 108
 115 T.L. 205
Bralley, George E. 125
 Jack 125
Bram, Viola 240
Branch, Henry 162 J.G.
 162 Maude 222
Brandon, James 163
 S.D. 163
Braudaus, Albert 7
Bray, Addie S. 254 Alvin
 254 Alvin H. 86 Hersel
 C. 254 Hershel 254

Bray (continued)
 Thomas 86
Breeding, Andrew J. 91
 I.T. 209 J.K. 91 Mattie
 C. 209 William 91
Brewer, Calvin A. 218
 Lizzie 218 Nettie 218
 Willie 100
Bridgeman, A.J. 60 Janie
 167 Mandie 3
Bridwell, Gertrude 247
Briggs, Nancy 5
Bright, Pegie 103
Brisco, Dave 123 Jack 123
 James S. 235
 J.S. (Mrs) 235
Briscoe, David 123 James
 239 Lyne 123 Matthew
 239 Richard 123 David 98
 Herriel 98 J.H. 98
 R.E. (Mrs) 98
Broce, Harvey Payne 40
Brooks, Andy 136 Andy
 (Mrs) 136 Bettie 191
 Jennie 211 Mary Ann 72
 Maynard 209 Moses 73
 Nellie 136 P.M. 148 P.M.
 (Mrs) 148 Sam 148
 William 209
Brose, Hattie 254
Brout, Fred M. 228
 John 228
Brown, Albert 194 Annie L.
 223 Arthur 253 Bettie
 47 Charlie 155 Elizabeth
 25 Ellen 254 Emma T. 199
 Enon H. 193 E.B. 99 Fred
 251 252 F.E. 187 George
 154 H.B. 251 H.C. 155
 Infant 225 James M. 81
 James W. 241 Josephine
 75 J.R. 81 Lee 225
 Lucian 194 Lucy 223
 Luther 215 L. 254
 Malinda 122 Martha 56
 Mary 56 Mary E. 208 251

Brown (continued)
  Matthew J. 223 Matthew
  L. 223 Maude H. 127 May
  206 Nettie 227 Orville
  252 O.S. 187 252 Rhoda
  81 Rhoda Hughes 82 Roy
  81 Rufus 14 R.E. 127
  Sarah A. 104 Thelma L.
  155 Tilden 144 Webb 215
  Will 193 253 William 199
  215 Winnie Bell 144 W.B.
  99 W.M. 182 Z. 187
Broyles, Allen 74 H.L. 74
  Lola L. 192 Louis S. 192
  Louis S. 74 Maria 88 R.L.
  192 Washington 132
Bruner, Arthur N. 252
  Matilda 234 Oma 234
Brushan, Nannie 78
Bryan, Alice 75 Charles E.
  84 Henry W. 84 W.H. 84
Bryant, Barbara 137 Ben
  137 Bessie 84 Eliza O.
  110 Jessie 84 R.L. 110
  Stella 229 T.J. 110
  Vesta 110
Bryson, Margaret 183
Buchanan, Abe 243 A.J.
  78 F.A. (Mrs) 130 John
  243 John (Mrs) 243
  Martha 168 Samuel B. 78
  W.B. 78
Buck, Tom 204
Buckeless, Sarah 156
Buckels, Rachel 84
Buckles, Arthor P. 238
  Frank J. 78 Grace 197
  Jake 240 Jane 240 John
  134 Martha 148 Mary E.
  134 Mary Jane 78 Mollie
  104 155 Robert 238 Rube
  240 S.L. 238 __ 84 90
  __ G. 24
Budgeman, Gordie 220
Budgman, A.J. 220
  Fora 220

Bueler, Andy 111 John 80
Buison, Mattie 80
Bullian, Hyathis 47
Bullion, Connie R. 185
  James 185
  Kennith M. 185
Bullis, Andrew 252 Bessie
  37 Ida 37 Ruby L. 252
Bullock, A.T. 145 Blanche
  145 Clarence 115 Ella
  167 Henry 180 Infant 177
  John 115 Joseph 177 J.A.
  70 Letta S. 70 Maggie
  246 Marion 172 Martha
  165 __ 107
Bumgardner, F.W. 226
  Infant 188 J.D. 188
  Sallie 226
Bunder, Carolina 198
Bunting, Lindsay 102
Burch, __ 149
Burchett, Jetta 209
Burford, Sylvester 183
Burger, Harry S. 79
Burgess, Sena 12
Burk, Sarah 124
Burke, Melvina 166
Burkett, Herbert 149 Lee
  Lina R. 207 Nathaniel 95
  William 149
Burkhart, Amanda 154
Burkhart, C.D. 180
  James W. 180
Burn (?), Absolom 25
Burner, Allen 252
Burnett, Andrew J. 61
  Decatur 211 Eliza 26
  Greenbury 211 Mary 130
  Nannie 167 Ollie 24
  Saraphenia 26 Sary Akers
  6 Simon 182 Tishie 182
Burns, John W. 82 J.B. 82
Burringer, Alfred H. 148
  Thomas 148
Burroughs, Thomas 219
Burrow, Robert 85

Burrow (continued)
  Thomas J. 85 W.M. 214
  W.M. (Mrs) 214
Burshell, Jetta 252
Burton, E. 105 George W.
  105 J.P. 105 Nannie 67
Bushong, Elizabeth 141
Buten, Mack 27
Butler, Charles 216
  Charlie 216 Lelia 216
  Myrtle 204 William E.
  243 W.E. 244
Byers, Andy T. 58
Byington, Carr 127
  Henry C. 127
Byrd, George 198 G.T. 237
  Marjorie E. 237
Cable, Charles B. 63
Cain, Abe 32
Calahand, Thomas 16
Caldwell, Cicero 237 Mary
Calhoun, J.H. 250
  Polly 131
Callahan, Clarence 171
  William 171
Callahand, Lillie 42
Calland, Infant 17
Calloway, Gladys 26
  Leachie 87 Richard 81
Calthan, Lillie 16
Campbell, Alfred L. 13
  Calie L.M. 152 Callie 22
  Corthena 13 Debora 113
  Elizabeth 78 E.L. 197
  George W. 152 Iva 229
  James 120 Julia 197 J.L.
  74 102 110 118 Katy 229
  Lucile 150 Martha 12
  Rebecca 184 Sallie 179
  Smith 66 Trigg 86 T.W.
  131 164 Vadella 86
Campell, Sallie 152
Campie, F.M. 230
  Gordon 230
Cannon, Polly 216
Canoy, Joseph P. 111

Canoy (continued)
  R.A. 111
Canter, John Jr. 5
  Myrtle 7
Cantrell, Jessie 233
Caraway, Katherine 242
Carberry, Sarah 166
Carden, Elbert 127
  Elizabeth 124 Emma Line
  41 James 11 26 Lizzie
  130 Cecil M. 130 C.C.
  101 215 Robert T. 101
Carinas, Tennessee 97
Carlton, Elizabeth 68
  Julia 63
Carmack, William 30 __ 140
Carpenter, A.J. 131
  J.N. 131
Carr, Amanda K. 178
  Charles 87 Chester 113
  Eleanor 29 Ellen 162
  Infant 162 James 92
  Jerry 46 Julie 183 Nola
  46 N.F. 221 O.H. 162
  Robert 113 178 Rowena
  255 Vance 87 Vestal 189
  Walter 189
Carrier, Bessie B. 150
  Brookie 37 Cain 209
  Catherine 101 Clarence
  164 Cora 95 David 28
  Elizabeth 254 Emma 123
  Fannie 211 Frank 101 212
  224 Henry 95 H.A. 98
  Infant 76 164 Isaac 203
  James 213 James R. 161
  Jennings 40 Jim 176 John
  224 Jonathan 135 161
  J. Hugh 135 Leather 176
  Lucy 198 Maggie 154
  Martha 68 Matt 224 May
  209 Mose 209 Nancy 68
  Orvill 17 Pollie 169
  Polly 142 Sarah 161
  Thomas 28 Thomas H. 203
  Thomas (Mrs) 203 T.E. 22

Carrier (continued)
  T.H. (Mrs) 150 Vera Mae
  213 Will 176 William C.
  76 W.W. 169 __ 77
Carroll, Andy J. 121 Bill
  220 Bob 226 David 210
  244 D.F. 177 Elbert 220
  Feornil 196 Francis 154
  G.W. 244 James A. 257
  John 154 John E. 238 257
  J.E. 257 Lucille 240
  Mary 92 177 Mary L. 238
  Robert F. 29 Sendia 207
  Starlin 210 Thomas 9 Tom
  256 Walter 244
  Wilrie 224
Carrowell, Nancy 195
Carter, Aggie 96 Bettie
  111 Ella 236 Emma 12
  Enoch 184 H.W. 69 John
  28 John R. 184 J.E. 236
  Lucy 205 Lula 225 Martha
  181 Mary M. 69 M.L. 110
  Nick 94 Pollie 110 Polly
  184 Ruth A. 190 R.B. 190
  __ Jane 198
Cartman, Susan 207
Cartwright, Abija 100
  David W. 100 Eliza 212
  Fannie 1 Fred 24 Jennie
  1 Lettie 188 Lida E. 100
Carunchael, James 260
Carver, Lou 251
Case, Walter 189 Wanna 189
Cash, Anna 120 Lehoy 57
  Sarah 112 William 96
Casteel, Lily 11 Sarah 11
Caster, Charlie 69 P. 210
Castle, Georgia 204
  John 204
Cate, Charley 21
Cates, Thomas J. 30
Cathey, Mary L. 244
Catron, Alice 182
  Maxia B. 55
Cattidett, Eliza 100

Caufman, Eva 100
Cautern, Infant 65
Cecil, Henry L. 178 Witten
  178 W.T. 179
Chafin, Charles (Mrs) 52
Chambers, Belle 135 136
  Jennie 200 Jerry 173
  John 235 John R. 83 J.B.
  83 Lillian M. 235 Willam
  135 William 136 W.M. 200
Chandler, Elizabeth 251
Chapin, L. 116
Chapman, Doc 50 Evelyn 102
  James 187 J. 222
  Lizzie 222
Chappel, James 18
Chappell, Lila 228
Charlton, Mary 133 134
Chase, Addie Maxie 117
  G.C. 228 Harvey 137
  Isaac 228 Isac P. 64
  Jary 223 John T. 166
  Mahola J. 259 Nancey 223
  Nancy 93 Neva 162 O.M.
  191 Richard D. 166
  Roland P. 108 Thomas J.
  228 Walter F. 117
Chateman, George 245
  May 245 Sam 245
Cheek, J.E. 256 Paul 256
Chester, J.M. (Mrs) 218
  J.W. 218
Chestnut, M.J. (Ms) 158
Childers, Jonah 118 J.B.
  118 William J. 118
Childress, Ann 211 Ann B.
  116 Bertha V 109 Charles
  168 Elizabeth 192 Ethel
  198 Evaline 248 F. (Dr)
  74 George W. 104 I.T. 79
  198 Mary A. 79 M.M. 49
  Noah 130 Rahcel 106 Ruth
  193 R.F. 104 109 114 R.T
  116 Sarah A. 168 T.C.
  156 Will B. 183 Willie
  Willie 219

Chisadys, Jessie 17
Christian, Dave 249 Edith 157 John 249 J.C. 249 Landon 157 Nany 166 William 24
Chrtcher, __ 196
Church, George 156 Infant 125 James H. 156 Jarvis C. 125 Jim 215 Joseph 156 Minnie 122
Churchwell, Infant 260 William H. 260 W.C.C. 23
Cilfford, John 54
Clamon, Jane 171
Clark, Andrew 135 Caroline 97 Claude 143 Harrison 229 Ida 156 Isaac 104 James 113 143 229 Jane 190 Job H. 20 J.B. 126 143 Lafayette 22 Lucinda 96 Margaret 46 William 104 William F. 113 Zora 229
Clarke, Elizabeth 104 Robert 141
Clarkson, Edd 257 James 257
Clay, Alla 45 Amanda 253 Diadema 48 Dora M. 178 Henry L. 178 Nellie 178
Clayman, Emaline 129 F.S. 192 Infant 192 J.A. 129 Maud 134 Robert F. 190 R.F. 190
Cleek, Margaret 122 Rufus 8
Clemmons, Annie 246
Click, Elizabeth 77 Henry 244 J.J 200 Lenna J. 200 William Lewis 77
Clifford, Joseph 70 William 70 William M. 70
Cloud, Benjamin 101 Carter 180 Cathleen R. 14 Cora 169 Emalin 59 F.S. 82 Jane 257 Jestie 101

Cloud (continued) Mildred E. 82 M.M. 218 Nettie 258
Cloyd, Cornelia H. 215 Grace 30 Hazel 153 John 153 J.C. 215 M.M. 153 215
Clyce, Samuel A. 79 William 79
Coates, Martha E. 219 Robert N. 125 Robert W. 125
Coats, Arthur 162 Blain 178 196 Dan 200 David L. 162 Dewitt 122 Eliza A. 200 Infant 122 John 194 196 McKinley 196 Myrtle 194 Nelson 127 Ralph G. 178
Cobbs, Jane 132
Coffee, John 37
Coffer, Giles 99
Coffman, Daniel 158 Roy A. Wiola C. 158 Walter A. 158
Coldwell, Frank 118 H.C. 118 220 J.H. 118 M. 216 Sallie T. 220
Cole, Bertie M. 173 Charlotte 171 C.D. 8 George C. 162 Ida 5 Isaac 199 Jack 84 170 Joel A.G. 20 Landon 245 Louise 151 Mariah 227 Mark 227 Marshal 84 Mary 170 Mary E. 241 Nancy Nannie 130 Neoma A. 173 Oakley 204 Sarah 227 Stephen 218 Winnie 218 W.H. 81 W.J. 241 __ 156
Coleman, Albert 159 Chester 135 Eva 159 Frank 176 George M. 176 John 142 Lena 159 Nancy 142 __ 215
Coley, Belle 137 Emmaline

Coley (continued)
  208 James 137 J.L. 145
  Sinora F. 93 Thomas 137
  208 213 T.A. 182 __ 244
Colier, Alice 174
Collars, Betsy 132
Collier, Alice 202
Collins, Adam 218 Alice
  209 Blanche 250 Burly 64
  Corda 196 Cordie 218 Don
  218 Dora 164 Fannie 145
  H.C. 157 Infant 64 Jake
  155 James E. 165 Jessie
  207 John T. 102 J.A. 80
  J.r. 127 Lark 207 Lizzie
  138 Mary 127 Maxie 138
  M.J. 249 Noah F. 165
  Nora 98 Rebecca M. 68
  Sullins 188 S. 219
  Virginia E. 68
  William A. 79 William D.
  68 Woodrow 188 W.D. 68
  Zollie 237 __ 234
Collons, Sallie 188
Colpers, Harry 89
Colton, Clarence 129
  James 129
Combes, __ 205
Combs, Docia 25 D.L. 22
  E.A. 72 William 11
  W.L. 135
Comes, Lucy 175
Compton, Everet 159 177
  E.M. 177 Louisa 142
  Nannie 159 Newt 184
  Omega 177
Conkin, Charina 108 Cordia
  76 Daniel 108 David 110
  Florence A. 124 Infant
  237 James 152 165 Jane
  Parker 89 Jerome 108
  John, Jr. 237 J.M. 124
  Katie 132 Laura 246
  Margaret 246 Novel 153
  S.H. 77 95 Thomas 124
  Thomas J. 93 Usely 93

Conkins, Emmaline 159
  J.B. 152 Roosevelt 33
Conklin, J.K.P. 103
  Lida 2
Conty, R.J. 218
  William 218
Cook, Alex 259 Cora A. 136
  Elbert 255 Elizabeth S.
  196 E.J. (Mrs) 235
  Infant 255 James 259
  J.W. 107 M.H. 259
  R.O. 196
Cookenhour, Betsy 196
Cooper, Anna L. 235 Cecil
  73 Charles R. 96
  Charmis 73 Infant 81
  James 170 Jess 170 John
  235 Landa 233 Landon 233
  L.A. 73 Maggie 81 Ronle
  W.F. 96
Copass, Connie 61
Copeland, Nancy 139
Copenhaver, Jonathan 239
  J.C. 128 Nancy C. 128
  Sallie 239
Copess, John J. 63
Cornett, James 142 Lelia
  164 Polly 131 __ 131
Cornice, Alex 73 Bessie 73
  Isaac 73
Cornville, Payton B. 172
Cornwell, W.M. 172
Corum, Howard R. 153
  R.C. 153
Corvin, Maggie 77
Coussell, Mollie 100
Cowan, Addie 30 Andrew 218
  Andrew (Mrs) 218 C.M.
  146 Elizabeth 4 George A
  140 Infant 97 140
  J. Booker 146 Nathan D.
  146 Sarah 148 Thomas H.
  97 T.H. 140 Gracie 62
  Rebecca 62 Texie 62
Cox, Abram 127 Anne 14
  Annie E. 183 Aris 172

Cox (continued)
  B.A. 50 Caroline 105
  Charles 163 Edna 96
  Ethel 184 Francis J. 34
  George P. 48 Grover C.
  110 G.C. 103 Hal Moore
  144 Ida May 110 Infant
  76 110 185 Jacob 103 214
  James 232 James D. 24
  James Gilbert 43 Jane 64
  John Emory 76 John L. 74
  Joshua 74 Josie D. 34
  J.H. 56 J.N. 54 J.R. 256
  J.T. 88 Lillie M. 144
  Martha 103 Martha L. 88
  Mary 143 Mary Lou 120
  Mollie 143 Monic L. 117
  Morris 120 Noah 8 Norma
  82 Roxy 13 Sallie 256
  Samuel B. 144 Samuel
  Carl 54 Samuel R. 127
  Susie 187 S.E. 54 S.P.
  120 S.R. 163 Thomas 83
  Thomas J. 83 Thomas W.
  187 190 T.A. 22 T.W. 187
  U.H. 139 Virgil T. 185
  Virginia 113 William F.
  190 Willie 33 __ 184
Crabtree, Benjamin F. 206
  Catherine 206 Jane 244
  Samuel 196
Cracey, Roberta 205
Cradae, Charity 123
Craft, Andrew 136 Ann 226
  H.V. 136 H.V.(Mrs) 136
Craig, Nancy 179
Crainford, Clarence 240
Crainford, John 240
Crane, Elizabeth 55
  Julia 234
Crawford, Ann 137 A.L.
  158 Berbitha 111 Bersty
  201 Birtha P. 214
  Bonnie 202 Claudie H. 76
  Coy C. 33 C.R. 111
  Daisey 228 David 96 104

Crawford (continued)
  D. 239 Ealey 242 Ed 214
  228 Ed (Mrs) 228 Edith
  33 Edmon 214 Edward 111
  Elizabeth 234 Eva Lee
  100 Fannie 158 Georgie
  R. 44 G.H. 82 Infant 61
  109 James A.W. 195 James
  N. 201 James O. 177
  James W. 253 James W.
  Jr. 253 John 82 87 95
  201 221 256 Lawrence 76
  Lucile 256 Mary C. 108
  Mary J. 95 108 Mat 239
  Nathan 100 Nathan M. 108
  Nellie 246 Olie 163
  Oliver 202 Ollie 242 Ray
  221 Ray R. 167 Robert
  239 Sam 87 Samuel 10
  Sahdrack 77 Thomas 77 82
  Thomas M. 177 Verlin 23
  Will 109 167 William 114
  195 Zachariah 111
Cress, Emma 204 John 32
  W.A. 204
Cretsinger, Ethel 5
  Wilmer A. 221
Cridlen, G.P. 179
  Sallie C. 179
Crockett, Helen 168 Mary
  256 S.S. 213
Crofford, Bessie 170
Croosenberry, Mary E. 41
Cross, Amanda 146 Anna
  Lee 154 Blanch 245
  Catherine 167 Charles H.
  187 C.B. 226 David 48
  148 Ellen 75 Elvese 140
  Ethel Cate 1 Fannie C.
  67 Fannie Kate 9 George
  133 187 Harvey William
  67 Infant 152 Jack 152
  Jacob 45 Jake 114 Jean
  218 Jennie 146 Joe 254
  John 137 211 250 254
  John F. 179 John Jr. 137

Cross (continued)
  John (Mrs) 218 Julia 54
  J.J. 250 J.W. 179
  Madeline 208 Marshall
  148 Martha Nell 218 Mary
  126 232 Mary E. 113
  Mattie 11 Mattie 254
  Mollie 232 M.E. 1 Nannie
  211 Nellie B. 182 Neoma
  98 Rebecca 106 Reece 54
  Sam 133 154 Sarah Jane
  48 S. 6 Virginia 102
  Wiley 5 William 15 17
  133
Crosswhite, Flemings 183
  Robert 183
Crouch, Lillian M. 136
Crow, Anis 175 Bessie 100
  102 James 99 Jim 175
Crowell, John W. 86 Joseph
  116 Mary H. 86 William
  H. 86 W.M. 86
Crudgington, Millie 197
Crum, Charles (Mrs) 97
  C.M. 91 Infant 91 173
  James B. 56 John (Mrs)
  206 J.R. 91 R.K. 173
Crumley, D.J. 35 George
  28 James (Mrs) 233 J.
  Milton 228 Luther 228
  Mary 71 218 Susan 125
  William O. 28
Crusenberry, Mandy 193
Crussel, William 127
Crussell, Elbert 12
  George 242 Willie 12
Crysel, John S. 97
Cunningham, A.B. 171
  Gerile R. 171 ___ 130
Curric, Joe 32
Currier, J.A. 18
Cursiea, Cinthy An 17
Curtis, Clyde 65 Ed 63
  Hannah 76 Infant 63
Cutshaw, Lula 184
Daggett, James 173

Daggett (continued)
  Joseph 173
Daggs, James 97 John 53
  Maggie 245 Robert 97
Daily, C.W. 180
Dake, Saphia 236
Dalton, Charles A. 202 209
  C.A. 174 Dan 97 111
  Infant 57 Mack 174
  Phoeba E. 202 Walice F.
  30 Worley 209
Dancey, Charles 108
  Infant 108
Dancy, Charles 184
Darter, George W. 128
  George (Mrs) 129
  John T. 128
Daugherty, James 98
  James Jr. 98
Davenport, Michael 54
  M. (Mrs) 148
David, Ira 112
Davidson, Eliza A. 248
  J. 19
Davis, Amanda 93 Andrew
  190 Andy 224 Becka 256
  Charlie 30 C.E. 157
  Duncan 190 Hariet 188
  Infant 51 Irene H. 102
  Jefferson 169 Joe 188
  John D. 199 Joseph 205
  J.D. 225 Lillian F.M. 81
  Lucy 24 Lucy A. 224 Lyda
  Kate 57 Mary 169 Mary F.
  86 Myrtle 157 Nannie W.
  199 Nick L. 81 Rena 55
  Will 179 William R. 188
  (Mrs) 47 ___ 90
Day, Fred Keever 93
  James 93
Deakens, Charlie 225
  Jim 225
Deakin, French 9 Mattie 64
Dean, Frank 257
Deboard, ___ 236
Deck, Eliza 167 Mary N.

Deck (continued)
  W.B. 230
Deen, Madison 79
Defreece, Laura C. 116
Defreese, E.Q. 106 Jennie
  106 Robert H. 106
Delaney, Ford 141 Infant
  243 J.R. 188 Martin 38
  Mary 180 N.J. (Dr) 12
  William 243
Demcy, Clifford 46 John M.
  34 Sarah E. 34
Dempesy, W.P. 217
Dempsey, Ivan G. 217
  Robert A. 230 W.P. 230
Denauff, R.H. 215
  William P. 215
Denney, B.R. 255
  Infant 255
Denton, Kate 57 Robert 207
  Ruth 207 R.C. 207
Depew, Elbert S. 244
  Elijah 69 Ernest 90 E.
  Orville 244 Fannie M. 137
  137 George 117 Haley 142
  Infant 90 James 137 J
  J. Delaney 97 Lillian 69
  Maria C. 37 Matilda 237
  Oscar 90 Ray H. 244 Roby
  137 Sarah J. 117 William
  (Rev) 23
Derey, Laura 241
Detherage, C.C. 78 John T.
  78 Walter M. 78
Dethrage, Wade 46
Dethridge, Bessie 238
  Bessie V. 87
Detron, Annie E. 57
Devalul, J.W. 245
  Daniel 72
Devalut, Elizabeth 250
  James Miller 72 Georgie
  249 Guy E. 235 J.
  Henderson 235 J.M. 235
  Martha E. 152 Mary 127
  Mary E. 44 Samuel P. 235

Devalut (continued)
  S.P. 111 D.R. 65
Dewell, Infant 97 James
  149 Margaret 149
Dezeiern, Louisa H. 78
Dickens, Arthur J. 88
  Harry 88
Dickerson, Charlie 239
  Dora E. 138 Eva 24 239
  Frank 113 Hugh 193 239
  Jessie 113 Mary 151 164
  Robert 3 Walter 113
  Will 113
Dickey, B.F. 73 Mary A.
  73 S.J. (Mrs) 73
Dickinson, Dora E. 83
  Frank 228 Sarah 233
  W.H. 207
Dickison, Thomas 118
Dickson, Allie 68 Charles
  E. 198 Della 252 Edgar
  198 George 195 Horace
  252 John 17 J. William
  74 Noah B. 104 Rae 54
  Sarah A. 195 T. 125
  William B. 104
Dilap, Ira 131
Dillard, Blanch 144 Elbert
  225 E.S. 125 George 69
  Jordan 153 Lonzinda 153
  Ruth A. 225 Wesley 69
  153
Dillon, Alice V. 212
  Phoeba 104
Dillons, Thomas J. 93
Dillow, Elbert 34 Myrtle
  140 Peter 113 Sarah 27
  Simpson B. 181 Simpson
  B. Jr. 181 Thomas J. 113
Dingus, Jenny 256
Diral, Infant 105
  Walter 105
Dishner, Andrew J. 215
  Cora D. 178 Fannie 159
  George H. 121 Infant 173
  John 126 158 215 J.L.

Dishner (continued)
    178 215 237 Kyle D. 173
    Martha 158 Minnie 145
    Palsey 126 Sara A. 121
    William 12 145
Dixon, Bessie 72 Calvin
    249 Eppie 84 Frank 84
    F. Fulton 105 Hugh 72
    Infant 14 John 201 203
    259 Jthan 201 Margareta
    129 Mary A. 259 Maxel 201
    201 Mildred 249 Reuben
    105 Tom 90 W.M. 15
Dizecrn, John 78
Doan, A.B. 211 Nannie E.
    211 Elacnah 69 George 69
    William 69
Dobbins, Lizzie 217
Dobbs, Melvina 105
Dobyns, Lucie 42
Dodd, L.C. 241 R.J. 241
Dolen, A. 187 David 113
    David P. 124 D.P. 103
    Ed 113 Fannie P. 209
    Isaac 124 John N. 124
    187 Mary 192 254 Matilda
    A. 74 Nelson 113 187
    Pixie E. 120
Dolls, Elbert 232
    Rachel 232
Donahue, Ida E. 253
    J. Kyle 253
Donnelly, Katherine 139
Dooley, Martha 13 Mary 154
    W.T. (Mrs) 222
Dorris, Lena Cook 52
Dotson, Arthur Virgil 31
    A.E. 210 Will 80
Dougherty, Grace 197
    Infant 197 J.C. 197
Douglas, Elbert S. 181
    George W. 193 Jacob 181
    J.A. 181 T.J. 193 258
    William 193
Dove, Buckner 137 Charles
    B. 137 Fannie 137

Dove (continued)
    George R. 137 Georgie 39
Dow, Columbus 62
Dowell, Infant 72 73 208
    James 72 73 John A. 137
    Noah 117 Sarah 117
    Thomas 117 Will 208
Dowler, Fannie 55 Isaac
Doyle, Isaac 131 Isaac
    (Mrs) 94 Maud 151
Draper, Elizabeth 206 John
    206 William T. 206
Droke, A.J. 31 A.W. 31
    Catherine 174 Christina
    M. 77 J. Benjamine 39
    J.B. 77 Linnie 173 Ralph
    S. 68 William 157 W.M.
    W.M. 148
Duff, Martha E. 205
Dufreece, Infant 50
Dugger, Fannie 99 Mary 149
Dulaney, Alice 232 George
    198 Hanibel 155 Janie
    199 John 72 Nathan 198
    William R. 181
Duncan, David 143 Dora 217
    Ellen 162 Hannah 187
    James 128 Lydia 74 Susan
    101 257
Dunn, Eva 238 Frank 88
    Hollie 30 Mollie 44 Odom
    C. 88 Samuel 55 Sarah K.
    76 Venita 254
Durham, Emory L. 103 F.D.
    144 Infant 103 221 Marsh
    B. 144 Mary E. 53 Willia
    L. 221 W.M. 119
Dyer, Alice 85 Bessie
    Poore 77 J.R. 85 160
    Lillian B. 73 Nellie 160
    William 92 W.J. 75 W.J.
    Jr. 75 W.P. 73
Dykes, Berdie 228 Elbert
    132 Louisa M. 124 162
    Molly 184 Sallie 251
    Silas G. 251 Susanna 206

Dykes (continued)
 Susie 74 Thomas 110
 W.R. (Mrs) 167
Dyre, Jennie 248 Sarah
 182 195 Sarah A. 170
Eades, Annie Lorena 96
 Charles 96 Cora 44
Eads, Charlie 85 David 111
 David C. 111 Dora Bessie
 111 __ 85
Earhart, Joseph 116 J.T.
 116 R.R. 116 Sidney 15
Early, E.E. 251 Martha 187
Easley, Infant 260 Jane 23
 Lucy A. 82 Nancy 196
 O.M. 89 William W. 260
 W.W. 82
East, Mary 98 Robert W.
 101 Thomas 101 __ 225
Eastman, Charlotty 210
Eaton, George 70 Infant 70
 70 Johnnie 56 Vergie 56
Edmonson, Lula 130
Edwards, Ada Gertrude 2
 Cora 191 David C. 68
 D.C. 169 Ed 168 Gertie 8
 Hannah 181 Infant 68
 Mame 168 May 156
Eggers, Clair 95 Irma 231
 W.D. 231
Elam, Infant 164 W.C. 164
Eldridge, Wallie 155
Eller, John 94 Maggie 99
 Mattie 94 Steven Lee 60
Ellinger, Jearette 121
Elliott, Andrew 94 F.T. 94
 Infant 138 Julia 209
 Montie 138 Sarah J. 104
Ellis, Daniel 19
 Nancy 175
Elsea, Louise 70 Melvin 32
Elsom, Loula 187
Elswick, Catherine 17
Ely, Belle 212
Emerson, David 107
Emmert, Hal 39 John 173

Emmert (continued)
 John W. 173 J.C. 173
 J.W. 247 Mary L. 247
Emmett, Mollie 258
English, Annie May 62
 Charles A. 242 Clara 130
 C.C. (Mrs) 216 Eliza 130
 J.A. 242 Mary 129
Ensley, Sarah 2
Ensor, J. Kass 49 Lizzie
 139 Mary Wilson 140
Eperson, Mary I. 174
Epperson, Elbert 199 Jake
 199 Mary J. 116
Erwin, Charles S. 152
 T.S. 109
Estep, Cora 169 E.M. 147
 250 J.E. 194 Loyd 147
 Susan 250 __ 233
Ettor, Margaret 182
Eubank, Iren 166
Evans, Ella 126 Eva 75
 N.H. (Rev) 75 __ 232
Everett, Cicero E. 234
 H.E. 99 John H. 234
 John V. 99 J.H. 42 99
 W. 234
Ewing, Henry Wood 80
Eyler, C.E. 152 Reesi 152
Fagan, T.J. 43
Fagans, Charlie 232
 Evaline 104 John 163
 232 Samuel H. 258
Faidley, Ed 122
Faine, Jane 172
Fair, Caroline V. 164
 Gussie 198 Harmon 198
 James 70 James N, 198
 Jeanette G. 70 Laura
 Gerturde 11 Sarah P. 164
Fairbanks, Mary 153
Fairfax, Annie E. 183
Falin, Hezakiah 78
 Ludie 187
Falines, Patti 86
Falk, Bordie 159

Falk (continued)
　Infant 159
Falls, Sarah 236
Farifax, R.R. 183
Farr, Bettie 79
Farrety, James 123
　J.A. 123
Farris, Kate 145 Nancy 90
　Ruth 90 53
Farther, Lewis 131
Farthing, Robert L. 236
　R.B. 236 William Y. 236
Feagins, Andrew 258
　J.W. 154
Feagons, Bertie 237
Feathers, Flora 120 Flors
　256 James H. 155 Jennie
　92 John 22 Mary 123 216
　Rahcel 90 Susan 93
　William 158
Felick, Nancy 193
Fellers, Amelia 77
Felts, Joseph 91
Felty, Charles 115 Ella
　100 George W. 186 G.F.
　186 John W. 58
　Margarette 40 Nina V.
　152 R.D. 152
Ferguson, Jane 85 John 2
　Lucil 61 Maggie E. 189
　Margaret 229 Phoebe J.
　177 Walter 62
Fickle, Jane 215
　William 215
Fickles, Cora 1
Fields, Florence 112 Grace
　V. 259 Lonisa 197 Mary
　L. 226 Sam 166 Silas 112
　Steve 72 226 Thomas 259
Filon, Elizabeth 216
Fincher, Elizabeth 220
　Thomas W. 33
Fink, D.P. 128 George 136
　George W. 128 244 Infant
　244 Jacob K. 244 Joseph
　B. 128 Ossel 207 Sarah

Fink (continued)
　136 Thomas B. 115 T.C.
　207 W.E. 244 W.M. 27
　W.R. 115
Fish, Elvira 103 Isaac P.
　174 I.P. 197
　Mary L.O. 174
Fitch, Finnie 184
　Henry 181
Fitsworth, Sam 129
Fitzgerald, Lee S. 247
　Lola 228 Margaret 221
　Willie A. 141
Fitzpatrick, Mary M. 152
Flanigan, C.M. 229
　W.M. 229
Flannery, T.C. 102
Fleener, William 134
Fleenor, Emmie 156 George
　133 infant 258 James 193
　John O. 215 J. 218 J.W.
　100 Katheryn 128 Martin
　128 Mary E. 219 Mary M.
　181 Norah P. 109 Patsy
　189 Ruby 134 Sarah 59
　Selvia M. 193 S.G. 129
　William 14 133
　William W. 258
Flemming, Isaac 175
　J.C. 175
Flencher, Clarence 235
　William 235
Fletcher, Elbert 205 Elia
　V. 239 Homer 205 Louisa
　188 L.C. 168 Stacy 239
　Stacy 239
Flick, Rosy 189
Flynn, Emiline 13
Foalden, Andrew J. 138
　A.J. 83 G.W. 138
　Infant 83 Woodrow W. 138
Fogarty, John 72
　Raymond F. 72
Foglesong, Elias 103
Ford, Annie E. 183 A.O.
　183 B.L. 43 Catherine 32

Ford (continued)
  Dana 206 Darthula M. 71
  Eddie 240 Ernest 202
  Ezekiel 222 F.M. 207
  G.H. 230 Hanna 107 Hazel
  230 Henry 207 Henry A.
  207 H. Arthur 144 Infant
  14 John 14 91 240 Kiltie
  36 Lelas 48 Lelas 48
  Lizzie Naoma 23 Lona 173
  Lula E. 237 Mahaley S.T.
  120 Margaret M. 144
  Marion L. 202 Martha 103
  Mary 121 Mary A. 162
  Mary J. 226 Richard 91
  Sabra 172 William 206
  William H. 206
  Winnie 222 __ 227
Foster, Ella 151
  Nancy 116
Fouch, Aaron J. 82 Clide
  213 Cora 213 Hannah 181
  James 82 John D. 213
Foust, David V. 175
  James E. 175 J.E. (Mrs)
Fowler, Jane 153
Fox, Hannah 239 Lizzie
  59 Magie 232 Nanje 154
Foy, Galdys 244
  William 244
France, Harriett 143
  S.W. 143
Francis, Helen 254
  T.A. 254
Franklin, Charles 98
  Infant 98
Frannell, __ 210
Frazier, David 72 Henry
  Etta 10 James 242 Mary
  32 Melvenia 76 Ollie 201
  221 Rachel A. 72 Cyniha
  238 Flora 250
Frick, Burl 141
  Charles 141
Fritts, Louise 170
  Martin 170

Fritz, Lillie 190 Nancy 20
Fry, Ethel 89 109
  Nannie 140
Frye, Ethel 79
Fugate, C.D. 132 Ester 86
  Francis 132 N.B. 132
  Tennie 257 __ 91
Fulk, Eliza 81
  Sallie H. 55
Fulkerson, Irene 212
  Margaret 215 Selina P.
  212 S.V. 212
Fuller, Erwin 189 Infant
  189 231 I.N. 231
Fulton, Mary E. 186 __ 217
Fulwilder, Abraham 97
  Ethel 97
Gaines, John 155 Lula 126
  Lydia 155 Martha 113
  William H.H. 49
Gains, Mamie F. 86
Galey, Pearl 230
Gallaher, Polly W. 235
  Walter Jr. 237 Walter E.
  237 William 235
Gallenhon, Sarah 128
Galloway, Annie M. 220
  G.H. (Mrs) 223 Infant 35
  71 Jacob 217 J.R. 78
  Lemon 112 Mary E. 91
  Noah 71 109 Ruby I. 217
  Samuel 112 S.P. 71 S.R.
  109 Thomas 103 Thomas M.
  91 130 William 109
Galuding, Ida 140
  Laura B. 140
Galyon, Hamilton 232
  J.R. 204 232 J.R. (Mrs)
  232 Mary B. 204
Gambill, Katie 195 W.W.
  W.W. 195
Gamble, Annie 232
Gammon, Julia 198
Gardner, Alberta 52
Garland, Emeline 209 Joe
  209 Johnathan 50 Laura

Garland (continued)
  255 Mary 209
  Serenal 218
Garrett, Elizabeth 169
  Fanny 171 George 20
  Infant 20 Zilpha 21
  __ 227
Gaulding, Sarah V. 130
  Theodore 140
Gearhart, Edd 220 Johnston
  220 W.E. 220
Geary, Julia 143
Geavins, Lula 230
Geisler, Caroline 259
  Ernest J. 83 Hayns
  Ernest 35 Infant 20 83
  Lucy 48 Margaret A. 59
  Susan 111
Gentry, Betsy 179 E. Roy
  89 Fannie 165 Infant 89
  Lee 57 Lucy 165
George, Ancil 73 Clara 151
  Eliza 73 James 73 John
  151 Mary 151
  Myrtle E. 151
Gibson, Agnes 174 Clem 4
  Infant 119 James 104
  Malindy 4 Margaret W. 86
  Neal 119 Neil 86 S.P.
  220 T.M. 86 William 86
  __ 222
Giles, Jessie F. 242
  Mary L. 183
Gillenwater, Joel C. 72
Gillespie, G.S. 73 John R.
  73 P.F. 73
Gilley, Amanda 144
Gilmore, A.B. 136
  Mary E. 189
Glenn, Bersheba 196
Gloor, Edward 95 Infant 95
Glossip, John 130
Glover, Andrew 57
  Bessie B. 256 Charlie
  129 Dick 140 Ethel 135
  Fannie 171 Hebert 179

Glover (continued)
  Infant 129 Jane 70
  Jennie 122 Jim 179
  Lillie 140 Louisa 146
  Mollie 147 O.F. 122
  Rebecca Ann 46 Rebecca
  A. 217 Sarah 34 Susan
  129 W.M. 167
Goad, Claissa C. 191
Gobble, Fanny 135 Mollie
  146 Sarah A. 215
  Washington 146 Alex 197
Godsey, Alex 197 Andrew 69
  246 Andy 197 Ann 71 Anna
  E. 146 Cain 85 Charles
  Q. 258 259 Charles (Mrs)
  151 Cora L. 137 C.J. 258
  C.Q. 258 Drury S. 259
  Earling M. 219 Ellen 246
  248 E.S. 118 Frank 141
  219 246 Hana 69 Henry P.
  85 Infant 186 Jackson 85
  James C. 258 Jennie 161
  Jessie M. 258 John T.
  186 Johnie F. 199 J.L.
  258 259 J.S. 151
  Lextisue 211 Lillie 141
  Lissie 102 Louisa 208
  Lucie 160 Nellie E. 209
  Rosa 53 W.C. 119 W.J. 26
  209 W.L. (Mrs) 229 W.M.
  137 W.R. 199
Godsy, Phoebe 134
Godwin, Dora 155
Goff, Katie 227 W.L. 227
Goforth, Joseph 16
Goheen, Hezia 202
  John W. 202
Goins, Mary 72 Rose 247
Golf, Martha 248
Golie, Blanch 28
Golloway, William 197
Good, H.P. 116 Lola E. 116
  William R. 116
Goodman, Amanda 156
  Andrew 49 A.H. 225

Goodman (continued)
　Dorthy 144 Fannie 142
　G.R. 115 Infant 225
　Jola 185 Marda 53
　Mary E. 56
Goodwin, B.F. 225
　Loura M. 225
Gornes, Josie 78
　Nelson 78
Goss, Robert 242 R.W. 242
Gott, C.E. 106 Elbert A.
　106 Nannie 118 Rolen P.
　106 W.O. 16
Graham, D.F. 197 201
　Infant 197 201
Grant, Ellen 173 Jackson
　173 John 157 Mary 234
　Nannie 229
Grass, __ 191
Graves, Dr. 127 136 142
　159 170 176 178 183 185
　195 220 235 237 248
Graves, F. (Dr) 103
Gray, Alexander 164
　Burleigh C. 125 Burley
　186 Caroline E. 53 Edith
　Evelyn 83 Elbert 146
　Elizabeth 95 191 Ell 224
　Ellen 146 E.P. 179
　Harriet 175 Infant 186
　238 Isaac 164 Jack 221
　224 James 81 Joe 221
　Joe (Mrs) 224 John 101
　149 John S. 1 Joseph R.
　101 J.S. 238 Laura Pet
　146 Lillie 191 Lucy 70
　Mack 129 Mamie 155 Mary
　149 Mary M. 186 May 81
　Rachel M. 141 Robert 141
　155 Roy 129 Sallie 164
　191 Walter 125 William
　83 Willie (Mrs) 83
　W.H. 221
Green, Amanda 219 Clide
　216 Daniel 50 David 138
　Frank 42 Geneva 198

Green (continued)
　Haskel 216 Hettie 138
　Hiram 157 Infant 182 186
　Jack 182 186 256 James
　62 James 149 Joseph 138
　154 Joshua 77 Kate 122
　Katherine 149 Madison
　Maggie C. 79 Nathan 79
　Richard 154 Sarah F.
　256 Tabor 198 Toben 138
　W.F. 163 __ 235
Greenway, Chassie B. 29
　Nathan 76 Nettie 148
　Theopholis 15
　William C. 76
Greer, Rena 169
Gregg, Annis 183 Charles
　124 162 Debbie J. 204
　Guy 33 John H. 162
　Joseph G. 204 Josephine
　204 Mary E. 124
　Samuel P. 162
Gregory, Dolly 153
Grier, Cecilia 67
Griffin, George 159
　Lillie 209
Griffith, R.W. 205
Grills, Bettie 156 Effie
　162 Henry 156
　Sallie G. 156 197
Grimes, John 32 154 John
　154 Nancy E. 154
Grimsley, Georgie E. 71
　Laura Etta 71 Sam H. 71
Grindstaff, Wilburn 123
Griner, Infant 69 J.W. 69
Grogen, Lillie 168 Myrtle
　168 W.W. 168
Groseclose, Levi 60
Gross, David 112 Eliza 95
　Eliza A. 176 Ellie 111
　Sallie 110 William 95
　Wilson 176
Grow, James W. 204 Joseph
　E. 204 Lucy 204
Grub, Lizzie 66

Grubb, David 231 Jack 21
  James C. 22 John 165
  J.B. Clinton 213
  Mattie 165
Grubbs, George (Mrs) 168
  Martha 236 Owen 123
  Sarah 233 Sophia 168
Grudgington, Milly 109
Gruff, Bruce Adam 50
  Nathaniel 4
Gudger, Katie 227
  Lucile 227
Guess, Stella Gale 41
Guin, Charlotte 10 James
  N. 35 John 11
Guinn, John G. 184
Gump, S.A. 121
Guthrie, Janie E. 245
G___, Elalina 16
Hagan, C.F. 118
Hage, John 137 Dewey 30
  Jack 146 Mary 241
  Robert L. 146
Haidly, A.J. (Dr) 11
Hale, Adiline 104
  Alexander 183 Beck 183
  Bettie 176 Eliza 137
  Fred 47 J. Melvin 177
  J.E.C. 18 Mary 222 Mary
  M. 177 Mike 183 Mose 176
  Phoebe J. 177 Susie 4
  Thomas 79 Will 176
  Will (Mrs) 176
Haley, Thomas 96
  William 96
Hall, Annie M. 214 A.H. 21
  B.B. 199 B.H. 260
  Cromwell H. 205 C.F. 234
  Etta Vestie 83 E.M. 71
  152 Frank B. 205 Hattie
  136 Ida 204 Infant 234
  James 70 Maude 188
  Minnie E. 112 O.M. 205
  Ruth 110 Soloma 89
  Thomas W. 116 William
  260 Willie B.R. 199

Hall (continued)
  ___ 72 215
Hamilton, A.A. 10 Charles
  M. 236 Ed 239 Elizabeth
  251 Fannie 178 George
  95 Infant 89 James B.
  95 236 255 John 239
  Joshua 185 J.A. 214 255
  J.B. 89 Mary 255 Sarah
  89 Thomas 171 William P.
  89 Wilson 21 W.A. 236
Hamlett, J.M. 155
Hammer, Elizabeth G. 149
  James 122124 J.K. 120
  Kate 119 Kizzie 233
  Lizzie 148 Lula 203
Hammett, G.W. 73 Infant 73
Hammons, Callie 100
  Nathan 24
Hampton, Rachel 120
Handcock, Berry 78
  Sarah 79
Hanpt, Kate 80
Hanshaw, Jessee 114
Hansom, M. Elizabeth 10
Hansor, Rachel 257
Harbour, Lillie 197
Hardaway, E. (Mrs) 242
  E.T. 171 Thomas S. 170
Harden, John 84 Noah 84
Hardin, Okie 173
Harding, Lizzie 131
Hardy, Alice 187 Eliza 213
  Erschel 62 Infant 141
  Niles 212 Perry 212 Roy
  188 Strenela 141
Hargass, Mary 105
Hargis, Daniel 156 Feona
  104 John 211
Harker, ___ 192
Harkeroad, Leonard C. 219
Harkerode, Lee 219
Harkleroad, Andrew C. 60
  88 Cynthia A. 171 Daisy
  242 Ella 201 Helen 57
  H.L. 171 Infant 203

Harkleread (continued)
　James M. 159 Jess J. 203
　J.T. 92 Lillie 200
　Maggie 155 Margaret 101
　Mary Ann 68 Mary E. 49
　Owen 101 Pauline 92
　Sarah 176 William L. 68
Harland, Maria 149
　Sarah 221
Harleroad, Sarah 223
Harless, Elizabeth 146
　J.P. 198 W.M. 198
Harmon, Carrie S. 35
　Clair 95 Fred 247 Henry
　Walter 45 Howard 95
　Infant 36 John 95 Luther
　247 Malissa 24 Ralph
　Gentry 10 Sarah 117
　Victoria 185
Harmon, Victoria 185 Helen
　H. 172 Will 232 Zola 232
Harr, Anna 236 Elizabeth
　121 Ellen 31 Frank 27
　George 12 Lola 11 Lydia
　31 L.B. 16 Mary 236
　Medie 22 Rebecca 68
　__ 77
Harrell, L. Beulah 77
Harrigan, Ella 219
　Thomas 92
Harrington, Dan 141
　Elizabeth 126 Joe 247
　Lizzie 231 Nettie 223
　Sallie 141 William 247
Harris, Eva 136 Fannie 164
　Harvey 135 Henry 136 164
　245 Infant 135 Joe 229
　Lonnie 245 Mary E. 229
　Mollie 209 Nellie 245
　Sarah 145 228 Will 164
　__ 203
Harrison, Annie 198
　Coleman 87 Cora 158
　Cyrus 142 Effie 193 199
　J.C. 183 222 J.J. 205
　Martha 130 Mary E. 240

Harrison (continued)
　Matt 87 Mearia 87 Nannie
　149 Nannie J. 222
　Nathaniel 107 W.H. 107
　W.H. (Mrs) 107 __ 207
Harropp, Sarah 186
Hart, J.T. 143 Lawrence
　143 Viola 111
Hartess, John W. 33
Hartman, Polly 95
Hartsel, Viola 160
Hartsock, Anna 96 J.W. 239
　Malissa 184 R.E. 239
　Sallie E. 77 William 235
Harvey, Vice 186
Hass, J.C. 154 W.H. 153
　W.J. 153
Hatcher, Alf 179 A.M. 128
　A.M. (Mrs) 128 Eliza 70
　Eliza Alice 87 Emeline
　127 Estella I. 4 E. 93
　George 246 John P. 246
　Katie 246 Kniciley 5
　Laura J. 179 R.L. 87
　Sallie 225 Sidney 18
　Stacy 48 Tom 225 Tom
　(Mrs) 225 Willie 43
　W.B. 2
Hauk, Allie G. 259 Herbert
　259 Myrtle 152 O.S. 259
Haun, J. 90 Pleas A. 90
　P. 158 Roy N. 158 R.N.
　R.N. 90
Hawk, George D. 74
　Isabeller 223 Ivan L. 86
　James 195 John A. 223
　J.A. 86 223 Martin R. 74
　Nancy Hamilton 95 Robert
　211 Rosana 157 Sarah 28
　Tack 35
Hawkins, Callie R. 101
　215 Joe 248 Mary 222
　Will 248
Hawks, R.E. 151 R.M. 151
　T.M. 151
Hawley, John 242

Hawley (continued)
Magie E. 242
Hayatt, Infant 221 ___ 221
Hayes, Alex 90 153 Edward
H. 100 Effie B. 86
George 100 Henry 90 153
Leon 90 Mary 99
Hayett, Albert 140 Alphard
201 Arthur 148 Hazel 148
Henry 93 James 93 Nannie
93 Preston 201 Robert
140 Edgar 47 Elmer 47
Elmer J. 4 George W. 162
Gretchen 239 G.C. 149
Hal 195 John W. 162 J.
163 Mary 151 Nannie 204
Polly 148 Robert V. 149
R.J. 151 ___ 232
Hays, Dorcen 221 Frank
222 Julia 222 Lucy 222
Mary K.A. 236 Nancy 180
W.H. 236
Hazzard, Cynthia 255
Harrison 214 Mary 6
Wesley 214
Wesley, Jr. 214
Heaberlin, Elbert H. 63
Headen, George E. 29
Heartley, James 165
Heatherly, ___ 241
Hedrick, Clementine 128
Helton, Adeh 184
Hemphill, Infant 98 James
98 210 James L. 210
Henby, Essie 126
Henderlite, George E. 179
George E. Jr. 179 J.H.
179 Florence 170 M.J.
(Mrs) 46 W.M. 193
Hendman, Jennie E. 94
Hendricks, Green 254
Johnson 254 Moses 254
Hendrickson, Lorena 13
Mary 32
Hendrix, ___ 98
Heneger, Infant 107

Heneger (continued)
J.F. Jr. 107 Malinda 73
John H. 226 John L. 226
Henley, Addie 160 Carrie
Ruth 40 Droke 114 Hettie
114 J.M. 241 J.P. 105
Naomi R. 133 Pearl 207
Sam 199 241 Samuel G.
133 W.H. 150
Hennessy, Sarah 121
Henning, Huelah 83
Henninger, J.T. ___ S.L.
255 William P. 255
Henry, Alace 242 Elizabeth
109 Essie 208 James C.
106 Mahaley 86 Robert N.
85 Thornton 209 Visa 182
William 106 ___ 198 237
Hensley, A.D. 175 Infant
175 Irene 172 Maryan 246
William 210
Henson, Jane 173 Joe 114
236 John 114 Luther 236
Mollie 236 S. (Mrs) 111
Herren, R.D. 184
Walter C. 184
Hervell, Andrew 100
Hess, Mary Jane 100
Heyett, Infant 65 66 133
James 133 Polly 133
Hickman, Ann 142 Bersheba
14 C.H. 130 Elizabeth
239 Fanny 83 George 14
Infant 51 74 130 243
Janett 256 Joseph 174
J.D. 105 J.T. 239 Martha
E. 165 Nancy 23 Sam E.
206 Simon 239 243 S.E.
206 Thomas 242
Wilma E. 206
Hickok, Caroline 220
Hicks, Abe 100 Alice 80
Annie Loura 15 A.M. 94
Belle 124 C.M. 89
Earnest 207 Eliza 203
Elizabeth 141

Hicks (continued)
　Elizabeth K. 157 Ellen 19
　Ellen 255 Ethel 253
　Fannie 218 Frank 94
　George 250 253 George W.
　193 Glen 124 Henry 247
　H.B. 255 Infant 21 124
　Isaac 227 Jacob N. 25
　James 227 Jesse L. 238
　John 110 207 John Elbert
　80 John W. 55 193 J.E.
　122 J.W. 110 Katie B. 227
　Lester 231 Lillian 91
　Lorina 133 Marshall 238
　Mary 88 Matilda 9 Mattie
　114 M. 238 N. Darhula 34
　Rachel I. 94 Ruben 80
　122 Stella 247 Susan 45
　Tommy 19 William P. 122
Hight, ___ 247
Hikin, Harriett 129
Hill, May 227 Nora 97
　Pearl 173
Hillard, Evaline 148
Hilliard, Robbie 18 Silas
　139 William O. 139
　W.O. (Mrs) 139
Hillman, Sabra C. 147
　Walker 147
Hilton, A.S. 250 C.F. 96
　103 Daniel 37 Daniel T.
　16 Frank M. 250 George
　H. 103 Infant 2 John H.
　145 Lelona 2 Lizzie 42
　Lula 152 Mary 96 Robert
　145 Robert C. 145 Lula
　152 Mary 96 Robert 145
　Robert C. 145
　William 103
Hina, Mountiful 122
Hinard, Fannie 141
Hinderson, Luther 38
Hines, James Clive 39 J.J.
　181 William C. 181
Hinkle, William 101
Hitchens, John 203 John

Hichens (continued)
　(Mrs) 203 Sevanius 203
Hite, Bethel G. 144 Evalin
　245 Gastona 70 Infant 8
　Jackson 132 Julia 148
　Maggie 44 Mairah 240
　Mary Jane 26 Matilda 187
　Nora May 138 Rebecca 122
　Tenny 23 Theodore H. 122
　William T. 144
　Zolia E. 122
Hix, George 202 Mary L. 69
　Mollie 202 Nancy 202
Hixon, Rockett V. 242
Hobaugh, Mary A. 92
Hobbs, C.D. 143 Eliza J.
　138 Ella 146 Gertrude 15
　J.A. 138 Mattie S. 29
　Nathan 96 ___ 231
Hobson, Arthur 244
　Jake B. 56
Hodge, Anderson 191
　Barbara 140 C.M. 10
　E. 235 G.H. 218 Hubert
　180 Jim 175 John 191
　Julia 180 Landon 235
　Lena Mae 235 Louise 22
　Lucy 175 Mary 141
　Nora 142
Hodges, Eliza A. 76 Evan
　135 Hester 68 James 142
　John 77 John C. 220
　Laura G. 77 Lee (Mrs)
　138 Loyd 135 Lucy 48
　Marion 220 Pearl 48
　Sara 135
Hoebauch, Sallie 185
Hoffman, Aron 115
Hogan, Susa H. 257
　William R. 257
Holden, John 116
Holder, Ella 252
Holdsclaw, Mary 191 Ruth
　191 West 191
Holley, Anna Belle 196
　James 194 Nora 119

Holley (continued)
　Wade 196 Wade E. 196
Holly, Martha 12
Holmes, Lillie 168
　Mary E. 42
Holoman, Callie 223
　M.E. (Mrs) 223
Holt, Belle 20 Emeline 175
　Emma 105 Infant 203
　Lessie 23 Louvena 8 L.E.
　(Mrs) 9 Tom 203 Will 105
　W.A. 8
Holton, Infant 114 260
　J.T. 114 260 Lizzi 94
Holtsclaw, Lydia 165
Homel, John 200 Rosa 194
Hommel, Rosa 194
　Rosa E. 192
Honecut, Litha 162
Honk, Barbra 111 Don 111
Honser, Sallie R. 37
Hood, Annie 89 Annie Eldon
　71 Benjamin F. 156 B.F.
　103 Cora 222 Cynthia M.
　213 Dutton 115 156 219
　Henry H. 93 James 127
　Johnathon 156 J.D. 208
　Lafayette 89 Nancy 138
　177 Nellie 2 Robert L.
　93 Sinora F. 208 Thomas
　M. 213 T.O. 93
Hoofnagle, Emily L. 161
Hooper, Infant 234 Mat 234
Hoover, A. 75 Bettie 73
　Claud 224 Elizabeth 81
　George 3 Infant 96
　Infant 224 Jacob 96 181
　Lucy 137 Mattie 91
　Valentine 208
Hopkins, Adeline 121 James
　121 Malinda 254 Martha
　208 Mattie 210
Horn, Cecil 59 David 33
　Ida M. 207
Horn, Missouri C. 97
Horne, Alice B. 213

Horne (continued)
　A.P. 117 Charles 109
　Elizabeth 117 George 134
　G.W. 134 J.C. 213 Lelia
　E. 201 Sarah 74
　Simon 109
Horner, Annie May 84
　Martha 166 William 166
Horton, Arthur 207 Bradis
　158 Cecil 160 Charlie
　207 Eugenens 191 Infant
　160 Julia 154 Martha 107
　Prince E. 191 William 66
Hoss, James 200
Houchin, Martha 80
Houck, J.W. 189 Laura B.
　202 Rebecca 202
Houk, Beechie 213 C.A. 213
Houke, Kate 157
Houpt, George 243
　Rebecca E. 243
Houser, Mina 203
Houshell, Alpha 137
Housley, Viola 171
Houston, Alex 250 Charlie
　250 Sarah 250
Houtz, Lulu May 30
Howell, Sarah 183
Huddle, Jacob 103
　Margaret 103
Hudgens, Florrie 108
　__ 183
Hudson, Alice 131 Charles
　R. 106 Clarence E. 49
　Clyde E. 227 Ella 226
　Fannie 148 George 66
　Infant 173 James 227 Jim
　173 Mary 140 201 Nannie
　81 Polly J. 106 Robert
　148 218 William L. 238
　Willie 55 W.J. 238
Hues, William 123
Huffman, Infant 49
　Mary C. 15
Hughes, Bettie 142 Daniel
　W. 131 Elenor 119 Infant

Hughes (continued)
  Infant 148 James P. 148
  Jese 82 Jesse 81 J.P.
  Maria 246 O.F. 41
  Preston 153 Samuel 41
  S.F. 15 Theodocia 90
  William 123 ___ 260
Hughett, Etta 145
Hughs, George R. 193
Huhn, Malinda 70
Hull, Amelia 226 David 68
  David W. 226 D.H. (Mrs)
  226 John C. 12 Noah 168
  Rebecca M. 68 Rolland
  226 Vernie 225 ___ 227
Hullett, Paisey L. 82
Hulse, Mary 128
Humphrey, ___ 83
Humphreys, Eula D. 192
  James H. 15 John 155
  P.G. 5 Amanda 159
  Lucinda 155
  William T. 192
Hunley, Nancy 96 104
Hunt, Adam 40 Charlie 258
  Ernest V. 84 George 14
  Harold P. 258 Infant 84
  James C. 214 James H. 26
  John 256 258 Kate M. 214
  Lizzie 93 M.L. (Mrs) 108
  Parmelia 113 Sallie 214
  Thomas 14 William M. 256
Hunter, Agnes 75 Hudson
  238 Infant 238
  Selina 212
Huntington, Mary 179
Hurst, Cordie Ray 88 Flem
  H. 171 George T. 88
  George W. 88
Husley, Nancy 254
Huston, Martha 194
Hutsell, J.C. 172
Hutson, Charles 198
  Charlie 176 Claud 198
  Claude 176 Dorrie 88
  Elsie 243 Jim 247

Hutson (continued)
  Johnson P. 198 Lillie 72
  Martha 230 Mary 200
  Samuel N. 247
Hyatt, Charlie 163 Vennie
  163 Edward 147 Sam 147
Ingle, Infant 62 L.D. 62
Inman, Infant 156 Lee 152
  156 Lola 151 William 151
Irvine, Eliza 148
Irwin, George W. 152
Isam, Ursula 162
Iseley, A.L. 74
Isenberg, Daisy 94
  Jacob I, 204
Isenbert, A.J. 204
  Nicholas 204
Isley, Alice Marie 33
  Clarence 257 Hattie 257
  J.S. 184 Mary R. 8
  William 157
  William I. 157
Jackson, A.S. 74 Effie P.
  234 Elizabeth 158 James
  251 Jim 169 J.W. 187
  Nathan 102 Ora E. 187
  Priscilla 31 Samuel 132
  Sara 169 Will 169
Janes, C.P. 45 Elizabeth
  253 Laura 28 L.W. 36
  Martha E. 28 Robert 253
Jarret, Emma L. 105
  Sanday 105
Jayn, Elizabeth 206
Jayne, Hattie J. 27
Jefferson, Leon 150
  Windham 150
Jenkins, Ben H. 82
  Benjamin 82 Bob 143
  Bonnie L. 187 Debby 165
  Ed 249 Elbert 187 Evalyn
  M. 207 G.E. 143 Harnin
  249 Harsie 25 Infant 185
  James 25 Laura 218 Maud
  114 Mollie 244 Nathaniel
  207 Robert 143

Jenkins (continued)
  Robert T. 143 Rollin 164
  Theodore 82 Thurston 31
  William 143 185
Jennings, Cora 230
  E.L. 115 Infant 115
Jessie, Angie 249 Blanch
  249 Blanche 244 Jess 244
  Jess (Mrs) 244 Mattie E.
  45 Will 249 ___ 186
Jeter, Infant 165 James 55
  John 198 Lydia 165 Mary
  206 Mike 165 Paul 198
Jett, Irene 119
Jobe, Francia E. 101 Mary
  76 Minnie 174 Rice 101
  Will 174 William M. 101
John, Madison 147
Johnson, Ada 122 Allen 212
  Anderson 51 Annise 65
  Avery 256 A.C. 159
  Bessie 199 Blanche 153
  Carl D. 222 Cecil 196
  Charlcie L. 149 C.E. 222
  Edward S. 57 Elic 40
  Ethel 87 Fannie L. 186
  Flora E. 222 George L.
  170 Hanna 12 Hannah 51
  Herbert L. 222 Infant 17
  James 122 155 196 James
  A. 122 144 James P. 122
  Joe W. 163 John 199 John
  A. 170 Julia 239 J.E.
  149 Lucy 202 Maggie 247
  Matilda 249 Nannie 50
  157 Peter 168 Rich 155
  R.M. 85 Sam 222 Sam F.
  159 Surilla 122 Susan 64
  S.R. 222 Virginia B. 163
  Walter 69 196 Wanita E.
  159 W.H. 122 ___ 91 226
  245
Johnston, Mary E. 192
Jones, Anna Mae 235 Annie
  B. 208 Benjamin 135
  Bernita 215 Bill 196

Jones (continued)
  Bob 145 Charles 128 234
  Charles F. 35 Charley 21
  Clide 197 C.H. 236 C.P.
  (Dr) 216 Daniel 213
  Donald B. 259 Dove 164
  D.B. 69 122 Emma 182 Esy
  John 134 Evilen C. 145
  E.T. 102 Floyd 20 Gay 81
  George 100 166 180
  George J. 149 Grover 100
  G.W. 72 83 216 Haskell
  200 201 Infant 20 110
  145 189 201 208 Jacob 54
  James K. 145 Jane 75 105
  139 Jay Fred 120 Jennie
  258 John 34 147 John
  Henry 59 Jonathon 216
  Joseph 75 149 Joseph C.
  149 Joseph T. 208 Julia
  90 J.H. 209 J.L. 118
  J.R. 176 Leila E. 200
  Loucinda 206 Lucy 199
  213 L.W. 36 Mahala 254
  Mamie 158 Margaret
  Louise 52 Margie 69 Mary
  4 129 164 166 Minnie 178
  Mollie 125 Mollie C. 72
  Morrel 52 Nancie C. 236
  Oscar 147 Palmer G. 120
  Peter 88 Quinten V. 120
  Raugleigh 189 R.W. 102
  Sallie 84 Sallie L. 128
  Saphina 236 Sara M. 208
  Sarah 17 211 Susie 216
  S.C. (Mrs) 56 Thomas H.
  210 Thomas (Mrs) 161 210
  Tom 208 210 Tom (Mrs)
  208 T.D. 132 Urbana H.
  132 Viola 160 Walter 213
  259 Wiley 259 W.E. (Dr)
  85 W.H. 120 218 W.T. 110
  W.W. 215 ___ 165
Jordan, Dr. 174 Hester 112
  Stella 99 Walter 99
Joyce, Gladys 194

Joyce (continued)
  Infant 227 John 89
  Ora Anna 192
  W.H. 192 194 227
Joyner, Adeline 138
Kagle, Isaac 133 Magie 189
  Mary 189
Kanah, E.K. 259
Kaylor, L.P. 135
Keaton, Rauley 246
Kee, Samuel 98 W.M. 98
Keeling, Martha 172
Keen, Eliza 69
Keener, Frank 84 Fred 230
  G.G. (Mrs) 58 Nina 163
Keesee, Mattie 94 R.M. 94
  W.B. 94
Keesling, Infant 238 John
  A. 87 J.A. 238 Madeline
  3 W.D. (Mrs) 256
Keeton, Fannie 209
Kegley, Bessie G. 188
Keith, Allen 138 Edith 203
  Lena 138 Martha 194
Keller, Cora 214 Lucey M.
  169 Martin 169 Lannie
  207 Will 157
Kelsey, Charles N. 194
  C.M. 150 Sallie E. 150
Kendoff, William F. 116
Kene, Abraham A. 106
  Isaac A. 106
Kenedy, Elizabeth 79
Kennedy, C.O. 51 E.B. 121
Kenney, Samuel B. 112
  Wade K. 112
Kerin, Katherine 139
  Montie 179
Kern, James F. 202
  Oscar J. 202
Kesery, Peter Mimish 56
Keshier, David 87
Kester, Polly 91
Ketron, Alice Agatha 55
  A.B. 201 A.C. 181 A.E.
  (Mrs) 101 Blanche A. 195

Ketron (continued)
  Della 234 Elizabeth 15
  Ella 198 Eula 138 Ida
  202 Infant 144 James C.
  196 Joe 230 Joseph 196
  Maggie 79 Malinda 85
  Mary C. 230 Maud E. 15
  Melvin A. 49 Nora 169
  O.E. 144 Philip 230
  Suella 15 S.G. 195 T.M.
  79 Walker D. 49 William
  162 W.D. 27
Key, G.M. 148
Keys, Sarah 230
Kibler, Steve 175
Kidd, Cora 249 Eliza J.
  119 W.J. 76 119
Kidwell, Elija 222 W.H. 8
Killinger, ___ 179
Kincer, Ella 168
Kindrick, Mollie 150
King, Amanda 103 Barbara
  196 Bertie 135 Bessie E.
  159 Bettie D. 5 Corda
  111 David O. 120 Dorothy
  203 Dottie 257 Elanor
  Elisha 195 Elizabeth M.
  19 Ella 89 E.W. 235
  George 7 Gladys V. 120
  G.W. 159 195 Irene V.
  195 Jacob L. 120 John L.
  259 John P. 103 259
  Kittie 128 Lester 36
  Lila 133 Lucinda 91 Lue
  243 Martha A. 103 Mary
  36 97 234 Mattie Oliver
  203 Maud J. 119
  Priscilla 220 Robert
  (Mrs) 46 Rutledge 111
  R.F. 19 T.C. 91 114
  William 235 William H.
  259 ___ 190 220
Kinkead, Mary 3
  W.D. (Mrs) 60
Kiss, John 130 Julia 130
Kistner, Charles 139

Kistner (continued)
  Elizabeth 139 Hiram 139
  John 139 Sarah A. 257
Kitts, Cora K. 193 Ganim
  193 Nathaniel G. 193
Kitzmiller, John 36 165
  Judson 36 J.M. 165 M.A.
  165 Stachis 165
  Stasha 165
Kriger, S.S. 186
Kuhn, Joseph 70
Kuhnart, J.G. (Mrs) 75
Kuyle, Elizabeth 85
Kyle, Charles H. 181 David
  W. 111 J.W. 181 182 Mary
  111 Robert 88 111
Lacy, Elizabeth 133
  Emeline 69
Ladd, J.R. 120 249
Lady, George W. 76 Infant
  234 J.D. 54 Mary E. 8
  Pet 173 Richard C. 234
  William 76 __ 188
Lambert, Ethel 182 Nannie
  E. 67 Sarah 182
Lampkin, Beatrice P. 166
  Walker 166
Lampkins, Callie 246 Floyd
  253 George 97 Helen 253
  Infant 196 Samuel 97
  Walker 196 253
Lane, Buck 116 Infant 32
  J.L. 222 Lola Birdwell
  60 Margaret 243 Mary 160
  Mildred 145 Nancy 68 219
  Samuel 116 William 116
  145 __ (Mr) 4
Langhorne, Elizabeth 214
Langley, James 161
  John 161
Langorne, Matilda 167
Large, Pattie 254
  Polly 51
Larkins, Infant 61
  John 115
Latture, David 169

Latture (continued)
  Susan 258 259 Will 169
Laughtus, Harvey 25
Lavison, Viv 10
Lawson, Callie 250 Christa
  B. 260 C.W. 260 Kittie
  110 Zina 114
Lay, Mary 193
Layne, George 179
Leatherwood, Mary E. 157
Lece, Bob P. 228 W.M. 228
Ledbetter, Alfred 171
  Modest 171
Ledford, Eliza 159
Lee, Edna 78 Edward 78
  W.W. 100
Leedy, James B. 105 L.B.
  84 Samuel 105
Leeper, L.F. 244 Robert
  244 Sallie M. 244
Lenard, Polly 87
Lenton, Fred 171 Jane 171
  Mattie 171
Leonard, Abe 12 Abram 126
  A.C. 150 Benjamin F.
  188 Bert 175 B.B. 174
  B.F. 188 Carl 209
  Catherine 117 Cynthia
  101 C.A. 252 David 251
  Ed 175 Ewell 156 Casper
  161 Hattie 126 Helen 252
  Ike 56 Infant 209 I.B.
  38 James 26 J.J. 178
  J.M. 161 J.M. (Mrs) 158
  K.A. 175 Lilburn 138
  Lura Lee 56 Margaret 27
  51 182 Mattie L. 150
  Mike 156 M.B. 174 Nancy
  175 Noah 126 Olena 188
  O.E. 252 Penelopia 174
  P.H. 161 Rauster 251
  Rebecca 253 Sallie 138
  Susie 145 S.K. 233
  W.F. 156 __ 150 239
Leroy, J.H. 126 J.H. (Rev)
  137 M. Ellen 137

Lerue, E. (Mrs) 92
Leslie, John 194 John J.
  31 Sarah 194
Lessley, S.P. 159
Lester, Infant 33 Lydia
  173 Pearl 200 201
Lethco, Chalmas M. 124
  C.L. 124 Ethel 212 E.F.
  212 Fannie 213 John 213
  Sallie 213 Sandy A. 124
Lewis, A.P. 203 Elizabeth
  176 F.L. 176 Hattie Lee
  203 Pearl Beard 74
  Tom 203
Light, Albert G. 138 177
  Arlie L. 214 A.G. 94 115
  Basil F. 250 Cecil C.
  156 Delia P. 207 Della
  C. 156 Emeline 242 Eva
  173 247 George W. 94 214
  250 G.W. 250 Henry (Mrs)
  14 Infant 94 John R. 156
  J.E. 142 Mabel Ann 113
  Nancy 115 Nora M. 144
  Pearce 207 Samuel 49
  Thomas 15
Lillard, Jordan 114
Lilley, Andy 124 A.J. 110
  Bill 148 Clarence 148
  Clide 124 David B. 110
  David (Mrs) 110 Tena 221
  Josie 201 M.L. 201
Lincolnfelt, Jess 142
Linconfelt, James 142
Lindsey, Feubia 208
  M.J. 132
Lineweaver, Catherine 230
  Henry 230
Ling, __ 144
Linkons, Pearl 129
Lipps, Cage 139 G.S. 133
  Hiram 55 Infant 139
Lisemay, Alfred K. 14
Lisenbey, Sarah J. 215
Lisenby, Ida J. 260
Lita, J.W. 196

Lite, Clarence 84 Eva 227
  Georgie 10 Ida 167 Maxie
  84 Mollie 225
Little, Bettie 228 George
  80 Henry 80 Laura 80
  Leonard 187 Sarah E. 230
  W.J. 82
Littleford, John H. 40
  Richard 121 Willis 121
Litton, Emerson 240
  Loura 240 Margie 240
  Oliver 240
Litz, Henry 97 Joel 196
  John H. 196 Loucinda 57
Lloyd, Woodson 91
Lockett, Mary 136
Lockhart, William 186
Lockwood, E.A. 153
  E.M. 153 Zelotis 153
Logan, Lizzie 202
Logins, P.H. 220
  P.H. (Mrs) 220
Lomax, George 217 Lizzie
  217 Mary C. 217
Londy, Norman P. 128
Lonet, E.D. 20 Infant 20
Long, Earl J. 174 Ellen B.
  108 Frank J. 174 James
  74 108 Joseph 83 Lucinda
  74 L. 83
Longacre, Matilda 141 142
Longley, Lizzie M. 223
  Samuel 223
Lossip, Sarah 140
Loudewill, John 76
Loudy, Claten 21
Louis, Winny 205
Love, Alfred 118 Alice 85
  Anna 86 Buford 26
  Georgie 25 James 56 146
  Jane 194 Nancy 156
  Thearthur M. 146 William
  G. 118 W.G. (Mrs) 118
Lovegrove, Burnie 39
Lowe, Annie J. 82 A.J. 82
  Harry 24 N.L. 166

Lowery, Susan 221
Loyd, Adrian A. 189
  Carrie A. 106 Charlie
  29 J.L. 189 Katherine
  200 Mary 4 Pearl 167
  Sallie 170 Stephen W.
  170 Venia 260
Lucas, Allie 109
  Linda A. 109
Lunceford, Laura 248 Mary
  Mat 114 Syndy 79 __ 79
Lundy, C.E. 128 Louisa 177
Lunons, Will 106
  William M. 106
Luster, Edna 147 James 210
  Jim 207 Tom 252
Luttrell, Infant 126
  Jessie J. 62 S.M. 126
Lyle, Belle 85
Lynn, Charles A. 204 James
  204 Joe 8 John G. 29
  Sallie E. 22 S.B. 204
Lyon, Thomas 120
Lyons, Beulah Edith 53
  Landon 146 Mary 109
Madon, Pearl 216
Magee, Julia 243
Mahaffey, Infant 15
Mahatha, Everett 186
  James 186
Maiden, D.W. 202
Malone, Callie 228 Ellen
  127 F.B. 194 F.L. 241
  Infant 12 29 John 237
  Josie 217 Julia A. 194
  Robert 228 V. 228
Malonee, Alfred M. 90
  R.F. 90
Maness, Mitchell 149
Mann, Mary 188
Manuel, Canzadia 108
  Cawzadia 74 Mary 105
Marce, Jane 140
Marden, Emma 95
Marion, Dorth 144 Eliza
  97 Frank H. 144

Marion (continued)
  Mathey 159 __ 144.
Markland, Sarah 123
Marks, Jack (Mrs) 186
  Tina 130
Marsh, Ida 52 John 179
  Luther C. 179 Mandie
  179 Sarah 153
Marshal, Ben 172 Frank 172
Marshall, E.L. 241 Infant
  241 Mary L. 194
Martin, Alfred 237 Bell 93
  Charles P. 93 Clarence
  250 Clyde Paul 80 Conias
  216 Ed K. 134 Edna 180
  Ed 80 Elnora 216 E.K.
  145 Glen 112 John 237
  J.A. 180 Ralph K. 134
  Rosa 216 Sarah E. 145
  U.G. 112 Verden R. 93
  Wilburn E. 180
Marton, Ellen 172
Mason, __ 228
Mass, Abraham 178 Ananias
  178 John 183
Massengill, Jane 5 Norman
  148 Sam 148
Massey, Catherine 75
  Henderson 113 Lucy 13
  Wash 75 William A. 113
  W.E. 113
Massingale, Precilla 247
Massingill, H.H. 134
  Jane 165
Massy, Ella K. 257
  John 257
Master, Victoria 19
Matherly, Fannie 257
  Garfield 257 George W.
  257 Mary J. 116
Mathews, Mary 195
Mathis, J.C. 81
Mattox, Nannie 9
Mauk, Andy 217 Iva C. 145
  John 226 Sarah 217
Maury, Catherine E. 98

Maury (continued)
  C.E. 73 Katherine
  A. 73 Mary 98
  Thomas W. 73
Mawk, Bessie 221 Gilbert
  221 Sallie 221
Maxwell, Bettie M. 81
  Clarence 117 Jake 117
Mayne, Henry 165
Mayo, Anna 247 Thomas 247
  Walter 247
Mays, Bill 172 George 171
  Jake 171 Jake 171 Jim
  228 Julie 211 J. (Ms)
  147 Nat 125 Ollie 228
  Ora 198 William 125
Mayse, J.A. 139
Maze, Mollie 67
McAfee, Hester 205
McCamey, Mollie 152
McCaney, Infant 110 Jullie
  112 Sam 110
McCannis, ___ 243
McChessney, M.W. 120
McClain, Minnie Pearl 31
McClaury, Mollie 148
McClay, Mary 40
McClellan, Belle 62 C.T.
  258 Jane 164 John 258
  J.B. 153 J.H. 153 Robert
  153 Robert W. 258 A.B.
  200 Octar 200
  Octar (Mrs) 200
McClellern, Abraham 113
  John 113
McClure, P.F. 71
McColley, Melvina 225
McConnell, Arther G. 231
  David 149 George 149
  Lillie B. 231 Mary 204
  Sue 149 W.P. 142
  W.S. 142
McCorkle, J.J. 130
  Martha F. 130
McCormick, C.M. 221 Infant
  221 James L. 217

McCormick (continued)
  J.L. (Mrs) 217 R.B. 217
McCoy, Mary 171 Rebecca J.
  167 Will 184
McCracken, George 190
  Gladys 190 John 190
  Sallie 210
McCrary, Columbus 124 Dora
  Y. 162 Edward 124 George
  C. 49 John 127 Liza C.
  130 Lizzie 127 Lum 130
  L.B. 196 Margaret 28
  Sallie 24
McCue, Charles W. 71 John
  M. 71 J.H. 71
McCulley, Beatrice 94
  Jeremiah P. 94 Jerry 59
  Lillie A. 82 S.N. 76
McCullough, Sallie 250
McCully, Elizabeth 23
McCurry, Belle 252 George
  233 John 233 L.B. 233
McDaniel, John 38
McDowell, B.S. 131 Irene
  131 John 131
McElyea, Alice 253
  Badger 252
McFaw, Martha Jane 31
McFerris, Jospeh J. 174
  M.M. 174 Samuel 174
McGarry, Annie 118 Jud E.
  38 R.J. 140 Sarah E. 66
McGavock, Mary 168
McGee, George 202
  James 202
McGentry, Lucy 176
McGoldric, John 47
McGowen, G.V. 244
McGuffie, Mamie 155
McGuinn, Martha 234
McHorris, J.C. 150
McIntosh, George 134 James
  134 Lucy 243 M.B. 134
  Robert 24
McKay, Clara 94
McKenzie, D.C. 255 H.W.

McKenzie (continued)
 H.W. 220 John 255 John M.
 185 John Ross 185
 J.C. 185
McKinndy, Nat 114
McKinney, Benjamin H. 187
 Infant 114 James 194
 Johnathan 194 Mollie 36
 Zolla 187 Addie L. 5
 Annie 130 Annie M. 91
 Maud 58 William L. 88
McLaney, Nanny 124
McMahan, Bertie E. 237
McMillan, G.W. 130 Henry
 130 J.C. 205 S.L. 130
McMin, Infant 156 O.L. 156
McMurray, E.L. 75 Joel 210
 Martha 210 Nelson W. 75
McMurry, A.G. 172 Henry
 172 Joal 144 145 163
 J. 166 Ocia 172
 Sallie 166
McNeil, E.S. 87
 Lillian 87
McNutt, Infant 135 Letcher
 50 T.A. 135
McPherson, Frank 128
 Joseph F. 128
McPoland, Nell 98
McQueen, R.C. 45
Meadow, Alice 150
 Wildie 150
Meadows, Mary 211
Melear, Infant 33
Melior, Nancy 122
Mellon, Horace 111
 Mollie P. 111
Meltzer, Lizzie 115
Merrill, Emma 115
Merry, Bill 122
 Elizabeth 42
Messick, Mary 188
Metcalf, Allen 142
 Mary M. 137
Micklas, Sarah 17
Milam, W.J. (Mrs) 123

Milam (continued)
 James 108 Martha E. 108
Milard, Sallie 9
Miles, Dave 134 166
 George S. 166
Milhorn, Annie 153 G.W.
 205 Henry 182 Infant 237
 Mary K. 224 Nora 205
 Sealey E. 182
 William 237
Millard, C.B. 53 Dr. 163
 Frank 3 J.B. 160 170
Miller, Alvin 111 Andrew
 100 102 Anna Jeeter 11
 A.M. (Dr) 147 A.S. 99
 Barbara 26 Bonnie A. 178
 Charlotte 176 David 129
 D.M. (Dr) 33 Godfrey 118
 Grover 100 Grover W. 102
 Infant 118 James 75 254
 Jane 99 243 Jane C. 259
 Jean 143 Jeasie 64 Jesse
 259 John 88 Joshua 219
 J. Parks 25 Margaret 139
 Martin (Mrs) 209 Mary 79
 Miles 45 Nora 3 Perry 34
 Polly 219 Rhena 92
 Robert H. 75 Sam 107
 Samuel B. 56 Sarah M.
 249 Susan 9 129 S.W. 232
 Thomas 254 William 61
 William R. 260 W.H. 111
 W.H. 176 ___ 111
Millerd, Sallie E. 55
Millhorn, Grace E. 238
 Harrison 170 Henry Clay
 70 Minnie 76 Nancy A. 70
 Ray 76 Robert L. 170
Milliom, John M. 195
 Virginia D. 112 Mary 102
Mills, Mollie C. 187
 Pearl 85 87
Milsap, Fannie 157
 Walter 157
Minga, James 1
Mingea, Marinda 193

Mingus, Will 162
Minnie, Kathleen 47
Minnick, Cora 163
　Elizabeth 71 Emma 71
　Isaac 101 Jake 182 James
　K.P. 11 Jim 71 Kate 87
Minoy, Emmatin C. 152
Minton, Oliva 48
Mise, F.S. 205
Mitchell, Alice 196 200
　A. 180 Bessie L. 103
　Charles 253 Clara 120
　Claud 123 Columbus 97
　David 200 Ed 88 Ellie
　97 Etta 72 73 Floyd 144
　253 Henry 88 Hiram 243
　Isiah 217 James 200
　Julian 163 J. Walter 163
　J.J. 222 Millie 88
　Nellie 196 Ollie 198
　Perlina 200 Robert L.
　217 Ruby Mae 144 Sallie
　A. 222 Sarah 83 Turk 90
　William 42 Yetava 252
　___ 97
Moats, Thomas B. 111
　Willie B. 111
Mobley, Mary 79
Mock, Arthur 248 Arthur
　(Mrs) 248 Isaac 59
　Mary 25
Moerly, M.B. 117
Moffit, Andrew T. 195
　Dan 195
Moffitt, Gertrude 247
Momel, John M. 65
Mondy, Bert 127 James W.
　127 Mary B. 214
Mongle, Lynn 125
Monk, Emaline 35 Emma 10
　Ossie 214
Monroe, Evaline 81 Henry
　M. 107 Robert 81
　W.H. 107
Monteith, Julina 136
Montgomery, C. 75 C.M. 148

Montgomery (continued)
　Mamie 148 M.J. 132
　Sallie 6
Montieth, Mark 191
Moody, Adam 212 Amanda
　Ethel 72 74 Annie 1
　Carrie A. 170 Clarence
　H. 189 Dalton Delaney
　68 D.C. 189 Edna 189
　Eliza Bishop 212
　Elizabeth 22 Ethel 207
　George 152 George W. 106
　G.W. 72 74 Infant 208
　J.R. 208 J.S. 135 Lula
　152 Martha E. 74 Mary
　79 Roxy M. 152 Sallie
　208 Thomas 135 V.W.B.
　135 William H. 106
　William L. 68
　W.H. 106 170
Mooer, Agnes 96
Moore, Alfred 76 Alice 136
　Anne 113 A.P. 126 Beky
　11 Bertha 232 Ebonezer
　M.P. 188 Elizabeth 92
　Fuller 232 Hattie May 89
　Hazel Lynn 99 Infant 51
　150 James 51 108 121 188
　James S. 108 Junior 232
　J.A. 76 128 J.T. 221
　Leonda F. 221 Louisa 4
　Maggie 41 Mart 92 Martha
　76 May 192 Nancy E. 128
　Nathan 76 Nathan T. 183
　Ray C. 99 R.C. 99 183
　Thomas 150 Vollie 57
　William 183 William A.
　204 William G. 11 W.A.
　204 W.M. 202 ___ 122
Moorman, Harriett J. 47
More, Cliff 199
　Johnathon 199 Susie 199
Morefield, Bessie 111
　Callie 166 196 253 Jack
　246 John C. 80 Joseph
　80 Landon 160

Morelock, Ada 165 Alpha
258 C.H. 252 Hannah 233
Infant 252 Martha 90
Matilda 115
Morely, E.L. 117 E.W. 117
Moretz, John 79
Morgan, Dr. 152 Elizabeth
259 E.P. 108
Morley, Eva C. 210
Morrell, Abe 183 Albert 66
Annie 199 A.B. 129
Billie 82 Brooks 206
Brooks M. 202 Burtie 101
B.W. 245 Catherine 77
Dana 156 Dorsey 156 202
Dosie 197 Ellen 38
Fannie 212 Frank 2 Frank
A. 39 Frank B. 245 Fred
Walker 39 George 66
George W. 64 Infant 197
Isaac 125 Jack 212 James
92 Joe 212 John 206
Lafayette 18 Lucy 212
Maggie 85 Marry 7 Martha
E. 152 165 Mary 156 202
Mary C. 9 M.J. 202 Nancy
176 Patsy 115 Paul 18
Polly 140 Rebecca 129
Rosana 36 Rufus 133
Rufus W. 125 Sallie 38
Samuel 77 Sarah 231 S.W.
77 Victoria 118
Morris, Charlotte 171
George 196 Henry 99 Mary
145 Peral 238
Morrison, Ellen 61 Hellen
61 Riley 166
Morrow, Isaac H. 251 J.C.
251 Lillie S. 193
Morse, Clara Lee 63
Paskel 10 William G. 11
Mortin, Aleck 180
Morton, Alice C. 7 A.O.
107 George 140 G.C. 140
James 77 Jonthan 172 J.M.
53 107 Robert 107

Morton (continued)
R.L. 180 Sarah A. 180
Mosely, A.W. 104
Mildred 104 __ 179
Moser, Jennie 78
Moses, Rena A. 219
R.A. 219
Mosly, Ann 97
Moss, Abe 143 Beckie 143
Emaline 195 John 195
Will 252
Mottern, Mary 80 Mary A.
154 Polly 122
Mottit, George 195
Moudy, Isaac D. 61 J.W.
190 Mary Bessie 94 Mary
B. 250 Wilkey K. 190
William 190
Mulholtz, Margaret 177
Mullens, Alice 152
Lorenzo 152
Samuel R. 152
Mullinnix, Sallie 93
Mullins, Weeka 2
William 246
Mumpower, Etta 215 Etter
153 Henry 184 Lettie 72
Mignon 81 Ossie 229
Will 229 __ 244
Murcery, Mike 3
Murphey, Hattie 102 James
123 Joseph 123 Kemp 216
Murray, Byrd 152 Catherine
233 Charlotte E. 238
George 26 Infant 152
James D. 162 James W.
162 John A. 238 J.A. 162
Mary 137 Roller 159
Rollie P. 219
W.H. (Mrs) 219
Murrell, Henry 147
Pauline 218
Murry, Abbie 124 Andrew
107 Bill 148 Catherine
124 Elizabeth 42 Frach
148 Lizzie 3

Murry (continued)
　Marquise B. 124 Mary 210
　Thomas W. 124 Walter 107
Musgrave, Samuel (Mrs) 226
　Bettie 139
Music, Cora 161
　S.E. (Mrs) 161
Mussleman, Issac 71
　Mary 71
Mutter, Edward 131
　William 131
Myatt, George 41
Myers, Bettie 250
　Christine 155 Elizabeth
　165 Katherine E. 28 Mary
　27 Mary E. 55 Polly 106
　Samuel K. 249 Thomas 249
Myres, Claude 173
　Montie F. 173
Nall, John B. 205
　John B. Jr. 205
Nave, David 257 David
　(Mrs) 220 Henry W. 257
　Maggie 66 Marry J. 66
　Virginia 18 W.H. 257
Neal, Bee 109 Emerson 214
　Infant 63 J.C. 111
　Sallie 109 Samuel O. 109
Necessary, Daniel 136
　T.J. 136
Neff, Rashel H. 201
Neil, Mary Cloud 101
　W.D. 100 101
Nelms, Ada 224 Bruce 115
　Frank (Mrs) 212 Hellen
　M. 115 Joseph 192 L.L.
　192 Minnie 247 Thelma L.
　163 Thomas L. 221 Trigg
　247 Walker 163 221
　William 192
Nelson, Della 97 Infant 95
　Isaac 94 Margaret 99
　Nannie 144 R.E. 114
Nester, Edna E. 164
　John 164
Netherland, Eva 193

Netherland (continued)
　July M. 14 Mary 228
　Nancy 101
Neviston, Neal 38
Newlan, Margaret 215
Newland, Infant 35 Joseph
　78 Loura D. 229 Mabel 10
　W.H. 229
Newman, Dolly 248 John 228
　J.W. 248 Katie 102
　Sallie 118
Newmans, Jasper 7
Newton, Calvin 222 Dorcas
　142 Elizabeth 176 John
　90 J. 142 Nellie 90
Nialom, David 132
Nichols, Evaline 2 James
　171 J.A. 171 J.A. (Mrs)
　171 Mary D. 202
Nickels, Robert 34
　Sarah 125
Noah, Grant 151 Martha 151
Nodrike, James 71
Noe, John M. 45
Nordike, Warneda 71
Nordyke, Annie 255
　James 255
Norman, Roy S. 182
　William 182
Norton, ___ 129
Nushborne, Patrick 256
Oaks, Nancy 163
Oberbay, C.C. 214
Odell, Andy 219 A.B. 165
　Cyris M. 218 D.T. 218
　Earl 61 Infant 219 Jane
　S. 64 John 165 Joseph
　165 J.D. 167 Kate 134
　135 Lauretia 28 Lddia
　100 Lydia 102 183 Martha
　104 Mattie 80 Paul Henry
　80 Ralph 165 167 Robbie
　162 Ruby 165 Stella 23
　S.L. 112 Thomas 101 102
　104 105 Will 80 183
　William 71 102 105 162

Odell (continued)
    William 218 ___ 208
Offield, George 75 Infant
    17 243 King 243 Ollie
    243 Ollie (Mrs) 243
    Wesley 178 William 29
    Zora 75
Offiels, Jake 243
Oler, J.M. 249
Olinger, Albert 114 Isaac
    Ruby H. 176 Sallie 176
    Thomas 176
Oliver, Bill 146 David
    203 Emma 180 Francis 257
    George 179 James 249
    Martha 146 Mary 65 163
    Sam 249 Walter 257
    William 179
Olliver, C.C. 205 Pete 237
    Tom 237
Openmeyer, Gerd 166
    Infant 166
Ornduff, James 166
    James W. 166
Osborn, Charles 91 Eula
    Fay 91 Isaac 37 William
    200 W.M. 172
Osborne, Martha 199
    Rousie 94
Overbay, Elijah 151 152
    Ethel 190 George 151
    George J. 152 G. 189
    G.A. 138 Margaret 106
    Ralph V. 189
Overby, Albert L. 76 Ben
    (Mrs) 34 Jacob 76 John
    76 M. Ethel 127
Overholser, J.W. 104 138
Overstreet, G. Wayne 251
    G.W. 251
Owen, Andrew 81 John Henry
    81 J.H. 191 Laura L. 176
Owens, A.A. 191 Charlotte
    13 Clyde 257 Elish 257
    Eliza 44 201 203 259
    Emma 226 Hender Etta 190

Owens (continued)
    James 163 James R. 190
    John 206 John H. 190
    Lula 206 Martha 207 Mary
    179 190 Ruth 174 Sam 226
    Samuel 45
O'Brien, David 208
    William 48
Pace, Binks 69 J.J. 69
    Lillie 69
Page, Claud 175 Elizabeth
    175 Jane 191
Painter, Caroline 119
    Caroline E. 120 C.S. 251
    E. (Mrs) 251 E.S. 63 151
    Infant 63 James 119 J.W.
    7 Louise 151 Louise H.
    151 Mary 121 Philip 120
Pane, Hannah 1
Pare, Ann 22
Parett, Henry A. 229
Parker, Albert 183 Allie
    189 Annie L.M. 183 Cleve
    157 Clive 106 Fannie 253
    Frank 129 221 George 138
    Henry (Mrs) 183 Infant
    101 129 221 Joe W. 163
    Lucy Ann 215 Minnie
    Mable 59 Mollie 183
    Pearl 221 Samuel W. 163
    S.P. 189 Thomas 58 138
    183 Walker 101 Walter
    183 William 85
    Wyatt 85 ___ 191
Parks, N.D. 57
Parlier, Ida May 69
Parmilee, Abner 55
Parris, Amey 172
Parrott, H.A. 178
Parton, Peggy 187
Partrum, Andrew 252
Pasion, Carrie 156
Patrick, Edna 17
Patterson, D.A. 87
    Infant 87 Rutledge 258
Patton, Barton 107

Patton (continued)
  Della 150 E.K. 150
  Infant 86 150 Jennie 117
  Lena 86 Martha 147
  Nannie 107 Sam 193
  W.S. 86
Pauel, Nettie 246
Paxton, Peggy 113
  Sarah 124
Payne, Ada J. 81 Celia 83
  91 Hugh L. 245 Ida 245
  Infant 62 Margeurite L.
  245 Norris A. 209
  N.V. 91
Peaks, Andrew 154 Charlie
  154 Mary E. 1
Pearler, Lottie A. 123
  Mary 106 Mollie 131
Peaver, Annie F. 219
Peavler, William 120
Pectol, F.H. 129
  Sally T. 129
Pelport, Pearl 174
Peltier, J.W.T. 59
Pemberton, T.D. (Mrs) 230
Pemberton, William 200
  W.B. 200
Pendigrass, Lula 248
Pendleton, Sylvinia 236
Peniter, Josephine 223
Penix, Infant 109 Laura C.
  79 Preston 79 109
  Miles 43
Penley, Caroline 253
  English 234 F.M. 253
  Gladys 234 L.M. 234
  Monerie 201 Sam 201
Penn, Lucy 184 Matilda 63
  Robert 153 224 Ruth 153
  224 R.D. 218
  Susan T. 224
Pennington, Bessie 233
  J.R. 233
Pense, Annie 170
Peoples, Ada 113 Henry 83
  Lueretia 89 Sallie 135

Pepper, C.R. (Mrs) 102
Peppin, Fannie 255
Peregay, Sally 92
Peregoy, S. 260
Perkins, Abe 222 Charles
  160 Charles Sr. 160
  George 106 107 Harve 222
  Lucinda 106 107 Minnie
  May 58 Ottie 166
Perry, Carson 143 Charles
  81 Ella J. 120 Fannie
  188 Infant 143 Jessie D.
  89 John 188 Maria 249
  Minie 115 Nannie 188
  Nellie M. 229 Ollie 28
  Preston 89 Thomas 229
  William 81 144 W.A. 120
  W.H. 157
Persinger, J.P. 184
  Worley 184
Pervine, H.C. 126
Peters, Abe 203 A.P. 203
  Cathern 21 Elsie 225
  Floyd 37 George 211
  Hattie 174 Henry 225
  John E. 233 King 6 Mag
  213 May 226 N.S. 154
  Pleas G. 203 Roy 211
  Sam A. 225 Samuel E. 233
  Sarah 142 233 Savery 92
  S.H. 194 Will 225 Winnie
  C. 40 W.D. 205 W.J. 225
Petteres, Pleas H. 200
  Roubin 200
  P.H. (Mrs) 200
Pettyjohn, J.H. 109
Pewler, Rachel 182
Phelps, Infant 39
Philips, James 224
  Theona 224
Phillips, H.H. 133 James
  96 Joe 93 Rachel 108
  Rebecca 94 Rosa Bell 96
  T.J. 220 Viola V. 119
  W.E. 108 W.H. 222
Phipps, Edith L. 121

Phipps (continued)
  George P. 146 Gernia 114
  Guy 102 H.F. 255 James
  146 John 6 J.M. 121 194
  J.Z. 179 Kyle Z. 179
  Mary C. 259 Mattie 158
  Maude 194 Pink E. 107
  Rowena 146 Ruby 255
  Seebert T. 39
  William D. 102 ___ 219
Phips, Mattie 235
Pickens, Emma 144 Sarah
  244 Virginia 252
  W.D. 144
Picking, Mary 167
Pickle, James 248 Martha
  180 Sarah T. 135 Tom 248
Pierce, Amanda 43 Infant
  69 Isaac 134 James M.
  134 James (Mrs) 30
  J.H.C. 5 65 William 69
Piercy, Francis 213
  Wesley 213
Pierson, Amanda 13
Pile, George Thomas 31
  John L. 58 Margaret V.
  138 W.R. 138
Pindergrass, Infant 21
  John 21
Pinn, Eddie 7
Pippin, Bertie 153
  E.H. 170 Gordon I. 170
  Hugh J. 6 H.G. 153
  Luther (Mrs) 4
Pits, Myrtle 10
Pitts, Guy D. 235 J.G. 235
  Pattie Rose 235
Pleasant, Mollie 210
Pless, Rothern 37
Poe, Belle 242 Elkanah 184
  Eralin 243 Evert 243
  Hannah 203 Hassie 48
  Infant 208 Lizzie 225
  Perry W. 109 Wesley 225
  Will L. 208
Pointer, W.Y. 42

Pooer, Alice 144
Poole, Sinthy 94 Bessie 73
  75 Bob 182 David W. 125
  Elizabeth 110 Floyd 155
  Hiram 182 John 174 Laura
  E. 29 Mary 174 Mary A.
  182 Pank N. 29 Rachel D.
  155 Robert 125 R.J. 75
  Wiley B.65 Will 73
  Will C. 77
Porter, Henry 223 James
  223 James B. 205
  Peggy 201
Portwood, Toby 5
Poston, Clara E. 169
  Patton 61 Tom K. 169
Potts, Ferdinand (Mrs) 233
  Maude 211 Rachel 165
Powell, Emma 13 Jessie S.
  103 Nettie 211
  Rody 60 ___ 195
Powers, Alfred 141 J.S.
  249 Lindsey 141 Lula 249
Pratt, Mary 127
Prayter, Rose 90
Prescott, C.S. 252
  Infant 252
Presley, Charisey 82
Presnell, Garfield 65
  Garfield H. 46
Pressley, Tennie 247
  William 247
Preston, Dinah 237
Price, Annie 5 Birty Ann
  64 B. 102 Eliza J. 107
  Infant 65 James 107 Joe
  65 178 John 253 John W.
  98 Mildred 102 Nettie 84
  Prescilla 201 Ruth 154
  W. 98
Prichard, Susie 157
Pritchard, Bessie 191
  Isom 60 Infant 112 James
  H. 112 Viola 107
Privett, Clyde 67
Proffitt, Granville 65

Proffitt (continued)
　Infant 97 Wade 97
Prter, Mary 147
Pruett, Addie 181 D.F. 181
　D.K. (Mrs) 237 J.P. 150
　D.F. 160 Infant 160
Pruski, Julia 130
Pulliam, Virginia 71
Pyle, Dorothy F. 240 D.A.
　93 209 Henry Clay 93
　Lora V. 209 Mattie 84
　Nannie 85 Pearl 93
　Samuel P. 93 Sue E. 21
　S.J. 190 W.R. 240
Quailes, Benjamin S. 118
　John 118 R.M. 118
Quails, Elizabeth 180
　James C. 249 John 249
Quarles, David E. 57
　J.A. (Mrs) 67
Quarls, Bessie Lee 8
Quillen, Ollie 253
Rader, Bob 221 Eva V. 50
　Minnie 86
Ragan, Daniel 82
　John W. 82
Ragen Earnest 82
Ragland, C.L. 86
Rambo, Ben 233 Kate 122
　Margaret 124 Nancy 259
Ramey, Benjamin 199 Bertie
　H. 204 Francis 172 Jack
　204 Johnathon 199
　J.E. 106
Ramsey, Maggie 232 Mary
　119 William 75
Ramy, Francis 126
Randolph, Hazy 225
Range, Howard E. 107
　Sallie 81 W.T. 107
Rasine, Marie 81
Ratcliffe, Eliza 23
Ratliff, Hester 162
　Julia A. 125
Ray, A.F. 115 Henry
　Stewart 27 Jessie 172

Ray (continued)
　Mary M. 69 ___ 245
Read, David E. 253 James
　253 Rebecca 253
Rearden, Mike 227
Reed, Alice 238 Ben H. 254
　Eugene 254 Hardy 80 110
　Infant 30 80 110
Reese, D.M. 163 220 D.M.
　(Mrs) 163 Helon 220
　Nancy 163 Wilber 163
　William 240 W.F. 240
Reeser, Dr. 154
Remiul, H.C. 236 N.B. 236
　N.B. (Mrs) 236
Remmion, Mary M. 250
Reposs, Alace 242 Carrie
　192 Elic 242 Hattie 242
　Henry 226 Infant 199
　John 192 Lafayett F. 140
　R.F. (Mrs) 140 Vernon L.
　192 Viola 226 Will 140
　Will 199 ___ (Mrs) 224
Resgue, Sparriel 84
Rethford, Vine 22
Retter, Mattie L. 119
Revess, Mattie 159
Reymond, Francis 96
Reynold, Mary E. 259
Reynolds, Ann 132 Arther
　184 Clarence E. 168
　Frank 184 Henrietta 168
　Moses 53 Niles 132 Rhoda
　132 Robert 60 168
Rhea, A.T. (Mrs) 142
　Bertie 67 Dr. 114 John
　256 John P. 141 John P.
　(Dr) 142 Joseph 15 J.P.
　141 J.P. (Dr) 142 167
　J.P. (Mrs) 141 Lucy 139
　Myra 256 M.P. 116 Newton
　42 Sarah H. 256 S.W. 256
Rhodes, George 193
　Martha S. 193
Rhyston, John 116
　Lilburn 116

Rice, J.D. 3 Submit D. 116
Richard, Carrie 113 Leland
　195 R. 147 ___ 147
Richards, Emma 67 E.H. 99
　Flora A. 251 Infant 34
　Jane 99 121 Joe 212
　Lizzie 111 Mollie 186
　Sam (Mrs) 142 Samuel R.
　142 Tom 142
Richardson, Bessie 205
　Cynthia C. 168 C.A. 243
　F.N. 214 George W. 166
　H.G. 137 Infant 243 John
　168 Leona 87 Mary 115
　Mildred R. 214 Rhoda 137
　Ruby C. 166
Richarson, J.R. 168
Rickets, Sarah 166
Riddle, Urias 13
Rider, Myrtle E. 76
Riggs, Alfred A. 89 H.L.
　181 248 Jack C. 181
　Jackson C. 248 Janie May
　7 Paul J. 181 Samuel M.
　89 William B. 89
Rigsby, Cordelia 226
Riley, James 231 John M.
　231 William 80
　William B. 80 ___ 205
Ritchardson, Sallie 34
Ritchie, Harold C. 223
　I.K. 223 Mary 216
Rivers, Infant 186 W.D.
　186 W.M. 186
Roads, George 192
　Sallie 192
Roar, Jane 232
Robbinett, Fred 227
　T.B. 227
Robbins, Hazel E. 174
　M.C. 174
Roberson, Isaac 33
Roberts, Benjamin 107
　Carrie E. 88 Edwin 171
　194 Edwin B. Jr. 171
　Eliza 107 E.B. 171

Roberts (continued)
　Ferby 38 Jessie 230 J.M.
　230 Magnolia 87 Mary K.
　177 M.C. 194 Ruben 88
　Susan 230 W.E. 230
Robertson, Byrd A. 117
　Fannie 117 George (Mrs)
　149 John B. 117 Windham
　C. 170 ___ 170
Robins, Matilda 198
Robinson, Andy 141 Artie
　175 Frank W. Jr. 119
　F.W. 119 Howard 175
　Infant 90 Jessie 80
　J.R. (Mrs) 180 Nancy 123
　Pat 90
Rock, Addie 204
Rodefer, Infant 134
　J.R. 134
Rodgers, Bernita 215 John M
　M. 47 Lacy E. 47 Luisy
　47 Margt 47 William 215
　Winie 101
Roe, Auston 169 Frank 227
　Frank G. 169 F.G. 229
　H.C. 84 James L. 229
　Lelia Belle 84 Oscar 227
　Virginia 227
Rogan, Charlie 232 David
　232 Lula 252 Lynn G. 232
Rogers, Abe 224 Bud 133
　Clara B. 144 Doc 64 Ira
　A. 219 James C. 105 John
　53 John D. 195 Julia V.
　43 J.D. 144 Logan 224
　Mary E. 224 N.E. 189
　Robert 105 R.D. 105
　Susan 13 18 William 161
Roggers, Elvina 9
Roller, Almedia E. 159
　Amos 231 A.C. 242 Burnel
　Burnell 3 Dalis 16 David
　245 E. Paul 173 E.P. 144
　Hiram 231 Jacob 190 John
　167 J.f. 167 Lura E. 84
　Mary 72 162

Roller (continued)
    Maxine N. 173 Nellie 5
    Sarah 201 Sarah J. 68
    Susan 33 242 William 159
Rominger, Mary 118
Rose, Bettie 23 C.D. (Mrs)
    143 Infant 89 Leashey
    152 Lizzie 154 Maggie
    175 Marsha R. 129 Oscar
    89 Susan Suviller 108
Rosenbalm, Infant 38
    Roxie 186 Sam 102 Robert
    L. 102 Emma 110 Sam 160
    Verrey 160
Ross, Allen P. 96 James
    32 John 136 J.H. 145
    Lela 217 Neal 96
Rouse, Dora 229 Felick 193
    flick 189 Gladdis 27
    Jane 229 John 189 John
    C. 193 Lillie Bell 27
Routh, J.H. 216
    Mary A. 216
Rowe, Jack 233 Martha 175
    Robert 175 ___ 170
Royston, Belle 74 Ernest
    J. 4 Frank 212 217
    Infant 74 212 John 217
    Lizzie 189 Margaret V.
    134 Mary J. 194 Orpha
    134 Roderick 75 Samuel
    217 T.B. 194
    William B. 68
Ruben, Mariah 210 Ralph B.
    160 Ralph B. Jr. 160
Rudy, Jack 157
Rumbley, Gorden W. 170
    Mildred B. 170
Rupe, Dennis C. 84
    Robert Earl 84
Rush, Gordin 16
    Nelley E. 16
Russell, Albert 84 A.R. 84
    Charlotte 161 David A.
    125 Elizabeth 12 James
    A. 125 Lizzie 50 ___ 135

Rutherford, Dora 27 Infant
    27 James 66 John 131
    John P. 79 J.C. 131 J.H.
    151 Lola 147 Maria 238
    Mary 73 Mary J. 79
    Thomas R. 249 William 24
    William 249
Rutledge, Dave 23
Rutledge, George D. 41
    Infant 44 Kate 185 Katie
    8 Lillie 85 Lizzie 223
    Marie V. 41 Mary A. 203
Rutter, R.B. 185
Ryan, Millie 171
Sagi, William 233
Saliers, Jennie 251
Salts, ___ 223
Sampson, Hassie J. 94
    ___ 251
Sams, Abe 93 Annie 167
    A.J. 123 Bart 167 Canie
    C. 174 Carrie 213 226
    Charles 194 Emmert 226
    Etta 239 George 78
    George (Mrs) 142 George
    W. 121 Henry 200 Infant
    113 167 James 78 Landon
    239 Lucinda 139 Maggie
    226 Martha 139 Mary 198
    Minnie 123 Monroe 226
    Owen 28 142 Robert T.
    250 Roof 113 Sallie 123
    Sindy 142 Virgie 234
    William E. 250 William
    T. 250 Wils 121
    Wilson 139
Sanders, Della L. 209
    JOhn 45 140 John H. 219
    Joseph 214 Nellie 255
    William 219
Santiago, Infant 151
    James J. 151
Saul, Infant 57
Sauls, Minnie F. 154
Saunders, Jesie B. 70
    J.B. 70 Sallie 91

Sawyers, Catherine E. 178
  Sarah 177
Scalf, Charles Howard 46
  William 58
Scharf, William 3
Scifres, G.M. 251 L.M. 251
Scoraft, Charles 56
Scott, Belle 71 Ben (Mrs)
  158 Benjamin H. 158 222
  Betsy 99 Carl J. 183
  Caroline 169 Emma 180
  E.P. (Mrs) 201 Fannie
  203 Frank 223 George 158
  John 201 John A. 149
  Josie 223 J.M. 141 149
  205 222 Lillian 158
  Millie 236 Nannie J. 205
  O.J. 141 Pete 223
  R.F. 141
Seahrest, John E. 230
  John (Mrs) 230
Search, Frank (Mrs) 39
Seavers, May 83
Seeeney, Eugene 231
Sell, G.W. 151 Sarah E.
  151 Barbara 37 Benjamin
  L. 48 Elizabeth 165
  Emaline 1 Infant 48 John
  P. 165 J.B. 165 Lula 36
  Magie 201 __ 229
Semkin, Sallie 7
Senebough, Joe 176
Seneker, Allice M. 180
  David 118 Elenaora 118
  James K. 141 John E.L.
  141 O.H. 141 Thomas 118
  W.R. 180 __ 180
Seniker, John M. 66
  Mamie Eliza 20
Senter, Sinde 213
Setles, __ 191
Setzer, Happyann 127
Sevier, D.R. 80
Sevier, Jane 177
Sexton, Henry 24 Jane 190
  Leonard 184 W.P. 184

Shafer, Ella 140 John 140
Shaffer, Bertie 75
  Blanche E. 247 James
  208 J.H. 247
Shankle, Eliza 255
  Lafayette 116
  Robert W. 116
Shankles, Malinda 128
Sharp, A.M. 186 Elbert 186
  Harret 35 James A. 214
  James William 17 Jasper
  186 John J. 214
  Julia 245
Sharrett, Amanda 260
Sharrott, Earl 231
  Willie 231
Shaver, Mary K, 98
Shaw, Shelby 206
Shazer, Fannie 121
Sheen, Mary Holden 116
  Will W. 116
Sheets, Daniel 63
  Robert 63
Sheffey, Bessie May 20
Shell, Infant 95 Maggie
  121 Mary 149 Thomas 95
  __ 113
Shelley, D.M. 206
  Mary Ann 206
Shelly, Jennie 6
Shelton, Bidy May 153
  J.H. 117 Lottie 117
  M.E. (Mrs) 153
Shepard, D.N. 189 S.H. 81
  Wilbur H. 81
Shephard, J.B. 154 LaSalle
  87 William 83
Shepherd, Ala May 259 L.R.
  Henry 83 L.R. 154
  Mary E. 154
Shepshire, Samantha 153
Sherfey, Isaac 78 J.S. 78
  90 Mary 90 William H. 78
Sherman, James 135 Maggie
  135 Mattie 54
Shipley, Adam C. 139

Shipley (continued)
　Alice 197 Allie 236
　Amanda E. 225 Anna L.
　185 Asa 104 Benjamin 139
　Caroline 146 Daniel O.
　66 Diman 110 Edmond 146
　Edna A. 217 Enoch 197
　E.L. 225 Faustine 185
　Frederick 70 George 221
　G.R. 195 H.H. 195 Ida
　221 John K. 104 John L.
　139 Joshua 225 J.K (Mrs)
　104 J.M. 217 J.T. 222
　Laura 7 Lula 20 Lydia
　102 105 Margaret 122
　Martha 110 Martin 245
　Mary 207 228 Mary Ann 70
　Mary A. 197 Mattie 130
　Maurice 197 May 228
　M. 177 Noah 130 Orbin F.
　44 Park 195 Rachel 74
　Ray B. 245 Rena 148 221
　Rosa 104 Sarah 71 Sarah
　f. 222 S.P. 21 Tolbert
　248 William 79
Shipp, J.S. 122 R. 192
Shoecraft, Annie 160
　Clide 243 Eva 225 E.V.
　(Mrs) 127 Maud 199 M.B.
　243 Nanie 243
Shoemaker, Ellen 119 Emma
　3 Jonathan 218 Lola 218
　Mary 106 227 Mary E. 233
　May 227 Nancy 92 Soloman
　227 W.C. 131
Short, Dan 23 Eliza B. 103
　Ellen 59 Maggie 127 Mary
　30 Minnie 125 Talmage 59
　William 103 122 127
Shoun, Callie 231
　Elizabeth 161 Ham 46
　Hampton 18
Showalter, Charles 252
　C.P. 252 Hugh F. 252
　Mildred A. 191 W.N. 191
Shrinkle, Bertie 169

Shrively, Nannie 30
Shriver, Celia 6
Shroley, Nannie 28
Shufflebarger, Eliz 178
Shufflestreet, John 21
Shultz, J.W. 112
Shumaker, Elbert 256
　Jonathan 256
Shuman, Henry 189 Hershel
　180 Isaac 180
Shupe, Annie B. 243
Shuttle, Margaret E. 235
Siefors, John B. 83
Sigman, Daniel Milton 35
Simerly, Amanda 185 Bessie
　256 Clarence 244 Daniel
　244 Flora 84 Infant 120
　L.P. 120 256 Mary 147
　Mary E. 249 William 64
　W.B. 167
Simmons, Ben 178 Charles
　37 Ike 25 James 167
　James A. 167 R.L. 135
Simpkins, Sammie 52
Simpson, Joseph 166 J.W.
　189 Lawrence 189 Sudie 2
Sims, Hyder 34 Mary 176
Sinon, Henry 233
　Mary E. 233
Sissell, Easter 168
Sitgnaves, O. 86 John 86
Sizemore, Hogan 127
　Louisa 125
Skaggs, Hattie 175
Slagle, Jane 188
Slaughter, Charlie 137
　Elizabeth 236 255 251
　G.a. 70 Mary E. 208
　Mollie 50 Sara 137
Sloan, Polly 78
Smalling, Florence O. 241
　J.E. 241 Sallie 207
　Sarah C. 40 ___ 255
Smallwood, Bessie 39
　Mamie 79 Maude 176
Smiley, Bob 44

Smiley (continued)
  Hazel A. 169 Pierce 169
Smily, Mirinda 59
Smith, Alex 98 Alex (Mrs)
  98 Alice 96 Allice 258
  Annie D. 193 A. Robert
  150 A.C. 161 Barnet 100
  Benjamin 22 211 Bertha
  114 260 Burt R. 62
  Casper Sr. 120 Charles
  Nelson 60 Cora 177 Cora
  Lee 189 Cordelia 1 C.C.
  150 207 Dave 100 David
  95 96 193 Dennie 243
  Dennis 88 Dorothy V. 208
  Earl 43 Elbert 242
  Elbert (Mrs) 242 Eliza
  A. 26 Elizabeth 42 Emma
  24 Fannie J. 37 Fannie
  M. 177 Florence 249
  Frank 242 Franklin C. 40
  G.E. 197 G.W. 126 208
  237 Henry W. 159 Homer
  H. Jr. 13 Infant 63 126
  140 157 255 Ira 144
  Isaac 80 Isaac Enoch 80
  Isaah 157 Isabell 82
  I.V. 243 Jackson M. 241
  Jacob 54 James 177
  James A. 208 219 Jennie
  117 John 96 144 208 219
  246 John Ernest 36 10
  John J. 88 Julia Ann 54
  Julia A. 219 J. Millard
  255 J.A. 258 J.J. 51
  J.L 121 J.L.C. 179 J.M.
  150 J.N. 36 J.W. 63 112
  Lancaster 100 Lee 177
  Lena 234 235 Lillie 100
  Louisa 11 Louriene 181
  Lovie M. 85 Lutissia 207
  Lydia 119 Lydia H. 105
  L.C. 177 Maggie 193
  Mahalia 119 Malissa 240
  Mamie R. 225 Mary 96 129
  154 245 Mary Ann 93

Smith (continued)
  Mary Elizabeth 73 Mary
  E. 116 Maud 150 M.B. 16
  Nannie 137 P.O. 224
  Rachel 65 Reba 30 Rhoda
  120 Rite 139 Robert 102
  150 225 Robert K. 150
  Roy B. 159 Ruth B. 224
  R. Floyd 189 Sallie 205
  Sam E. 140 Sarah 129
  Susan 102 200 S.C. 1
  S.C.W. 161 Tenny 212
  Thomas 3 67 Toy A. 197
  Walt 194 Walter 178
  William 173 William A.
  150 William J. 37 W.T.
  180 219 ___ 170 175 178
  187 208
Smithton, Adie 7
Smothers, John M. 235
  Johnie 235
Smyth, Jane 224 Joseph
  175 May 172 Rosanah 232
Smythe, Mandy 134
Snapp, Belle F. 161 Dr.
  112 162 Ellen R. 112
  Harriett 31 Jacob 119
  Mary 157
Snodgras, Patricia W. 162
  Valina 258
Snow, Jane 151
Snyder, Bula 161 P.T. 161
Soloman, Hannah 180
Sols, Meme 98
Sourbeer, Infant 119 Julia
  191 J.H. 119
Sourbur, Katy 182
South, Dora 247 Elizabeth
  191 Kenney 50 Mariah
  176 Mose 191 M.A. 140
  Ollie M. 164 Virgie 223
  William P. 47
Southerland, C.C. 234
  James B. 234 T.H. 234
Sox, S.E. 54
Spaha, Infant 140 Will 140

Spangler, Bonie 30 David
154 Fannie Jane 50
J.R. 154
Sparger, William 186 W.H.
186 Zebulon V. 186
Sparges, Merlin 131
W.A. 131
Sparks, Elizabeth 71
Sparp, Mildred 214
Sparr, Rebecca 126
Sparry, Ira 35
Spear, Elizabeth 186
Spears, Charles H. 209
Della L. 214 Edna 174
Georgia A. 209 Gracie
213 Infant 193 James E.
193 Ross 200
Ross A. 174 213
Speer, Elizabeth 102
Speers, Cora M. 115
Harriott 234 James B.
115 John 234 John D. 115
Julia 170
Spicer, Gary 64
Spivey, Infant 167 225
Will 167 William 225
Spotts, Marie L. 172
Sprager, Susie 260
Spriggs, Mary 260
Sprinkle, G.W. 83
Mary A. 83
Sproles, Gordon 135 John
71 Johnathon 117 J.K.
Lizzie 117 Lucy 108
Nancy F. 70 Robert S. 71
Sallie 242 Samuel 70
William M. 117 W.S. 70
Spurgeon, B.D. (Mrs) 168
Elizabeth 226 Joseph 226
Raymond 169 Sarah J. 232
St John, A.C. 232 Berry
187 Carrie D. 181
Elizabeth P. 253 Nancy
214 N.C. 187
William B. 181
Stacey, W.R. 130

Stadman, Laura 163 Mary 44
Stafford, Charles 228
Infant 228 Nora 132
Stanley, Polly 183
Starbock, Infant 128
M.C. 128
Starbuck, Elizabeth 213
Infant 115 W.I. 115 213
Starnes, Bettie 92 Eliza
189 Elizabeth 231 E.M.
92 J.S. 110 Mary C. 110
Staten, Albert 234 Charles
W. 235 John 234 235
Staubur, Eleanora 118
Steadman, C.J. 176 C.W. 85
Edna M. 254 Infant 85
James 19 John 162 166
254 John M. 254 Larry E.
176 Minnie L. 162 Mollie
M. 192 Patton 166 192
254 Sarah 115 S.P. 196
William 103
Steel, Infant 233 John 233
J.H. 233
Steele, Abigal 193
G.W. 241
Stegall, Henry 227
Mary S. 227
Stephenson, Jessie 196
Mable 196 Sallie 126
Sterne, Leon 121
Minnie 121
Stevens, Elbert 17
John N. (Mrs) 242
Steward, Jennie 77
Joseph 116 S.T. 232
Voley M. 232
Stewart, Jane 174 Olive M.
71 Ollie 41 Sallie 131
Sam 238
Stidman, George 109 James
P.H. 108 Sarah J. 119
Stillfe, Tiner 123
Stine, Hattie 133
Stinnette, Robert H. 240
R. Nicholas 240

Stitt, J.A. 189
  Mary L. 189
Stoats, Lizzie 158
Stoffel, ___ 229
Stoffle, Abe 123
  Hannah 220 Lina 176
  Owen 123 ___ 157
Stokes, Elizabeth 82
Stone, C.D. 173 Francis
  234 F.M. 87 Georgie 61
  G.E. 147 Infant 87
  Joseph A. 177 J.C. 189
  J.T. (Mrs) 181 Mart 6
  Mary Elzora 20 Mary
  Luther 94 Sarah 106
  William 177 William H.
  22 William R. 177
Stophel, Christine M. 155
  David 155 Davy 158 Jake
  244 Joseph 244 Margaret
  158 Susannah 171
  Valentine 171
Stouk, William 158
Stout, Carrie 117
  Cora 196 Dr. 161
Stover, Sarah D. 78
Strain, James B. 126
  Robert R. 126
  R.C. (Mrs) 126
Straser, Lola 146
Stratton, Mary 80
Strickler, Nanie 21
Strickley, W.S. 151
Strols, Infant 208
  Luther 208
Strother, Mary 131
Strukley, Addie 258
Stuart, Henry M. 236
  John W. Jr. 89 J.W. 89
Stuffle, Clarence F. 252
  Mack 252 M.R. 252
Stump, Mary 129
Sumerlin, ___ 216
Summers, Anna 143
  Catherine 138 Claude
  138 Mollie 122

Susong, George 246
  Polly 164 Susan 175
  ___ 211
Swan, Alexander 86 R.A.
  (Rev) 86 Susie C. 86
Sweeney, James 231
Sweet, Abe 207 Maud 43
  Varginer 207
Swift, David C. 57
Swiney, Sarah 22
Swinney, Jacob 229 Lizzie
  102 Tennie 229
  Rebecca 84
Swoops, Sallie 166
Tadlock, Mollie 201
Tarter, Andrew 137
Tarver, Sallie 118
Tate, William 119
Taylor, Abram 92 Al 155
  Alfred 94 Alfred (Mrs)
  94 Alice 197 Amanda 146
  Dan 245 David T. 238
  Gensie 219 George 143
  George W. 143 155 Infant
  15 49 155 James 51 190
  John P. 238 J.W. 238
  Kate 37 Liddie 248 Lidie
  158 Lue Ray 245 Manuel
  190 Margaret 128 Mary
  181 May 16 M.K. (Mrs)
  216 Nancy 102 Polly 94
  Rober Rhea 41 Robert S.
  205 Robert L. (Mrs) 187
  R.L. (Mrs) 253 Sallie
  143 244 Sarah 126
  William H. 190 W.C. 205
  W.N. 92 ___ 233 241
Teaster, Thomas 206
Tellwoody, Maggie 246
Tester, Aris 35 Ethel 167
  240 Fred 240 Smith 240
  Wiley 167 William 167
Teters, Loudema 134
Tevis, Ernest 227 Harry A.
  227 H.A. 227
Tevis, H.A. 227

Thier, Mary 142
Thomas, Annie 42 Charles
  O. 186 Daris 186 Edd 249
  Elizabeth 206 Ella 146
  Hallie V. 7 Henry 25
  Jacob 121 James 121 223
  John 69 J.E. 242 Lee 223
  Mattie 223 Nydia 170
  Rosie 94 136 Sam 21
  Samuel 26 S.L. 249
  W.D. 249
Thompkins, Walter T. 31
Thompson, Ann 172 Aura D.
  58 A.J. 133 Henry 3
  Infant 258 James 143
  Lizzie 146 Mary J. 146
  Patton 258 Walter P. 247
Thorpe, Maria 99
Thrall, Harry E. 178
Thurman, Cornelia 102
Thurston, Lucy 184
  Thurman 45
Tickle, Ira L. 172
  Mary E.F. 172
Tiffany, H. 172
Tilley, Emory 176
  Millard 176
Tillison, James K. 124
  J.T. 124 Virgie Lee 39
Tilly, Edmond 161 Edmond
  A. 161 E.A. 161
Tiltsworth, George W. 201
  Thomas 201
Tipton, E.W. 209 214 E.W.
  (Mrs) 205 George A. 209
  L.W. 128 William 216
  Z.W. 128
Tobert, Revely A. 132
Todd, G.F. 113
  Lilly May 113
Tolbert, Charles 85 94 132
  182 Cleo C. 94 Infant
  182 Joe 164 John 85 251
  Myrtle 164 N.T. 85
Tolley, Elizabeth 210
  Infant 200 James 210

Tolley (continued)
  John 210 M.L. 200
Tollman, John 13
Tomlinson, Adelia 33
  George S. 100 Hiram P.
  100 LaFayette 41
  Mary E. 100
Torbet, ___ 175
Torbett, Alen M. 163
  John 163
Tower, Augustus 220
Traubarger, Mary 134
Treadway, Jennie 76
Trent, George 248 Hattie
  248 Mary 249 William 249
  W.E. 248
Tribble, John 114
  Robert C. 114
Trickle, Annie 9 John 9
Trigg, Sallie 141 223
Trimble, Ada 111
  William 111
Trimmer, Joseph 189
Trinkle, George 91 Hazel
  232 Infant 160 Joseph
  91 J.E. 232 Lee 160
  ___ 250
Trinner, Mary E. 136
Triplett, Ernest 192
  Ernie C. 192 Martha 192
Trivet, Mary 18
Trivett, Elijah 256 L.T.
  248 Mary 173
Trobaugh, Elizabeth 240
  Mary 73
Trull, Nancy J. 188
  Laura 187
Tucker, Alijah 96 104
Tuell, A.W. 224 Daniel H.
  224 Ellen S. 224
  J.W. 224
Tunnell, Isaac 103
Turner, Alex 122 Fannie
  99 Fin 69 George 70
  Georgie 70 Jacob 226
  Mary 88 Mary A. 164

Turner (continued)
  Roy 122 Thomas J. 226
  ___ 243
Tyre, M.G. 77
Umbarger, B. Ballard 185
  D.L. 185 Luce 185 M.
  Lafayett 185
Umphras, Lucinda 155
Utsman, John 92
Vail, ___ 99
Van Hoesen, Gerturde 210
  Isaac 210
Van Miller, A. 210
Vanburen, Cash 52
Vance, Ada 209 Charles R.
  63 Earl 133 Earnest 248
  Elbert 255 Elizabeth 185
  Ethel 211 E.G. 248 E.J.
  249 Hugh 133 Infant 158
  194 255 James H. 177
  J.L. 49 J.S. 79 178
  Kiziah 177 Margaret 78
  194 Margaret Jane 78
  Mary 249 Mary M. 252
  Mattie 211 Nick 194
  Ollie 4 Peter 211 R.H.
  194 Susan 82 S.J. 158
Vanderpool, Orpha 220
Vandeventer, Nannie 213
Vanover, Emma 254
Vargas, James T. 97
Vaughn, Cleve 138 C.W. 166
  251 Elizabeth K. 215
  George 237 George W. 215
  Moria 166 Mollie 239
  Nanie E. 138 Sallie Ann
  ___ 68
Vaught, George 211 G.C.
  164 Infant 164 209 211
  Mary 38 S.N. 209
Vault, Mamie 75
Venable, Reba 163
  Brady 240
Vernon, C.J. 236 Mary 106
  Ward 24
Verron, Ellen 151

Vestal, Alice 252 George
  253 Jesse 206
  Wade 252 253 259
Vester, Robert 52
Vickers, Lizzie 180
Viles, Nannie 260 Sam 79
Vires, Clara 132
Virgie, ___ 53
Vowers, Clary 182
Wadkins, Rufus 31
Wagner, Alzenia 132 A.G.
  136 Charles M. 216
  George 153 Mary 153 M.F.
  153 Nancy A. 123
Wake, Agnes 141
Walker, Charles R. 177
  Cyrus 90 Elmira 194
  Infant 177 William 90
Wallace, G.W. 254 James
  201 Jesse Albert 65
  John 154 John E. 154
  J.A. 201 Lanettie 154
  Luther A. 254 Rose 201
Walling, Joe 240 Mary V.
  160 Sue 240 Thomas 240
  Vernon 160
Walsh, Sam 140
Wampler, Gray A. 2 Infant
  211 John 211 J.W. 211
Ward, John 162
  Vernie M. 159
Warden, Mary R. 170
Warick, ___ 186
Warren, Claud W. 226
  Claud W. Jr. 226 Eli P.
  104 Eliza K. 205 Gerogie
  188 G. 243 H.C. 104
  Infant 255 John 255
  John 255 Martha 2 Sue
  251 S.K. 205
Warwick, Zettie 82
Washington, A.P. 73
  Bertha M. 216 Charles
  40 Charlie 248 Dink 246
  248 Ellen 246 Howard
  248 Howard 248 Infant

Washington (continued)
Infant 87 Jim 217 Lornes
87 Maude 41 Nellie 87 217
Octavia 217
Wassom. Lucinda 123
Waterman, L.D. 49
Waters, Zilphia 63
Watkins, Arch 224 Cordelia
259 James 54 Nancy 92
Ressie 96 William 141
Watson, Anner 25 Bettie
214 Edith 203 Ernest
203 E.M. 147 George 92
Infant 78 John 147 John
W. (Rev) 93 Johnathon 93
Lillie 95 Lizzie 131
Mary 93 M.C. 131 M.J.
73 Robert 91 Sam 93 T.P.
131 Vada 15 Wiley 78
William W. 91 W.H. 147
Wattenberger, Fannie 133
Wayman, J.W. 199
Willie G. 199
Weaver, Eliza 78 Elizabeth
116 Elsira 78 F. (Dr)
212 Jacob 56 Jacob E. 86
James E. 86 Jane 110
J.E. Sr. 221 Lockie 158
Minnie 221 Ollie 134 145
Ribie Lee 6 Routh A. 134
W.A. 139
Webb, Adam L. 65 Agnes 157
Amanda 224 Bery F. 99
Carl 119 Catherine 241
Cleo 52 Darbey 72 David
99 Harold D. 126 Henry
D. 151 H.C. 250 Infant
5 119 James 259 James D.
250 Jane 191 John 147
J.W. 157 Lucinda 168
Martha 173 Mary 173
Mike 134 135 143 Mike B.
126 250 Mike B. (Mrs)
126 Rachel 110 Ruby 134
135 Sarah 99 Sousan 134
Susan 114 W.C. 5 __ 97

Wells, Elizabeth 96
Welsh, John D. 147 John W.
257 Sarah I. 147
West, Becky 75 Effie 231
Fannie R. 231
Wexler, Alice 200 H.H. 128
156 E.B. (Mrs) 60 George
156 Henry 133 Infant 133
Joseph R. 213 Nellie 245
Whaley, L.H. 8 Nancy L.
211 Nany 156
Wheatly, Joseph 38
Wheeler, James 79 Nany 79
Whesel, Bonnie M. 33
Whifler, Fannie 233
Whisman, J.A. 236 J.R. 236
Whitaker, Addie 254 A.B.
131 A.B. (Mrs) 61 G.H.
167 245 Julia B. 163
Nannie 10 Polly 108 117
W.G. 55 __ 43
White, Bettie 151 Carrie
Daisey 194 Deliah 75
Dr. 237 Elizabeth 88
Eugene 126 231 Eugene A.
231 E.B. 240 E.H. 194
E.H. (Mrs) 194 Fannie
143 Francis 181 Freddie
198 F.L. 180 F.L. (Mrs)
180 Harnie C. 185 Henry
198 Ida 90 Jacob 180
Jane 91 169 Joseph 7
J.J. 93 185 J.P. 24 Lena
237 Lula 185 Mack 72
Maggie 243 Mary 101
Perry P. 126 Rosana 43
Ruby 246 Rufus Logan 2
Sallie Kate 72 Susan
Susan 239 T.J. 168
Virgie H. 168 William
William 121
Webster, Ella 258
Weeks, Amelia 143
Weing, L.M. 80
Victoria G. 80
Welch, Henry 3 Lucinda 145

Welch (continued)
  Lula 215 Mart 198
  Martin 198
Whitlock, Barbara A. 95
  Infant 69 Lillie 95
Whitsel, Jess 132 Margaret
  J. 77 Nathan W. 255 N.W.
  255 Oscar 255
  Paulser 132
Whitt, ___ 246
Whittaker, Infant 142
  Jessee 142
Whitten, Lucile 25
Widener, Jennie 60
Widly, Bertie 117
Widner, Bettie 182 Clyde
  136 Gladus 43 P.V. 136
  Willis 231
Wilborn, Emma V. 208
  Sam 208
Wilcox, John W. 256
  Joseph 256 Lilly 114
Wilder, Kate 185 Palser
  185 William B. 185
Wiles, Bonnie 125
Wiley, Jane 219
Wilherin, William 248
Wilkes, Lula 97
Wilkins, Joe 173 John 160
  Joseph 160
Wilkinson, Judith 161
Willard, Dulaney 97
  Elizabeth 134
  Mariah C. 244
Willett, George M. 60
Williams, Allie 128 Anna
  153 Bettie 74 Carrie 253
  Cora 237 C.H. 202 Delia
  245 D.J. 231 D.T. (Dr) 7
  G.A. 51 Harry 190 James
  62 Jerry 1 Joseph R. 231
  Josephine 235 J.T. (Mrs)
  231 Katheryn 202 Mattie
  219 251 Millhom 45 N.
  213 Polly C. 213 Samina
  K. 235 S.J. 83 144

Williams (continued)
  Tate 190 Zellie 205
  ___ 139
Williamson, James 125
Willis, Eveline 134
  W.E. 158
Whiteaker, Alexander 214
Whitehead, Belle 224
  Callie 126 William 224
Williss, S.P. 151
Willoughby, Mary 248
Wills, C.G. 155 Effie 155
  Emeline B. 155 Geneva
  190 Joe 218 John W. 135
  Kenneth E. 155 Martha C.
  134 Noah 127 Ottie 231
  Susan 216 William B. 135
Wilson, Annie 103 E.J.
  (Mrs) 87 Grover A. 162
  Hollie 212 H.K. 136
  Infant 155 Irene 212
  Jack 212 Jennie 256
  Josie 169 Julius 109
  J.H. 136 J.H. (Mrs) 136
  Lacy 98 Lillie 138 L.S.
  155 Mary 109 Moses 169
  Sam 109 162 Sinda 69
  Thad 109 Tom 138 169
  William 81 98 ___ 132
  229 230
Wine, Susan 9
Winegar, Anie 218
  William 218
Wingfield, Mary 216
Wingford, Bessie 246
  W.T. 246
Wisdom, Charlie 40 Ellen
  192 Shadrack 192
Wise, Janie 227
Wisner, Sarah A. 238
Witcher, D.R. 256
  Elizabeth 184 Hubert 211
  James R. 256 Joe 184
  Mary 184 Mary L. 211
  Sallie 211
Witt, Martha 86

Wods, W.E. 183
Wolf, Infant 96 103 126
    172 201 Samuel 103
    Walter 201 Will 96
    William 126 172
Wolfe, E.W. 102 E.W. (Mrs)
    102 John B. 260 S. 260
    Virginia A. 51
    Winfred 20
Wolford, E.D. 31
    Mattie 105
Wood, Henry 169 H.C. (Maj)
    47 Infant 77 118 James
    O. 146 Juliett J. 146
    Laura 229 Margaret 98
    Mary 98 Mary L. 163
    Robert 169 R.D. 77 R.L.
    118 Sharlotte 224
    T.F. 126
Wooding, Nellie M. 128
Woods, Charles 163
    Fransinah 154 F.G. 86
    G.W. 210 John H. 210
    John L. 198 J.L (Mrs)
    198 Margaret 133 Rahl A.
    72 Robert 174 Stella
    219 Thomas G. 198 Tracy
    174 Veby 119 William M.
    2 W.W. 72
Woodward, __ 220
Woody, Bertha 195 G.W. 186
    Lillie 186 Robert 188
    Robert Jr. 188
Workman, James E. Sr. 175
    William 175
Worley, James P. 113 Joe
    210 Joe (Mrs) 87
    John (Mrs) 216
Worsham, Mattie V. 62
Wright, Alfred 210 Alice
    L. 136 Birthy 195 Claud
    210 C.L. 72 Ellen Parlee
    72 Tibitha 114 Tobitha
    109 William 16
    Winfield 191
Wyatt, A.A. 213 C. Jim 251

Wyatt (continued)
    Hue 251 Steven 57
    W.F. 258
Wysong, Charles R. 204
    Ethel 204
Yoakley, George W. 157
    Hazel C. 238
    M.H. (Miss) 158 Noah 157
    W.J. (Mrs) 100 __ 70
    100 __ 70
Yokley, Elizabeth 242
    Jane 219
Yonce, Mollie M. 132
York, Elizabeth 240
Yost, Rebecca P. 162
Younce, Addie 41
Young, A.H. 75 Haynes G.
    119 J.B. 184 J.B. (Mrs)
    184 J.P. 75 S.J. 119
    William 44
Youous, Jane 210
Zimmerman, Benjamin F. 168
    Daniel 128 Isaac 152
    Jacob C. 89 Polly B. 156
    Samuel 89 126 Sarah 89
    213

www.ingramcontent.com/pod-product-compliance
Lightning Source LLC
Chambersburg PA
CBHW060554230426
43670CB00011B/1819